Dubious Gastronomy

FOOD IN ASIA AND THE PACIFIC

Series Editors: Christine R. Yano and Robert Ji-Song Ku

Dubious Gastronomy

THE CULTURAL POLITICS
OF EATING ASIAN IN THE USA

Robert Ji-Song Ku

University of Hawai'i Press | Honolulu

© 2014 University of Hawaiʻi Press
All rights reserved
Printed in the United States of America

19 18 17 16 15 14   6 5 4 3 2 1

Library of Congress Cataloging-in-Publication Data
Ku, Robert Ji-Song, author.
  Dubious gastronomy : the cultural politics of eating Asian in the USA / Robert Ji-Song Ku.
       pages cm.—(Food in Asia and the Pacific)
  Includes bibliographical references and index.
  ISBN 978-0-8248-3921-5 (cloth : alk. paper)
  1. Food habits—United States. 2. Food in popular culture—United States. 3. Gastronomy—United States. 4. Cooking, Asian. I. Title.
  GT2853.U5K8 2014
  394.1'20973—dc23
                                                                  2013017500

University of Hawaiʻi Press books are printed on acid-free paper and meet the guidelines for permanence and durability of the Council on Library Resources.

Designed by Westchester Publishing Services.

Printed by Sheridan Books, Inc.

Contents

Acknowledgments vii

Introduction 1

PART I INAUTHENTIC GASTRONOMY
  1 California Roll *17*
  2 Chinese Take-Out *49*

PART II DISREPUTABLE GASTRONOMY
  3 Kimchi *81*
  4 Dogmeat *120*

PART III ARTIFICIAL GASTRONOMY
  5 Monosodium Glutamate *159*
  6 SPAM *190*
    Conclusion *224*

    Notes 231
    Glossary 259
    Bibliography 267
    Index 281

Acknowledgments

This book is the result of an unsettled literary scholar's mid-career realization that it is more pleasurable to deconstruct a meal than it is to ruminate on the meaning of a novel. Switching over from the path of literary studies to food studies has been nothing short of revivifying. It has allowed me to conceive of and express my intellectual and pedagogical endeavors in a whole new—and hopefully meaningful—way. The publication of this book signals the first sojourn stemming from the switch, and, I must say, I am enjoying the view—not to mention the viands—here very much. In fact, I relish it so much that I cannot wait to see what lies just beyond that bend ahead.

I am told that there is an old Korean proverb that says something to the effect of "Not even a monk can cut his own hair." As with the shaving of heads, so too the writing of books—evidently, neither is a solitary endeavor. In the long, slow, and often interrupted process of writing this book, countless individuals have provided aid and comfort. I would like to thank my family, friends, and colleagues whose advice, inspiration, encouragement, and patience sustained me through the many years it took to complete this project.

I began to conceive of this book soon after I joined the faculty of Binghamton University. My thanks go first and foremost to Lisa Yun, my Asian American studies sister-in-arms, not only for her indefatigable belief in this book, but for her invaluable friendship throughout the many years that I have known her. I have had the good fortune to share the department hallway with a group of distinguished scholars of Asian studies as well as Asian American studies, whose knowledge and insights I continue to shamelessly poach. I would like to acknowledge John Chaffee, John

Cheng, Sungdai Cho, Fa-ti Fan, Nick Kaldis, Immanuel Kim, Sonja Kim, Yoonkyung Lee, Dina Maramba, Cynthia Marasigan, Rumiko Sode, Roberta Strippoli, and Shu-Min Tung-Kaldis. I am deeply appreciative of the collegiality and friendship of many others at Binghamton. In particular, I would like to recognize Elisa Camiscioli, Frances Goldman, Praseeda Gopinath, Robert Guay, Kendra Hansen, Kevin Hatch, Douglas Holmes, Matthew Johnson, Joe Keith, Sebastien Lacombe, Tom Mcdonough, Monika Mehta, Pamela Smart, Kathleen Sterling, Jennifer Stoever-Ackerman, Julia Walker, Deanne Westerman, and Melissa Zinkin. The Harpur College dean's office provided me with the time and material support that proved indispensable to the completion of this project. My gratitude goes to the deans past and present, namely, Jean-Pierre Mileur, Ricardo Laremont, Donald Nieman, and Wayne Jones. And I thank the knowledgeable staff at the Binghamton University libraries for reminding me why there is no "research" without "search."

During the process of conceiving, researching, and writing, I have benefited from the collective wisdom, brilliance, and friendship of Asian American studies scholars from across the country and beyond. In particular, I am grateful to Ibrahim Aoudé, Vivek Bald, Victor Bascara, Jason Oliver Chang, Kandice Chuh, Mary Yu Danico, Diane Fujino, Jennifer Hayashida, Jennifer Ho, Grace Hong, Joseph Jeon, Mary Kao, Maryam Kashani, Santhi Kavuri-Bauer, Elaine Kim, SanSan Kwan, Soo Ah Kwon, Heather Lee, James Kyung-Jin Lee, Kyoo Lee, Marjorie Lee, Russell Leong, Kathleen Lopez, Margo Machida, Martin Manalansan, Yong Soon Min, Lisa Nakamura, Don Nakanishi, Franklin Odo, Gary Okihiro, Jane Chi Hyun Park, Junaid Rana, Zohra Saed, Cathy Schlund-Vials, Shalini Shankar, Sandhya Shukla, Rajini Srikanth, Karen Su, Eric Tang, and Linta Varghese.

Anita Mannur, Min Hyoung Song, and Jenefer Shute each read portions of the manuscript at various stages, and their generous feedback not only helped to make this book better than it would have been otherwise, but also gave me the confidence I needed to actually finish it. I thank them and also the two anonymous readers who, besides offering numerous spot-on suggestions for improving this book, recommended the publication of this book in the most effusive manner.

Also providing me with the confidence that I sorely needed was the amazing reception I received from the organizers and audiences at conferences, symposiums, and lectures to which I was invited to present portions of this book. My heartfelt thanks go to the organizers of Eating Chinese:

Cuisine, Commerce, and Culture, a symposium sponsored largely by the Center for Race and Ethnicity at Brown University in 2009, and in particular I am indebted to John Eng-Wong, Evelyn Hu-DeHart, Marie Myung-Ok Lee, Robert G. Lee, Naoko Shibusawa, and Mark Swislocki. I also thank the following institutions for their invitations and gracious hospitality: the Asian American Studies Institute and the Asian American Cultural Center at the University of Connecticut, Storrs; the Asian American/Asian Research Institute of the City University of New York; the Asian American Studies Program at the University of Illinois, Urbana-Champaign; the Ethnic Studies Department at the University of Oregon; the Department of Ethnic Studies at Cal Poly, San Luis Obispo; and the Midwest Asian American Student Conference. In addition, I am deeply appreciative of the feedback I received from audiences at conferences hosted by the following organizations: the Association for Asian American Studies, the Association for Asian Studies, the New York Conference on Asian Studies, and the Association for the Study of Food and Society.

Although I no longer reside there, the friendships I have forged during my life in New York City carry on and have left an ineffable mark on this book. How would I have managed without Jane Bai, Moustafa Bayoumi, Jonathan Blazon, Jane Bowers, Christy Carrillo, Melissa Cerezo, Lillian Cho, Mark Chung, Una Chung, Elena Georgiou, Tomio Geron, Beth Harris, Marina Henriquez, Parag Khandhar, Karlyn Koh, Cynthia Lee, Sara Lee, Lorraine Leong, Margot Liddell, Harriett Luria, Leyla Mei, Kelly Nishimura, Rene Ontal, Janice Pono, Ai-jen Poo, Eun Rhee, Shara Richter, Bill Spath, Seung Hye Suh, and Joe Ugoretz? Of course, my other lifelong friends whose localities lie elsewhere deserve equal consideration: Charise Cheney, Gisele Fong, Joyce Garrigus, Curtis Hardin, Alice Hom, Emma Hunt, Bob Kim, Wonil Kim, Richard Ko, Ed Lin, Jean-Paul Manceau, Kurt Mueller, Maxine Park, Connie Rho-Kim, Yolanda Tiscareño, Lynne Waihee, and Christine Wang.

If I must name a single individual most responsible for taking what was merely a fledgling manuscript and actually transforming it into a full-fledged book, it is undoubtedly my intrepid editor, Masako Ikeda. The fact that I grew up in Hawai'i has made the acceptance of this book by the University of Hawai'i Press singularly meaningful, and I cannot be more delighted and proud. To Masako, who championed this book from the moment that I brought it to her attention, *mahalo nui loa*.

Finally, I would be remiss if I failed to acknowledge the role of my extended family in writing this book—not just those on my side ("the Kus") but my wife's side ("the Ums") as well. Starting with the Kus, I thank my parents Chong Sun Ku and Chi Yun Ku, my sister Shireen and brother James, my sister-in-law Sandra, my niece Hannah, and my nephews Colin and Grant. As for the Ums, I thank my parents-in-law Manok Um and Young Um, my sister-in-law Janet, and her husband Brian Hogencamp.

For the past decade my wife, Nancy Um, has been my constant friend and loving companion. Together we have moved across the country twice and she has shown me parts of the world that I would never have dreamed of visiting on my own. To say that the past twelve years have been the happiest of my life because of her would be an understatement. I started to write this book just as our twin boys Eliot and Oliver came into the world. What joy they bring to our lives every day! It is to the three of them that I dedicate this book.

Introduction

It is an altogether plausible tale: the Orient, once upon a time, was *there*, over yonder where the sun ascended to the heavens each day. Tasting the true flavors of the Orient, then, meant arduous journeys over mountains, oceans, and deserts. No longer. Today, the peoples of the Orient[1]—be they Saracens or Celestials—reside by the multitudes in major metropolises and minor townships beyond the geographic Orient, including across the breadth of the United States. And, of course, found alongside these outlanders, no matter the country, region, or neighborhood, is an endless assortment of exotic delights, the culinary first and foremost. The Orient—or at least the gastronomic Orient—is now global, as diners far and wide need only walk down their own streets or make a quick phone call to make a meal of it.

Not everyone is pleased, however. Culinary purists protest that Anthelme Brillat-Savarin's old reliable adage, "Tell me what you eat and I'll tell you what you are," is now sadly obsolete, as anyone anywhere can at any time eat just about anything. As a consequence, to say that Chinese, Indian, Japanese, or another *cuisine orientale* is global might be stating the obvious, but to contend that kung pao, vindaloo, or sushi everywhere is equally authentic is, for many, a cause for alarm, if not an invitation to a quarrel. Blame it on the masses of ignorant diners who neither know better nor care, the purists say. And blame it also on lax culinary and unscrupulous business practices of food professionals who prey upon them. Complicating matters further is the unavoidable condition of modernity—or was it postmodernity?—characterized by shifting geographic borders, transnational flows of labor and capital, fluid ethnic identities, and flexible cultural citizenships. The stench of fear—the fear for the demise of the authentic Orient—sours the air breathed by both venturesome epicureans and homesick immigrants alike. A shared longing for a return to a more delicious past, a gastronomic golden age just out of reach, makes these otherwise strangers unusual dinner guests.

The Battle Begins

The tale continues: nourished by the milk (soy milk, of course) of nostalgia and nauseated by the bitter taste of industrial globalization, the armies of the gustatory right wing, the defenders of culinary authenticity, with the marketplace as battleground, dig deep their trenches. The rumored destabilization of discreet traditional identities and the declining significance of the nation-state as cultural arbiters of the authentic, mourned and elegized by a litany of fashionable cultural theorists, are greatly exaggerated, they argue. As cuisines around the world undergo the inexorable process of transformation, amalgamation, and fusion that has been the hallmark of human gastronomy since the dawn of the species' digestive history, the indefatigable knights of authenticity don their aprons, sharpen their cleavers, and season their woks. A procession of indignant voices cry out:

> "Not on our watch."
> "Give us the unsullied food of your ancestors."
> "Give us the foods enjoyed by *real* natives not yet compromised by technological innovations, standardized recipes, and surrogate ingredients."
> "Oh, woe is me, woe is me, why so fake must my kimchi, *dosa*, and *harissa* be?"

The lament does not end here, and neither does the tale: the battle for the future of authentic foods is now afoot. Up against the army of gastronomic authenticity stands the phalanx of the apocryphal. Unlike the other side, which subsists on the elixir of transcendental certainty, this group feeds on the ordnance of the interpretative, derivative, ephemeral, and hybrid. In unison, they taunt and provoke their foe:

> "Wake up and smell the coffee!"
> "Give up your dream of culinary Shangri-la."

"The authentic Orient is a figment of your overheated imagination and authentic food of your overindulged palate."
And the most cutting of all: "The apocryphal is the new authentic."

This conflict, as with all momentous conflicts, demands that each diner, aka consumer, choose a side. You are warned: if you're not with us, you're against us. The battle, however, is not limited to the kitchen. The zones of combat extend far and wide: atop restaurant tables, in grocery store aisles, in corporate offices of the food and advertisement industries, in cookbooks, in travel and tourism literature, on television cooking shows, and in the hands of industry lobbyists to the back pockets of politicians. Authenticity is big bucks, and when it comes to matters of food, authenticity is always supersized, especially when so-called ethnic, native, regional, or national cuisines are on the plate.

Today's postindustrial, cosmopolitan diners fear the McDonaldization of the globe will lead to the suppression—and ultimately extinction—of diversity and integrity of traditional fare. Thus they demand that the marketplace, first and foremost, satiate their desire for pristine culinary experiences with a steady supply of newly discovered and sufficiently authenticated autochthonous foods. Business-savvy ethnic entrepreneurs, be they humble immigrant cooks supported by measly family savings or classically trained chefs backed by big-money financiers, are ready and willing to comply, as are mammoth transnational hotel and travel conglomerates. "Welcome to our authentic restaurants," they say with a wink and a smile; "come taste the true flavors of the Orient."

These are fighting words. Both sides stand ready with their onions diced and nerves on edge, their *mis en place* fully prepped for the clash. All that is left now is for Chairman Kaga of *Iron Chef* to shout (in his odd pidgin French): *"Allez cuisine!"* In this battle of gastronomic authenticity versus gastronomic apocryphal, whose cuisine reigns supreme?

Linguistic Analogy

Admittedly, the above is an overly dramatic and purposefully exaggerated rendition of what I believe is the primary binary that dictates much of the current discussion of the globalization of Asian food: either it is authentic, meaning as the "true natives" know it, and therefore delicious, or it is apocryphal, meaning altered by alien forces, most notably via "Americanization," a process often construed as coercive, if not corrosive, and thus rendering food unpalatable. This book is an attempt to challenge the absolutism of authenticity by considering the cultural politics of the dubious, with the hopes of demonstrating that authenticity is both an illusion and a trap. To believe in authenticity is to rely on transcendental means to answer questions posed by a reality deemed untidy and undesirable. Authenticity, in a manner of speaking, is a coping mechanism.

The field of cultural linguistics proves instructive here by way of analogy. So-called authentic cuisines are to standard languages (e.g., Standard American English or middle-class Parisian French) as apocryphal foods are to pidgins and creoles (e.g., Hawaiian Creole English or Haitian French). As any self-respecting linguist will concede, however reluctantly, the belief that a standard language is inherently more proper, superior, or pure is spurious at best. As argued by Peter Trudgill, James Milroy, and many others, standard languages, by definition, are simply dialects within the category of languages to which they belong—no more and certainly no less.[2] The high status enjoyed by standard languages is not a function of inherent linguistic endowments but of cultural and political prestige and power. (Hence the quip generally attributed to Max Weinreich: "A language is a dialect with an army and navy.") Standard British English, for example, is the dialect of the privileged class in the United Kingdom; it is a variety of English native to perhaps less than 12–15 percent of its inhabitants.[3] Those who insist that Standard English is the correct, proper, pure, or authentic English betray their ideological dogma—one that favors a uniform, standard nation, a place where cultural differences, heterogeneity, and hybridity are viewed as undesirable. By stigmatizing alternative forms of English—a notable example is African American English Vernacular—language purists, aka prescriptivists, attempt to discipline the nation by punishing the tongues of its heteroglossic citizenry.

What is true for language is apparently often true for food. Arjun Appudurai reminds us that "all cuisines have a history: tastes shift, regional distinctions go in and out of focus, new techniques and technologies appear."[4] He could very well have been describing a linguistic process. In both instances, the tongue is the legislator—if not the dictator—of taste, not only within the nation, but also, as I hope to demonstrate, increasingly across the diaspora. Consider the immense variety of Englishes that exists around the world.[5] In *English as a Global Language,* published in 1997,

David Crystal estimated that some 2.1 billion people in the world employ English in one significant fashion or another on a daily basis. He estimated as a lowest estimate "a grand total of 670 million people with a native or native-like command of English."⁶ Of course, it does not take a linguist to know that the English utilized by these masses of native users is not linguistically uniform. A whole host of factors, including class, education level, national origin, regional particularity, and ethnic affiliation, contribute to the global diversity of English. And it is not just the United Kingdom, the United States, Canada, Australia, or New Zealand that boast unique expressions of English. The countries that are now either primarily Anglophone or becoming increasingly so are legion: Barbados, Belize, Cameroon, Dominica, Eritrea, Ghana, Guyana, India, Ireland, the Netherlands, Pakistan, Singapore, South Africa, Swaziland, and Zimbabwe constitute a mere tip of the global English iceberg.

Just as London is no longer—if it ever was to begin with—the linguistic center of the English language, Asia is not the standard bearer of all "Asianness," least of all of food. Rather, Asia, like the rest of the world, is in a state of continual flux and perpetual mutation, hybridization, and transmogrification. Moreover, today one need not necessarily reside or travel to the geographic Asia in order to *be in* Asia. Communities of Asians, a multitude of them, in fact, live in a vast array of locations. They not only reside in Beijing, Manila, Mumbai, and Hanoi, but also Toronto, Berlin, Los Angeles, Durban, and São Paulo. If it can be said that the health and vitality of a cultural practice are directly connected to innovation, adaption, and progress, then the changes to food culture taking place in, say, Flushing, Queens, are just as significant as those taking place anywhere in Asia proper.

By exploring the other side, as it were, of what is generally understood as authentic Asian gastronomy, I wish to suggest that expressions of Asian food cultures taking place in "far-flung" locations such as Los Angeles, Honolulu, New York City, or even Baton Rouge are no less critical to understand the meaning of Asian food (provided such a thing exists) than the culinary expressions that took place (or perhaps took root) in the Orient, say, Tokyo, Seoul, or Shanghai, centuries ago. In other words, just as a cultural linguist might argue for recognizing the legitimacy of a nonstandard language vis-à-vis the stigmatizing and repressive process of language standardization, I argue for the legitimacy of Asian identities, experiences, and cultural forms *beyond* the geographic and political imaginings of Asia. When it comes to culinary matters, diasporic Asia—including Asian America, the principal site of this book—matters a great deal more than most mavens of gastronomic authenticity are willing to concede. But instead of vying for the equal legitimacy of Asian culinary practices beyond Asia, I wish to challenge the saliency of the very notion of authenticity, a concept I find troubled, troubling, and troublesome.

Dubious Gastronomy

As the title suggests, this book meditates on foods that belong to a gastronomic category that I call dubious Asian foods, especially as they are manifested, consumed, discussed, and contested in the United States. I devote individual chapters to six specific edible subjects: the California roll, take-out Chinese food, monosodium glutamate (MSG), dogmeat, factory-made American kimchi, and the canned meat product called SPAM. Several notable features bring these foods together.

First, each is strongly associated with Asians and Asian Americans. California roll is a type of sushi, which is arguably the best-known Japanese food outside of Japan. With avocado, a fruit unknown in Japan until recently, serving as the signature ingredient, California roll is generally assumed to be a Japanese American invention. Take-out Chinese, of course, is self-evidently Chinese, and in the United States it is almost exclusively Chinese immigrants who are in the business of selling it. Often considered synonymous with bad Chinese food, MSG was in fact invented by a Japanese chemist a century ago and widely marketed in Japan and its colonies (principally Korea, Taiwan, and China) during the first half of the twentieth century. Although dogmeat is an idiosyncratic part of the diet of a relatively small number of people in Southeast and East Asia, its culinary significance as a traditional Asian food looms much larger in the popular American imagination. Kimchi is perhaps the most representative Korean food and is widely considered the "national dish" of Korea. Finally, SPAM is a highly regarded and sought-after commodity in parts of Asia (especially in Korea and the Philippines), the Pacific (most notably in Guam and Hawai'i), and among Asian Pacific Americans (especially those of Korean, Filipino, Japanese, and Pacific Islander backgrounds).

Second, each is commonly found beyond Asia, and in the United States in particular, if not materially in any significant way, then certainly as a topic of contentious conversation or debate. California roll is undoubtedly the most popular type of sushi in the United States; its wide appeal is due largely to the absence of raw fish, which most Americans equate with sushi itself. Chinese food is arguably the second most popular "ethnic" food in America, trailing only Italian. Although invented in Japan and powerfully linked to Chinese food, MSG appears on the list of ingredients of umpteen numbers of food products sold in the United States; nearly all canned soups and frozen meals contain it, often under various aliases. While widespread rumors of Asian immigrants feasting on their American neighbors' dogs have been proven entirely spurious, the fact that such canards comprise a documentable category of urban mythology indicates that the specter of the dog-eating Oriental has much currency in the United States. Kimchi is now a hot global commodity; a 2011 PBS series called *Kimchi Chronicles*, hosted by Marja Vongerichten, is one indication that the fermented product has begun to enter the US culinary mainstream. And despite SPAM's immense popularity in some parts of Asia and the Pacific, Americans are the largest bulk consumer, especially during times of economic downturn, when SPAM production typically increases to keep up with the rise in demand.

Third, each is (or once was) an object of ridicule, scorn, disgust, and bemusement, particularly to Americans—that is to say, each has been regarded as a dubious Asian food. Deemed the epitome of bad sushi, California roll is dismissed out of hand by sushi aficionados on both sides of the Pacific. In the United States its appearance on a restaurant menu is often regarded as a sign of a subpar sushi establishment. American diners have had a love-hate relationship with Chinese food since the nineteenth century, when Chinese immigrants first arrived on the West Coast. Although among the most popular ethnic foods in America, Chinese food is perhaps the most pilloried; it is the target of endless complaints regarding its sanitariness (or the lack thereof), healthfulness (or the lack thereof), and about the desirability (or the lack thereof) of the people (namely, the Chinese) who sell it. A key part of what I call the "culture of complaint" that surrounds Chinese food in the United States is the obsession many diners have with the possibility that MSG is the root cause of a litany of bodily ailments—headaches, nausea, bloating, and dizziness, to name only a few of the countless reported symptoms. This has proven to be such a burden on Chinese restaurants that a near-universal requisite of all Chinese menus is a "No MSG" disclaimer. If a single word describes the feeling most Americans experience when faced with the idea of dogmeat, it is most certainly disgust, an emotion that is not limited to culinary concerns but extends to the people who are purported to consume it—Asians and Asian Americans. Although many gourmands now regard kimchi as a "superfood" due to its healthful claims, it was not that long ago that it was largely unknown in the United States; the few non-Koreans who knew of it typically described it in less-than-flattering terms—as rotten, spoiled, dangerously spicy, and, above all, malodorous. SPAM, widely adjudged as the antithesis of wholesome food, is commonly treated as if it was scraped off the pages of Upton Sinclair's *The Jungle*. It is popularly regarded as kitsch, more suitable as a punch line to jokes than an edible object.

Finally, each provides an ideal opportunity to ponder the question of gastronomic authenticity—or, rather, the lack thereof—because each is commonly understood as an example of bad, ersatz, or corrupt Asian food, or not Asian at all. With the possible exception of dogmeat, which most Americans associate exclusively with depraved Asia, each of these foods, in one way or another, is strongly associated with the adulterating apparatus of Americanization. Each is suspect because it either presumably originated in or has crossed over too far into mainstream United States. Both the California roll and take-out Chinese food are considered American inventions that would not be recognized in the country of their supposed origins. MSG and SPAM are both synonymous with artificiality. The fact that the American food supply is currently awash with MSG is taken as predictable, given that Americanization is often equated with artificiality. SPAM, a product of the American food industry, is perhaps the original "mystery meat." Having only recently gained the attention of American eaters, kimchi is still considered "unsullied"; this, however, is due to change, as Korean food undergoes a process of assimilation similar to that experienced by Japanese and Chinese foods upon their introduction to the United States. Dogmeat, meanwhile, is an example of how something that resists mainstreaming can be considered depraved and dangerous, and serves as a reminder of the limits not only of globalization but also of authenticity.

I argue that the privileging of authenticity serves as a reproof not merely of so-called dubious Asian foods but also of Asian *peoples* who are viewed as complicit in the ruination of their own culinary tradition. In the United States the burden, if not blame, of Asian inauthenticity falls most heavily on the shoulders of Asian Americans, who are construed as human analogs of inauthentic cultural products. Discursively positioned neither as truly "Asian" nor truly "American," they are read as doubly dubious. The Asian presence in the United States is commonly seen as watered down, counterfeit, inauthentic—at least when measured against a largely mythical if not entirely imaginary standard of people of so-called real or authentic Asia. What I suggest is that the dubious Asian foods explored here share a special fellowship with Asian Americans—an intellectual, cultural, political, and discursive fellowship—that forms the foundation of this book.

Of course, any attempt to address a subject as vast as Asian food (or even Asian food in the United States) must delineate terms and boundaries as well as acknowledge limitations. The category is simply too expansive, too nebulous, too heterogeneous not to. I do this by limiting my discussion primarily, but not entirely, to gastronomy associated with East Asia, specifically Chinese, Korean, and Japanese. These are not without drawbacks, as any bracketing of "Asia" or "Asian America" must take into consideration not merely East Asia but Southeast Asia, South Asia, Central Asia, West Asia, and potentially the entirety of the Middle East as well, including North Africa. Therefore, whenever possible, I refrain from remarking categorically about Asians or Asian Americans in general and instead direct my comments to a specific national or ethnic group in question.

It is perhaps important for me to point out that the principally East Asian focus of this book is neither arbitrary nor accidental. Rather, it developed as a result of the specific foods, themes, and questions that materialized as the book came together. When the culinary subjects of this book are considered in concert, it is East Asia that generally, but by no means exclusively, comes into most obvious and lucid shape. The East Asian focus of the book, moreover, is a result of my own personal gastronomic coming of age vis-à-vis geographic journey: birth in Korea, childhood in Hawai'i, and adulthood in Southern California and New York City. In short, these are foods I have been around all my life—either eating or thinking and brooding about. That said, had I had the culinary experience or intellectual wherewithal to go beyond an East Asian scope while writing this book, I might have very well included such dubious foods as the South Asian chicken tikka masala (and other dubious curries) and Southeast Asian balut (and other so-called "bizarre foods" regularly featured, say, on the Travel Channel).

Also, I situate the book's point of departure not in Asia proper, but the United States, where significant populations of Asians, both immigrant and American born, reside. In doing so, I dislodge the very notion of what is or is not legitimately Asian from its dynastic, nation-state, and ethnic myths of origins and relocate it to a place whose name is often synonymous with cultural imperialism, bastardization, and dubiousness—a seemingly dishonorable phenomenon known worldwide, including in the United States, as "Americanization."

The observations, theories, arguments, and conjectures of *Dubious Gastronomy* are explored using a wide range of narrative strategies. The book is part cultural studies, part political polemic, part food history, part food science, part literary analysis, and part anthropological critique. It is a work that overlaps a number of academic interests, including the fields of American studies (and Asian American studies in particular), Asian studies (especially within a transnational or diasporic context), and literary and cultural studies, as well as the newly burgeoning intellectual field of food studies. More so than overlapping these areas, however, I believe the book fulfills the important task of amalgamating them and putting each of these fields into conversation with one another. In this sense, the book is truly interdisciplinary.

What this book is *not* is a food reference guide, objective history, or detailed description of Asian American food and food practices. It is, rather, a series of critical contemplation of both the "metabolic" and "symbolic" meaning of food vis-à-vis the people who consume it. The narrative voice I employ is a fusion of the scholarly and the popular, the empirical and the subjective, the sociological and the semiotic, and the political and the personal. In other words, the book eschews the linear, rational, and deductive modes of argument that are standard to traditional academic writing for a more multidirectional—if not whimsical or idiosyncratic—exploration of the issues at hand. The novelist Bharati Mukherjee once wrote, "The zigzag route is the straightest."[7] In terms of this book's narrative mode, this is as apt a characterization as any. Thus you might say this book is as dubious as the foods that appear in it. I hope to show that this is not necessarily a bad thing. Rather, it might be quite delicious.

The book is organized into three parts, with each part corresponding to three possible meanings of the word "dubious"—inauthenticity, disreputableness, and artificiality. Part I, "Inauthentic Gastronomy," focuses on a pair of culinary sites that are often treated as paragons of counterfeit or fake Asian food in America: "California Roll" (chapter 1) and "Chinese Take-Out" (chapter 2). Part II, "Disreputable Gastronomy," meditates on "Kimchi" (chapter 3) and "Dogmeat" (chapter 4) as examples of how foods that are strongly associated with the perceived moral depravity of a particular ethnic or racial group can either become rehabilitated (as with kimchi) or remain permanently suspect (as with dogmeat). Part III, "Artificial Gastronomy," examines "Monosodium Glutamate" (chapter 5) and "SPAM" (chapter 6), two comestibles that are often seen as synthetic or simulated substitutes for an actual taste (*umami*) or real food (meat).

Narrative Arc

Recalling the creative beginnings of *M. Butterfly*, the Tony Award–winning play about a French diplomat's decades-long love affair with a Chinese male spy masquerading as a Chinese actress, the playwright David Henry Hwang credits a two-paragraph story in the *New York Times* as the spark that ignited his interest in writing the play. But instead of investigating the "true life" incident further, Hwang opted for a counterintuitive approach: "I purposely refrained from further research, for I was not interested in writing docudrama. Frankly, I didn't want the 'truth' to interfere with my own speculations." He speculated that the French diplomat, who claimed not to know that his lover was a man until the bitter end, saw in the Chinese spy not the reality of the actual, but rather the "fantasy stereotype" of Asians as "bowing, blushing flowers." The spy, on the other hand, "must have played up to and exploited this image of the Oriental woman as demure and submissive."[8] Yes, for both the diplomat and spy it was "pretty to think"—to borrow a phrase from Ernest Hemingway's *The Sun Also Rises*—that they were in fact what each pretended to be.

Hwang recalls that he came up with the basic "arc" of the yet-to-be written play while driving along Los Angeles' Santa Monica Boulevard: the Frenchman and his Chinese lover are entangled in a very adult game of pretend in a deconstructed version of Puccini's *Madam Butterfly*.[9] The unconventional reshuffling of the players' parts, each playing the other's role at different junctures, gives the play the necessary subversive quality that makes it Hwang's most engaging and entertaining work to date. Hwang felt certain that the audience would instinctively engage the political and sexual truisms of the play, despite its reliance on a diegetic contrivance: "From my point of view, the 'impossible' story of a Frenchman duped by a Chinese man masquerading as a woman always seemed perfectly explicable; given the degree of misunderstanding between men and women and also between East and West, it seemed inevitable that a mistake of this magnitude would one day take place."[10] It is worth noting that the entirety of the play is rendered exclusively through the point of view of the Frenchman, who, in isolation, addresses the audience from his private prison cell. The events replayed on the stage, including every word attributed to the Chinese spy, are therefore the Frenchman's version alone. It is left up to the audience to decide whether to accept his ventriloquial performance at face value. How reliable a narrator is he? Apart from his monologic pantomime, are we privy to any other source of information or perspective? Given this dramatic conceit, and even if Hwang may reject this idea altogether, the Chinese spy remains nameless, sexless, and nationless throughout the duration of the drama.

In locating the basic arc of this book's gastronomic stories, I endeavor to enlist Hwang's tripronged dramaturgical strategy: first, the use of speculation in filling in the blanks without relying solely on the factual or veridical evidence of a matter; second, the deconstructivist tactic in blurring powerful discursive binaries; and third, the public scrutiny of private performances in the transformation of the quotidian into the spectacular and translation of ordinary fare into extraordinary epicurean delights.

In *Orientalism*, his 1978 critique of the West's discursive and administrative structuring and control of the Orient, Edward Said stresses that the notion of Orientalism as he defines it means several interdependent things. This includes an academic definition in which anyone who "teaches, writes about, or researches the Orient—and this applies whether the person is an anthropologist, sociologist, historian, or philologist—either in its specifics or its general aspects, is an Orientalist, and what he or she does is Orientalism."[11] Another definition is more general: "Orientalism is a style of thought based upon an ontological and epistemological distinction between 'the Orient' and (most of the time) 'the Occident.' Thus a very large mass of writers, among whom are poets, novelists, philosophers, political theorists, economists, and imperial administrators, have accepted the basic distinction between East and West as the *starting point* for elaborate theories, epics, novels, social descriptions, and political accounts concerning the Orient, its peoples, customs, 'mind,' destiny, and so on."[12] To the list of activities that define Orientalism I would add contemporary food discourse (cookbooks, television cooking shows and competitions, food films, etc.) on Asia, in which the East-West binary, expressed as essential differences between the twain, more often than not serves as the starting point for whatever else is to follow.

Where Hwang and I part ways is at the intersection of the East-West binary. While I believe he employs it as a starting point for the dramatic gulf he believes exists between the Orient and Occident, I seek to undermine it from the outset. Does a successful marriage of East and West on a plate presage, harbor, and reflect the so-called real conditions on the proverbial ground? That is to say, does it point in any meaningful way to the relationship between the *peoples* of the East and West? Of course, this question is meaningful insofar as the categories of East and West and the rhetorical binary they engender are meaningful.

Given the immense political, cultural, and representational schisms that separate "citizens" from "immigrants" of a given nation (as Lisa Lowe postulates in *Immigrant Acts*),[13] as well as between the "Occident" and "Orient" (as Edward Said does in *Orientalism*), the divide between the lofty idea of authentic Asian food and vulgar reality of dubious food is not only inevitable but synecdochical: the semiotics of eating Asian in the United States is emblematic of the larger questions facing the nation in what is decidedly a transnational and diasporic dynamic of the twenty-first century.

Matters of gastronomy are a matter for a nation's sense of collective self as much as they are for its sense of collective taste. The ambivalence over eating Asian in the United States is reflective of a general tendency, and a considerable irony, in American immigrant history. As Matthew Frye Jacobson has argued in regards to fin de siècle US encounters with the darker, alien peoples of the world, "Immigrants provided the basis of self-flattering portraits of openness of the nation's democratic order and yet they bore the brunt of some of the nation's fiercest antidemocratic impulses."[14] Asian Americans have always been and continue to be emblematic of the unassimilable American, not only in body politic but in gastronomic culture as well. Asian food is America's culinary stepchild, technically part of the family but never quite entirely. This, however, does not mean that it isn't good to think—or eat.

Part I
INAUTHENTIC GASTRONOMY

1 | California Roll

Recall that it was not that long ago, despite its lofty status in the current US culinary scene, that sushi, synonymous with raw fish to most Americans, was a frequent object of derision, ridicule, and, above all, dread. When the *Ladies' Home Journal* introduced Japanese cuisine to American women in 1929, the magazine discreetly dodged the subject, fearful that it might disturb the genteel constitution of its female readership. "There have been purposely omitted," the article ran, "any recipes using the delicate and raw tuna fish which is sliced wafer thin and served iced with attractive garnishes." The magazine did, however, offer the tenuous assurance that raw fish "might not sound so entirely delicious as they are in reality."[1]

In countless films, TV shows, commercials, and popular American discourse in general sushi was routinely represented as nothing more than slimy, smelly, and spoiled orts of raw octopus, squid, or some other bizarre sea creature, more suitable for fish bait than a blue-plate special. One notable example from my cinematic salad days is *The Breakfast Club,* John Hughes' 1985 meditation on white, middle-class, suburban teenage angst. When the "rich girl" Claire Standish (played by Molly Ringwald) takes out a box of sushi for lunch (signifying her snootiness), the other highschoolers serving detention with her look on with a mixture of trepidation and disgust. The "rebel" John Bender (played by Judd Nelson) asks what "that" is. Standish responds that it is sushi, "rice, raw fish, and seaweed," to which Bender remarks, "You won't accept a guy's tongue in your mouth and you're going to eat that?" Another example comes via television: in a 2001 advertisement for 10-10 220, a long-distance phone service, a pair of football stars, Terry Bradshaw and Doug Flutie, sits at a sushi bar. "Man,

Claire Standish (Molly Ringwald) eats sushi for lunch. Frame enlargement from *The Breakfast Club* (1985).

I'm hungry," declares Bradshaw. When the sushi chef places pieces of *nigirizushi* in front of them, Bradshaw, the Hall of Fame quarterback who won four Super Bowl titles with the Pittsburgh Steelers during the 1970s, and Flutie, who was awarded the Heisman Trophy in 1984 as a quarterback for Boston College, look down at their plates with trepidation. Seeing their nonplussed expressions, a young woman seated next to them tells them it is sushi. "Sootchi? Where I come from we call that stuff bait," barks an incredulous, pronunciation-challenged Bradshaw. At the end of the commercial Bradshaw leans over to the sushi chef and adds sotto voce, as if he is bestowing confidential sage advice, "Hey, you forgot to cook this."

You've Come a Long Way, Baby

Sushi once possessed the ultimate "yuk!" factor, grossing out grown-up Americans the way spinach might repulse a finicky child or head cheese a vegan. As anyone who has recently purchased a pre-prepared box of sushi from a local supermarket might attest, the popularity and prestige of Japanese food, and sushi in particular, have soared since the 1980s, leading to the shrine-like status of restaurants such as Nobu and Masa in New York City, and transforming chefs like Masaharu Morimoto into culinary rock stars. The novelist Jay McInerney recounts how when he first braved sushi while visiting Tokyo back in 1977, he saw himself as "an intrepid culinary adventurer who, if he survived the experience, would return to America to tell the incredible, unbelievable tale of the day he ate raw fish on rice ball." He would tell his children about it "someday," he thought. Little did he realize that within a couple of years sushi bars would mushroom in Manhattan and nigirizushi would soon "become the signature forage of the Young Urban Professional." McInerney's children eventually became so undaunted by sushi that they began to eat it three or four times a week, having developed the habit while living in Nashville, Tennessee, of all places.[2] But perhaps the ultimate symbol of sushi's triumph over America's Puritan palate might be a 2006 episode of HBO's *The Sopranos*, in which Tony Soprano, the brutal but oddly endearing mob boss, not once but twice in a single episode dines on a plate of artistically arranged *tekkamaki* at a posh Japanese restaurant somewhere, I imagine, not far from the New Jersey Turnpike and the Bada Bing!

Sushi is a rare example—or a *raw* example, rather—of a foreign dish that has, within the relatively short span of my adult life, undergone a thorough reputation makeover. Initially regarded as dubious, it has now gone mainstream, and, remarkably, it did so while retaining most of its exotic aura. Indeed, considering the hostile reception sushi received during its early years in the United States, who could have predicted this remarkable reversal of fortune? In fact, I can think of no other dish so thoroughly identified with another nation's gastronomy that shares this backstory of culinary rags to riches. Sushi in America is symbolic of a bilateral culinary redemption, a two-way reminder of how far both sushi and American foodways have come.

On the one hand, sushi has altered itself in form and substance to better assimilate into the norms of US gastronomy, principally in the form of California roll and countless other elaborate and imaginative avocado-centered *makizushi*, such as Philadelphia roll (typically made of salmon, asparagus, cream cheese, and avocado), dragon roll (eel, crab, cucumber, and avocado), spider roll (soft-shell crab, cucumber, and avocado), and rainbow roll (California roll wrapped in five different types of raw fish).[3] On the other hand, American diners have learned to better embrace the

A shopper looking over an assortment of premade sushi at Wegmans Market in Johnson City, New York. Photo by the author.

exotic palate—so much so that in 2006 the Japanese minister of agriculture, forestry, and fisheries calculated that there were already "9000 Japanese restaurants in the US alone, with their number increasing at a rate of 8.5 per cent a year."[4]

In *The United States of Arugula: How We Became a Gourmet Nation*, David Kamp contends that during the 1980s at least three factors merged to increase sushi's popularity in the United States, signaling Japanese food's coming of age: James Clavell's novel *Shogun* became a hit television miniseries (starring Richard Chamberlain and Toshiro Mifune), "which spurred a faddist mania for all things Japanese"; "diet-conscious Americans" began to see sushi as a healthy, pure, clean, and organic alternative to the overly processed, deleterious foods that dominated the American foodscape; and "status-conscious Americans" began to increase their consumption of raw fish because it seemed "hip" and "cool."[5] But while the cosmopolitan crowd may have altered the status of sushi from outlandish victual to food fad to haute cuisine to mass-market fare, all within a couple decades, its legacy as one of the most mocked, if not feared, foreign foods has not entirely been erased.

The popularity of frozen fish sticks, McDonald's Filet-O-Fish, and the Red Lobster restaurant chain notwithstanding, to mainstream America seafood was and to a great degree still is caught with a can opener, not chopsticks. It is something gathered not from the oceans, seas, and other waterways but pulled from the pantry and freezer. The actress-singer Jessica Simpson's much lampooned question about whether tuna was fish or chicken reveals the extent to which much of landlocked Middle America still experiences anxiety over the idea of eating fish—even cooked fish. (In a 2003 episode of MTV's reality show *Newlyweds: Nick and Jessica*, Simpson expresses confusion over the moniker "Chicken of the Sea," thinking it read either Chicken "by" or "of" the Sea.) This attitude was on full display even in a presumably high-end gourmand environment like the Bravo network's *Top Chef*. In the "Eastern Promise" episode of the 2006–2007 season, a contestant (Mia Gaines-Alt of Oakdale, California) gags histrionically when told by the host Padma Lakshmi (aka Ex-Mrs. Salman Rushdie) that the day's challenge involved handling raw fish to create a scrumptious sushi meal. Be that as it may, considering where it once was a mere decade or two ago, sushi, at least in the United States, has come a long way.

Row over California Roll

If the thought of raw fish, despite sushi's prominent place in the current American food scene, makes your stomach heave, there is, of course, California roll, the most commonly consumed form of sushi in the United States, if not the entire Western Hemisphere. Typically prepared using crabmeat (usually imitation), avocado (the signature ingredient), cucumber (at times carrot), mayonnaise (from a jar), and rolled "inside out" so as to hide the nori from the view of diners turned off by the idea of seaweed, California roll is not only benign enough for the gastronomically squeamish, but also for finicky children and expectant mothers, the latter of whom are medically advised in the United States to abstain from consuming raw fish.[6]

If tortilla chips, tomato salsa, guacamole, and nachos can be said to be "entry points for Mexican food for a lot of Americans," as Rick Bayless, the famed Chicago-based Mexican cuisine restaurateur, has observed,[7] then California roll, along with tempura, teriyaki, and, of course, instant ramen, are the gateway dishes for Americans wishing to venture into the daunting world of Japanese cuisine. "For Caucasians," writes David Kamp, "the California roll proved to be an ideal gateway drug to the hard stuff; once you got over the weirdness of a cold piece of something-or-other brushed with wasabi and rolled in vinegar-seasoned rice and seaweed, it wasn't so crazy to try sushi made with uncooked scallops or slices of velvety, high-quality raw tuna."[8]

After all, what is there not to like about California roll? First and foremost, it is delicious—or at least a large segment of the world's sushi-eating population thinks it is. Second, like a Big Mac and unlike, say, tuna tartare or ceviche, California roll is gastronomically anodyne; it is eater friendly and universally appealing. For the novice epicurean not yet swayed by the hoopla surrounding raw fish (or raw-like, in the case of ceviche, where the seafood is technically "cooked" not over heat but in acid), California roll minimizes most of the dangers—psychological or otherwise—associated with uncooked fish while maintaining the thrill of the exotic. Indeed, if McDonald's were to ever put sushi on its menu, it certainly would start with California roll, which, one could argue, is sushi with training wheels. Representing the training wheels in this admittedly flimsy analogy is the absence of raw fish, which, as stated earlier, is synonymous with sushi in the United States. (In Japan, sushi is not so much about raw fish as it is about seasoned rice—more on this later.)

This is perhaps why most self-appointed sushi mavens treat California roll as the bane of their avocation, a fishbone in their throats. Often made in the United States by Korean, Chinese, Filipino, Thai, and at times Mexican, hands, this dubious concoction befits more the all-you-can-eat pavilion of a Chinese buffet just off the interstate than a dignified sushi shop in Osaka, Japan, the sushi pundits say. California roll is emblematic of an ancient, once-noble Japanese product that has been "Americanized," a multipronged euphemism for "mass produced," "compromised," and "vulgarized." In short, California roll is said to embody culinary apocrypha and ersatz gastronomy in our increasingly globalized, technologized, corporatized, and standardized world, where indigenous foods near and far have begun to go the way of the samurai, to exist only as fodder for museums, Hollywood, and other theme park ventures. (California roll! Hardly are those words out when a vapid image out of Fast Food Nation troubles our tongues. Surely the sushi apocalypse is at hand. Surely the end of real food is at hand. And what rough beast, the sushi cognoscenti ask, its hour come round at last, slouches toward Benihana to be born?)

California roll's reputation as a dubious variety of sushi stems largely from the fact that it is seen as ersatz, imitative, and artificial—in a word, fake—both on the level of individual ingredients used and as an assembled dish. A key ingredient that is incriminated is crabmeat, since what most often passes for crabmeat in California roll is not really made of crab but minced fish, or what the Japanese calls *surimi* (which in Japanese means "formed fish"). Composed of fish scrap, such as pollock, that is minced to a gelatinous paste, washed, pressed (to remove the water), salted and seasoned, shaped, and boiled until solidified,[9] surimi is what often stands in place of crabmeat in garden-variety California roll. And the inclusion of avocado and mayonnaise, both of which are strongly associated with American food, makes California roll appear not merely imitative but brands it as an American—to wit, crass—imitation at that. Moreover, the absence of raw fish, which gives sushi the aura of adventure and danger, adds to the sense of dubiousness. Take that away and most of sushi's exoticness, if not essence, is subdued. Consequently, California roll is construed as a symbol of counterfeit and therefore second-rate gastronomy. More so than that, to serious sushi devotees it is no less a harbinger of the end of real or whole food as we know it.

But is it really? Is California roll a sign of the culinary apocalypse, a regrettable consequence of Americanization of the world, as its critics declare it to be? Or is it simply a great culinary invention, a paragon of fusion cuisine, an ingenious amalgamation of sumptuous ingredients that cannot but taste good? Is this, moreover, simply a question of taste (both gustatory and aesthetic) or is it something much more?

The Global Pantry

Pantry item one: "They're calling it a soy sauce smackdown," began a 2002 *San Francisco Chronicle* article. "In one corner, led by the Japanese, are the soy sauce traditionalists," who tout their "centuries-old method of fermenting soybeans." Standing across the ring are the Americans, who support a newer soy sauce made not with soybeans, but with "a quick recipe that combines hydrolyzed vegetable protein, caramel coloring and corn syrup." The wrangle started years earlier when Japanese officials proposed to the Codex Alimentarius Commission, a United Nations–backed food arbiter that regulates standards for the international food trade, that brands such as La Choy and Chun King, both owned by the US industry goliath ConAgra Foods, be barred from using the term "soy sauce" when exporting their nonbrewed, nonsoy products overseas. True soy sauce, at a minimum, ought to contain soy, the Japanese contingent argued.[10]

To the US soy sauce producers and members of the International Hydrolyzed Protein Council, the actions of the Japanese were nothing less than a declaration of war. "All we want is for the standard for soy sauce to be all-inclusive," said a Codex delegate for the United States. "We have people who make naturally brewed and the hydrolyzed. We just have to make sure that the product is safe and compatible, that's all." The US soy sauce makers have a good reason for taking on this fight. While nonbrewed, hydrolyzed soy sauces ruled America thirty years ago, today, Kikkoman, a Japanese brand, dominates the US market.[11]

In asking the Codex to rule in their favor, the Japanese soy sauce lobby wanted to make sure Japan kept its market share in not only the United States but around the world, where the nonbrewed variety is primed to compete against the traditionally brewed soy sauces for new customers. In framing this story, the *San Francisco Chronicle* article pitted Japanese tradition against American modification of that tradition. Question: does it matter that soy sauce did not originate in Japan but in China during the Zhou dynasty (1134–246 BC)?[12] And what if the technique of producing the nonfermented, so-called American version made with hydrolyzed vegetable protein was invented not in the United States but in Japan, with Kikkoman and not ConAgra playing an important role both in the production and marketing of it as early as the 1920s?[13]

Pantry item two: in Mexico "the red-hot chili pepper is under attack from abroad," declared a 2005 story in *USA Today*. As it has done with other exports such as cheap shoes, China has flooded the Mexican market with Chinese-grown *chile de árbol*, which now accounts for a full third of all such chiles consumed in Mexico. While the Chinese- and Mexican-grown chiles appear visually identical, Mexican chile sellers insist that dried Mexican chiles are superior in taste and better suited for cooking Mexican dishes such as salsas and *moles*, and thus often charge up to 20 percent more for them. Mexican consumers, however, seem to neither notice nor care, as they more often choose the less expensive Chinese chiles. This has prompted Mexican lawmakers to urge protection for Mexican chile farmers. "If we don't pay attention, the cultivation of this crop could disappear in just a few years," warned a representative from Zacatecas, a state where cultivation of domestic chiles is a vital economic resource.[14]

What makes this situation especially galling to Mexican officials is the knowledge that pre-Columbian America is the origin of the chile. For untold millions of years before the arrival of humans, different varieties of chiles (genus *Capsicum*) grew wild in South America. In all probability, the plant was first domesticated in the Bolivian highlands before spreading to the Peruvian highlands.[15] According to Dave DeWitt's *The Chile Pepper Encyclopedia*, chiles have been part of the human diet in the Yucatán Peninsula and southern Mexico since 7500 BC, "and thus their usage predates the two great Central American civilizations, the Maya and the Aztecs." The development of the Olmec culture (1000 BC) and Monte Albán culture of Oaxaca (500 BC) included the culinary use of chiles.[16] This raises a question: are Mexican chiles superior to Chinese chiles by virtue of their origin? That is to say, by being indigenous to the Americas? If a case can be made that they are, can similar cases be made with any and all other edible matter, say, coffee (most likely West African origin), potato (South America), or Buffalo wings (upstate New York)?

Pantry item three: In October 2005 a team of Chinese scientists published in the journal *Nature* a surprising discovery made while excavating an archaeological site in northwestern China on the upper reaches of the Yellow River. "Noodles have been a popular staple food in many parts of the world for at least 2,000 years," began the article, prior to presenting a startling announcement—the unearthing of a "prehistoric sample of noodles contained in a well-preserved, sealed earthenware bowl discovered in the Late Neolithic archaeological site of Lajian." Based on their analysis of the remains, the scientists concluded that the ancient bowl of noodles, made of millet and resembling "the La-Mian noodle, a traditional Chinese noodle that is made by repeatedly pulling and stretching the dough by hand," dates back four thousand years.[17]

It did not take long for news of the discovery to travel far and wide. That same day, news outlets from New York to San Francisco, from Taipei to Glasgow, from Sydney to Bahrain, from Calcutta to Detroit, in unison declared China the victor and Italy the loser. Under the headline "Use

Your Noodle, Of Course the Chinese Served it First," the *Brisbane Courier Mail* declared, "A wrangle lasting decades as to which culture gave birth to the noodle has finally been settled—and the winner is China." "Old Noodle Settles Pasta Row," announced Australia's Special Broadcasting Service. "Chinese take away the credit for inventing noodles," proclaimed the UK's *Independent,* while the *Sun* suggested that the archaeological find is "possible proof for the argument that China invented pasta before Italy."[18]

The *Los Angeles Times,* meanwhile, printed the victory proclamations of two well-known Chinese American food personalities—Ming Tsai, the owner-chef of Blue Ginger restaurant in Wellesley, Massachusetts, and Martin Yan, perhaps the most beloved Chinese cook in America. "I can't imagine a more conclusive piece of evidence than this," Tsai is quoted as saying. "This definitely proves that the Chinese were making noodles way before the Italian Marco Polo came," said Martin Yan. "I take pride in that, even though I have a lot of Italian friends."[19]

Sushi Religiosity

The case against California roll appears as ironclad as the case for Japanese soy sauce, Mexican chile de árbol, and Chinese noodles. It rests on a single, all-encompassing premise: sushi originated in Japan. Among the most enduring myths Americans, and Westerners in general, have about Japan and Japanese people is that they are unrivaled in terms of cultural punctiliousness, and nowhere is this more evident than in the discourse surrounding comestibles, including beverages (e.g., tea, sake) and food, especially sushi. "Japanese cuisine is world renowned for meticulous presentation and refinement in presentation," begins the entry on Japan in Alan Davidson's *The Oxford Companion to Food.*[20] M. F. K. Fisher, the literary dame of American gastronomy, describes Japanese cuisine as "inextricably meshed with aesthetics, with religion, with tradition and history," and the Japanese people as "austere by nature" and "basically more aware . . . of the functional beauty of a bowl or plate" than your average American.[21] According to Michael Ashkenazi and Jeanne Jacob, authors of *The Essence of Japanese Cuisine: An Essay on Food and Culture,* the Japanese people consider food a "part of a complex, interrelated artistic tradition." Food is "clearly intermeshed into other threads of expressive endeavour," they argue, making it "possible to draw associations between other Japanese art forms and food, which illuminate the choices Japanese have made about their food and its presentation."[22]

Reputedly, chief among the culinary choices made by the Japanese is taking sushi—its history, artistry, and tradition—seriously, if not ascetically. To Ashkenazi and Jacob, sushi "exemplifies, perhaps more than any other Japanese dish, the cultural ability to find the essence of an activity, or object." They place sushi in the category of Japanese arts, alongside "dance, ink-brush painting, calligraphy, flower arrangement," positing that "minimalism of expression is the height of art" and that sushi, more than any other Japanese art form, embodies the essence of minimalism.[23]

Indeed, the degree to which a sushi eatery in Japan faithfully adheres to what is commonly perceived as a "proper" sushi creation is said to either make or break that establishment.[24] Moreover, highly regarded sushi chefs—or sushi artisans, rather—undergo years of apprenticeship, learning their crafts under the tutelage of venerable sushi masters. Theodore Bestor, author of *Tsukiji: The Fish Market at the Center of the World*, an ethnographic account of the famed Japanese fish emporium, cites a "folklore of artisanal apprenticeship" that has a sushi chef devoting "ten years as an apprentice, the first two just learning how to cook rice, before even beginning to wield a knife."[25] Ashkenazi and Jacob believe that a good sushi chef is an "artist" and report that it takes "at least five years to master the basics of the craft."[26]

Kinjiro Omae and Yuzuru Tachibana, authors of *The Book of Sushi*, break down a typical apprenticeship timetable in the following fashion: the first two years of a "young man aspiring to become an *itamae-san* are delegated to routine kitchen chores and making deliveries." (Figuratively, *itamae-san* refers to someone who is the master of his own establishment; literally, it means someone standing before the cutting board.) The next two years are devoted to proper rice making, a task that demands such a careful study that a "Japanese housewife who prepares this staple food daily" could not possibly live up to the precise standard expected of the sushi apprentice. Finally, the following three or four years are devoted to learning "the ins and outs of buying and preparing fish." This brings the total number of years spent training to seven or eight. And it is only at this point that a properly trained apprentice can begin to embark on a career as a sushi chef—in other words, to stand before the cutting board of his own establishment.²⁷ Thus in Japan a young man with dreams of becoming a sushi chef knows exactly the road before him, a road "firmly established in the culture of the sushi bar as the code that bound a samurai."²⁸ Or so it is said.

A young woman, of course, dares not dream such a dream. The art historian Linda Nochlin once asked, "Why have there been no great women artists?"²⁹ Taking her cue, we can just as easily ask: why have there not been any women sushi chefs, great or otherwise? "Because—some men say—women's hands are warmer than men's and hence adversely affect the flavor of raw seafood."³⁰ A woman's basal temperature, according to sushi mythology, is a shade higher than a man's and thus might compromise the freshness of the ingredients if she were to put her hands on them.³¹ (This notion persists despite the fact that a 1998 peer-reviewed study published in the medical journal *The Lancet* found men's hands to be on average warmer than women's.³² That said, even if a woman's hands were a fraction of a Fahrenheit warmer, would that really make any difference?) Others claim that since sushi is prepared with bare hands, "it would be intolerable for the fragrance of cosmetics on a woman's hand to be transmitted to the food."³³ (Never mind that a woman can just as easily choose not to use such products as men can.) Some, meanwhile, offer a more bluntly chauvinistic rationale, contenting that "the area behind the sushi bar is sacred space and would be defiled by the presence of a woman."³⁴

And there is yet another rationale for the absence of female sushi chefs: knives, it is said, are "boy's toys."³⁵ The sushi knife, like the samurai sword, is regarded by sushi traditionalists as no mere kitchen utensil but a sacred symbol of masculine Japanese pride and manly honor. Naomichi Ishige, author of *History and Culture of Japanese Food*, referring to the samurai as "Japan's warrior of the past," notes that a "sword embodied the samurai's soul: it represented the character of its owner." Ishige then opines that the "Japanese kitchen knife" is the "equivalent of the samurai's sword." Superior versions of both are handmade and engraved with the name of the bladesmith, and the wielder of both treats his blade with the utmost care and respect. In a professional kitchen, the pots, pans, and other kitchen utensils usually belong to the establishment. The knife, however, "is the private possession of the one who uses it" and moves with him if he were to take another job. And it is often the "top chef" of a kitchen who wields the knife (hence the moniker itamae) and upon him is bestowed not only the highest rank, prestige, and respect, but also the task of "artis-

Professional kitchen knives on display at Korin, a Japanese knives and kitchen supply store in New York City. Photo by Shara Richter.

tically slicing *sashimi*, the preparation of which requires no cooking as such but demands the highest skill."[36]

There is, however, an important difference between the samurai sword and the kitchen knife: while the former is a holy relic, an artifact of a mythologized past fetishized by the likes of Yukio Mishima and Tom Cruise playing dress-up as the "last samurai," the latter is believed to be very much a living force, the most essential implement of the sushi chef, the closest facsimile that contemporary Japan has to a sword-wielding warrior. (The samurai-sushi connection is brazenly touted in Trevor Corson's 2007 book on sushi, *The Zen of Fish: The Story of Sushi from Samurai to Supermarket*.) In Japan the cult of the blade is said to be exclusively a male domain, be it on the battlefield or behind the sushi bar. What this testosteronic legend camouflages is the material fact that sushi making is highly coveted because, relative to other professions in the food industry, it is better paid and has a higher status.[37] It is seen as "one of the last occupations that still maintains the proud manliness of the Edo workman."[38] Thus women who insist on pursuing the profession against these chauvinistic odds "simply leave Japan for America."[39] Once there, they, like most other US-based sushi chefs, are doomed to an ignominious career, fated to churn out roll after roll of—you guessed it—California rolls.

California roll, like the notion of female and non-Japanese sushi chefs, demeans sushi's sacrosanct legacy, the sushi purists charge. In keeping with the inherited relationship between notions of purity and sanctity, no cuisine is couched more lavishly in the language of religiosity than Japanese and no dish more so than sushi, which is discursively positioned as a symbol of Japanese culinary impeccability. French cuisine at times comes close, but it is perhaps more accurate to describe the critical genuflection before the presence of such revered restaurants as Le Meurice in Paris or Le Bernardin in New York City as aristocratic or regal more than religious. The reverence shown to Sukiyabashi Jiro, a sushi establishment in Tokyo and the subject of a 2011 documentary film, *Jiro Dreams of Sushi*, on the other hand, can only be described as spiritual—in an exaggerated Zen sort of way.

For an archetypal if not stereotypical example of how not only the food but the entire experience of eating Japanese food can be draped in the language of piety, consider the *New York Times* review of Sushi Yasuda published in 2011. In it, the food critic Eric Asimov refers to the Manhattan Japanese restaurant as a "standout shrine." He reports that the owners "staked the restaurant's reputation on a pure, uncompromised expression of the traditional art of sushi making" and that they "succeeded brilliantly" in this regard. "The effect is to be transported to a calm sanctuary where one may experience sushi artistically, pleasurably and, dare I say, spiritually," he opined—and without a shred of irony. A slice of *kanpachi* that he places in his mouth is described as "supremely pure" and the sea urchin so "intense, complex, and subtle and soulful it sends shivers" down his spine. "For a moment nothing exists but me and the sushi," gushes Asimov—again absent of all irony. The last item he tries, an omelet, is described as "perfect" in flavor and "beautiful to observe." He ends the review with a bold claim that defines sushi eating as a religious experience above all, while characterizing American influence as the primary defiler of that experience: "With its devotion to sushi in its purist form, unalloyed with other Japanese cuisines with American twists, Yasuda occupies a singular position in New York's sushi landscape."[40]

Asimov does not say it outright, but for an expression of sushi in its *impurist* form, alloyed with vulgar American twists, we are asked to look no further than the California roll. He strongly implies this idea when he remarks that at Yasuda "the creative liberties taken with sushi are a world away" (in Japan, it is assumed) where avocado is "an unknown," as are jalapeño and mayonnaise.[41] This disdain for avocado as a sushi ingredient is aptly encapsulated in a 2008 *Wall Street Journal* profile of three American sushi establishments—Sushi Nozawa in Los Angeles, Sasabune in New York City, and Sawa Sushi in Sunnyvale, California. If you find yourself sitting at the sushi bar at one of these venerable restaurants, the article warns, "Don't try to order—the chef will decide what you eat. Use extra soy sauce at your own risk. And don't ask for a California roll. You might get kicked out." Referring admiringly to the head sushi chefs of these establishments as "sushi bullies" and "sushi dictators," the article notes that each has his own set of pet peeves, which includes patrons who use too much soy sauce, disassemble a piece of sushi, ask for miso soup or extra rice, or linger at the sushi bar too long. And they all "loathe the ubiquitous California roll." Why? "Not only is it a newfangled American invention that combines avocado and cucumber, but it usually contains imitation crab—anathema to chefs who have spent so much of their energy and money securing pristine seafood," according to the article. Asking for it could result in customers—including "Hollywood bigwigs"—being ejected from the premises. Sawa Sushi even has a ban on California roll because the concoction is believed to epitomize the very opposite of what is considered "authentic" sushi.[42]

The Profane Fruit

When it comes to the sheer number of questions generated about the etiquette of consumption, it seems no other single dish, foreign or otherwise, comes close to rivaling sushi. Can I use my fingers or must I use chopsticks? (Either, according to most sushi mavens.) Am I supposed to mix the wasabi with the soy sauce to form a slurry into which sushi pieces are dipped? (No.) What do I do with the pickled ginger—eat it before, with, or after the sushi? (Between bites of sushi as a palate cleanser.) When eating nigirizushi, do I dip the rice side or the fish side into the soy sauce? (The fish side.) When putting it into my mouth, which side faces up? (Most mavens say fish side up, but a select few insist on fish side down.) Am I supposed to put the whole thing in my mouth at once or am I allowed to eat it in two or three bites? (All at once; if the piece is too large to eat in a single bite, your sushi chef needs to go back to sushi school.) Is it better to drink beer (Yes), sake (No, since it is also made of rice), wine (Why would you?), or tea? (Yes.) Can I have a Diet Coke with it instead? (Sigh.) To serious sushi aficionados, these are not trivial or rhetorical questions. They are, rather, imperative, and each has a correct answer.

But does it, really? As is often the case with activities that are severely rule driven, such as, say, grammatical usage, answers to questions about propriety often vary depending on which so-called expert is consulted. Question: is it okay to end a sentence with a preposition, split an infinitive, or begin a sentence with "however"? Answer: it depends on which grammarian you ask. In this regard, sushi eating is among the most prescriptive of all restaurant experiences. And it can also seem the most intimidating, especially for a sushi tyro sitting at a sushi bar for the very first time. Given the religiosity of sushi discourse, perhaps this is to be expected. In fact, it appears the intimidation factor is something serious sushi eaters not only expect but desire—and the more high end the sushi establishment, the more intense the desire for the intimidation factor. (Hence the requisite admiration for and excessive kowtowing to sushi chefs who behave in the most autocratic and draconian manner.) A major element of sushi is getting it right, of knowing how it is supposed to be done and doing it properly, not only by the sushi artisans but also by the patrons themselves. This, however, applies only to proper sushi creations. When it comes to California roll, given that the concoction itself is seen as a violation of sushi's innate spiritual integrity, do these rules even matter?

As a culinary symbol that stands as the most serious transgressor of sushi purity and propriety, avocado is without rival. Ashkenazi and Jacob recount the response of one Japanese sushi chef to the question of avocado, California roll's signature ingredient: "What *is* that? And why put it on sushi?"[43] What avocados are, of course, besides no longer being an unknown in Japan, is the bulbous fruit of a tree that belongs to the laurel family. Unlike other laurel plants, such as cinnamon and bay tree, which have Old World origins, avocados (*Persea americana*) are New World, meaning it did not exist outside the Americas prior to Columbus. The fruit is best characterized by its "unctuous oily flesh, a trait shared only with the olive and the coconut in the edible plant world," according to Sophie Coe, author of *America's First Cuisines,* a book that surveys pre-Columbian food cultures.[44]

Avocado plant. Painting by Pierre-Joseph Redouté (1759–1840).

Due largely to the use of avocado (dubbed sushi's "eternal interloper" by a *New York Times* restaurant critic in 2012)[45] as a primary ingredient, California roll is described by *The Dictionary of American Food and Drink* as a form of sushi created for the "American palate" and offers "carifornia" as an alternate spelling.[46] In *Why We Eat What We Eat: How Columbus Changed the Way the World Eats*, Raymond Sokolov describes California roll as an "American-Japanese neologism," while Katarzyna Cwiertka, author of *Modern Japanese Cuisine: Food, Power and National Identity*, calls it an "American standard."[47] And in the words of a Japanese ministry of foreign affairs official, California roll is an American "imitation" of Japanese food, but it is a "good thing" because "imitation is the sincerest flattery."[48] In each of these instances (with Cwiertka being the possible exception), "American" is not merely meant as a descriptor but also a pejorative.[49]

In this global era there is perhaps no greater insult to the perceived integrity of indigenous cultural expressions than to designate something as "American" or to describe it as having undergone a process of "Americanization." For example, in much of equatorial cuisines that rely heavily on chiles and other piquant spices, to say that a dish has been Americanized equates it to being "watered down," its heat shamelessly subdued in order to cater to what is understood as a craven American taste. Since the mid-twentieth century, and today more than ever, a legion of detractors has regarded the United States as the leading agent of cultural imperialism, a system of exploitation that relies not so much on explicit military or political coercion, but instead on the hegemonic transmission of cultural forms—popular culture in particular—under the aegis of powerful corporations, with Disney, Microsoft, Coca-Cola, and McDonald's leading the way.[50] In this regard, as Youchi Shimemura has observed, globalization is assumed to be "another name for world dominance by American capitalists," which inevitably leads to, in the view of more radical critics, the eventual erosion of "local and regional cultures and spreading American consumer goods and the American way of life to every corner of the world."[51] Donald Pease, meanwhile, points to the "relationship between recent changes in the understanding of U.S. diplomatic history and the emergent interest in the importance of imperialism to cultural constructions in general and for critical multiculturalism's understanding of race, class, and gender as culturally constructed categories." As a result, "the concept of U.S. imperialism has itself become the subject of political and scholarly debates," he writes.[52]

Thus to label sushi, which Alan Davidson considers "perhaps the best known internationally of all Japanese specialities,"[53] as "American" is a not-so-secret code for implying that some sacred cultural convention has been desecrated as a result of US hegemony. The alternative possibility, that California roll might be an American product that has been Japanized, is a concept that cannot be sustained in the current discussion of cultural imperialism, since the hegemonic flow is primarily seen as unidirectional—from a more powerful source to a weaker destination. This is the case even in the face of Japan's brawny economic standing on the world stage; it is, after all, the third largest economy in the world according to most measures (and only recently surpassed by China as the second largest after the United States). When the United States appears in the picture, the cultural materials associated with all other nations, even relatively privileged ones such as Japan and France (the ninth largest economy in the world), appear to teeter on the brink of permanent defilement or extinction. The general consensus is that California roll is, at best, pseudo-Japanese and, at worst, not Japanese at all, that this New World product fails the litmus test of sushi authenticity, that it is American at the core. This is despite the fact that, as Sonoko Kondo puts it in *The Poetical Pursuit of Food: Japanese Recipes for American Cooks*, the recipe had, as early as the 1980s, "reached the shores of Japan, becoming a favorite with all sushi lovers."[54]

Pretty to Think So

If California roll cannot be considered authentic sushi, what does authenticity on a plate look like? What makes a dish—or an entire cuisine, for that matter—authentic? If vindaloo, must the protein be pork, not lamb, using none other than Kashmiri chiles, without the addition of potatoes, prepared by an actual Goan in Margao, and not a Bangladeshi short-order cook on Manhattan's East Sixth Street? If *bulgogi*, must it be closer to the version prepared by the expert chefs at the Shilla Hotel's Sorabol Restaurant in Seoul, South Korea, with thinly sliced rib eye marinated in rice wine and Nashi pear, rather than the Rachael Ray version, which calls for a whole flank steak rubbed with McCormick Montreal Steak Seasoning, served atop a bed of faux kimchi, a godawful mess of sautéed bok choy, red bell peppers, and canned sauerkraut?[55] (Surely if the gastronomic apocalypse is indeed at hand, the slouching rough beast, its *30 Minute Meals* and *$40 a Day* come round at last, has to be Rachael Ray, doesn't it?) Is the qualitative gulf between *this* and *that*—between what could be called apocryphal gastronomy and authentic gastronomy—unmistakably self-evident, irrefutable, and as wide as the Orient itself? Bottom line: do authentic foods simply taste better?

To attempt to answer these questions, let alone pose them, is to play along in a game of make-believe; it is to put one's faith in the fictive or imaginary as a discursive strategy for making sense of and coping with the world as it is. It is to deliberately reenact the conversation between Lady Brett Ashley and Jake Barnes, the accidental platonic lovers, as they ride off into the Madrid sunset in the back of a taxi at the end of Ernest Hemingway's *The Sun Also Rises*. "Oh Jake, we could have had such a damned good time together," the wanton Brett says wistfully. "Yes," the impuissant Jake replies. "Isn't it pretty to think so?"[56]

Likewise, isn't it pretty to think of the eternal virtue and wholesomeness of gastronomic authenticity, pretty to cling to a vision of wholly discrete foodscapes undamaged by the passing of time and the ceaselessness of human activities? To contemporary diners, the answer to the question "What should I eat?" is unduly complicated, as chronicled by Michael Pollan in his gastro-opus, *The Omnivore's Dilemma: A Natural History of Four Meals*. "When you can eat just about anything nature has to offer," Pollan reminds us, "deciding what you should eat will inevitably stir anxiety." Shall I eat organic or conventional, wild or farmed? Should I remain a carnivore or convert to lacto-vegetarianism, or perhaps veganism? Pollan compares the plight of today's American diner to a long-ago hunter-gatherer contemplating the edibility of a wild mushroom picked off the ground, with the supermarket aisle replacing the forest floor. We select a packaged victual, eyeball the baffling label, and fret over the cryptography of "cage-free," "range-fed," "TBHQ," and "xanthan gum."[57] Enter the salve of culinary nostalgia, accompanied by authoritative reassurances in the form of connoisseurship of authenticity. If we feel hemmed in by the minefield of synthetic and potentially toxic foodstuffs that clutters our edible environment, then the promise of gastronomic authenticity is a welcomed portal that leads us to a land of milk, honey, and incredibly scrumptious heirloom tomatoes.

To desire to eat authenticity is to combat the weariness of the modern condition as an endless romantic might, disdainful of the present and wistful of the past. The trick is to pull this off as Jake Barnes would, with *aficion*, or passion backed by thorough knowledge of a subject, and in a manner that would gain you entrance into Montoya's hotel, where the true bullfighters come to stay each year. Accordingly, you must at all costs avoid coming off like the drippy Robert Cohn, former Princeton middleweight boxing champion and failed knight of latter-day chivalry. (In other words, you must be a culinary Indiana Jones, à la Anthony Bourdain of the Travel Channel's *No Reservations*, and not a mere culinary tourist, à la Jeff Smith of PBS' *Frugal Gourmet*.) You must be worthy of having your photograph framed by Montoya and hung on his wall, not thrown into his desk drawer. As Jake said of true aficion, "there was no password, no set questions that could bring it out."[58] Likewise, gastronomic authenticity is something that is defined as either is or isn't; like all cultural matter that depends on taste, either you have it or you don't. As the noted African art dealer Henri Kamer has said of connoisseurship and expertise, you must have an "instinct for quality," "a sixth sense" with which "to feel the quality."

And while much can be gained through the study of books and firsthand field experience, as far as Kamer is concerned, "taste and a feeling of quality are never acquired"; it is, rather, "innate."[59]

To attach one's faith to gastronomic authenticity, to borrow an allusion from Milan Kundera, is to prefer the "unbearable heaviness" to the "unbearable lightness" of food, but not in a sense of richness of ingredients or tallying calories. It is the Beethovenian *ess muss sein* view of food, of believing that food must be a certain way, that it has to adhere to a prescribed order of things.[60] Arjun Appadurai contends that authenticity "measures the degree to which something is more or less what it *ought* to be." To "ought" I would add *must, shall, should*. The alternative modals—*may, could, might, can*—are too capricious for such a weighty rhetorical game. But given that authenticity is a "norm of some sort," Appadurai wonders who or what exactly—to borrow a George W. Bush-ism—is the decider? Does authenticity emerge from the thing itself? Is it an "immanent norm, emerging somehow from the cuisine itself? Or is it an external norm, reflecting some imposed gastronomic standard? If it is an immanent norm, who is its authoritative voice: the professional cook? the average consumer? the gourmand? the housewife? If it is an imposed norm, who is its privileged voice: the connoisseur of exotic food? the tourist? the ordinary participant in a neighborhood cuisine? the cultivated eater from a distant one?"[61] Unable to come up with satisfactory answers, Appadurai likens authenticity to a "mirage," which the diner obsessively pursues even as it "invariably vanishes just when we think we have it" within our reach.

In this respect, authenticity is the White Whale of modern epicurism, tirelessly pursued by hungry Ahabs (e.g., cosmopolitan foodies and displaced migrants) in search of the perfect "native" meal despite heavy tolls of spiritual anguish and material oblation. Authenticity is also Godot, the anticipated company that never manages to arrive despite encouraging rumors, signs, and promises. When something does finally arrive, accompanied by extortionate fanfare, it rarely—if truly ever—lives up to expectations. Unlike a Snicker's candy bar, it never really quite satisfies. The best that can be hoped for is a conciliatory simulacrum of some uncanny essence that is hankered for, a diminutive but true-to-scale proxy of the thing itself, say, the Eiffel Tower on the Las Vegas Strip in place of the genuine article on the Champ de Mars, with one crucial difference: imagine Alexander Gustave Eiffel never built a tower, that the Exposition

Universelle never took place, that the Las Vegas Chamber of Commerce made it all up. Imagine if what happens in Vegas really doesn't happen at all.

Had John Berger opted to write *Ways of Tasting* instead of *Ways of Seeing*, he might have equated the desire for culinary authenticity with the bogus religiosity of food, with full-color illustrations of how the fear of the present—the fear of the demise of authentic dining experiences due to modernity, globalization, and industrialization of food—leads to the mystification of the past, where inequalities appear noble, hierarchies thrilling, and everything is magically delicious.[62] This is a condition unique to modernity that I call the cult of gastronomic authenticity, a quasi-religious, fashion-driven system of veneration directed toward a particular set of comestibles, commonly organized along a racial, ethnic, national, or regional axis. I use the term "cult" quite deliberately, as I wish to maximize the "shamanistic" or "priestly" dimensions of gastronomic authorities who wield a special kind of cultural, economic, and emotional power over not only the words that come out of their mouths, but also the viands that go into ours. A pronounced characteristic of the system is an excessive admiration for and pursuits of culinary elements that faithfully re-create or attempt to resemble undisputed origins. As Appadurai puts it, authenticity "seems always to appear just after its subject matter has been significantly transformed" and is indicative of a profound doubt over a culinary tradition that is believed to have undergone some sort of inimical disturbance.[63] The result is a search for the so-called authentic, if not original, version of a cultural product deemed to be damaged, contaminated, or interrupted via imaginative travel to a place and time assumed to be more glorious, faraway, and bygone.

Here, I follow the semantic lead of Edward Said, who, in *Beginnings: Intention and Method,* describes *origin*—in contrast to *beginning*—as "a unique miracle" that "cannot be duplicated or incarnated within the absolute boundaries of human life." Said posits that between the words "origin" and "beginning" "lies a constantly changing system of meanings," where the former possesses a more "passive" meaning and the latter a more "active" one. "Origin" is a term that is almost "theological," Said argues, "in that it must be understood in the strictest sense possible." This is the word best suited to buttress mythological beliefs or religious entitlements, systems that are diminished by rigorous demands of reason or ocular proof. "Beginning," however, is "eminently secular, or gentile, continuing activities." In short, while origin concerns itself with what we construe to be mythical, mystical, or sacred, beginning inaugurates something temporally historical. (E.g., while the origin of all human souls may be attributable to biblical Eve, it can be said that the beginning of all *Homo sapiens* is mitochondrial Eve.) "To complicate matters further," Said asserts, "we generally locate origins before beginnings, since the Origin is a latent state from which the beginnings of action move forward: retrospectively considered, then, the Origin is a condition or state that permits beginning." The power of origin, therefore, is arbitrary, if not divine, and beginning is often placed under its rhetorical jurisdiction. Given the passivity of ideas that rely on claims of origins and the original, Said even goes so far as to say that they "ought to be avoided" in honest criticism.[64]

Unless, of course, you believe in magic or the occult, upon which, I believe, transcendental notions such as culinary authenticity rely. All food-related claims of authenticity are passively derived through a narrative of origin, which transports the modern eater back to the golden era of human gastronomy, a mythical time when every fruit was organic and livestock hormone free—a prelapsarian Larder of Eden, if you will. The empty stomach gives way to the restless tongue, which in turn sits second fiddle to the bored ear. The decision behind each bite of food must be accompanied by a credible Scheherazade story—be it a creation myth, a narrative of origin, a chain of custody, or a documentable *terroir*—in order for another to be taken. Foods haloed with the rose-colored aura of nostalgia, often for someone else's invented past, is the holy grail of today's recreational diners and forlorn expatriates, whose need for subsistence is trumped by a need to fill a more urgent spiritual void.

To cope with the unbearable ennui of the present, we must travel to a nobler if not more vibrant past so that a worthwhile future might be secured—or so we are told. In this regard, culinary authenticity functions as a time-travel vehicle, and in the driver's seat are culinary authorities whose job is to manipulate and profit from this arrangement. This is not to say that the ceaseless activities of gastronomic professionals are necessarily dishonest entrepreneurship, however. They are, rather, savvy capitalists who know exactly who their customers are (hopeless romantics) and know exactly what they want (another delectable bite). They are also lowbrow versions of high modernists, charged with the awesome task of bringing the impenetrable poetics of luminaries such as T. S. Eliot, Ezra Pound, and Thomas Keller down to the pews.

Whence Sushi?

Unlike sukiyaki or tempura, "sushi is completely Japanese," writes Sylvia Lovegren, author of *Fashionable Foods: Seven Decades of Food Fad*, a book chronicling US food crazes from the 1920s to the 1990s. Sukiyaki, the best-known Japanese dish in the United States before World War II, is either Dutch or Portuguese in origin, she asserts, and remained a "foreign" dish in Japan for over a century after having been introduced to the islands in the sixteenth century. Another well-known Japanese dish, tempura, was also introduced to Japan in the sixteenth century by the Portuguese, and it too remained "foreign" for a century, until the Japanese adopted it as "one of their own favorite foods." According to Lovegren, the origin of sushi, by contrast, is strictly insular: "Some say sushi was invented, much like the Occidental sandwich, by Japanese gamblers too busy to tear themselves away from the gaming tables to eat. Others say that vinegared rice was used to separate layers of salted fish, and when a hungry worker tasted the rice, sushi was born. Whichever story is true, sushi is completely Japanese."[65] Based on Lovegren's line of thought, it is the place of origin and the moment of inception that determine whether an item of food is "Japanese" or "foreign." In her view, neither sukiyaki nor tempura, although having thoroughly been assimilated into the nation's gastronomy for over a century, is wholly Japanese, given its European origins. What makes sushi completely Japanese is that some autochthonous inhabitants of Japan (e.g., a Japanese gambler) are principally, if not solely, responsible for its birth, even if the details of that birth are murky, to say the least, as evidenced by her use of "some say" and "others say" in the narrative.

Lovegren's sketchy account of sushi's origin differs dramatically from Theodore Bestor's more specialized rendering, in which the modern form of sushi is linked to an atavistic sushi that survives today as *funazushi*, a regional specialty from Shiga Prefecture near Kyoto.[66] (*Funa* is a freshwater fish, a type of carp, and is most strongly associated with Lake Biwa, located about six miles east of Kyoto at the nearest point.) According to Naomichi Ishige, the origin of the word "sushi" is linked to this original sushi.[67] In point of fact, funazushi is the best-known example of *narezushi*, a fermented fish product that takes months and often over a year to prepare. After capture, the funa is salted and packed inside a crock between layers of vinegared rice. Over time, lactic acid is produced by the rice, which essentially pickles the fish and keeps it from spoiling. This method of fish preservation coincided with the introduction of rice cultivation in Japan during "prehistoric times," assert Kinjiro Omae and Yuzuru Tachibana. They also note that the rice of narezushi was discarded by the ancients, and it was not until the fifteenth and sixteenth centuries that the people of Japan grew not only impatient with the long duration of fermentation but began to feel that the entire undertaking was a waste of an extremely valuable commodity, namely rice.[68] Bestor, meanwhile, relates that culinary historians date the origins of sushi in the form of funazushi not to prehistoric times but to "perhaps as early as the seventeenth century." He also stresses that "the rice itself was simply discarded before the fish was eaten."[69]

The fact that this earliest sushi was one in which the rice was not consumed but cast aside is significant for a simple reason: as Trevor Corson reminds us in *The Zen of Fish*, the term "sushi" does not, by definition, entail fish, raw or otherwise, as commonly assumed by most Americans. To the Japanese, the essential component of sushi is "rice seasoned with rice vinegar, sugar, and salt," and "any food made with this seasoned rice can be called sushi."[70] Corson finds this to be "ironic because the original sushi chefs threw the sushi rice away."[71] (Provided this is true, Corson is unaware of another irony, namely the title of his book. If indeed his book is about sushi, why not call it *The Zen of Seasoned Rice* instead of *The Zen of Fish?*) Michael Ashkenazi and Jeanne Jacob reinforce the centrality of rice in sushi by repeating the words of an unnamed sushi chef: "Rice is the soul of sushi."

Question: if vinegared rice is indeed what makes sushi *sushi*, would it make sense to consider the precise moment when freshly (i.e., unfermented) seasoned rice was first consumed (with or without fish, raw or otherwise) as the birth of modern sushi? If so, when exactly did this occur? Not until the Tokugawa period, according to Bestor.[72] (He, however, does not specify exactly when during the Tokugawa period, which lasted from 1603 to 1867.) And the individual responsible for introducing freshly vinegared rice that would be paired with unfermented (i.e., fresh) raw fish? According to Omae and Tachibana, it was the brainchild of Yoshiichi Matsumoto, a doctor who lived in Yotsuya, Edo, and was employed by Ietsuna (1641–1680), the fourth Tokugawa shogun.[73]

And what about the origin of perhaps the most iconic sushi of all, nigirizushi, the bite-sized block of rice with a slice of raw fish placed on top?

According to Bestor, nigirizushi "became the rage of Edo in the 1820s or 1830s" and is thus also known as *edomaezushi*. (Edo was renamed Tokyo in 1868 by the Meiji government.) Although he briefly alludes to Hanaya Yohei (1799–1858), "who invented or perfected the technique in 1824" at his Edo shop, Bestor does not elaborate further on this famed sushi chef but instead refers to this account merely as a "common story" of nigirizushi's origins, strongly implying that there are others versions out there.[74] Omae and Tachibana augment the story by calling nigirizushi "an instant improvement on the older, more venerable sushi dishes," adding that the stall that Yohei opened in the "bustling Ryoguku district of Edo caught on at once."[75]

But even if Matsumoto's status as the originator of vinegared rice and Hanaya Yohei's as the father of nigirizushi can be authenticated, the precise origin of sushi itself still remains unsettled due largely to the legacy of narezushi, which, contrary to Lovegren's Japanese gambler hypothesis, did not spontaneously originate in Japan. By all accounts, this so-called earliest version of sushi instead was brought to Japan by ancient settlers hailing from the Mekong River basin of Southeast Asia some twenty-five hundred miles away. Narezushi, which is essentially fermented fish, is in this regard directly related to other fermented fish products, most notably fish sauce (e.g., *kecap ikan, nampla, nuoc mam*) and fish paste (e.g., *bagoong, kapi, padec*), that are key elements to Vietnamese, Thai, Filipino, Cambodian, and other Southeast Asian cuisines.

If modern-day sushi, which typically uses the freshest and the least adulterated seafood, bears no resemblance to fish sauce, look no further than the vinegar in the sushi rice for a reminder of this common culinary ancestry.[76] (The vinegar is said to mimic the acidic note typical of the taste imparted by the lactic acid in fermented foods.) In this regard, sushi's origin might very well be tied to the *shiokara*, the "salt-cured preserve of fish, mollusks, and their entrails,"[77] which is the Japanese version of fermented seafood. In his retelling of the story of sushi's origin, Corson likewise locates the place of sushi's birth to somewhere along the Mekong River, "in what is now landlocked southern China, Laos, and northern Thailand." As for sushi's date of birth, he takes us back as far as the Jomon period, to 3500 BC. And although it is unclear when sushi, in the form of narezushi, exactly made its way from southern China to Japan, Corson cites an AD 718 government document listing sushi as an acceptable form of tax payment, indicating that sushi goes at least that far back.[78]

Question: given the probability that sushi in fact did not spring forth autochthonously in Japan but that its origins lie somewhere in Southeast Asia, can it really be considered completely, purely, or indigenously Japanese? That said, how do we know for sure that the trail stops in Southeast Asia? If we rewind the story even further, where might we end up? India? The Fertile Crescent? The savannahs of East Africa? The Garden of Eden?

Whence California Roll?

Fast forward to the twentieth century, to the late 1960s. By all accounts, this was when California roll first came into existence. But as Sasha Issenberg, author of *The Sushi Economy: Globalization and the Making of a Modern Delicacy,* puts it, the "story of the California roll's creation varies slightly depending on who is telling it."[79] In 1989 Molly O'Neill of the *New York Times* wrote that in Los Angeles' sushi bars "Japanese immigrants used American avocados to confect the 'California roll.'" This was part of what she called the "Chop Suey Syndrome" to describe the process of "Americanizing the Exotic." The Chinese American chop suey, Afghan American kofta kebab, Italian American lasagna (laden with meat), Tex-Mex nachos (piled high with beans, cheese, guacamole, and sour cream), and Japanese American California roll were cited as examples of how "new arrivals"—meaning immigrants—often play the role of "culinary ambassadors" by fabricating versions of traditional dishes that are "easily produced and tuned to current tastes." But before these dishes "move from pushcarts to storefronts and on toward mainstream America," they first must be "tamed" in order to "suit the shy American palate." By making the "exotic familiar," O'Neill argues, immigrants transform these ancestral dishes into "ethnic icons" that "say more about where immigrants have arrived than where they have left."[80]

O'Neill's rhetorical use of chop suey is significant in that the dish has long been regarded as the paragon of a shoddy "ethnic" American dish that bears little or no resemblance to anything eaten by a so-called true native back in an immigrant's place of origin. Is California roll the chop suey of Japanese food? Is it a jerry-built invention of Japanese immigrants who settled in America over a century ago? Does it bear only the slightest resemblance to the "authentic" sushi in its ancestral homeland? Indeed, perhaps more than any other dish associated with Japan, it is California roll, made tame by subtraction of raw fish and made familiar by addition of avocados, that plays the role of cultural ambassador to Japanese food in America.

The chop suey–California roll analogy, however, is muddled by the question of California roll's origins (not to mention chop suey's).[81] Specifically, whence did it arise? Were the originators in fact Japanese *Americans,* as Molly O'Neill presumes, or were they Japanese *nationals,* who just happened to be in California at the time of California roll's creation? In other words, does California roll say more about how Japanese immigrants and their descendants manifest their cultural presence in the United States or about how, in the words of Iris-Aya Laemmerhirt, a traditional Japanese food such as sushi is "reimagined in the United States" and becomes a participant in "a transnational exchange, thereby communicating across cultural and national boundaries"?[82] Or perhaps the two processes are inextricably linked and inseparable, like the two sides of a single sheet of nori?

What appears to be undisputed with regard to California roll's origins is the birthplace—the Little Tokyo neighborhood of Los Angeles at a restaurant called Tokyo Kaikan, first opened in 1963. As for the individual—or individuals—credited as creator, according to David Kamp it was a pair of Japanese sushi chefs named Ichiro Mashita and Teruo Imaizumi.[83] Trevor Corson also identifies Tokyo Kaikan, which he calls "one of the first restaurants to open a sushi bar, and the premier Japanese eatery in L.A." during that time, as the place of origin. He, however, names only a single person as the creator—Ichiro Mashita.[84] Issenberg, meanwhile, names both men but refers to Mashita as "Chef" and Imaizumi as "his broadcheeked and sideburned young assistant." He also points out that the two men were there on a business assignment, meaning they were not immigrants. Tokyo Kaikan was part of "the EIWA Group, a Tokyo-based food-business conglomerate that had purchased a Chinese restaurant going out of business in First Street in Little Tokyo," and Mashita and Imaizumi "had been imported from EIWA's Tokyo restaurants."[85]

Thus we have a rough consensus, at least among Issenberg, Kamp, and Corson, on an approximate *when* (the 1960s), a most likely *where* (Tokyo Kaikan in Little Tokyo), and *who* (Mashita and Imaizumi). To better understand California roll's origins, however, we need to also understand *why* and *how* this concoction came to exist in the first place. This is crucial if, as the sushi cognoscenti believe, origin is in fact inextricably linked to authenticity. What inspired Mashita (and Imaizumi) to put avocado, an ingredient hitherto unacquainted with the concept of sushi, in the mix? Who was it first intended for? That is to say, was it designed for Tokyo Kaikan's clientele of Japanese nationals, who presumably knew what authentic sushi was by the virtue of their Japanese nationality, or was it for benighted Americans, for whom sushi was essentially culinary exotica? If the former, perhaps California roll can be rescued from its current low status and reputation as a dubious sushi and allowed to join the ethereal rank enjoyed by other so-called proper sushi types. If the latter, perhaps California roll can be justifiably compared to chop suey and is deserving of all the disparagement heaped upon it. Whichever the case, if in fact Mashita and Imaizumi were the inventors, then the dish was not the product of Japanese American culinary adaptation as Molly O'Neill suggests, and thus it would be erroneous to lump California roll with chop suey, kofta kebab, meat laden lasagna, Tex-Mex nachos, and other "exotic familiar" dishes made possible through immigrant entrepreneurship.

According to one myth of origin, an executive of the Japanese conglomerate that owned Tokyo Kaikan came to America and suggested that sushi be made to appeal to Caucasians. Mashita and his assistant took heed and came up with a king-crab leg, avocado, and mayonnaise amalgam. Issenberg, however believes this to be "company lore" and offers another story, placing Mashita's culinary genius at the center. During the 1960s in California, fresh tuna was available only during the summer months. When his American (i.e., Caucasian) customers, having taken to the taste of *toro* (a cut from the fatty belly of tuna), complained of its absence during the off months, Mashita experimented with fatty beef and chicken but eventually settled on silky avocado, "accented, for good measure, by creamy mayonnaise"—and presto, ersatz toro![86] "Mashita first prepared the avocado as *nigirizushi,* placing a slice upon a mound of rice," writes Issenberg. Seeing his customers taken aback by the odd green hue of avocado, he decided to roll it up along with king crab, creating the makizushi form that we are familiar with today. (Today's inside-out form, a type of makizushi called *uramaki,* which has an outer layer of rice and fillings surrounded by nori inside, reportedly occurred at a later date.) Issenberg notes that California roll was not cheap at first, as avocado was relatively expensive at the time, as was king crab, which was shipped from Alaska. Industrial surimi (e.g., imitation crabmeat) used in most massmarket versions today was not yet available.[87]

Kamp, meanwhile, tells a slightly different story, one that takes place in 1964. He begins by quoting directly from an interview he conducted with Imaizumi, Mashita's assistant: "It wasn't because we were trying to make something more palatable for Americans, but because of the poor variety of fish back then.... The tuna was just a seasonal thing in LA, available in the summertime, so we were thinking, 'What else can we use? What else can we look for?'" According to Imaizumi, then, California roll was originally intended for Japanese customers. "Cut into little cubes, ripe avocado flesh had an unctuousness that approximated the texture of fatty fish, and the two sushi chefs combined it with king crab, cucumber, and ginger, serving their creation as a *hand roll*," writes Kamp.[88] The Japanese diners were initially wary of the absence of raw fish. But soon a new clientele emerged: "Caucasian diners—executives and financiers who had business with Japanese companies, and fearless diners emboldened by the new spirit of ethnic adventure afoot in the seventies." Apparently it was they who would take California roll into the culinary stratosphere and make it into the most popular form of sushi ever invented.[89]

Premade supermarket California roll. The classic version consists of avocado, imitation crabmeat, and cucumber rolled "inside out." Photo by the author.

Another detail worth noting: provided Kamp's version is correct, the original California roll was not the more common type of makizushi, such as *futomaki* or uramaki, that is rolled into a cylinder with the aid of a bamboo mat (called *makisu*) and cut into bite-sized pieces. Rather, it was a type of makizushi called *temakizushi*, which is "rolled by hand" and is typically conical in shape. This distinction appears to be reinforced by what might be the first ever mention of California roll in the *New York Times*. In a 1982 review of a Japanese restaurant in Glen Cove, New York, Florence Fabricant refers to California roll as "a West Coast invention for those who may be timid about trying sushi." Although she does not cite the term, she unmistakably implies that it was a temakizushi, describing it as "the size of a small ice cream cone, rolled in a thin sheet of papery pressed seaweed and filled with rice, cooked crabmeat, avocado and mayonnaise."[90]

Corson offers yet another variation of California roll's origins. Like Kamp, he asserts that California roll was not initially created to appease timid American eaters, but to satisfy discriminating Japanese palates. Tokyo Kaikan's sushi bar, he notes, primarily served a Japanese—not American or Japanese American, even—clientele. Unable to obtain toro, Mashita found in avocados a stand-in that "melts in the mouth sort of like fatty tuna." He first mixed the avocado with shrimp before settling on crabmeat. While Issenberg remarked that avocados were expensive at the time, Corson claims they were available by the "truckloads" and presumably quite cheap—this, after all, was California. And Mashita prepared his invention as a traditional sushi roll (i.e., makizushi) to remind his Japanese customers of the fatty tuna back home. "According to one report, three months passed before someone came up with the name 'California roll,'" writes Corson.[91]

Let us say we follow either Kamp's or Corson's narrative to its logical end: it turns out California roll is not so American after all. That is to say, the inventors were not amateurish Americans but highly trained Japanese sushi chefs employed at a highly respected Japanese restaurant that catered to highly knowledgeable Japanese eaters. The fact that the act of creation took place in Los Angeles is perhaps incidental and is meaningful only so far as it involved avocados. Had Mashita and Imaizumi been stationed elsewhere, say, somewhere in Europe, perhaps they would have found another substitution for toro that was just as ingenious and appetizing.

Then again, perhaps there indeed is something exceptional about the taste and mouth-feel of avocado, allowing it to be a singularly ideal simulacrum of toro. That said, perhaps there is something singularly exceptional about the state of California, the city of Los Angeles, and the neighborhood of Little Tokyo. After all, where else during the 1960s could so many disparate factors—a growing number of expatriated Japanese businessmen longing for a familiar meal, a truckload of cheap avocados, a seasonal shortage of toro, a pair of highly trained sushi chefs sent to a culinary hinterland by their corporate employers, and an ethnic business district established by emigrant Japanese who settled in America earlier—have so perfectly collided to produce what is arguably the king of all sushi in the twenty-first century?

If indeed the priests of the cult of culinary authenticity have it right, if origin is indelibly linked to authenticity and authenticity cannot be detached from quality, perhaps it is possible to argue that California roll is an authentic sushi. The ostensibly disparate components of California roll, fused together using meticulous, time-honored sushi preparation methods, did somehow commingle perfectly, and thus was loosed upon the world something not only utterly cutting edge but also wonderfully familiar, and, given its principally Japanese pedigree, utterly authentic. So let us not hate California roll for its popularity, for its ubiquity. Let us look beyond the illusion of its dubiousness, for it is as authentic, and therefore as delicious, as Mexican chiles, Japanese soy sauce, and Chinese noodles, is it not?

Yes, it's pretty to think so.

2 | Chinese Take-Out

On a hot, sultry day in the summer of 2011, an irate woman in Savannah, Georgia, called 9-1-1. An audio recording revealed the nature of the emergency: "I need the police. It's this Hong Kong restaurant type to go. I ordered food and they done bring me the wrong food. I done brought it outside and they ain't going to give me my money and I need my money. Uh-uh, I need to [sic] someone to handle this. They ain't going to do me in any kind of way."[1] Instead of charging the woman with abusing the 9-1-1 service, as they could have, the police instead let her off with a reprimand and a valuable lesson: a mix-up with the order at a Chinese take-out does not an emergency make.

This incident serves as an ideal backstory to an uncontestable gastronomic fact: Chinese restaurants in the United States are beset by a culture of complaint. This appears to neither bear out nor belie the fact that Chinese is without question one of the most popular cuisines in America. Other cuisines prevail, of course, when considered regionally: Creole and Cajun in New Orleans, Mexican-inspired (such as Tex-Mex) throughout the West, and barbeque in the South and Midwest—each rules its respective geographic roost. But when viewed from a nationwide perch, Chinese easily ranks above Thai, Japanese, Middle Eastern, Greek, Indian, and virtually all other so-called ethnic foods, with the notable exception of Italian, the cuisine that gave pizza and spaghetti to the world.

As the artist Indigo Som contends, "Chinese restaurants are so ubiquitous throughout the United States that they constitute an integral part of American life." She reminds us that while Chinese restaurants are the primary point of contact with all things Chinese for most non-Chinese Americans, "this potent influence remains generally unacknowledged, even invisible." Through a composite of photography, instillations, and words, Som asks why, "despite its position as a fixture in the American foodscape," Chinese food "remains an exoticized outsider to the usual consideration of 'American' culture and identity."[2] In what she calls the Chinese Restaurant Project, Som embarks on road trips to areas of the country where, despite the absence of discernable Chinese American populations, Chinese restaurants are nonetheless omnipresent, a phenomenon that hints at the commonness of Chinese food in, for example, Baton Rouge, Louisiana, and Yazoo City, Mississippi.

Equipped with a twenty-dollar Holga camera, a Chinese product renowned for a design flaw that produces distorted images, including vignetting (the softening or shadowing of the edges of a photograph), Som photographs a series of random Chinese restaurant exteriors whose motley designs range from an imitation of a lavish imperial Chinese palace to a tumbledown building that once perhaps housed a Taco Bell.[3] No matter the location or appearance captured, these photographs reaffirm the quintessential American character of Chinese restaurants, placing them on par with, and in the company of, burger joints, coffee shops, barbecue shacks, and other definitively American—to borrow a phrase from the Food Network's Guy Fieri—diners, drive-ins, and dives.

Most foods synonymous with American gastronomy have thoroughly shed their Old World origins. Hamburgers, French fries, pizzas, pretzels, hot dogs, macaroni and cheese, and apple pie, for instance, are such fixtures at the nation's lunch counters that they appear natural, indigenous, routine, and incontestable. Trace the mythical roots of a typical pizza pie and we are as likely to end up at Gennaro Lombardi's grocery store in turn-of-the-twentieth-century New York City, Papa's Tomato Pies in 1920s Trenton, Frank Pepe Pizzeria Napoletana in 1920s New Haven (where the dish goes by the name "apizza," pronounced *ah-BEETZ*), or even Pizzeria Uno in 1940s Chicago, as we are in tenth-century Naples. Follow the hot dog back to the dawn of its creation and we are as liable to see the handiwork of Charles Feltman, a German American butcher in 1860s Coney Island, or Antonoine Feuchtwanger, a German American sausage vendor in 1870s St. Louis, as we are any eighteenth-century *brühwurst* maker in Frankfurt.[4] In contrast, foods identified as specifically Chinese—say, chow mein, chop suey, or wonton soup—retain an aura of perpetual foreignness despite a lengthy presence in the United States that dates back to the nineteenth century. Or, to be more precise, Chinese

Chinese Restaurant Project, South China, Natchez, Mississippi (2004–2005). Photo by Indigo Som. Courtesy of Indigo Som.

Chinese Restaurant Project, China Garden, Yazoo City, Mississippi (2004–2005). Photo by Indigo Som. Courtesy of Indigo Som.

food is treated as an alien presence in America despite a lengthy American provenance.

Records indicate that Norman Asing, aka San Yuen, who wrote a letter in 1852 challenging California governor John Bigler's call to deny Asian immigrants full legal rights, opened a Chinese restaurant in San Francisco perhaps as early as 1850, which would have made Asing's eatery one among at least five that were concurrently open for business.[5] New York City's Chinatown had by the 1870s already become known to outsiders for its restaurants. By 1903 there were four on Mott Street alone and one each on Doyers Street and Pell Street. Among the more notable of these was the Chinese Tuxedo Restaurant, located on 2 Doyers Street on the corner of the Bowery, which featured a richly decorated exterior façade of a large wooden carved dragon and dining rooms with pressed-tin ceilings and mosaic tile floors. First opened in 1897, the Tuxedo, like its nearby competitors, which included Chinese Delmonico on Pell Street and Port Arthur Restaurant on Mott Street, catered to "high-class" clientele and to both Chinese and white Americans alike.[6]

As Robert G. Lee reminds us in *Orientals: Asian Americans in Popular Culture,* the words "foreign" and "alien," while often used interchangeably, convey different connotations. "Foreign," he explains, "refers to that which is outside or distant, while 'alien' describes things that are immediate and present yet have a foreign nature or allegiance." While the foreign is a temporary condition (like, say, the tourist) the alien is a permanent pollutant, a defiler of neat categories that separate "us" (i.e., real Americans) from "them" (i.e., immigrants). The alien, Lee posits, is "always out of place, therefore disturbing and dangerous."[7] Chinese food is an alien American cuisine. As such, Chinese restaurants go hand in hand with culinary ambivalence, as Americans flock to them en masse to consume simultaneously the foreign and familiar alongside a serving of sweet and sour.

Samantha Barbas, author of "'I'll take Chop Suey': Restaurants as Agents of Culinary and Cultural Exchange," cautions that the popularity of Chinese food in the United States does not necessarily "correlate with racial and social attitudes." She argues that the corporeal—as opposed to strictly culinary—presence of Chinese Americans continues to stir deeply held racial anxieties but "may seem far less threatening to dominant social groups when placed in context of food and dining."[8] As Frank Wu puts it in *Yellow: Race in America beyond Black and White,* "Eating at a Chinese restaurant is not the same as 'breaking bread' with Chinese people."[9] In other words, it is one thing to relish Chinese food but altogether another to tolerate Chinese people.

Culture of Complaint

In Warren Zevon's 1978 song "Werewolves of London," a werewolf is spotted with a "Chinese menu in his hand, walking through the streets of Soho in the rain." We are told that he was "looking for a place called Lee Ho Fooks" in order to "get a big dish of beef chow mein." This satirical song aptly illustrates how Zevon, an American rock singer, imagines Chinese food to play an ordinary part of daily life in the United Kingdom. Of course, in reality, Chinese food is even more quotidian in the United States. Recent estimates indicate that there is a Chinese restaurant for every ninety-three square miles, or seventy-five hundred people, in the country. Numbering more than forty thousand, Chinese restaurants exceed the total number of—and no doubt deliver more calories than—McDonald's, Burger King, and Wendy's franchises combined.[10] This ubiquity, however, is not without detractors and gadflies who recognize not only a dependable meal in Chinese restaurants but also danger, fear, and loathing. While criticizing some aspects of the restaurant experience (the décor, service, food quality, price, etc.) may be as much a consumer's inalienable right as complimentary tap water, complaints brought on by visits to Chinese eateries are especially shrill, at least compared to other ethnic eateries such as Italian, Thai, Japanese, or French. Indeed, one wonders whether there is a "kick me" sign taped to the back of all Chinese restaurants, the Rodney Dangerfield of American gastronomy. Chinese food, at least in the United States, gets no respect.

The pervasiveness of the grievances is strongly suggested by the number of urban legends that lampoons the perils of eating out—and taking out—Chinese. Urban folklorists have found Chinese restaurants a subject substantial enough to merit several separate categories, placing them alongside such classic food fables as the "Kentucky Fried Rat" and "Mouse in the Coke." Jan Harold Brunvand, author of several books on urban legends, posits that conspiratorial stories about the remains of pets, pests, and even human bodies unexpectedly appearing in Chinese food rank as among "the most venerable categories of food-contamination legends." One such legend tells of a severed finger found in a dish of chop suey, which is traced to a Chinese leper who loses one digit after another over the course of his career as a cook. Another popular story has a scientist of some sort, after finding a mysterious, stringy piece of meat in his kung pao chicken, discreetly taking it back to his lab to discover the remnants of a dog, cat, or rat. A frequent reputed whistleblower of Chinese restaurant shenanigans is the government health inspector who turns up unannounced to find pelts, bones, and severed heads of cats or dogs in kitchen refrigerators or garbage bins.[11]

The radio personality and song parodist Bob Rivers capitalized on this legacy of culinary Sinophobia with a song titled "Cats in the Kettle," sung to the tune of Harry Chapin's "Cat's in the Cradle."[12] The parody begins,

> Did you ever think when you eat Chinese
> It ain't pork or chicken but a fat Siamese
> Yet the food tastes great so you don't complain
> But that's not chicken in your chicken chow mein
> Seems to me I ordered sweet and sour pork
> But Garfield's on my fork
> He's purring here on my fork

The song, for which no less than thirty-five different homemade video accompaniments can be viewed on YouTube, concludes,

> There's a cat in the kettle at the Peking Moon
> I think I gotta stop eating there at noon
> They say that it's beef or fish or pork
> But it's purring there on my fork
> There's a hair-ball on my fork.

More widespread and recurrent than legends about catflesh, however, are rumors of dogmeat served in Chinese restaurants. Indeed, the specter of not just Chinese but a general Asian proclivity for dogmeat looms large enough to reach far beyond the arena of ethnic eateries to the backyards of average Americans. A typical urban legend features a mystery of someone's missing pug and the suspicious behavior of an immigrant family—typically Korean or Vietnamese—that recently moved to the neighborhood.

These "mystery meat" stories constitute just the tip of the urban legend iceberg. Rumors of the unsanitary practices of Chinese restaurant workers, identified as outlandish aliens, are commonplace in all regions of the

United States. Often scatological in nature, these rumors typically concern sickened diners who take leftovers to health officials only to discover to their horror some sort of bodily discharge—saliva, urine, or semen—mixed with the beef and broccoli. American diners have long joked that no matter how much you eat, Chinese food leaves you hungry an hour later. A 1991 episode of *Seinfeld* about an endless wait for a table due to the inscrutability of a Chinese restaurant maître d' and a 2000 episode of *Sex in the City* about a phone mishap while ordering Chinese take-out are considered television classics.

In 1995 the American pop group Lyte Funky Ones (aka LFO) released a song called "Summer Girls" that included the line, "Chinese food makes me sick." The song was a huge hit. A decade later, in a nationally televised commercial, a portly man standing over an all-you-can-eat Chinese buffet drops a utensil and appears to suffer a heart attack. To his relief, it is only heartburn, which is quickly quelled by a new antacid his nephew offers him. In recent years health- and consumer-advocacy groups have dubbed Chinese restaurants a nutritionist's nightmare. Accused of peddling products that contain dangerous levels of sodium, fat, and sugar in popular dishes such as General Tso's chicken and orange-flavored beef, Chinese restaurants are now grouped with fast food chains, carbonated soft drinks, processed foods, and sedentary lifestyles as leading causes behind the nation's reputation as the most overfed but undernourished population on the planet.

In New York City diners lament that dishes sold at countless Chinese take-outs scattered throughout the five boroughs are too uncannily similar for it to be a mere coincidence. A well-circulated joke conjectures that a single centralized source, a gargantuan factory in a secret underground location, mass produces and distributes the same batch of food to every Chinese restaurant in the country via an elaborate subterranean plumbing matrix. Also, a legion of apartment dwellers complains of the unregulated proliferation of take-out menus, likening them to lethal banana peels strewn across hallways and stairways by a horde of Chinese-food deliverymen leaving a trail of leaflets in their wake. As a result, a common fixture in the entranceway to many apartment buildings is a "No Menus" sign—in English and often Chinese—specifically directed at Chinese-food deliverymen.

And there is, of course, the pinnacle of complaints, the granddaddy of them all, the inscrutable malady whose moniker, "Chinese restaurant syndrome," brazenly identifies not the alleged poison but the poisoner. Despite

"No Menus" (2012), a photographic collage of signs posted in apartment building entrances in New York City, by Cynthia Ai-fen Lee. Courtesy of Cynthia Ai-fen Lee.

the absence of conclusive medical evidence that identifies monosodium glutamate (MSG) as the root cause, several generations of Americans since the late 1960s have complained of bodily ailments—most notably headaches—stemming from consuming what they believe to be MSG-laden Chinese food. Exasperated by what he sees as a collective irrational fear of MSG among Americans, an irked Jeffrey Steingarten once characterized those who claim to get sick from MSG as "psychologically troubled" people who "see things that don't exist." You are an "MSG crybaby," accuses Steingarten in an essay titled "Why Doesn't Everybody in China Have a Headache?"[13]

The culture of complaint that tails Chinese restaurants is not limited to the bounds of the dinner plate or the take-out container, but spills over to the larger entrepreneurial aspect of the Chinese restaurant business itself. Accusations of corrupt or illegal business dealings have joined the litany of consumerist quibbles, as Chinese restaurateurs, whether deservedly or not, have increasingly become targets of legal and political rebukes, reprimands, and punishments. A close scrutiny of these complaints and their fallout indicates that consumerist objection to Chinese restaurants is often not a matter of food per se but of the nation's collective uneasy feeling about the perceived foreignness or alienness of the people who are in the business of selling it. In sum, the culture of complaint that hounds the Chinese restaurant in the United States is the gastronomic reification of anti-Chinese sentiments that began during the days of the Gold Rush a century and a half ago and persisted throughout the twentieth century. The message behind this sentiment is still palpable: Chinese Americans, along with their cultural trappings, including food, are alien to the United States, which makes them at best dubiously American. Serving as instructive cases in point are recent newspaper items of the pillorying of two Chinese restaurants in New York City prompted by disgruntled customers and backed by locally elected officials.

Case Number One

It is spring 2007. As reported by Manny Fernandez in a May 4, 2007, *New York Times* article, "When Pennies Fail to Pay the Bill, a Bronx Man Pushes for Change," a man named Wayne Jones orders four pieces of fried chicken wings at a neighborhood Chinese take-out and proceeds to pay with exact change, which includes ten pennies. The cashier, a Chinese woman named Juan Lin who speaks very little English, refuses to accept the pennies and a quarrel ensues. Outraged, Jones returns home and e-mails several elected officials with details of the incident, arguing that the restaurant's rejection of pennies discriminates against the poor and the homeless. Soon, a swarm of protestors, reporters, and the simply curious descends upon the humble take-out, the Great Wall Restaurant in the Soundview neighborhood of the Bronx. The aggrieved patron stands among the gathering crowd, which includes several Christian ministers and a state senator, Rubén Díaz Sr., who promises to take up the issue in Albany. One of the ministers demands that the city shut down the business. When questioned by a journalist, Lin denies the charge and breaks down in tears. A good while later, after the crowd has dispersed, Jones, now feeling vindicated, shakes hands with the humiliated Lin, who, perhaps not knowing what else to do, apologizes to him. Jones then orders four pieces of fried chicken wings and pays with exact change, which includes ten pennies.[14]

This news item, carefully crafted as a self-contained narrative in the morning paper, appears wondrously pithy and perfect, like a Baudelaire prose poem, Kawabata Palm-of-the-Hand story, or O. Henry tale. It is symmetrically equipped with a narrative arc that contains a beginning, middle, and end. With newsprint in hand, an entire saga comes full circle in less time than it takes to travel a single subway stop during the morning commute. Serving as a modern-day parable or object lesson, this sort of news tidbit invites readers to tease out for themselves the moral—as in the "moral of the story"—embedded in a random, offbeat incident snapped up from real life. Complete and tidy as they may appear, it is also true that social conflicts rendered in such abbreviated fashion are merely the leftover remains of fuller, more nuanced affairs, picked clean by the distorting powers of tabloid journalism.

Within this convention there is little if any need to offer up a more substantive dish garnished with extraneous narrative complexities, which, truth be told, only gets in the way of the winsome morality tale. This is especially true in cases involving conflicts that can easily be defined as oppositional. It is an added bonus if the conflict can be structurally characterized as one that pits a member of an "in-group" against a member of an "out-group." The newspaper coverage makes little or no attempt at neutrality, as the narrative willfully hinges on the perspective of the crusading "American" customer rather than that of the "alien" Chinese merchant, who is cast as the unscrupulous profiteer, a modern-day version of a Chinese Shylock.

An observation made by Toni Morrison in her essay on the literary imagination of whiteness and the Africanist presence in American literature helps to elucidate an important point. "For reasons that should not need explanation here," she writes in *Playing in the Dark: Whiteness and the Literary Imagination,* "until very recently, and regardless of the race of the author, the readers of virtually all of American fiction have been positioned as white."[15] In placing such luminaries as Cather, Poe, Hawthorne, Melville, Hemingway, and Twain under her critical microscope, Morrison leads us to a not altogether unexpected verdict: "Deep within the word 'American' is its association with race." Specifically, "American means white." This, however, is not to say that there is an absence of nonwhites in American literature. On the contrary, dark figures (e.g., African Americans) abound. Morrison believes the Africanist presence in American literature informs in "compelling and inescapable ways the texture of American literature."[16]

In a potent demonstration of her thesis in play, Morrison interrogates a single sentence in Ernest Hemingway's 1937 novel, *To Have and Have Not.* While the novel is told through a voice that alternates from that of the main character, Harry Morgan (a fishing boat captain and smuggler of contraband goods in the Caribbean), to a third-person point of view (presumably Hemingway's), the sentence in question occurs through the former. Among Morgan's crew is a black man who remains nameless for four chapters and is referred to most commonly as "nigger." Early in the novel, while Morgan tends to a customer who has hired his boat out for recreational fishing, the black man is the first to see promising signs of good water ahead while tending the wheel. Through Morgan's voice, Hemingway pens an ungainly sentence: "The nigger was still taking her [the boat] out and I looked and saw he had seen a patch of flying fish burst out ahead."[17]

The specific fragment of the sentence Morrison underscores is "saw he had seen," which, for her, is "improbable in syntax, sense, and tense but, like other choices available to Hemingway, it is risked to avoid a speaking black." How does a writer, after all, "say how one sees that someone else has already seen"? Morrison contends that the awkward locution preserves the black character's "nameless, sexless, nationless Africanist presence" that Hemingway presupposes. Usually praised for his terse if not flawless prose, Hemingway in this instance opts for inelegance of diction over allowing the black man "a verbal initiative of importance." But why? "What would have been the cost," Morrison wonders, "of humanizing, genderizing, this character"?[18] Likewise, we might wonder what it would have cost—or have been lost—to give the cashier of the Chinese take-out *her* verbal initiative of importance in the newspaper coverage. What is the price of humanizing and genderizing this character? Can it be said of American newspaper readers what Morrison says of readers of American fiction, that they are virtually always positioned as white?

In the annals of the nation's cultural self-portraiture, the figure of the crusading-white-citizen-consumer is as emblematic of what is traditionally construed as the quintessential American character as any other possible sequence of descriptors. Consequently, the opposite, or the quintessential *non*-American, is construed as an infidel-nonwhite-immigrant-merchant— such as a Korean grocer, Pakistani cab driver, Vietnamese manicurist, or Chinese restaurateur. This notion is aptly illustrated in Joel Schumacher's 1993 film *Falling Down*, in which the lead character, a white male played by Michael Douglas, indignantly asserts his rights as an American and a consumer before taking a baseball bat to a convenience store run by a pidgin-speaking Korean merchant. As the Douglas character demolishes the store, the immigrant merchant is seen cowering in fear. The film makes it clear that the Korean, due to his surly treatment of customers, got what was coming to him. The film invites the audience—positioned as white—to empathize with the anger and resentment experienced by Douglas' character, a white American Everyman and wronged consumer, and not with the fear, shock, and awe experienced by the Korean merchant played by the third-generation Chinese American actor Michael Paul Chan.

Perhaps Morrison is onto something when she asserts that in American literature the word "American" always equates to someone who is white. But if we expand the discursive arena further to include, say, the news account of the beleaguered Chinese take-out, then her assertion falls short in a particularly crucial way. Yes, the word "American" first and foremost means white. But when the nonwhite presence of a story, instead of being solely Africanist, also happens to be Asianist, that is to say, someone Chinese, Korean, Filipino, Pakistani, etc., then American can also mean black.

As Asian American scholars and activists have repeatedly pointed out, Asians in the United States, regardless of their citizenship or immigration

An enraged William Foster (Michael Douglas) berates a terrified Korean merchant curled in a fetal position on the store floor. Convinced he was overcharged for a can of soda, Foster goes on to demolish parts of the store with a baseball bat. Frame enlargement from *Falling Down* (1993).

status, are habitually regarded as perpetual foreigners. This tendency was displayed during the 1998 Winter Olympic Games, when Tara Lipinski, a white American, edged out Michelle Kwan for the gold medal in figure skating. Immediately after the Chinese American Kwan was awarded the silver metal, the headline "American beats out Kwan" appeared on the MSNBC website. The Asian-American-as-perpetually-foreign perception was also evident during the 2011–2012 National Basketball Association season, when a surprising breakout performance by the American-born Jeremy Lin forced many in the mainstream media to reassess the differences between what it means to be a Chinese American (à la Jeremy Lin) versus a Chinese national (à la Yao Ming).

Paying the biggest price of all for being perceived as a foreigner was the Chinese American Vincent Chin, who died on June 23, 1982, from a brutal beating he received on the night of his own bachelor party. Two white men, Ronald Ebens and Michael Nitz, blamed Chin for the decline of the US auto industry due to the rise of Japanese imports. "It's because of you little motherfuckers that we're out of work," Ebens reportedly shouted during a verbal argument that eventually escalated into physical violence, culminating in Chin's skull being cracked open by a baseball bat repeatedly swung by Ebens. Charged with second-degree murder, Ebens and Nitz pleaded guilty to manslaughter. If the crime was not shocking enough, the sentence the two men received was truly outrageous: three years of probation and a fine of three thousand dollars. The men never served a day in jail. The case would become a rallying cry for widespread Asian American protests across the nation.[19]

Five years after the deadly incident, the filmmaker Michael Moore interviewed Ebens for an article published in the *Detroit Free Press* on August 30, 1987. The occasion for the interview was the acquittal of criminal charges and the settlement of a civil suit the US Department of Justice had filed against Ebens. In the interview, Ebens tells Moore that he does not understand why the Asian American community is so against him. "They blew it [the killing] all out of proportion," he remarks. Moore asks why the Asian American groups were against him. "To show the plight of the Asian-Americans in America," he answers, adding, "I still don't know what their plight is." What are Asian Americans shooting for, Moore asks. "I don't know," Ebens answers. "Do you see any Asian-Americans around here? I don't even know them. I don't know what their plight is. I've never been around them. The only ones I had ever met are the ones in the

Chinese restaurants, and they were always nice and I was always nice to them."[20]

African Americans often face different sorts of racial hurdles than those encountered by Asian Americans. While it is undeniable that African Americans have had their rights as citizens routinely compromised and at times outright denied since emancipation, the fact that African Americans are citizens has rarely been questioned—at least not to the degree experienced by Asian Americans. This contrast is evident in Spike Lee's 1989 film *Do the Right Thing,* in which the American citizenship of the black rioters is never in question. As for the Korean merchants whose store is demolished by the angry mob, not only are they not regarded as true Americans, they are not even considered legitimate members of a neighborhood in which they spend every moment of each day working. (Korean-run delis in New York City are usually open twenty-four hours.)

Although not stated explicitly in the newspaper account, one can surmise that the Bronx man with the ten pennies is African American. Giving credence to this supposition is a photograph of the two adversaries that accompanied the article, in which Jones appears to be an African American. Also, the residents of the Soundview section of the Bronx, where Jones lives, are predominantly Latino and African American, and Jones is not a typical name among Latinos.

Moreover, it is probable that Jones is an individual who holds a keen sense of social and racial justice. This is indicated by the fact that the article identifies him as an active member (a preacher and community liaison) of the neighborhood Mount Zion Christian Methodist Episcopal Church, whose membership is almost entirely African American. According to the national Christian Methodist Episcopal website, the organization "came into existence as a result of the movement from slavery to freedom," in which "the emancipation of Blacks from slavery created the desire by Blacks to have and control their own church," and "formerly enslaved persons who had been members of the Methodist Episcopal Church South" started this independent religious organization.[21] Given the church's historical mission and his prominent role in the Bronx affiliate, Jones no doubt made public his grievance with the Chinese take-out by calling his state senator and rallying his church members because he sincerely believed that he was a victim of racial discrimination.

Although both Jones and Lin are nonwhite, the former is nonetheless a nonimmigrant citizen with the wherewithal to take his consumerist grievance to his locally elected officials, who immediately jumped to his aid. In contrast, the article implies that the restaurant worker Lin is a noncitizen immigrant, meaning she is treated as an outsider to a neighborhood in which she spends the better part of every day, morning to night, working. Thus, as journalistically rendered, it is the black man's verbal initiative of importance—manifested as a complaint against the Chinese take-out—that resonates with the general American readership, not the Asian woman's. This is possible because the word "American," while almost always meaning white, can also periodically mean black, as in moments like this, when a conflict between an African American and Asian American manifests as a tabloid-ready public spectacle. This is demonstrated not only in this case, but it also was on full display nationwide throughout the 1980s and 1990s with the so-called Black-Korean conflict, in which disgruntled African American customers confronted Korean American–run grocery and liquor stores with lawsuits, boycotts, and other forms of protest, including, some argue, a full-blown riot in Los Angeles following the acquittal of the police officers involved in the Rodney King beating.[22]

A brief culinary analogy can apply here: when compared to the foods most strongly identified with African Americans (e.g., soul food), whose American fiber is unassailable, Chinese food, as well as the people associated with it, appears perpetually foreign and conspicuously alien.[23] While it is possible to label black-eyed peas, collard greens, and chitterlings with a term that insinuates blackness (or regionally "Southern," as the two culinary categories often overlap),[24] it is unreasonable to call them foreign or alien. The same cannot be said of eggrolls, wonton soup, pork fried rice, and other Chinese menu options, which are essentially American fare of Chinese descent with origins that date back a century and a half to the earliest years of Chinese immigration. In other words, while the difference between what is African and African American appears self-evident to most Americans, so much so that to conflate the two can often seem racially problematic, the contrast between what is Chinese and Chinese American is not so obvious. Thus the factors that set soul food apart from Chinese food are not necessarily culinary; rather, it is the troubling and troublesome fact that only the former is associated with a group that can without much complication be regarded as authentically American.

Case Number Two

A few months prior to the squabble over ten pennies at a Chinese take-out in the Bronx, at the other end of the city a man walks into a Chinese restaurant, threatens the owner, and leaves with a pocketful of cash as the mayor of the city cheers him on. No, this is not one of those political corruption stories you see in movies—such as *City Hall,* the 1996 Harold Becker film starring Al Pacino and John Cusack—about an illicit relationship between the mayor of a major city and the mob. In this actual case covered in the city's tabloids (stories ran in both the *New York Post* and *New York Daily News*), a Wisconsinite tourist named David Lopez orders a meal at the Canal Seafood Restaurant in Chinatown but grows suspicious when he is told that a serving of rice costs a little extra. His suspicion increases when he notices nearby customers eating a similar dish served over a bed of rice. Lopez soon discovers that the restaurant gave out two different menus, an English-language version for non-Chinese customers like him and a Chinese version for Chinese patrons. He compares the menus and determines that the dishes on the English version are on the average a dollar more per item than those on the Chinese.

Convinced he is being discriminated against because he is not Chinese, the tourist takes his complaint to the city's Human Rights Commission. An investigation ensues and the commission sides with the complainant, formally charging the restaurant with price gouging based on racial or linguistic preference for Chinese customers. When a reporter asks for his comment, Mayor Michael Bloomberg urges a public boycott of the establishment. Threatened with multiple legal actions, including a fine of fifty thousand dollars in punitive damages, the restaurant agrees to settle out of court, paying Lopez one thousand dollars and promising to list and charge identical prices for the same dishes on all its future menus. The restaurant's counsel, however, insists that the terms of settlement are "absolutely no admission of wrongdoing." When asked about the outcome, the tourist replies that he is happy, adding that the food at the restaurant, incidentally, is "excellent."[25]

Perhaps Lopez, the tourist, did the right thing in exposing what he believed was the restaurant's policy of denying non-Chinese customers a gratis bed of rice and overcharging them a dollar more per item. It is quite possible that the restaurant did in fact gouge non-Chinese customers with separate but unequal menus. It is just as likely, however, that the two menus were just that—two separate menus intended for two separate but not necessarily unequal customers, where the price difference was either inconsequential or an unintended consequence of a commercial strategy in service of a greater cause. Generally speaking, in New York City's Chinatown, as in all Chinatowns around the world, different customers—Chinese, non-Chinese, or what have you—walk into a Chinese restaurant with diverging culinary expectations. It is not uncommon, therefore, for enterprising restaurateurs to employ the two-menu solution in dealing with this gastronomic reality.

It is not only possible but altogether probable that the two menus Lopez encountered listed a separate litany of dishes, each pointing toward an alternative universe of gustatory expectations. This bifurcation reveals not only the complex nature of what Chinese food is and means to various people in this era of culinary globalization, but also suggests that the meaning of Chinese food is not so much a matter of cost but taste.[26] For

Canal Seafood Restaurant in New York City's Chinatown. Following the media scrutiny, the restaurant changed its English name to Canal Best Restaurant. The Chinese name remains the same. Photo by Shara Richter.

Chinese restaurants that cater to a heterogeneous clientele (meaning almost all Chinese restaurants outside China and increasingly those within), the two-menu strategy is not only financially shrewd but represents a pragmatic assessment of the world as it is, as opposed to the world someone—say, some sort of a culinary purist or absolutist—thinks it ought to be. Akin to parents of young children preparing separate meals according to an individual child's gastronomic predilection, Chinese restaurateurs often attempt to offer the version of Chinese food that an alternate set of diners desires or believes Chinese food to be. To complicate this matter further, many Chinese restaurants in the United States are known to feature not merely two but three or more menus: an English version for "outsiders," a Chinese version for "insiders," a bilingual menu, a "secret" (i.e., unwritten) menu for the "very" insiders, and so forth. These different menus, moreover, although equal in terms of importance in serving as potential revenue streams, are unequal in terms of perceived "authenticity" of the food contained therein. To wit, the more a dish or set of dishes appears to be intended for Chinese diners, the more luminous the halo of "authenticity," meaning the more it strikes the non-Chinese as daring, adventuresome, and daunting. Hence the old adage that non-Chinese diners looking for "real" Chinese food seek out restaurants in which you, the non-Chinese, are a conspicuous minority. In theory, Chinese food in the United States is tastiest in places that are yet to be discovered by non-Chinese patrons.

It is noteworthy that none of the newspaper accounts about the Lopez story identified the precise dish at the center of the storm. This omission indicates that compared to the legal, cross-cultural, linguistic, and interpersonal aspects of it, the culinary aspect, or what was on the plate, mattered very little. What exactly did the tourist order? This story takes on a completely different tenor if he ordered, say, General Tso's chicken, perhaps the most popular dish among non-Chinese eaters of Chinese food in the United States today,[27] as opposed to *siu ngaap*, the ever-present and atmospheric Cantonese-style roast duck that hangs alongside other roast meats in the windows of many Chinatown restaurants. For that matter, why did he choose *this* restaurant among scores of others in Chinatown? Was it mentioned in a guidebook? Was it recommended by a friend? Did he walk into it randomly? Did the exterior or another environmental detail portend a promising meal? In fact, why come to eat Chinese food in New York City in the first place? Surely there had to be no shortage of Chinese restaurants in the state of Wisconsin.

Given the ubiquity of Chinese restaurants and the quotidian nature of Chinese food nationwide, one could argue that eating Chinese food in Chinatown is analogous to seeking out a Big Mac in Paris or Tokyo. You essentially eat there (at the tourist site) what you eat here (at home).

Perhaps operating under the assumption that Chinatowns are the closest thing to the "real" thing (i.e., China) without actually having to travel there, the tourist pilgrimaged to New York City's Chinatown in search of something familiar that has been rendered more "original"—that is, exotic—by the aura of an unadulterated China that Chinatown supposedly exudes. If so, what he searched for was not food per se but something that is best expressed *through* food; he was searching for the one thing tourists typically desire the most, a desire that in many ways defines the very essence of the tourist—a taste of the authentic.[28] Thus his belief that he was swindled by unscrupulous foreign merchants provided him with a greater sense of what eating in China would be like than eating a dish he ended up ordering. After all, mustn't Americans abroad always be on guard against the devious and underhanded chicaneries of the natives, especially natives of the so-called Third World? And despite the fact that the dish he ordered was from the English-language menu, he no doubt went away thinking that it was a more authentic, and therefore more delicious, version of a familiar taste he first experienced back home in Wisconsin.

Just as the Chinese cashier of the Great Wall Restaurant in the Bronx denied the charge that she rejected pennies as legal tender, so did the proprietors of the Canal Seafood Restaurant in Chinatown deny the charge leveled against their establishment—that the two menus listed different prices for identical items. In each case, a Chinese restaurant was accused of violating the civil rights of non-Chinese customers, of racially discriminating against the non-Chinese. The trouble in the Chinatown case appears to have begun when Lopez felt there was something fishy about a Chinese restaurant that charged extra for rice, especially since some of the other customers—namely, Chinese people—were served "similar dishes" over a bed of rice. Like bread and olive oil at an Italian restaurant, chips and salsa at a Mexican eatery, and assorted *banchan*, especially kimchi, at a Korean establishment, Lopez no doubt assumed rice was either gratis or a standard entrée accompaniment to a typical Chinese restaurant meal.

Of course, charging extra for rice is not an actionable offense, no matter how powerful or automatic the expectation. What is clearly illegal is for a business to charge different prices for the same goods or services in accordance to a customer's race, ethnicity, or language. The tourist concluded that he was discriminated against only after comparing the two menus side by side. What makes the legal outcome of this case a foregone conclusion is the fact that Lopez, by his own admission, did not know how to read Chinese. He may have had the capacity to calculate the discrepancy in prices, leading to the conclusion that the English version listed higher prices on average, but did the menus feature the same items? How plausible, really, is it for this or any Chinese restaurant to offer the same bill of fare to Chinese and non-Chinese customers, especially when both clienteles, whose gustatory disparity may be as wide as the starchy gulf between Uncle Ben's converted rice and Thai jasmine rice, represent equally indispensable sources of revenue? Surely the difference between the two menus—between what non-Chinese and Chinese believe and desire Chinese food to be—amounts to more than a dollar and a bed of rice?

Food for Barbarians

To E. N. Anderson, author of *The Food of China*, a highly regarded scholarly survey of traditional Chinese food systems, there is a vast difference between the version of Chinese food consumed by non-Chinese people, especially of the West, and that consumed by Chinese people, specifically in China. The difference is evidenced in what he sees as the deplorable state of Cantonese cuisine in the United States and Europe. In describing it, Anderson cannot help but inject the language with vitriol: "Much of what passes for Cantonese cooking in the Western World would sicken a traditional Cantonese gourmet. Canned pineapple, canned cherries, and even canned fruit cocktail; enormous quantities of dehydrated garlic, barbecue or Worcestershire sauce; canned vegetables, corn starch, monosodium glutamate, cooking sherry, and heavy doses of sugar are found in many of these bizarre creations." Anderson traces the origin of this "fusion of pseudo-Cantonese and pseudo-Polynesian food" to a "renegade" Cantonese chef who once worked at a Trader Vic's restaurant in California. He sums up the "basic formula" of the Western version of Cantonese cuisine thus: "take the fattest, rankest pork you can get; cook it in a lot of oil with the sweetest mixture of canned fruits and sugar you can make; throw on a lot of MSG and cheap soy sauce; thicken the sauce to gluelike consistency; and serve it forth." Anderson adds that this sort of corruption of their food is regarded as "proof" to the Cantonese people that "Westerners are cultureless barbarians." To make matters worse, in recent years "even many Taiwan Chinese (having eaten Cantonese food only in cafés catering to American G.I.s) are convinced that this is typical Cantonese cooking."[29]

As anyone fond of American-style Chinese food can attest, the vast majority of Chinese food sold in the United States does not resemble the mishmash that Anderson limns. (Given the profusion of Chinese restaurants in the United States, that would mean tens, if not hundreds, of millions of people.) In fact, it might be safe to say that Chinese food even at Trader Vic's looks nothing of the sort. If it is any indication, a recent dinner menu at Trader Vic's in Atlanta listed several Chinese dishes, such as Szechwan prawns, made with wood-car mushrooms, snow peas, and sweet peppers; kung pao chicken, made with red bell peppers, cashews, and spicy chile sauce; and special fried rice, made with chicken, prawns, and *char siu* pork—with nary a canned fruit in sight. To be sure, such a version as Anderson describes once existed in the United States, but how universal or widespread was it, really? In his attempt to illustrate the destructive power of Americanization on Cantonese food, Anderson, an otherwise objective gastronomic historian writing a straightforward book, suddenly and uncharacteristically resorts to hyperbole. But why? What is the motive behind the magnified complaint? What might he achieve by exaggerating, if not misrepresenting, Chinese food in the United States?[30]

A clue to his motive can be found in his use of highly charged words like "bizarre," "pseudo," and "renegade." For these words to relay the meaning Anderson intends, we must first acknowledge the other side of their locutions, their antonyms. That is to say, we must first believe in the existence of Chinese food that is "normal" or "conventional," "genuine" or "authentic," and "loyal" or "unchanging." In essence, what these words presuppose is a transcendental culinary standard that is violated or betrayed when Chinese food travels beyond the borders of China, and especially to the United States. In fact, according to Anderson, regional Cantonese cuisine needs to travel only five hundred miles or so to Taiwan—given the island's close political relationship to the United States—for it to undergo irreparable damage. Anderson's belief in "proper" Chinese cuisine is so absolute that he is able to identify the individual he believes was the first to set into motion Cantonese cuisine's diasporic degradation and downfall. And it just happens that the original miscreant, an unnamed apostate, was a native Cantonese chef who once worked at a California restaurant whose primary claim to fame is not food, but a drink. According to cocktail lore, propagated most zealously by the restaurant itself, Trader Vic's is the birthplace of the mai tai—a tropical drink, now considered the epitome of tiki-kitsch, originally made of Jamaican rum, Dutch orange curaçao, French orgeat (an almond-based sugary syrup), and fresh lime juice.

Founded in the 1930s by Victor Jules Bergeron Jr., Trader Vic's began as a modest pub in Oakland. The establishment was first called Hinky Dink's before it adopted Bergeron's nickname and grew into a global franchise worth $70 million, with numerous locations, including in the United States, Bahrain, England, Lebanon, Germany, Japan, United Arab Emirates, and China.[31] (In the aforementioned Warren Zevon song, the werewolf is eventually spotted not at Lee Ho Fooks, but at the London Trader Vic's, first opened in 1963, drinking not a mai tai, as one might expect, but another famous tropical drink, a piña colada. This is probably due to no intrinsic shortcoming of the mai tai other than lacking the required number of syllables to fit the lyrics.) Anderson's scoffing allusion to Trader Vic's is not without purpose: he clearly means to disparage Cantonese food in the West through guilt by association. For him, Trader Vic's is the contemptible yin of debased Americanized Chinese food to the sublime yang of authentic Cantonese cookery in native China. In other words, Trader Vic's is ersatz Cantonese, distorted, and therefore ludicrous and inedible.

Anderson is irked by what he sees as the low status consigned to Cantonese food—compared to, say, Hunan or Sichuan food—around the world. He calls the rumor of Cantonese culinary inferiority a "myth," a direct result of the cuisine's widespread diffusion overseas, where "a lamentable Cantonese tendency to seek the lowest common denominator in business practices" took root. Although he does not specify what these practices are, one can assume he means abbreviated cooking techniques and use of substandard or cheap ingredients, among other cost-cutting measures and culinary shortcuts.

Anderson lavishes praise on what he believes to be the uncorrupted version of Cantonese food, which, "at its best, is probably unequalled in China and possibly the world." He compiles a running list of Cantonese culinary achievements that no other cooks in the world, including those of other Chinese regions, can duplicate: "insist on such absolute freshness," "control cooking temperatures so perfectly," "insist on such quality in ingredients," "draw on such a wide range of ingredients," "can be so eclectic while maintaining the spirit of their tradition," "excel in so many techniques," "produce so many dishes," and so forth. As a cuisine, Cantonese has no rival anywhere in the world, "not even in France," Anderson avers.[32]

To him, what typifies Chinese food in the West are the awful, apocryphal dishes that most Westerners consume in bulk, such as sweet-and-sour pork ("Cantonese more often cook sweet-sour fish," he opines), fried rice ("not of the height of the true cuisine"), chow mein ("a counterpart of fried rice"), and chop suey (an Americanized Toisanese dish). These foods are all in the "nature of hash," he charges, "cheap, quick, easy ways to get rid of less than desirable leftovers and other scraps." In other words, "all the stuff that would otherwise have to go to the animals can be fed to people." (In this, Anderson parrots the British lexicographer Samuel Johnson, who, in his 1755 *Dictionary of the English Language,* notoriously defined oats as "a grain, which in England is generally given to horses, but in Scotland supports the people.") Anderson, however, adds an important caveat: these otherwise dreadful dishes are delicious when found in "traditional cafés and homes in Hong Kong." But diners had best beware, for versions served up in Hong Kong restaurants that specifically cater to Westerners are as atrocious as those found in the West.[33] Anderson's formula for good Chinese food is simple: made in China, presumably by Chinese hands, for Chinese people. The formula for bad Chinese food is equally simple: made anywhere but China or made in China for non-Chinese people.

Some two decades after Anderson published his polemic against Chinese food in the West, the creators of perhaps the most popular restaurant guides ever published—at least for New York City—made their own contribution to the fertile culture of complaint that surrounds the Chinese restaurant in the United States. In a June 21, 2007, *New York Times* op-ed titled "Eating beyond Sichuan," Nina and Tim Zagat, the brainchild behind the vast Zagat Guides franchise, bemoan the woeful state of Chinese food in America. In comparison to other Asian foods, such as Korean, Thai, Vietnamese, and Japanese, all of which have "soared" as of late, Chinese food in America has "stalled," they charge. Chinese food is the "same tired routine" American diners have experienced for years, "unimaginative dishes served amid dated, pseudo-imperial décor." They compare Chinese food in the United States to Chinese food in China and ask, "Where are the great versions of bird's nest soup from Shandong, or Zhejiang's beggar's chicken, or braised Anhui-style pigeon or the crisp eel specialties of Jiangsu?"[34]

Although phrased as a question, their query is strictly rhetorical since they presumably already know the answer—nowhere outside China, and least of all in America. "There is a historic explanation for the abysmal state of Chinese cuisine in the United States," they assert; blame it on the nineteenth-century Chinese immigrant railroad workers and their Chinese American descendants who, lacking access to proper ingredients, "improvised dishes like chow mein and chop suey that nobody back in their native land would have recognized." Anxious to cater to the "naïve palates" of Americans, pioneering Chinese American restaurateurs incorporated many deplorable culinary changes, including the replacement of the heat of "chili-based dishes served back home" with "sweet, rich sauces to coat the food."

But that was then. Today, unlike during the nineteenth century, proper ingredients from China are readily available in the United States, the Zagats point out. How is it, then, that things have not changed? Why is Chinese food still so lamentable here? We must hold the past and current population of Chinese food purveyors in America culpable, they argue, for it is they who have failed to live up to the standards set forth by their counterparts in China, where, due to the rise of capitalism, "restaurants have become a place for people to spend their newfound disposable incomes." Simply put, Chinese food in the United States is "lackluster" because "Cantonese, Hunan and Sichuan restaurants in this country do not resemble those you can find in China."

The Zagats then pose a solution: a joint US-China "culinary visa program that makes it easier for Chinese chefs to come here." Due to post-9/11 immigration restrictions, skilled chefs from the increasingly capitalist China, where the culinary scene is "thriving," find it difficult to obtain working visas, and this subsequently derails heroic efforts by Chinese restaurateurs in the United States—like the head of the Shun Lee line of restaurants in New York City—to revolutionize Chinese food in America. American diners have come a long way since the nineteenth century, the Zagats assure us. "Eating food prepared by an influx of Chinese chefs would be like opening up a culinary time capsule." Besides, we Americans are ready for ambitious dining, as evidenced by the noticeable popularity of sophisticated culinary offerings such as offal, *sous-vide* preparations, and tasting menus. "So, we welcome Chinese chefs to share their authentic cuisines with us," the Zagats proclaim. "American palates, unlike those of previous generations, are ready for the real stuff."

Only in China?

The charge put forth by Anderson and the Zagats is essentially the same: Chinese food in America is terrible because it is not the "real stuff," and it is not the real stuff because it is made in America, not China. It is, moreover, made by Chinese American hands, not by the hands of the "real" Chinese over there. By extension, then, it is only in China where we find real Chinese people, and it is only they who are capable of making authentic—and therefore delicious—Chinese food. Chinese Americans, by virtue of residing in the United States for too long, cannot qualify as bona-fide Chinese, and the food they cook up can best be described as ersatz Chinese, a poor imitation of the original, and not original in its own right. Chinese Americans, using this logic, are either poor imitations or irredeemable corruptions of the real thing; they, like their food, must therefore be considered not authentically Chinese. Moreover, given that Chinese American food purveyors have unscrupulously served and continue to serve corrupt versions of Chinese food to unsuspecting, if not gullible, non-Chinese customers, the entire Chinese food experience in the United States, according to Anderson and the Zagats, has to be considered a sham.

On the face of it, the belief in the infallibility of Chinese cuisine in China and the dubiousness of Chinese food in America appears plausible if not wholly valid. But for this assertion to remain incontrovertible, two conditions must hold true: first, there cannot be "good" Chinese food anywhere in the United States. We are asked to categorically condemn American-style Chinese food as entirely unpalatable. There is no way for quality versions of the type of Chinese food that Americans adore—egg rolls, sweet and sour pork, General Tso's chicken, beef with broccoli, and so on—to exist because the very notion of American Chinese food is illegitimate. We are also asked to put aside the possibility that excellent regional Chinese food of the sort Anderson and the Zagats rave about exists in the United States, and has been available for nearly half a century (if not longer), most notably in the vibrant culinary enclaves populated by new

Chinese arrivals. The three primary New York City Chinatowns—in lower Manhattan, Flushing (Queens), and Sunset Park (Brooklyn)—as well as Chinatowns in San Francisco and Monterey Park (near Los Angeles), for example, are sites where Chinese food that not only rivals but arguably surpasses the food of China proper might very well exist and may have existed at least since 1965, when the Hart-Celler Act reopened American borders to thousands upon thousands of new Chinese immigrants.

Second, for Anderson's and the Zagats' position to be tenable, there must not be any "bad" Chinese food anywhere in China (unless intended for Western visitors, that is). We are thus compelled to ignore the possibility that poor Chinese food abounds in China, too. Surely the notion of subpar native food that caters to local denizens, wherever in the world they might reside, is a culinary fact of life. In other words, there has to be bad Chinese food in China, just as there is bad Korean food in Korea and bad French food in France. It is through their failure to acknowledge these possibilities that Anderson and the Zagats rest their polemic—that Chinese food in the West, and especially in the United States, is nothing more than a culinary racket.

The notion that Chinese food in America might be a fraud is not new, but rather has a long history. In describing the popularity of chop suey among American diners since the late nineteenth century, Jennifer 8. Lee, author of *The Fortune Cookie Chronicles: Adventures in the World of Chinese Food*, labels it "the biggest culinary prank that one culture has ever played on another."[35] Andrew Coe asserts in *Chop Suey: A Cultural History of Chinese Food in the United States* that rumors of the "chop suey hoax" were in circulation as far back as 1904, when a Chinese cook who first worked in San Francisco materialized one day in New York City and claimed that he was the inventor of the dish. Chop suey "is no more a national dish of the Chinese than pork and beans," the cook reportedly said. "There is not a grain of anything Celestial in it." Stories of chop suey's fraudulence proliferated, according to Coe, when "American travelers just back from China or more often Chinese themselves, often highly educated diplomats or businessmen from anywhere but the hinterland of the Pearl River Delta," became the source of the accusation.[36] Although Coe's description is of a scenario that took place a century ago, he could just as easily have been referring to a similar sentiment expressed more recently by critics of American Chinese food, such as Anderson and the Zagats, who fancy themselves well-traveled culinary authorities. In fact, within the so-called foodie scene, American Chinese food is routinely singled out as the epitome of the inauthentic dining experience in a time of rapid McDonaldization of traditional foodways. In this, the critical reception of Chinese food in America is not unlike that of a certain monumental Hollywood product—a blockbuster film, which, like Chinese food in America, the masses tend to love and professional critics love to hate.

With global box office sales exceeding $1.8 billion, *Titanic*, the 1997 film directed by James Cameron and starring Leonardo DiCaprio, is the second most profitable film in cinematic history. It is also among the most decorated, with fourteen Academy Awards nominations and eleven wins, including Best Picture and Best Director. This, however, has not resulted in critical accolades. As David Lubin puts it, *Titanic* has been derided by critics as a "crude, tawdry, manipulative example of cinematic art," closer to the kitsch of *The Poseidon Adventure* and *The Love Boat* than the artistry of *Battleship Potempkin*.[37] The *Los Angeles Times* film reviewer Kenneth Turan once described it as "a witless counterfeit of Hollywood's Golden Age, a compendium of clichés that add up to a reasonable facsimile of a film." He also dismissed the legions of devotees who flocked to the film (many repeatedly) by accusing them of being "mainstream"—that is to say, of being conventional, conformist, and common. They are "desperate people," he averred, "deadened by exposure to nonstop trash" spewed forth by producers of contemporary popular culture.[38] In other words, while it may be cynical, immoral, and in bad taste for a filmmaker and his financial enablers to produce cultural trash, it is nothing short of foolish for the audience to blindly consume it. After all, that (producing junk) is what profit-minded companies do. The question Turan poses is, Why do so many people buy it? His answer: because they lack not only smarts but also taste.

The charge of the critics of American Chinese food is comparable. Yes, Chinese food is widely available in the United States, but why should anyone feel obligated to consume it? The fact that there are over forty thousand Chinese restaurants in America is seen as evidence that the product is tailored for the benighted masses. To paraphrase Turan, Chinese food, like McDonald's burgers (over 100 billion sold, and counting), is a witless counterfeit of a preindustrial gastronomic Golden Age, a compendium of throwaway animal parts and synthetic chemicals that adds up to a reasonable facsimile of human fodder. According to this view, Americans who eat Chinese food are no less desperate than those who flock to the multiplex to see *Titanic*, their higher senses of taste and refinement having been deadened by nonstop exposure to junk spewed out by our contemporary food culture. In this regard, *Titanic*-ization and McDonaldization are viewed as interrelated processes. Turan himself notes this parallel in comparing his job as a film critic to that of a restaurant critic who refuses to send diners "straight to McDonald's on the 'everybody goes there, it must be the best' theory."

Despite the copious amount of General Tso's chicken, beef and broccoli, and pork fried rice consumed in the United States (or perhaps due precisely to that reason), people who believe themselves to be "in the know" (i.e., self-professed gourmands) do not consider these foods to be legitimate examples of Chinese food. Instead, they are seen, to paraphrase Turan, as witless facsimiles of wondrous Chinese cuisine corrupted by dark forces of philistine Americanization. Moreover, it is often someone recently arrived from China, or someone with an extensive knowledge of China, who is especially dismissive of American Chinese food. More than dismissive, they are often annoyed at, if not down right hostile to, the idea that anyone could confuse ordinary Chinese take-out for real Chinese cuisine. A commonly expressed sentiment is that what popularly passes for Chinese food in the United States either does not exist in China or that a real Chinese person would not recognize, let alone eat, any of it.

Therein lies the rub (to misquote *Hamlet*). For all intents and purposes, the cultural legitimacy of Chinese food in the United States is measured against a standard that is impossible to live up to—a largely mythical benchmark that points to the food of so-called real or authentic Chinese people defined as those who live there (in China), not here (in the United States). Not only there, but a there that is frozen in cultural stasis and resistant to the march of historical time. The Chinese presence in America—whether gastronomic or corporeal—is therefore defined as a dubious thing, neither legitimate nor appropriate, neither completely this (Chinese) nor that (American). Taken to its logical conclusion, then, to consider American Chinese food as "not the real thing" is to argue that nothing innovated by and made with Chinese American hands can be authentic, which is a fancier way of saying that nothing Chinese American can qualify as culturally legitimate.

Most, if not all, of the numerous complaints levied against Chinese food in the United States—that it is unsanitary, that it contains suspicious ingredients, that it is calorically shallow, that it is unhealthy, that it is repetitious, that it is boring, that it tastes awful, that it is inauthentic, that the selling of it is corrupt—boil down to a single overwhelming perception: the Chinese presence in America is first and foremost alien. Despite a *longue durée* of cultural and corporeal history in the United Sates, Chinese America is still seen as out of place. It is regarded as neither entirely American nor authentically Chinese.

Question: how long must Chinese Americans wait before they are no longer compared unfavorably to their supposedly authentic relatives on the other side of the globe? What characteristics must Chinese food in America exhibit before it can be considered just one of many "regional" Chinese foods that exist around the world? Is it really that untenable to argue that Chinese food in, say, Hong Kong, is simply different—not better or worse, but *different*—than Chinese food in Beijing or Shanghai or Sichuan or Xinjiang or Taiwan or Japan or Korea or India or the Philippines or Cuba or New York City or Baton Rouge? And aren't the differences among these diverse versions of Chinese food more a matter of regional particularity, migratory history, diasporic taste, and the individual skills of a particular cook than they are a matter of innate worth, legitimacy, superiority, or authenticity? (Based on personal experience, General Tso's chicken can taste anywhere from dreadful to spectacular depending on the quality of the restaurant.) How long must we wait before Chinese food in the United States and the people associated with it are appraised on their own terms and merits? Stay tuned.

Part II
DISREPUTABLE GASTRONOMY

3 | Kimchi

On a cluttered shelf in my garage, intermingled with gardening tools, half-empty cans of paint, and cast-aside golf accoutrements, sits an empty one-gallon glass jar that once contained the most delicious kimchi east of California. The jar sits there still, several years after my wife and I completely finished off its contents in what was for us, only sporadic eaters of Korean food, record time—less than a week after my in-laws delivered it, declaring that this was the tastiest and most sought-after kimchi in all of New York, New Jersey, and Connecticut. Not only the tastiest, but also the most nutritious, my mother-in-law said, a special kimchi fortified with cutting-edge scientific technology. Supplies are limited, and thank God she was fortunate enough to procure two jars, one for us, one for them. Evidently, at the crack of dawn on the day of bestowal, my wife's parents drove two hours from their home near Hartford, Connecticut, to Queens on a resolute quest to procure this precious commodity.

But upon arriving at Kum Gang San, the popular Korean restaurant in Flushing that exclusively sold it, they were dismayed to find a long line of others who had arrived before them. Apparently news of the kimchi had spread not only far and wide but also speedily within the Tri-State Korean community. (My in-laws themselves had only just discovered the kimchi a few days earlier, when it seemingly appeared out of the blue at an after-service church potluck.) With two jars safely stowed in a large portable cooler, and feeling mightily pleased with their delicious find, my in-laws then drove four more hours along the picturesque New York State Route 17 to the frowsy upstate town of Binghamton, where my wife and I lived, in order to surprise us with our share. Early bird gets the worm, my father-in-law gloated, beaming with pride and chuckling in self-satisfaction.

The tastiest, most nutritious, and most sough-after kimchi in the entire Tri-State area? What a bold claim! Surely she exaggerates, I thought to myself as my mother-in-law slowly removed the lid of the cooler. Carefully nestled amid densely packed ice cubes were the two jars of kimchi. My mother-in-law paused for a moment, her eyes moving from one object to the other, as if yet undecided which bundle to give us. She finally made her selection. Then, in a manner suggestive not of an astute shopper (which she is) but a professional bomb defuser (which she is not), she gingerly unwrapped the jar from not one but three layers of plastic bags, each neatly double-knotted at the top.

In truth, I was more than a wee bit skeptical of my mother-in-law's claim that this was the preeminent kimchi of the entire Tri-State region. After all, the kimchi at Gahm Mi Oak Restaurant on Manhattan's West 32nd Street, the ultimate destination of *seolleongtang* aficionados everywhere, was pretty difficult to top. But everything changed with the first taste. How do I describe it? *Crunchy, crisp, and cool as a summer radish just plucked from a backyard garden. Fleshy, almost meaty, and sensual as a morsel of* otoro. *Faint traces of mineral and brine, as from a freshly shucked Blue Point oyster. Slightly acidic. Hints of citrus, jicama, and tomatillo. The subtle complexity of a top-notch Viognier. The effervescence of a classically pétillant Vinho Verde.*

What it was not, however, was spicy, fiery, piquant, pungent, or hot. (It was, in fact, cool as a cucumber.) And neither was it crimson, scarlet, or red. (More than anything, it was white, with a whisper of chartreuse.) Nor was it smelly, stinky, or malodorous. (It hardly smelled of anything at all.) In other words, this kimchi failed to live up to the three characteristics—spicy, red, smelly—most nonnative eaters associate with what is generally regarded as the "national dish" of Korea. A quick glance at the list of ingredients on the colorful label pasted to the jar revealed a clue as to why at least the first two characteristics were absent. Missing conspicuously was any mention of the one item, aside from cabbage, considered synonymous with kimchi and the sole ingredient responsible for the fiery taste and crimson hue most non-Koreans expect to see in kimchi—the red hot chile pepper. As for the absence of the disreputable odor, the label once again provided a clue: "Great-tasting Kimchi without the smell!" it blazoned in both Korean and English.

Upon closer inspection, I realized there was much more to the label than a mere list of ingredients and claims of product virtues. In fact, if we scrupulously examine the label, we just might locate the key to what can only be described as a twenty-first-century fermentation enigma. A scrupulous examination of the label and its bilingual content just might lead us to kimchi-Narnia, a world full of wonder, mystery, history, and mythology, replete with heroes, villains, exotic backdrops, and dramatic turns of plot. To fully comprehend the meaning of the jar (and, by extension, the kimchi itself), a sedulous, as well as fanciful, scrutiny of its signs, signifiers, and cryptograms might be required. In other words, we must treat the label as we might a mysterious Cro-Magnon cave painting in Lascaux of southern France's Vézère Valley; a difficult high modernist poem, say, a canto of Ezra Pound; or the Delphic symbols embedded in Leonardo Da

Label on the jar of the *baek* (white) kimchi sold at Kum Gang San Restaurant in Queens, New York.

Vinci's artwork housed at the Louvre or the Santa Maria delle Grazie. Yes, we must decode Da Kimchi Code. What might we discover about the meaning of kimchi—where it's been and where it's bound—by solving the riddle of the jar? Mind you, this kimchi was made nowhere near the dish's mythical birthplace, the Korean peninsula. Rather, it was bottled and fermented in heterogeneous and polyglot Queens, a place best known only a generation ago for being home to Archie and Edith Bunker of the 1970s television show *All in the Family*.

Fermented in Queens

Before my move to Binghamton, Queens was a place I once had the privilege to call home. For a short period of time (too short in retrospect), I lived just a few steps from the epicurean salmagundi that is Roosevelt Avenue, first in Woodside, then Elmhurst. Abutting the two neighborhoods, east of Woodside and north of Elmhurst, is Jackson Heights, arguably the most culturally diverse place in the country, if not the world. Perpetually overlaid by the latticed shadows of the elevated tracks and platforms that service the Number 7 train (aka the Orient Express), Roosevelt Avenue links the three neighborhoods. If we were to walk eastward from Woodside on Roosevelt for a span of thirty blocks or so, we would, as Martin Manalansan IV said about the borough as a whole, discover "a kaleidoscope of aural, aromatic, and gustatory delights."[1] We would encounter the multisensory contributions of the Philippines, Korea, China, India, Pakistan, Colombia, Ecuador, Mexico, Thailand, Puerto Rico, Guyana, Peru, and the Dominican Republic (to name just a few, and not necessarily in that order). Head farther east just a mere three or so miles and we cross into the neighborhood of Corona (the mythical home of Archie and Edith Bunker), then Flushing Meadows-Corona Park (home to the USTA Billie Jean King National Tennis Center, the site of the US Open tennis championship), and we eventually arrive in Flushing (the terminus of the Number 7 train and the point of departure of the kimchi that once graced the empty jar whose label we now contemplate).

The borough, of course, is significant for myriad reasons other than the fact that it was my former abode. For starters, Queens is where various members of the Lenape—meaning "Men" or "People" in the native Delaware language of Munsee—resided for some sixty-five thousand years prior to the arrival of the first Europeans. These included indigenous groups that called themselves Siwanoys, Matinecocks, Massapequas, Rockaways, and Merricks.[2] Then, just four hundred years ago, Dutch arrivals established a colony at the southern tip of Manhattan, naming it New Netherland, which included some farms in Queens on the banks of the East River. British settlers soon followed and, with the Dutch, drove out the Lenape. The British then took over the colony in 1664. Two decades later, the British divided the former Dutch settlement into ten counties, including Queens County, named after Catherine of Braganza, wife of King Charles II.[3] Since then, millions of settlers, ex-slaves, and immigrants from countless European, Latin American, Caribbean, Asian, and African countries have poured onto the land once exclusively occupied by the Lenape.

In land area, the borough of Queens is almost as large as the Bronx, Manhattan, and Staten Island combined. Only Brooklyn is more populous. More than 140 different languages are currently spoken there. It is home to nearly half of New York City's Asian and Pacific Islander population and the largest Chinese American community outside California. It is also home to the largest Argentinian community in the city. My favorite baseball team, the New York Mets, competes there (or at least tries to). It was the site of both the 1939 New York World's Fair, which included a pavilion whose façade was modeled after a Wonder Bread wrapper, and the 1964 New York World's Fair, which introduced Americans to the Belgian waffle (although some credit the 1962 Seattle World's Fair with this). Queens was also once home to George and Louise Jefferson, neighbors of the Bunkers—that is, until they finally got a piece of the pie (and their own spin-off show, *The Jeffersons*) and moved on up to the east side of Manhattan, to a deluxe doorman apartment in the sky.

Comedian Jerry Seinfeld and disgraced socialite Ruth Madoff (wife of Bernie, the greatest Ponzi schemer in history) attended college in Queens. Legends Harry Houdini, Louis Armstrong, Henny Youngman, Jackie Robinson, Lucky Luciano, Mae West, and some five million other dead souls, legendary or otherwise, are buried in dozens of graveyards scattered throughout the borough. (According to one estimate, the number of dead interred in Queens is more than three times the current population, which prompted the *New York Times* to describe the borough as the city's "cemetery central.")[4] Queens is "the valley of ashes," where Daisy ran over Myrtle while Jay rode shotgun in F. Scott Fitzgerald's 1925 Jazz Age novel

The Great Gatsby. And Queens is where a pair of black-clad intergalactic border agents exterminated a giant undocumented alien cockroach that was set to destroy Earth in Barry Sonnenfeld's 1997 film *Men in Black*.

Can kimchi made in such a place possibly cut the proverbial mustard? Or, to put it in theological terms (given that the majority of Koreans in the United States are churchgoing Christians), can kimchi made here, in Queens, ever taste as heavenly or smell as hellacious as the genuine article made there, in Korea?

The Heat That Conquered the World

In 1492 Columbus sailed the ocean blue—or so we are taught at an early age. (And as far as I know, this remains true.) We are also taught that in doing so, he proved to a superstitious, unenlightened world that the earth was not as flat as an American pancake but in fact as round as a Danish *aebleskiver*. (I was quite dismayed to learn later that this was decidedly untrue; it turns out nearly everyone of consequence knew the world was round during Columbus' time.) What we are seldom told, however, is that just decades prior the Ottoman Turks had established Constantinople as their empire's capital, all but cutting off Europe's terrestrial passage to the riches of Asia. Obsessively ambitious and in search of a direct sea route to the Orient and commercial access to its vast treasures (gold, spice, and everything nice), the Genovese explorer instead came upon an island in the Caribbean, one of the Bahamas, but, silly him, mistook it for India, or perhaps even China or Japan. No matter; let us call this place India, he and his followers said, and the semi-naked people upon it Indians. Thus the origin of the greatest nomenclatural blunder in history. No, not "Indian" for every indigenous person of the Americas. For the purposes of this discussion, that ranks second. And neither his corruption of the Carib Indians' name to *canibale,* which came to signify anthropophagy in the English and Spanish lexicons.[5] (That is to say, due to Columbus, the word for "Caribs became Canibs and eventually cannibals.")[6] Let us rank this misnaming third.

Columbus' greatest nomenclatural gaffe, at least from a gastronomic perspective, was mistaking the New World's chile for the Old World's black pepper. The latter was Europe's black gold, the hottest commodity of the time; it is the spice we call black pepper, as opposed to red pepper, its New World alter ego, its culinary doppelgänger. The red pepper is what the Arawaks of yore called *ají* (also rendered *axí*, *ajé*, or *agí*), a term still used in some parts of the Caribbean and South America.[7] The black pepper, meanwhile, is as apt a symbol as any of the financial motive behind Columbus, in his attempt to map an alternate route to the Moluccas (aka Spice Islands), sailing the ocean blue in the first place.[8] Due to his mix up, the two hitherto unrelated objects were to be evermore lexically blurred in most European languages. The Portuguese "pimento," Dutch "*Spaanse peper*," French "*piment*," Danish "paprika," and English "chili pepper" all are terms for the chile rooted in the masculine Spanish "pimiento," named after the feminine *pimienta*, the black pepper.

This nomenclatural conflation has prompted Jean Andrews, the world-renowned expert on the chile and author of *Peppers: The Domesticated Capsicums*, to wish "we had another name for what we call peppers, in order to distinguish them from the pepper of the spice merchants, which is obtained from the dried fruit of the *Piper nigrum* Linné, 1753, a climbing shrub of the family Piperaceae, native to India, whereas our peppers are of the genus *Capsicum* Tournefort, 1719, a member of the family Solanaceae."[9] Other major New World produce that belongs to the Solanaceae family includes tomatoes, potatoes, and tobacco.[10] Sophie Coe, author of a book on pre-Columbian food titled *America's First Cuisines*, remarks that the genus *Capsicum* seems "to have a magnetic attraction for confusing colloquial names."[11] There are two opinions as to the origin of *Capsicum*, both equally plausible. One camp believes it is from the Latin *capsa* or *capsula*, meaning "box" or "chest," while another insists it is from the Greek *kaptein* or *kapto*, meaning "to bite."[12]

To avoid confusion, I prefer to refer to the genus *Capsicum* simply and exclusively as "chile," reserving "pepper" for the small, dried fruit of *Piper nigrum* (i.e., the stuff that gets ground in a pepper mill) or to be used in conjunction with "bell" (as in green bell pepper or red bell pepper) in referring to the large, mild chiles the British call sweet peppers and Australians and New Zealanders call capsicum. In this I follow the lead of Mark Miller, formerly of the Coyote Café in Sante Fe, New Mexico, and others who insist on chile as the "general convention for proper usage" to refer to the plant or pod of the genus *Capsicum*, with chili, the conventional American spelling, reserved for the dish commonly made with chiles and meat, such as chili con carne.[13] And for reasons akin to why we Americans prefer "color" over "colour" and "civilize" over "civilise," I would rather we on this side of the pond leave "chilli" to those across it.

Exactly how many different chile varieties there are in the world is anyone's guess. Thus far about twenty-five wild and a handful of domesticated species have been identified. A reliable estimation is between two thousand and three thousand different cultivars, but even this vague figure is unhelpful given the chile's propensity to cross-pollinate without human involvement. The chile's tendency to hybridize readily has resulted in the emergence of innumerable local forms in nearly every conceivable climate or region the plant has laid down roots. Jean Andrews believes no other spice in history has proliferated so widely or so quickly. Regardless of the diversity, however, all chiles found in markets and kitchens around the world today are botanically similar to the varieties Columbus first encountered more than half a millennium ago.[14]

These include several species of undomesticated *Capsicums,* commonly called "bird peppers," along with the five major categories of domesticated varieties, namely *Capsicum frutescens* (which includes the tabasco chile, which gave its name to the famous Tabasco-brand pepper sauce), *Capsicum pubescens* (known in Mexico as apple or pear chile for its bulbous shape), *Capsicum baccatum* (called *ají* in parts of South America and the Caribbean), *Capsicum chinense* (which includes many of the hottest chiles in the world, such as the habañero), and *Capsicum annuum* (the most common and diverse of all, which includes Thai hot, cherry pepper, banana pepper, Hungarian paprika, Fresno, chile de árbol, Korean hot, cayenne, serrano, jalapeño, poblano, pasilla, sweet bell, and numerous ornamental varieties).[15]

Columbus' 1492 voyage initiated a back-and-forth flow of biological matter between the Eastern and Western Hemispheres that radically and irrevocably altered both worlds. Previously, the two hemispheres had been completely isolated from each other in all matters flora and fauna, and in human activities. This mutual isolation came to a sudden halt in a process Alfred Crosby Jr. has termed the "Columbian Exchange." And it was truly an exchange, as the two halves of the world indiscriminately traded biological matter that would become instrumental in both the population explosion of the denizens of the Old World and the population annihilation of many of the indigenous peoples of the New World.

The Old World settlers, who would eventually supplant much of the indigenous New World population, introduced to the Americas such important crops as wheat, oat, rice, sugarcane, banana, soy, garlic, onion, cucumber, carrot, and eggplant. In return, the New World contributed such essential viands as corn (maize), potato, tomato, squash, peanut, pineapple, cassava (manioc), and avocado. As for animals, the conquerors and settlers brought with them horses, cattle, pigs, sheep, goats, honeybees, pigeons, and rats, while the societies they left behind received turkeys, guinea pigs, llamas, and alpacas. Other exchanges included the New World's tobacco and cacao for the Old World's opium, coffee, tea, and milk.

Yet there was another biological exchange that proved to be as consequential as any other, with one side incontrovertibly losing out in the most cataclysmic fashion imaginable. For millennia prior to Columbus' arrival, New World denizens went about their business forming, as Crosby puts it, "unique cultures and working out tolerances for a limited, native American selection of pathological microlife." But after 1492, "the American Indian met for the first time his most hideous enemy: not the white man nor his black servant, but the invisible killers which those men brought in their bloods and breaths."[16] These invisible killers led to diseases such as typhoid, bubonic plague, yellow fever, leprosy, measles, small pox, chicken pox, malaria, tuberculosis, influenza, and the common cold. The New World, however, was not without its own microbial contribution, even if it was limited to a single type. As if some sort of comic relief would be necessary in the face of such great tragedy, some believe that the American Indian gave syphilis—aka the French Disease and Cupid's Disease—to the Old World.

In addition to possibly introducing to the Old World something that tickled its loins (syphilis), the New World also gave it something that titillated its tongue. There is a difference of scientific opinion as to the precise geographic origin of the chile. One group argues for what is now central Bolivia while another argues for southern Brazil. According to Andrews, the plant most likely originated "in the area south of the wet forests of Amazonia and the semiarid cerrado of Brazil." Their unique botanical features allowed these earliest wild chiles to be easily transported, and both birds and humans began spreading them widely "beginning any time after the formation of the Panama land bridge between North and South

America in the Pleistocene epoch," which lasted from some 1.6 million to 10,000 years ago.[17]

Archaeological remains point to chiles being the first spice ever to have been used by humans. Excavations in Mexico have revealed evidence of its consumption that dates back to 7200–5200 BC. It is believed chiles were first domesticated sometime between five thousand and ten thousand years ago.[18] By the time Columbus reached the New World, all of the major domesticated forms of the chile that now exist had not only already been formed, but had spread from South America to Central America and the Caribbean.[19] The traditional pre-Columbian use of chile went beyond the Nahuatl *molli* (or Mexican *mole*) and other culinary wonders, however. Although it proved futile, the Incas set ablaze mounds of dried chiles to temporarily blind the invading Spaniards, and the Mayas reportedly punished promiscuous women by rubbing fresh chiles on their genitals.[20]

Today, it is impossible to imagine innumerable cuisines of the world beyond the Americas without thinking first and foremost about chiles. Without them there would be no such thing as Indian vindaloo, Hungarian goulash, Spanish chorizo, Mozambican *piri-piri,* Ethiopian *berbere,* Moroccan harissa, Chinese kung pao, Thai *tom yum,* American Tabasco sauce, or Korean *yukgaejang.* And chiles continue to be used for martial and disciplinary purposes; the chemical that makes chiles pungent is the primary ingredient in pepper spray, for example.[21]

David DeWitt, author of over a dozen books on the chile, speculates that Koreans are the highest per capital consumer of chiles in the world.[22] Today there are perhaps more than a hundred varieties of chiles grown in South Korea alone, with different types named for the region in which they are grown, such as Yeongyang, Cheonan, Eumseong, Cheongsong, Jecheon, and Boeun.[23] South Korea is among the largest chile producers in the world. DeWitt ranks it fifth largest; India, Mexico, China, Thailand, Ethiopia, Malaysia, and the United States are other major producers. Chiles account for 35 percent of South Korea's vegetable agriculture, surpassing the other two major crops, cabbage and garlic, which, not so coincidentally, are also common ingredients in kimchi.[24]

This comes as a surprise to many, not least to Koreans: the practice of adding chiles, specifically dried red chile powder or flakes, to many types of kimchi is a relatively recent practice—that is, if you accept the premise that Korea is some five thousand years old, as national folklore purports. Michael Pettid, author of *Korean Cuisine: An Illustrated History,* notes that a fifteenth-century writer referred to kimchi as a "golden-yellow vegetable," indicating that the kimchi of that era was a far cry from today's emblematic version dominated by the color red.[25] According to Manjo Kim, the earliest record of chile use in kimchi is said to be 1715, when a Confucian scholar referred to the use of chiles in kimchi while discussing cultivated vegetables. Koreans have long enjoyed strong and bold flavors in food. Before chiles were introduced, mustard, black pepper, garlic, ginger, tangerine peels, and other pungent and aromatic ingredients enlivened the taste of kimchi.[26]

It is generally accepted that chiles entered Korea via Japan sometime after the Hideyoshi invasions at the end of the sixteenth century. The earliest recorded mention of chiles is in a 1613 document that referred to it as a "great poison" brought to Korea from Japan, but is now widespread in Korea. The document added that chile-laden foods were a common drinking-house nosh.[27] Some contemporary scholars, however, especially those who cannot stomach the idea that Korea owes something so vital as this to Japan, argue that chiles arrived directly via Portuguese soldiers included among the Ming reinforcements that fought alongside Koreans during the Japanese invasions.[28]

As to when chiles first appeared in Japan, this, too, is open to question. Most credit the Portuguese, who first reached Japan in 1549. Lizzie Collingham, author of *Curry: A Tale of Cooks and Conquerors,* notes that the Portuguese were the first to dominate the global chile trade and are responsible for introducing chiles to India soon after Vasco da Gama first landed near the port city of Calicut on the Malabar Coast in 1498.[29] Others, meanwhile, argue that chiles arrived in Japan independent of the Portuguese, through Japanese trading vessels such as the Red Seal ships that sailed to Southeast Asia, where the Portuguese had established commercial centers, and as far as to New Spain (present-day Mexico), the ancestral home of the chile, until access there was denied to Japanese ships in 1611.[30]

To most nonnative eaters, Korean food is synonymous with what the Japanese call *togarashi,* Senegalese *foronto,* Bhutanese *ema,* Thai *prik,* Gujarati *lilun marchu,* and Koreans *gochu.* More than any other criterion, the Scoville Heat Unit (SHU), a scale that gauges the hotness of chiles, dominates popular discussion of what constitutes "real" Korean fare. The SHU measures the level of capsaicin, the heat-producing chemical compound found in all chiles. The highest concentration of capsaicin is found not in the seeds, as many mistakenly believe, but along the vein-like placenta, or capsaicin glands, that run vertically within the inside wall of the chile pod. Capsaicin acts as a defense mechanism against animal predators that might otherwise choose to include chiles as part of their diet. It is believed that while mammals, including humans, are susceptible to the painful bite of the protective chemical, birds are immune. Hence many small varieties of chiles are called "bird peppers," which are believed to be consumed and then subsequently spread elsewhere via bird droppings. Under the Scoville scale, first devised in 1912, the mildest varieties, such as bell peppers, score zero SHU, whereas the hottest on record, the Bhut Jolokia from the Assam region of India, scores over a million.[31]

The hotter the dish, the more authentic the Korean taste, or so I often hear. Chile-laden Korean fare like *ojingeo bokkeum, bibim naengmyeon,* and *sundubu jjigae* is said to be "watered down," "westernized," or, worse yet, "Americanized" if it fails the native tongue taste—that is, if its SHU is lower than the idealized version consumed by a so-called "real" Korean, a figure shrouded in both anthropological and nationalistic intrigue. For better or for worse, the chile is the ingredient that comes first to mind

Assortment of red chile flakes and powder at a market in Seoul, South Korea. Photo by the author.

whenever Korean gastronomy is discussed, even if plain evidence—such as menus and cookbooks that contain a substantive number of dishes without chiles—indicates otherwise. *The Lonely Planet* guidebook, for example, describes the chile as Korea's "big spice," and offers the following rule for dining out: red = spicy.[32]

The tendency to distill Korean food down to its spicy essence is not only a nonnative trait, however. Increasingly, Koreans themselves are conceding to the power of the capsaicin. To Mi-ok Kim, the red chile powder in particular "occupies a permanent place on the dinner table of Korean families," making it difficult to imagine Korean food without it. This, she maintains, is especially true for kimchi.[33] The color red, moreover, occupies a special place in traditional Korean culture, including in food. Prior to the arrival of chiles, ingredients such as cockscomb, safflower, and violet leaf mustard were used to impart the desired redness to some kimchi.[34] To Kyung-Koo Han, it is the "red pepper that makes kimchi into the food of the Koreans."[35] This sentiment is echoed by Michael Pettid, who describes chiles as "an essential component in Korean cuisine" and most notably in kimchi, despite "a relatively brief history in Korea." He adds that some four hundred years after its introduction to Korea, "it is very difficult to imagine Korean foods without them."[36]

Thus, to return to our kimchi jar, a casual observer might find it even more curious to find no chile whatsoever in Kum Gang San's unspicy, odorless, white kimchi.

The Heterogeneous Kimchi

Of course, to those in the know, there is nothing remarkable about the whiteness of kimchi, as kimchi comes in all colors, shapes, sizes, and degrees of heat. (That being said, there is nothing remarkable about the whiteness of Korean food in general.) It is unclear as to exactly how many different types of kimchi exist. Reports vary widely: Cherl-Ho Lee indicates there are more than fifty types, while the Korea Food Research Institute, a South Korean government-sponsored research center charged with increasing the profits of the South Korean food industry, reports that 187 kinds were identified in a survey.[37] Manjo Kim declares that there have been more than three hundred different preparations.[38] But as Chun Ja Lee and others have pointed out, the exact number is ultimately meaningless given that

Koreans "can make kimchi out of practically any edible material," cultivated or wild, flora or fauna.[39]

Kimchi's boundless diversity indicates multiple factors at work, including regional, seasonal, agricultural, communal, and personal peculiarities. While this makes any effort to categorize kimchi a challenge, resulting in a number of alternate but overlapping organizing principles, the foremost factor is seasonal. The Korea Food Research Institute classifies kimchi into two main types, "winter" and "seasonal," with the former typified by whole-cabbage and whole-radish kimchi and the latter by young cabbage and cucumber kimchi.[40] Manjo Kim, perhaps the most prolific writer on kimchi in English, organizes kimchi along five seasonal types—winter, spring, summer, autumn, and year-round.[41]

Cross-referencing primary ingredients (e.g., cabbage, radish, leafy vegetables) with curing agents (e.g., brine, spices, soy sauce, soy paste, chile paste, fish sauce, fish fillets, rice wine, malted rice, fruit brew) is another way to make sense of kimchi's heterogeneity. This sorting method has reportedly resulted in the identification of ten major types of kimchi.[42] Owing to the Korean peninsula's numerous climatic zones, ranging from humid continental to humid subtropical, another important organizing principle is regional. Different regions of the peninsula boast distinct environmental, topographical, historical, and social idiosyncrasies. According to Chun Ja Lee, Hye Won Park, and Kwi Young Kim, authors of *The Book of Kimchi*, the kimchi of the northeasternmost Hamgyong province, which is not only the coldest but most remote part of the peninsula, is said to be "beautiful and bold," with "plenty of juice." Hamgyong kimchi is less salty and spicy, since the colder weather near the Chinese and Russian borders allows for a more moderate use of preservation agents such as salt and chiles. The southernmost Cheju Island province, by contrast, is noted for its lavish use of marine life, best characterized by its famous abalone kimchi and mixed-seafood kimchi. The mid-peninsular Gyeonggi province, meanwhile, due to its political centrality throughout Korean history, is known for "glamorous and extravagant" kimchi, typified by *ssam* (wrapped) kimchi and *chang* (soy sauce) kimchi.[43]

Other notable kimchi categories include royal palace kimchi, such as pomegranate kimchi (made not from the multiseeded, red-fleshed fruit but rather from stuffed radish blocks cut in a crosshatch pattern) and citron or *yuja* kimchi. Memorial service kimchi is usually a white radish variety that corresponds to the traditional Korean funereal color. Buddhist temple kimchi is characterized by the absence of animal products, such as seafood, and "hot" vegetables such as scallion and garlic, in accordance with Buddhist principles, and the inclusion of assorted mountainous herbs and other vegetation, such as dropwort. Filial piety kimchi is designed specially with the elderly—that is, weak teeth and sensitive digestion—in mind. And pregnancy kimchi pays meticulous attention to the precise shape and form of ingredients, such as radishes cut into exact measurements, as the formal beauty and precise proportion of the food consumed by the expectant mother are said to correlate to the child's "straight and sound body and mind."[44]

Today's most commonly consumed kimchi is unquestionably made with *baechu* cabbage (also known as napa cabbage, Chinese cabbage, or Korean cabbage). However, nearly every vegetable, cultivated or wild, found wherever Koreans reside, can be and has been used as the principal base for kimchi. Radishes, chives, Indian mustard leaves, soybean sprouts, leeks, onions, turnips, ginseng, spinach, cucumbers, watercress, burdock root, mulberry leaves, green tomatoes, Swiss chard, citron, sweet potato stems, bamboo shoots, perilla leaves, and eggplant hint at just the tip of the kimchi iceberg. Typically, some sort of fresh but more often preserved or fermented seafood called *chotkal*—oyster, shrimp, squid, or fish—is mixed in during kimchi preparation, reflecting Korea's peninsular geography and historical dependence on the ocean for foodstuffs.[45]

But if kimchi can be made with just about anything, and if the chile is but an optional ingredient, what makes kimchi *kimchi*? Not surprisingly, there are considerable differences of opinion as to the precise definition of kimchi, which, again not surprisingly, rests on its reputed origin. If kimchi is broadly defined as a vegetable that has been salted, brined, or pickled, then its origin goes back at least three thousand years to Neolithic China, reaching Korea through culinary diffusion during the Unified Silla period about fifteen hundred years ago.[46] In what is considered the earliest collection of Chinese poetry, *The Book of Songs* (compiled around 600 BC and containing lyrics composed between 1700 BC and 700 BC), a stanza celebrates the sliced and pickled cucumber, which, if offered to your ancestors, will bring long life and the blessing of Heaven for your progeny. Some believe the Chinese word for this pickle, pronounced *jeo* in Korean, is the progenitor of kimchi.[47] As for the etymology of kimchi, the word is said to have derived from Chinese characters for brined or salted vegetables, which nineteenth-century Koreans called *chimchae*, before evolving into the modern-day kimchi.[48] (At the 1966 International Academic Conference of Food Science and Engineering in Warsaw, Poland, participants reached an agreement to officially romanize the word as "k-i-m-c-h-i.")[49]

Thus it appears that what makes kimchi *kimchi* is neither cabbage nor chiles, but salt or perhaps acid, such as vinegar. The preservation of food by pickling or brining is among the oldest and simplest culinary practices known to humans. As Harold McGee, author of the essential *On Food and Cooking: The Science and Lore of the Kitchen,* points out, the technique is adaptable to all climates, requires no cooking, and thus expends no fuel. All that is required is a vessel and some salt, saltwater, or strong acid—and perhaps a hole in the ground.[50] Examples of such foods span the globe: sauerkraut, olives, preserved lemon, ham, corned beef, gravlax, and caviar are but a negligible sampling.

And while cabbage is mentioned in thousand-year-old Goryeo dynasty documents, the tiny and sparse core of that era's cabbage hardly resembles the current version. Today's baechu cabbage, whose large, densely

Assortment of kimchi at Super H Mart, a Korean market in Ridgefield, New Jersey. Photo by the author.

packed heads resulted from several generations of selective breeding by the Chinese and not grown in Korea until the mid-nineteenth century,[51] is now, for better or worse, the standard foundation of the twenty-first-century kimchi. In fact, when kimchi is referred to without any qualifiers, it is baechu kimchi made with red chiles that is most likely meant. The term "kimchi" is simultaneously narrow and wide ranging: specifically, it refers to chile-laden baechu kimchi; generically, it refers to the countless other kimchi varieties that currently exist, have once existed, and might one day exist.[52]

The Super Functional Food

While chiles do not appear as an ingredient on the label of our jar, the following items do: cabbage, radishes, garlic, ginger, salt, scallions, and, somewhat disturbingly, lactic acid bacteria. But rather than downplay this final, germy detail, the label counterintuitively highlights it. It not only divulges the type of bacteria used but the person responsible for it—a certain Dr. Kang (sans first name). In fact, it turns out that our white kimchi from Queens is named for the microbe: "Patent IH-22 Lactic Acid Bacteria Kimchi." Evidently, the kimchi makers want the world to know that their custom-tailored microbe—unlike, say, the dreaded *E. coli* O157:H7, the bane of Fast Food America's gastrointestinal tract—does not pose a health hazard. Rather, this newfangled, high-tech strain injected into Kum Gang San's kimchi is not only safe to eat, but is, more importantly, good for you.

Kimchi in recent years has become for Koreans what red wine has been for the French since the early 1990s—or since November 17, 1991, to be exact. On that Sunday evening, CBS' newsmagazine program *60 Minutes* first introduced the so-called French paradox to the mainstream American public. Despite a diet loaded with fat and cholesterol, there is something that seems to be protecting the French from heart disease, mused the segment. A meal consisting of pig's head pâté, black pudding ("which is very fat"), potatoes in oil, and double-fat sliced tripe was cited as "routine stuff" for the French. If Americans were subjected to this sort of meal, claimed a researcher, "we'd all be suffering from coronaries at an early age." So why is the French rate of coronary heart disease about half that of the United States? According to *60 Minutes*, the French drink more red wine.

Although this was the gist of the message that would be widely promulgated, in reality the matter was much more complicated and nuanced. First, the *60 Minutes* report did not single out red wine. Rather, it proposed the French love of cheese—as opposed to the American love of milk—as an equally important explanation for the paradox. Second, it was not simply wine but alcohol in general that was cited as an "all but confirmed" preventive for heart disease.[53] Regardless, over the next two decades the American media would repeatedly identify red wine as the primary—if not the sole—reason for the French paradox.[54]

And neither did *60 Minutes* imply that the wine ought to be French produced. Nonetheless, the French government immediately capitalized on the report by boasting about the miraculous power of their national viticulture. A governmental agency that promotes French food and wine overseas (Food and Wines from France) even purchased full-page advertisements in several American newspapers that fêted French wine while embellishing the facts. The copy of one such advertisement read, "According to a recent news report on CBS's '60 Minutes' entitled 'The French Paradox,' the intake of fat in the French diet seems to be counteracted by their drinking of French red wine. Yes, French red wine. The intake of wine per capita in France is higher than anywhere else in the world. In comparison, the United States per capita intake is among the lowest."[55]

What promptly followed was a boon for the wine business. In 1992, the year following the *60 Minutes* report, sales of red wine in the United States increased 42 percent and white wine 13 percent. And no doubt to the chagrin of Miles Raymond (the Paul Giamatti character in the 2004 film *Sideways*), the surge in sales of merlot was the most dramatic; it rose 92 percent from the previous year.[56] (Amusingly, sales of foie gras, which a French research team suggested was good for the heart, also spiked during this time.)[57] In 1996 an incredulous Harvey Levenstein made light of the French paradox, calling it a fortuitous break for the wine industry. "Don't expect that luck to last," he added.[58] Warren Belasco pressed this view with a reminder that 5 percent of the population drank 75 percent of the wine consumed in the United States. He predicted that the love of wine would never become widespread among Americans. Rather, wine drinking would disappear even in the Mediterranean world, as there was a greater likelihood of the Mediterranean "coming our way" than the United States adapting to the other's way of eating and imbibing.[59]

Levenstein and Belasco were not the only food pundits to publicly air their doubts. Some four years earlier, amid largely positive buzz about the French paradox, Marion Nestle prescribed a dose of restraint and perspective. She pointed out that the French diet was traditionally low in fat and had only recently begun to rival the American diet in this regard. "The French diet is newly high in fat," she asserted, "and heart disease rates just haven't had time to catch up." Jean Mayer took the criticism much further: "The French paradox is a hoax," she averred. "It's quite possible that 20 to 30 years from now the French may have as much heart disease as we (Americans) do."[60]

Just as news of the French paradox vivified the wine industry in the United States during the 1990s, reports of kimchi's health value proved similarly serendipitous for the kimchi industry a decade or so later. And just as the French government had done, the Korean government played a pivotal role in promoting the product. Somewhat predictably, it did so with the overt aim of bolstering the commercial potential for industrially produced kimchi in an ever-expanding overseas market.

Even as early as the 1980s, especially as the 1988 Seoul Olympic Games drew near, murmurs of a strange food from Korea called kimchi surfaced periodically here and there in the United States, and particularly on the two coasts, where significant Korean American populations resided. Back then, only a smattering of Americans had heard of, let alone tasted, kimchi, which led the *New York Times* to issue a primer on the rudiments of the dish on July 29, 1987. "Pronounced: kim-chee," began the article. "Produced: by women from Seoul to Pusan, from grandmothers to would-be brides." "Consumed: three times a day, year-round, by the majority of South Korea's 41 million people."[61] While the article touched on the origin, history, cultural importance, symbolic value, and emotional significance of kimchi, there was no mention of its nutritional value. A few months later, though, the *Los Angeles Times* would publish a major front-page profile of "the uniquely Korean dish" and report on the quaint but outlandish Korean belief in kimchi's "mysterious energizing quality" to "improve the performance of athletes."[62]

Over a span of twenty years, kimchi's reputation as a healthful food would undergo a dramatic transformation—from being regarded as an offbeat superstition of an eccentric people in the mid-1980s to a much-ballyhooed culinary truism for the cosmopolitan foodie crowd in the mid-2000s. In the March 2006 issue of *Health* magazine, for example, Korean kimchi is identified as among the five most healthful foods in the world, sharing the accolade with Spanish olive oil, Japanese soy, Greek yogurt, and Indian lentils. Kimchi "is loaded with vitamins A, B, and C" and is "part of a high-fiber, low-fat diet that has kept obesity at bay in Korea," reports the magazine.[63] In November 2009 the glossy food magazine *Saveur* devoted ten full-color pages to kimchi, calling it Korea's "national obsession." "In addition to being rich in vitamins B and C," writes Mei Chin, the author of the article, "kimchi has, according to more than one study I've read, even shown promise in preventing cancer. It is, apparently, a superfood."[64]

Kimchi's current reputation as a superfood is no chimera, however. It did not materialize out of thin air, nor did it magically emerge from the offices of South Korean government bureaucrats. The field of nutraceutical sciences, and Korean researchers in particular, had been paying scrupulous attention to the health-giving and medicinal potential of kimchi for quite some time. Kimchi, as such, is routinely defined as a functional food, a descriptor that Japanese researchers originated during the 1980s.[65]

Although "functional food" is freely bandied about among nutritional experts and commercial interests, there is no legal or uniform definition of it—at least not in the United States or Europe.[66] According to Glenn Gibson and Christine Williams, authors of *Functional Foods: Concept to Product*, a food is generally considered functional if it can be demonstrated to "affect beneficially one or more target functions of the body, beyond adequate nutrition, in a way that improves health and well-being or reduces the risk of disease." Moreover, a functional food must remain a food. That is to say, it must remain in its "natural" state or as close to it as possible. The food may be altered so that a positive component is included, deleterious component excluded, or one or more of its components modified to affix a benefit, but it must remain "whole" and not processed into, say, a capsule, tablet, or powder.[67] Of course, as some have pointed out, all foods are potentially functional, provided someone makes an empirical case.[68] For example, if it can be scientifically determined that flavonoids in grapefruits, omega-3 fatty acids in chicken eggs, sulforaphane in broccoli, lycopene in tomatoes, and resveratrol in red wine improve particular bodily functions or reduce the risk of certain diseases, then those foods are technically functional.

Kimchi is the epitome of functionality—if you trust the abundance of kimchi research that has proliferated since the early 1990s. According to Kun-Young Park and Sook-Hee Rhee, a research pair from Pusan National

University in South Korea, the functional characteristics of baechu kimchi include (but are not limited to) increased appetite, decreased body fats, prevention of constipation and colon cancer, decreased serum cholesterol, increased fibrinolytic activity, anti-oxidative and anti-aging effects, anti-atherosclerotic effects, anti-cancer effects, and increased immune functions. Kimchi is a low-caloric food that contains high levels of vitamins, minerals, dietary fibers, and "other functional components." Individual ingredients provide specific beneficial elements: vitamin C, potassium, and β-sitosterol from cabbage; polyunsaturated fatty acids, vitamins A and C, calcium, and capsaicinoid from chile powder; alliin, allicin, and diallysulfide from garlic; niacin, potassium, and gingerol from ginger; protein and iron from fermented anchovy; chlorophyll and sulfur compound from green onion; and so forth.[69]

But more than any other single factor, what makes kimchi a superfood is the very item that our kimchi from Queens has boldly blazoned on the jar—lactic acid bacteria.[70] As pointed out in the *Health* magazine article, kimchi's "biggest benefit may be in its 'healthy bacteria' called lactobacilli."[71] The presence of live microorganisms, and specifically lactic acid–producing bacteria, defines kimchi as much as any other single ingredient, including salt, cabbage, or chiles. What makes kimchi *kimchi*, in other words, is fermentation, a food-preservation method that encourages, in the words of Stuart Thorne, author of *The History of Food Preservation*, "the growth of harmless bacteria or other micro-organisms in the food to the exclusion of those that would cause the food to become harmful or unpalatable."[72] Kimchi is probiotic, meaning it is a food containing live active cultures, such as bacteria and yeast, that provide nutritional benefits. Other notable probiotic foods include dairy products like yogurt and some cheeses, and vegetable products like sauerkraut.

Aside from preserving food, fermentation converts indigestible matter, such as raw wheat or soybeans, into edible products like bread or tempeh.[73] All told, the category of fermented food consists of foods and beverages that span considerable historical time and cultural geography: both ancient and new comestibles, including meat products like salami, chorizo, and other cured sausages; bread products like dosa, *injera*, and sourdough; vegetable products like pickles, olives, miso, soy sauce, and poi; and all alcohol, including beer, wine, and spirits. Moreover, fermentation changes, if not improves, the gustatory character of the original ingredients, often imparting a tangy or zesty taste.

Perhaps unexpectedly, fermentation plays a crucial role in the production of commonplace foods such as vanilla, coffee, and chocolate.[74] Vanilla, a member of the orchid family indigenous to the rainforests of the Americas, develops its winsome aroma and flavor only after its string bean–like pods have been cured and fermented.[75] Likewise, the beguiling attributes of chocolate would not be possible without the proper processing of another New World produce, cacao beans, which must undergo several days of fermentation prior to toasting and grinding to produce cocoa, the basis for all chocolate.[76] And the seeds (i.e., beans) of the coffee plant, generally thought to have originated in east Africa and initially commercialized by Arab merchants, require fermentation prior to roasting and grinding before being metamorphosed into an espresso, café Americano, or Starbucks Frappuccino. Intriguingly, the world's most expensive coffee beans are reportedly found in the droppings of the civet, a nocturnal, catlike animal native to Southeast Asia. As described by Norimitsu Onishi in an April 17, 2010, *New York Times* article, the animal feasts on ripe coffee cherries and "eventually excretes the hard, indigestible innards of the fruit—essentially, incipient beans—though only after they have been fermented in the animal's stomach acids and enzymes to produce a brew described as smooth, chocolaty and devoid of any bitter aftertaste." This civet coffee from the Philippines and Indonesia can sell in Japan and South Korea, the product's biggest market, for about $227 a pound.[77]

In addition to keeping figures slim, impeding cancer, and slowing the aging process, kimchi is reputed to ward off diabetes.[78] During the 2003 SARS scare in Asia, Koreans boasted that kimchi kept them immune.[79] Riding this tidal wave of positive global publicity of kimchi's healthfulness, the Korean company LG Electronics launched a new air conditioner equipped with a filter made from kimchi, claiming that kimchi kills the H5N1, aka the bird flu, virus.[80] Not surprisingly, the miraculous health value and healing power of kimchi are not without detractors. Skeptics point to what might be called the Korean paradox—although kimchi may very well be a superfood for a number of scientifically credible reasons, gastric cancer among Koreans is ten times that of Americans. Most likely to blame is the high level of salt in the numerous variety of fermented foods that are the foundation of the Korean diet, including soy sauce, soy paste, chile paste, preserved fish, and, yes, kimchi.[81]

"Kimchi Is Korean Territory!"

Just as kimchi by nature takes many forms, our kimchi from Queens has many names. The label boasts no less than six descriptive epithets in two languages, including, "Specially Licensed Living Lactic Acid Bacteria Kimchi" (in Korean), "Patent IH-22 Lactic Acid Bacteria Kimchi" (in English), "White Kimchi" (Korean), "New York Kimchi" (English), "Great-tasting Kimchi without the Smell" (English), and, most confounding, "Dok-do Kimchi Produced by Dr. Kang and Kum Kang San Restaurant" (English). Look closely and you see that the Dok-do reference does not end there. It occurs again when the label proclaims in English, "Nutritional value increases when Dok-do Kimchi is fully fermented."[82]

There is also a third reference: at the lower right-hand corner of the label is a business logo (or so I assume), an iconic image of what appears to be a rocky island with a pair of gull-like birds hovering above. Below the island are the words "DOK-DO CORP." Encircling the top of the logo, like a rainbow, are the words, "Dok-Do (Dok Island) is Korea's Territory." Evidently, involved somehow with either the production or distribution of this kimchi is a company called Dok-Do Corp. But why does its slogan (if it is indeed a slogan) sound more jingoistic than mercantile? Who or what is Dok-Do and what does it have to do with this jar of kimchi from Queens?

While "Dok-Do" may not mean anything to most Americans, for contemporary Koreans it is no less than a matter of nation, self, and Korean identity. Embedded in the term is not only the tragic legacy of war and poverty of the previous century, but also the humiliation of ethnic impotency stemming from nearly a half-century of Japanese colonialism. The utterance of the term is enough to evoke in legions of Koreans a melancholy feeling that Koreans call *han*.[83] For some this is quite literally a matter of life, death, and limbs. This was aptly illustrated in 2005, when two South Koreans, in an unlikely act of synchronous auto-amputation, each cut off a finger at a public demonstration in Seoul. An elderly woman employed a pair of gardening shears, and her middle-aged son followed suit with a meat cleaver. In an apparent attempt to outshine this formidable mother and son tandem, another man set himself on fire. (He survived with severe burns to his neck and body.) Several other protesters, meanwhile,

Jar detail of Dok-Do Corporation logo.

chose instead to burn the Japanese flag as a phalanx of riot police struggled to restrain the chaotic demonstrations.

Only a couple of months earlier, however, the atmosphere was considerably more serene, if not deceptively sanguine. The South Korean and Japanese governments had, with great fanfare, just announced plans to commemorate forty years of diplomatic relations. (A momentous treaty to normalize basic relations between the two countries was ratified in June 1965.) This was the latest attempt by the two nations to put aside a history of hostility and rancor, at least diplomatically, and to let bygones be bygones so that they might mutually benefit from their close geographic proximity, common economic interests, and strong cultural ties.[84]

Unfortunately, the celebration imploded, leading to severed fingers and a scorched torso, when Japan chose that moment to reiterate its territorial claims to two tiny rocky islets nestled between the Korean peninsula and the Japanese archipelago. The name of these islets, situated some 133 miles off the Korean eastern shore and 99 miles from Japan's Oki Island, depends on whom you ask. Westerners call them Liancourt Rocks, a name passed on by mid-nineteenth-century French whalers and subsequently adopted by European explorers and writers.[85] The Japanese call them Takeshima. The Koreans call them Dokdo. ("Dok" is the name of the islets; "do" is the Korean word for island.)

A rancorous battle over territorial claim to the two islets, along with thirty-two or thirty-three even smaller outcrops, with a total surface area of a mere fifty-two acres, has raged since the end of World War II. With Japan's unconditional surrender to the Allies in 1945 came the end of Japan's colonial rule over Korea, which began in 1910. (At the end of the Russo-Japanese War in 1905, a Japanese protectorate was installed over Korea.) In addition to restoring Korea's independence, Japan was compelled to relinquish control of all Korean territories. This apparently included Dokdo, which the Supreme Commander for the Allied Powers specifically excluded from Japanese jurisdiction.[86] On January 18, 1952, President Syngman Rhee of South Korea issued a presidential proclamation that delineated what he believed was the Korean portion of the Sea of Japan, or, as the Koreans insist it be called, the East Sea. (Not surprisingly, the naming of this body of water is yet another hotly debated topic between the two countries.) This Peace Line (aka Rhee Line) placed Dokdo squarely on the Korean side. Japan, however, lodged a protest and asserted its own sovereignty over the rocks. The Rhee government in turn dismissed Japan's claim, insisting on Korea's ownership under historical and legal grounds.[87] The dispute between the two parties over Dokdo/Takeshima has remained acrimonious ever since.

According to a position paper released by Japan's Ministry of Foreign Affairs in 2004, Japan's claim to Takeshima dates back to at least the middle of the seventeenth century.[88] The paper asserts that authoritative maps and documents from the period clearly indicate that "Japan has long known about the existence of Takeshima." The Tokugawa shogunate granted two Japanese families feudal tenure of Takeshima, which was a stopover port for travelers to Utsuryo Island (aka Dagelet Island) and for Japanese fishermen. More important than these seventeenth-century circumstances to Japan's case, however, are the events of 1905, when, in the words of John Van Dyke, "Japan reaffirmed its intention to possess Takeshima by a Cabinet decision in January, followed by a notification by Shimane Prefecture in February, officially incorporating Takeshima as part of Shimane Prefecture."[89]

Japan's 1905 claim of Takeshima is under the legal cover of *terra nullius*, or "no-man's land." (Recall that 1905 was the year Korea was declared a Japanese protectorate.) Under international law, a land deemed *terra nullius* is subject to "discovery" and "occupation" so long as it is not "under any sovereignty" or "belongs to no state" at the time of occupation.[90] Australia, Canada, eastern Greenland, Western Sahara, the Hanish Islands in the Red Sea, the Island of Palmas in the Philippines archipelago, and the West Bank are notable examples in which terra nullius was evoked at one time or another by various parties to claim that a land was theirs to keep since it previously belonged to no one.[91]

The Koreans emphatically maintain that Dokdo has always belonged to them, or at least since AD 512, when the Silla kingdom conquered Ulleungdo, an island seventy-five miles off of Korea's eastern shore. The fact that Japan has never challenged Korean sovereignty over Ulleungdo is considered significant because Dokdo, which lies about fifty-five miles to the south of Ulleungdo, is a dependency or appendage of Ulleungdo, argue Korean scholars. (It is said that Dokdo is visible from Ullengdo on a clear day; this, to some, constitutes definitive proof of appendage.) Moreover, numerous maps and documents that date from the start of the fifteenth century to the end of the nineteenth reputedly confirm Korea's administrative control over both Ulleungdo and Dokdo. The Korean side points to Japanese historical records that, while making direct references to Ulleungdo and Dokdo, either fail to indicate them as Japanese possessions or allude to them as Korean territories.[92] As for the 1905 incorporation of Dokdo under the jurisdiction of Shimane prefecture, the Korean view is that Korea simply was unable at that time to prevent this illegal action from taking place due to its relative lack of power vis-à-vis Japan, which had by then forcibly assumed control of all Korean political affairs under the 1904 Protectorate Treaty.[93]

When it comes to Korean resolve over possessing ultimate control of Dokdo's destiny, the gloves are off—even if some of them have only four fingers. Following the Japanese protest of President Rhee's proclamation, there has been a continual Korean presence on Dokdo of one or two fishing families and a cadre of guards and police. In effect, South Korea has had de facto possession of Dokdo since the end of Japanese rule. Over the past decades, South Korea has assiduously expanded Dokdo's infrastructure by building a harbor, a lighthouse, a desalination plant, a helicopter pad, and tourist facilities.[94] Numerous nongovernmental groups with the sole mission of opposing Japan's claim to the islets have surfaced during this time.⁹⁵

Dokdo in name and image has become ubiquitous throughout South Korea. It appears on postage stamps (2.2 million were sold in three hours for the 2004 release) and even as the name of restaurants and other businesses. The slogan "Dokdo Is Our Land" (or "Dokdo Is Korean Territory") has become an unofficial national motto. The phrase is emblazoned on T-shirts and other apparel, flags and banners, and stuffed animals and various other toys; it also appears in popular songs and amateur YouTube videos. (And, as we have discovered, it also adorns American kimchi jars.) Schoolchildren and their grandparents alike utter the words with equal measures of pride and indignation. Mass protests are customary whenever Japan lays any sort of public claim over Takeshima. Demonstrators came out in droves in the early 2000s, when Japan approved schoolbooks identifying Takeshima as Japanese territory. They occurred again in 2004, when Shimane prefecture passed a resolution declaring February 22, the day the islands were incorporated into the prefecture in 1905, as Takeshima Day.⁹⁶

South Korean postage stamps depicting Dokdo. The caption in the large middle square reads, "Our Beautiful Land Dokdo!"

In 2005, as if fearful that its claims to Dokdo might go unnoticed, the South Korean government launched a 14,000-ton military transport ship, the largest of its class in Asia, capable of carrying up to seven hundred troops, ten helicopters, six tanks, seven amphibious vehicles, and two landing boats. It was christened *Dokdo*.[97] When Japan lodged a protest against the naming of the vessel, a South Korean Foreign Ministry spokesman replied, "Protests from the Japanese government are tantamount to a serious act of aggression on South Korean sovereignty."[98] When North Korea and South Korea entertained a short-lived idea to field a single team for the 2008 Summer Olympics in Beijing, the two sides decided on "Korea" as the team name, with Dokdo pictured on the team flag.[99]

Be that as it may, a perplexing question remains before us: why is Dokdo referred to not just once but three times on a bottle of kimchi produced by a restaurant halfway around the world in New York City? As a slogan, "Dokdo Is Korean Territory" is not so much an expression of legal reality but a flagrant rebuttal of Japan's claim over the disputed islets. It also reaffirms the unshakeable notion that Japan is a permanent symbol of Korea's abuser and injurer. Why would a Korean restaurant in Flushing, Queens (of all places), raise the specter of the evil Japanese Empire (of all things) in order to sell (of all things) a jar of kimchi? And why would it do so some sixty years after Korea's liberation from Japanese colonialism? What can our kimchi maker from Queens gain from perpetuating Japanophobia in this abstruse, if not underhanded, manner?

Odoriferous Food Fight

Once upon a time: before South Korea began to sparkle like a digital metropolis under the global spotlight of the 1988 Summer Olympics in Seoul; before South Korea's near-miraculous semi-final terminus at the 2002 FIFA World Cup co-hosted by South Korea and Japan;[100] before Korean popular music (aka K-Pop) groups like S.E.S., Dong Bang Shin Ki, and the Wonder Girls lit up music charts from Japan to Taiwan to the United States and beyond; before television dramas like *Gyeoul Yeonga* (Winter sonata), *Pul Hauseu* (Full house), and *Dae Jang Geum* (Jewel in the palace) became global exports every bit as significant as Korean-made cars and cellular phones; before these dramas were turned into Disneyfied theme parks that attract millions of foreign tourists to South Korea; before megastars like Yong-Joon Bae (aka Yon-sama), Young-Ae Lee, Rain (Ji-Hoon Jung), and PSY became household names in countries both near and far; before the figure skater Yu-Na Kim became the most beloved Olympic athlete in South Korean history and the American short-track speed skater Apolo Ohno the most despised; before the rival South Korean fried chicken chains Kyochon and Bon Chon vied for supremacy of Manhattan K-Town's lunch crowd; before the South Korean government's unlikely campaign to elevate Korean food into "the top five rank of world cuisines" by 2017;[101] before kimchi took on its global reputation as a miracle superfood; and before South Korea began exporting hundreds of millions of dollars worth of kimchi overseas—or, once upon a time: before *hallyu* (the Korean Wave) transformed contemporary Korean culture into a global and transnational commodity, kimchi was thought to be something utterly off-putting, unconsumable, and, most of all, miasmal by non-Koreans.

Writing in 1898, William Franklin Sands, an American, recalled the squalor of Korea, especially the horrid smell of kimchi, "the national condiment," he called it, "made of cabbage and turnips well rotted together."[102] In 1906 another American, Homer Hulbert, referred to kimchi as Korea's favorite sauerkraut, "whose proximity is detected without the aid of the eye."[103] In 1928 H. B. Drake, an Englishman, wrote of kimchi, which he called "the native pickle," "whose reek of sour vinegar pervades the whole atmosphere of Korea."[104] In a 1950 article about Korea's "Unpretty Pickle," the *New York Times* reported that Westerners were known to complain that kimchi was—"to quote the milder critics"—"highly malodorous," "abominable," and "offensive."[105] In 1951 Cornelius Osgood, then curator of anthropology at the Yale Peabody Museum, said of "the Korean national dish": "To the natives it smells good, to most foreigners it simply smells."[106] During the mid-1980s another Englishman, Simon Winchester, wrote of a Korean innkeeper's tureen of age-old cabbage and turnip soused in sour vinegar, brine, garlic, and red chiles: a "sorry-looking mess." When it was brought to him for breakfast, his stomach gave "an unpleasant little nudge to the back of [his] throat," and he desperately longed for a soft-boiled egg or a bowl of Weetabix with milk. Earlier, he had groused about "the pungent sourness of strong *kimchi* from the house next door."[107]

The field of cultural encounters between Koreans and foreigners is full of kimchi sagas of the following sort as reiterated by Kyung-Koo Han: a Korean traveler hand carries a jar of kimchi into a transpacific airline jet only to have the cap blow off due to air pressure changes in the cabin, forcing the other three hundred passengers to endure the hellish smell of kimchi for the duration of the overnight flight.[108] (This allegorical tale cautions us that kimchi is a rare example of a food—not a drink—that is carbonated and is prone to expand under pressure if stored in an airtight container.) Given its current lofty culinary status, it is hard to believe that for most of my lifetime kimchi, and particularly its funky smell, was a source of shame and self-contempt for Koreans from Seoul to Honolulu, from Los Angeles to New York City.

My, how things have changed. Koreans everywhere now proudly declare that kimchi is their favorite food, even as kimchi consumption among the younger generation is in steady decline. Once the symbol of poverty and embarrassment, kimchi has become a "legitimate food"—that is, a food any open-minded foreigner is sure to find delicious. Any non-Korean who disdains kimchi betrays his own cultural provincialism and culinary naiveté—or so Koreans are wont to believe. This attitude, according to Han, amounts to Korea's "declaration of independence of taste."[109]

But while Koreans continue to yearn for foreigners to embrace kimchi, it is the Japanese manufacturers who have had greater success internationalizing it. During the late 1990s the Japanese controlled a surprising 80 percent of the global kimchi trade, with export markets in dozens of countries. As a result, many around the world believe kimchi to be of Japanese origin and know it only by the Japanese name *kimuchi*. Koreans, of course, found this extremely annoying and irksome. And even before Japan had the temerity to lobby the Olympic Committee at the 1996 Atlanta Games to name kimuchi—not kimchi—as an official Olympic food,[110] the indignant Koreans took the case before the world's highest food arbiter, the Codex Alimentarius Commission.[111]

Established in 1963 by the Food and Agriculture Organization (FAO) of the United Nations and the World Health Organization (WHO), the Codex Alimentarius Commission develops "food standards, guidelines and related texts such as codes of practice under the Joint FAO/WHO Food Standards Programme." In other words, the commission establishes standards and guidelines as a way to settle disputes involving the international export of food between rival nations.[112] (John Feffer calls it the "Supreme Court of Food.")[113] As of 2010 official Codex Standards had been established for nearly three hundred food products.[114]

In December 1995 the Korean government formally submitted to the commission a proposal to establish a code of practice and Codex standard for kimchi. In June 1996 the Executive Committee at the Tenth Session of Codex Coordinating Committee for Asia approved the proposal. A year later the Korean delegation submitted its proposed draft standard to the Eleventh Session. Finally, in June 2001, after nearly five years of amendments and deliberation, the Twenty-fourth Session of the Codex Alimentarius Commission adopted Korea's draft standard as the official Codex Standard. (A year earlier, the Processed Fruits and Vegetables Subcommittee decided that products using the name "kimchi" had to be fermented according to methods codified by Korean manufacturers.) This immediately gave Korean exporters a leg up against Japan, their traditional nemesis in most things, in the battle for the world's kimchi markets.[115]

The Codex Standard (CODEX STAN 223-2001) defines kimchi as a product prepared from defect-free Chinese cabbage (*Brassica pekinesis*) that has been salted, rinsed, and drained; seasoned with mainly red pepper (*Capsicum annuum* L.) powder, radish, garlic, ginger, and other alliums (such as chive and leek); and "fermented before or after being packaged into appropriate containers to ensure proper ripening and preservation of the product by lactic acid production at low temperatures." Other allowable ingredients are fruits, vegetables, sesame seeds, nuts, sugars, salted and fermented seafood, glutinous rice paste, and wheat-flour paste. A limited number of additives are permitted, including flavor enhancers (e.g., monosodium glutamate, disodium guanylate), textualizers (sorbitol), and thickening and stabilizing agents (xanthan gum). The product must be red in color, with the redness "originating from red pepper." It must have a hot and salty (and an optional sour) taste and be "reasonably firm, crisp, and chewy." Moreover, the standard mandated that the "name of the product shall be 'Kimchi.'"[116]

Not kimuchi. Japanese makers rebuked the committee's decision to establish what they saw as a culinarily narrow, if not politically biased, definition of kimchi—and with reason. A principal factor in the global success of the Japanese product was precisely its milder taste, which appealed to a broader audience. Kimuchi was typically less spicy and salty, and not as sour as Korean kimchi. And many Japanese brands skipped the fermentation process altogether, once again to better suit a more general palate. (Recall that fermented foods have an added zestfulness and zing to them.)

Kimuchi, in this regard, is very much in keeping with the Japanese culinary tradition called *asazuke*, which are lightly or briefly pickled vegetables. The asazuke in turn belongs under the all-embracing category of *tsukemono*, which denotes all pickled foods. According to Shizuo Tsuji, tsukemono is a "vast domain in Japanese cuisine." He adds, "Rice and pickles are to the Japanese what bread and cheese are to the English, and French bread and wine to the French."[117] To Naomichi Ishige, pickles, as an accompaniment to the "equally indispensable rice," are a symbol of an "authentic" Japanese meal."[118]

There are several main methods or types of Japanese pickling, including salt (*shiozuke*), rice-brand (*nukazuke*), soy sauce (*shoyuzuke*), miso (*misozuke*), sake-lees (*kasuzuke*), vinegar (*suzuke*), and rice-mold (*kojizuke*). While the term "tsukemono" can apply to seafood, it more often refers to countless vegetable and fruit products, each with its own distinctive history and flavor. Among the more notable is *umeboshi*, a shiozuke made of a dried and pickled Japanese apricot called *ume*. Umeboshi is a common feature of *bento* (boxed meal) and is often found at the core of *onigiri* (rice balls). It is said the sourness and saltiness of umeboshi are so intense that the mere mention of it brings about puckered lips and salivating mouths to those familiar with it.[119]

Another prominent example is *takuan*, a nukazuke made of daikon (a type of radish). It is said that a seventh-century Buddhist priest named Takuan invented the pickle and introduced it to the Japanese diet. "Hot rice with *takuan* is as common on Japanese tables as bread and butter in America," remarks Tsuji.[120] Takuan is popular among Koreans as well. Called *danmuji* in Korean, it is an indispensable filling for and accompaniment with *gimbap* (Korean rolled sushi similar to the Japanese makizushi). It is also a standard side dish, along with kimchi and raw onions, for *jjajangmyeon* (the Chinese-Korean noodle dish topped with a black soybean-paste sauce). As a food category, tsukemono is analogous to the broader notion of kimchi, which is not limited to the baechu variety but refers to hundreds of preparations. Japanese tsukemono, however, is typically less pungent than Korean kimchi, keeping with the general rule that the Japanese prefer their food less fiery and fierce than the Koreans do. Both pickled products, however, are essential to the cuisines of either country, as they provide the necessary counterbalancing taste of saltiness and sourness to diets that revolve around the otherwise bland staple of rice.

To Korean kimchi producers, Japan's efforts to dominate the global kimchi trade was less an economic issue than a cultural one—or at least this is how their publicity and marketing strategy couched it. They charged that kimuchi eroded kimchi's "authenticity." "What the Japanese are selling is nothing more than cabbage sprinkled with seasonings and artificial flavoring," cried a representative of Doosan Corporation, which operates one of South Korea's largest kimchi factories. "This debate is not just about protecting our market share," he added. "We are trying to preserve our national heritage." The Japanese countered that once "ethnic" dishes gain international popularity, they are usually altered to fit the local palate. In effect, they argued, Korea does not have an inherent or automatic monopoly on kimchi—at least no more than, say, Italy has a monopoly on pizza, Germany on the hot dog, or Japan on sushi.

"Should the same standard be applied to curry?" asked an adviser to the Japan Pickle Producers Association. "Everyone knows that curry was invented in India, but the curry that Indians eat is quite different from the curry that Japanese eat."[121] As Lizzie Collingham has noted, "The Japanese love curry." They eat it with rice (*karee raisu*), with noodles (*karee udon*), and tucked inside bread (*karee pan*). In 1982 Japanese children voted curry as their favorite national school-lunch program meal, and it was once one of three dishes—along with pork cutlets (*tonkatsu*) and stir-fried vegetables—most often prepared for dinner in Japanese homes. Even as early as the 1890s an influential Japanese food critic deemed curry, as paraphrased by Michael Ashkenazi and Jeanne Jacob, "the food of the future, one that would bring Japan from an age of culinary barbarism to culinary and healthful heights of modernity."[122] As often repeated by both devotees and distracters, the contemporary version of Japanese curry is nothing anyone familiar with the cuisines of South Asia, or even the curries of Great Britain or the Caribbean, for that matter, would recognize. First introduced to Japan by British merchant ships docked at the port of Yokohama, curry—along with other *yoshoku* (Western foods) like cutlets, croquettes, ice cream, bread, and beef—became a favorite among the well-heeled and fashionable Japanese during the Meiji era.[123] The opening of a curry museum in Yokohama in 2003 commemorated the importance of curry's arrival to and everlasting legacy not only in Japan but also in Korea, where Japanese curry is much loved.

Be that as it may, in Japan's challenge for supremacy of the global kimchi market, Koreans found yet other reason to perpetuate a feeling of enmity toward their neighbor and one-time colonizer. In this regard the battle over kimchi is not so different from the battle over two tiny islets with a disputed ownership (Korea or Japan?) and name (Dokdo or Takeshima?) in the middle of a sea whose name (Sea of Japan or East Sea?), in turn, is also a battleground. When it comes to any squabble that involves Japan, Koreans find it virtually impossible to remain dispassionate or nonpartisan. Our Patent IH-22 Lactic Acid Bacteria Kimchi is proof that for Koreans even as far away as Queens, kimchi is not merely a matter of culinary culture but nationalist politics. Kimchi and Dokdo are one and the same. Kimchi is Dokdo and Dokdo is kimchi. Both are Korean territories. Neither is terra nullius. Any claim otherwise is tantamount to a declaration of war.

But even as Korean kimchi manufacturers struggled to defend their place in the global kimchi market against the Japanese challenge, China had by this time become an even greater threat. Import of Chinese-made kimchi to both Korea and Japan dramatically rose during the first decade of the twenty-first century. According to one estimate, in 2002 China sold a little over a thousand tons of kimchi to South Korea; just a year later it approached twenty-thousand tons.[124] Chinese kimchi, at nearly half the cost of locally produced kimchi, is consumed at highway restaurants, schools, and rehabilitation facilities throughout South Korea, and unlike the Japanese variety, most Koreans cannot tell it is imported due to its similarity to domestically produced kimchi.[125]

Nonetheless, claiming that test samples have been found to contain eggs of parasitic worms, the South Korean government temporarily banned the importation of Chinese kimchi in 2005. In return, Chinese manufacturers accused the South Koreans of "looking for any reason to crush Chinese kimchi." Beijing immediately retaliated by banning edible imports from South Korea, claiming Korean-produced kimchi and other foods were also infested with parasite eggs. Complicating matters further was the fact that Chinese kimchi factories were frequently owned and operated by South Korean entrepreneurs seeking cheaper materials and labor in China, and they apparently bore the brunt of this trade quarrel.[126] Ironically, the Codex Standard that the Korean manufacturers had feverishly worked to establish in order to compete against Japanese kimuchi contributed to the flooding of Chinese kimchi into the South Korean market.

The Declining Significance of Stench

Despite the remarkable reputation makeover enjoyed by the dish in recent years, the odorous power of kimchi has not been forgotten. If anything, it has only grown in legend. In fact, kimchi's funky smell has come to define the thing itself every bit as much as the dish's redness or spiciness. It seems the specter of kimchi's fetor rises whenever Koreans or Korean Americans are the subject of conversation, irrespective of whether the topic is food focused or not. In a 2005 *New York Times* article on the social etiquettes (or the lack thereof) of air travel, the "attack" on the nose by "strongly aromatic foods like the Korean kimchi," which "can really stink up a cabin," was lumped together with someone jamming a knee into the back of a seat or unabashedly viewing a pornographic movie on a portable DVD player as examples of impoliteness while flying coach.[127]

In a 2008 essay about the Los Angeles transit system, D. J. Waldie wrote of how passengers "redefine personal space and reorder social distinctions" and cited "the pretty girl talking in Tagalog," "the beaten-down domestic worker," "the man reading his Bible," "the iPod-addicted boy," and the "slight man reeking of kimchi" as examples of "a diminished version of real Angelenos."[128] That same year a sports reporter commented on the "smell of garlic and kimchi" in the halls of a hotel where several Korean members of the Ladies Professional Golf Association were lodged during a tournament in Danville, California.[129] And in September 2009, when First Lady Yoon-ok Kim of South Korea, with chef Jean-Georges Vongerichten and actress Moon Bloodgood by her side, visited a group of New York–area veterans of the Korean War, it was reported that the "strong smell of kimchi was a running joke among the American veterans."[130]

On July 23, 2009, the *Los Angeles Times* labeled kimchi one of the most "odoriferous global foods."[131] Of course, gastronomically speaking, this is not necessarily a bad thing. On the contrary, for devotees of durian, lutefisk, Limburger cheese, stinky tofu, and other foods that take olfaction to the edge, there is the sublime in miasma. But for a newly modernized South Korea, and among Korean Americans self-conscious about appearing too unsophisticated, bumpkin-like, or primitively exotic, the smell of kimchi is a predestined vexation—one that must be minimized by whatever

Advertisement for Daewoo Electronic's Klasse kimchi refrigerator.

means necessary. One strategy is provided by South Korea's electronic industry in the form of a product specially engineered to store kimchi—and only kimchi. The kimchi refrigerator not only maintains the optimal temperatures necessary for proper storage of different types of kimchi, but also quarantines it (and its socially pernicious fumes) from other foods. Samsung, Daewoo, LG, and Dimchae, among other companies, sell a long line of them, ranging in price from a few hundred to several thousand dollars per unit. Purportedly, kimchi refrigerators top the list of gifts desired by newlywed Korean brides.

Then there is the ontological solution to cope with the smell: many Koreans are convinced that the sole barrier standing in the way of Korean cuisine becoming truly global—like, say, Chinese or Japanese food—is the strong odor of kimchi, which accompanies most, if not all, Korean meals. Kimchi manufacturers, therefore, have resorted to what basically amounts to the nuclear option, doing what was no doubt unthinkable when kimchi was factory produced for the first time in history in 1967.[132] Many of today's mass producers of kimchi have begun—at least for the time being—to reboot kimchi to make it less spicy, less salty, and less odorous. In other words, in what can only be described as a cruel twist of fermentation irony, Koreans are modeling Korean kimchi after Japanese kimuchi.

Some have taken the challenge even further. Soon-Ja Kim, South Korea's first "kimchi master," a designation bestowed on her in 2007 by the South Korean Food Ministry, secured a patent in 2009 for the first deodorized kimchi. Her invention, a freeze-dried kimchi, remains odorless even after it is reconstituted. "When it soaks in water either hot or cold for a few minutes, it will become just like ordinary kimchi," claims the inventor. She wagers that the product will appeal not only to a potentially limitless number of foreigners, but also to Koreans who wish to avoid the all-too-common faux pas of, say, "kimchi breath," among other social embarrassments linked to irrepressible kimchi fumes. Perhaps unsurprisingly, the first order Kim received was from Japan.[133]

Which returns us to our kimchi from Queens, aka New York Kimchi, aka White Kimchi, aka Dokdo Kimchi, aka the "Great-tasting Kimchi without the smell!" By all accounts, this particular kimchi was no technological marvel. It comes nowhere close to rivaling Soon-ja Kim's deodorized kimchi or the "space kimchi" that South Korea's first astronaut packed for his journey to the International Space Station aboard the Russian spaceship *Soyuz* in 2008. According to Sang-Hun Choe's *New York Times* article, "Star Ship Kimchi: A Bold Taste Goes Where It Has Never Gone Before," published in February 24, 2008, the astronaut's kimchi was a bona fide space-age wonder that cost "millions of dollars and several years of perfecting" by three top South Korean government research institutes working to produce a "version of kimchi that would not turn dangerous when exposed to cosmic rays or other forms of radiation and would not put off non-Korean astronauts with its pungency."[134] (While lactic acid bacteria are harmless on earth, scientists were concerned the microbes might unpredictably mutate and turn dangerous in space.)

Despite my mother-in-law's contention that our Queens kimchi was a special kimchi fortified with cutting-edge scientific technology, compared to the space kimchi, it was quite ordinary. This isn't to say that it wasn't delicious, however. It absolutely was, but in a run-of-the-mill sort of way. In other words, it could have been served anywhere Koreans live in large numbers—say, Seoul, Honolulu, Los Angeles, Atlanta, Queens—and no native eater of kimchi would think it odd or in anyway dubious. In final consideration, then, the fact that it was produced in Queens, New York, had no bearing on whether or not this kimchi was authentic, the real deal. In fact, the only dubious thing about it was not something in the jar but on it. George Brown Goode, director of the United States National Museum during the 1870s, once said of the curatorial process, "The most important thing about an exhibition was the label."[135] A variation on the theme of his dictum applies nicely here: the most dubious thing about our Queens kimchi was the label.

As a *baek* (white) kimchi, our Dokdo kimchi from the land of Archie Bunker was by its nature less malodorous than the typical baechu kimchi. Boasting about the relative inodorousness of baek kimchi, therefore, is akin to bragging that a Chicago-style pizza has a thicker crust than a New York–style pizza. But in stating the obvious and making it appear to be a desirable technological achievement, our Queens kimchi becomes emblematic of the state of kimchi in the twenty-first century—a culturally chauvinistic, profit-driven, industrially produced commercial product that denotes, if not augurs, cosmopolitanism, sophistication, and a New Age wellness of body.

Coda

It is a common sight for those who frequent Korean restaurants in New York City, Los Angeles, Atlanta, and other cities with a sizable Korean American population: Latinos, mainly Mexican and other Central American men, busing tables, laying out place settings, pouring water, replacing dying embers with glowing red charcoal for tabletop grills, washing dishes, sweeping floors, and increasingly doing most of the cooking. Drop by these restaurants during off hours and you see these descendants of indigenous Americans, men whom Columbus, if he were alive today, might very well call "Indians," taking their meals before the rush. Look closely and see them devouring platefuls of kimchi with gusto—kimchi not only full of vitamins, fiber, and antioxidants, but also fiery red chiles.

How is this for coming full circle? Columbus gets lost, discovers America. He misnames the people and misnames the chile. Other Europeans soon follow, including the Portuguese, whose domination of the chile trade spreads to India, Japan, Korea, and beyond. The Koreans, although initially slow to act, rename it gochu and eventually make it an essential ingredient in their cuisine, especially in kimchi, their national dish.

Fast forward to the late twentieth century. Koreans in great numbers emigrate from their homeland to form multiple diasporic communities around the world, including New York City, Los Angeles, and Atlanta, where they join an even greater number of Central Americans who were always already there, even before Columbus made his navigational blunder. Today, many of these New World Indians find employment in Korean businesses, including in kimchi factories, where they are charged with making a dish that was once the exclusive domain of Korean women. They also find work in restaurants such as Kum Gang San in Queens, where they, along with the heterogeneous and multifarious customers they serve, consume large quantities of chile-laden Korean fare. In the process, they revel in the heat of the very item their pre-Columbian ancestors first cultivated and infused in the original cuisine of the Americas, but which is now spread worldwide, becoming the second most used spice in the world, second only to its culinary alter ego, the black pepper, Columbus' elusive white whale.

Yes, when it comes to diasporic and transnational Korean identity, blood, coagulated by nostalgic nationalism, is often thicker than water. However, given the contested state of kimchi in this era of rapid globalization, mass migration, and heightened industrialization of indigenous foodways, blood isn't as thick as kimchi juice, which is now, more often than not, the color of blood—and less odoriferous.

4 | Dogmeat

As the semester drew to a close in the spring of 2009, the police were dispatched to investigate a disorderly conduct call at the Binghamton University campus, where I had been teaching for several years. The call came in a few minutes before midnight and was made by a sixty-three-year-old university employee. While the exact details of the events that prompted the call are in dispute, this much is certain, as reported by the school paper, *Pipe Dream*, the following day: "Nearly four hours into a weekly Assembly meeting, three members of the Assembly and two Student Association executive board members moved outside a meeting room in the University Union and entered into an argument that four of the five involved said also included physical contact and racial slurs."[1]

Even before I had a chance to read the *Pipe Dream* article, a student in one of my Asian American studies classes told me of the incident. Everyone involved in the fracas was either Asian American or white. At the center of the conflict was the student government's vice president of finance, who happened to be an Asian American woman. Her main adversary, a student assembly representative, was a white male. Apparently the two had had long-standing ideological differences, which, that night, included disagreements about proper voting procedures and parliamentary etiquette.

"Professor, you won't believe what this white guy said to this Asian girl," my student said. I had to admit I was curious. "He told her to 'shut up and go eat a fucking dog.'"

"How did she respond?" I asked.

"She called him a white bastard."

Some sort of physical altercation then ensued. The Asian American woman's supporters claimed the white male took a swing at her. *Pipe Dream* reported that she had to be "physically restrained by friends."

The campus community reacted to this incident in a predictably variegated fashion: the vice president for student affairs instructed the director of judicial affairs to get to the bottom of what really happened. The student association's executive board issued a strongly worded statement condemning the actions of the individuals reported to have made racially charged remarks. And while some students felt that the whole thing was a bit overblown, a group of Asian American students organized a protest in front of the university's main administration building and called for the suspension of the white student.

Amid the hullabaloo, I asked a colleague, a fellow Asian American, what she thought of the incident. To my surprise, she appeared more bemused than outraged, "Of all the possible insults a white person could hurl at an Asian, why did he tell her to go eat a dog?" she asked. "Why not call her something conventional and common—you know, a chink or a gook or a slant-eyed bitch? But go home and eat a dog? Come on, you have to admit, that's interesting!"

Gastronomic Minstrelsy

In terms of food-related racist imageries, perhaps the closest equivalent to a bucktoothed Asian chewing on dogmeat is a wide-grinning African American gobbling up fried chicken and watermelon. As Psyche Williams-Forson argues in *Building Houses out of Chicken Legs: Black Women, Food, and Power*, a book that "examines the roles that chicken has played in the lives of black women from the past to present," the image of African Americans as "chicken lovers" is deeply rooted in American popular culture and is "one of the linchpins with which white racists claimed black inferiority." Something similar can be said of the dog-eating Oriental, for whom the moniker "dogmeat lover" equates to yellow depravity. Both are a form of minstrelsy—blackface for the former, yellowface for the latter. In Williams-Forson's words, these stereotypes reveal "sociopolitical correlations between the historical positioning and the current contemporary moment."[2]

Frank Wu, writing about the politics of dogmeat in *Yellow: Race in America beyond Black and White*, proposes that dog-eating accusations

General Electric magazine advertisement (1935).

are "an excuse to make Asians the butt of jokes" and to broadly define Asian cultures as "primitive." Calling the wholesale denigration of Asia as a dog-eating continent absurd, he posits that the stereotype "forms the basis for believing that Asians are inferior." For Wu, the question of dog eating is as useful a tool as any to scrutinize the limits and possibilities of multiculturalism in the United States. He argues that if Americans "can work out how to talk about dog-eating, we can grapple with the problem of how we think about diversity."³

There is, however, an important difference between the two versions of culinary minstrelsy. While most Americans do not regard chicken as a verboten food, dogs are an absolute taboo. In *Eat Not This Flesh: Food Avoidances from Prehistory to the Present,* Frederick Simoons attributes the anti-dogmeat feelings of certain societies, both ancient and contemporary, to two main factors: "the dirty eating habits of the dog, on the one hand, and its close associations with humans, on the other." He points out that a variety of groups, including followers of Indian religions such as Buddhism, Hinduism, and Jainism, loathe the scavenging nature of dogs. Moreover, the ritual killing of dogs in ancient times was directly associated with the animal's "carrion-eating propensities," which carried with it the specter of death, disease, and the supernatural agents that dealt with death and disease.[4]

James Serpell argues that the domestic dog "exists precariously in the no-man's-land between the human and non-human worlds." He calls the dog an "interstitial creature, neither person nor beast, forever oscillating uncomfortably between the roles of high-status animal and low-status person." The animal, as a consequence, "is rarely accepted and appreciated purely for what it is: a uniquely varied, carnivorous mammal adapted to a huge range of mutualistic association with people."[5]

Today, the most powerful reason for disqualifying dogmeat as a potential food source, especially in industrial and postindustrial societies, is the honorary human status bestowed upon dogs. As Nick Fiddes points out in *Meat: A Natural Symbol,* we tend to them, give them proper names, and feed them foods modeled on human tastes. "We treat pets more like individual subjects than the abstract objects as which we officially regard edible animals," he asserts.[6] Lynette Hart reminds us that dogs are "special" animals for myriad reasons, including their ability to display affection, loyalty, and devotion toward humans; play games with humans; touch or tenderly interact with humans; provide positive developmental, psychological, and overall health benefits to humans; act as therapists to humans; and act as buffers against grief and stress.[7] In other words, more than any other animal, dogs are capable of exhibiting behavioral and symbolic qualities that we not merely seek in other humans, but that most humans usually fail to find in other humans.

The more I thought about it, the more I had to agree with my colleague—a white male telling an Asian woman to go eat a dog *was* more interesting than calling her a chink or commenting on the shape of her eyes. Given that, yes, some Asians have been known to and continue to eat dogmeat, what do we really talk about when we talk about eating dog?

What complicates this question for me personally is the fact that I once actually went out of my way to eat dogmeat. As a Korean who grew up in the United States, I was no stranger to the dog-eater epithet. On more than one occasion I had been told to go eat a dog. It is probably safe to say that no one thought I would actually go off and do it.

Most older Korean men I knew in the United States—uncles, family friends, colleagues—spoke of dogmeat with reverence, as if eating it was a sacred part of the ritual of Korean machismo, on par with drinking excessive amounts of alcohol, smoking like a chimney, gambling your life savings away, or playing golf obsessively. It was quite delicious, I often heard, fiercely delicious, gamey, and odorous. Although no one said this outright, the message was clear: real Korean men eat dog. By insisting on the manly virtues of dogmeat, these Korean men who no longer resided in Korea were signaling to me that their long stay in the United States had failed to soften them; they were bragging that they had managed to impede the milksop tide of Americanization. By boasting of their love of dogmeat, these Korean American men, via the power of nostalgia, were equating a shift in the dog's meaning from food to pet to nothing less than a betrayal of Korean manhood.

Thus when I found myself in Seoul a few years ago I had to give it a try. After all, if I wanted to write about dogmeat (and, as a bonus, know firsthand what it felt like to be a "real" Korean man), wasn't I obligated to at least taste it? And so I did. If I had to distill the experience down to a single word, I would say it was a moment of intense *disgust*. I literally almost lost my lunch while lunching on it. If I had to come up with the closest gastronomic analog, I imagine it has to somehow involve human flesh.

The Culinary Abyss

It is the not-too-distant future—the year 2022, to be exact. Mired in irreversible greenhouse effect and wilting from a yearlong heat wave, earth is an overpopulated, environmental disaster. Potable water is limited and rationed by the government. A worldwide collapse of agriculture has left "real food"—eggs, milk, lettuce, beef—scarce and a luxury reserved for the privileged few. A powerful multinational corporate entity, the Soylent Corporation, rises from the ashes of the ecological wasteland to control half the world's food supply. It floods the market with an assortment of highly processed vegetable protein wafers branded as Soylent Red and Soylent Yellow. The launch of its latest product, Soylent Green, stirs public frenzy unlike anything previous. Demand promptly overwhelms supply, limiting sales to a single day of the week. The slogan "Tuesday is Soylent Day" blankets all media. Before long, each Tuesday becomes a day of riots as hungry mobs clash with heavily armed police at distribution centers.

While conducting a routine murder investigation, a New York City detective named Robert Thorn stumbles upon a carefully guarded secret about the integrity of the food supply. More than a secret, it is a full-blown conspiracy involving the powerful food corporation in cahoots with a covert sector of the government. The highly sought-after new wafers, a product Thorn himself consumes regularly, are not, as advertised, a "miracle food of high energy plankton gathered from the oceans of the world." Rather, Soylent Green is composed of recycled human remains, a by-product of the state-run industrial euthanasia complex designed to keep the human population in check. Now a potential whistleblower, the horrified Thorn finds himself on the other side of the law as shadowy security operatives pursue him unrelentingly. It is only when he is captured at the conclusion of this 1973 film titled *Soylent Green* that Thorn, played by Charlton Heston, finally utters the film's memorable signature line: "Soylent Green is people!"

Those familiar with modern Chinese fiction will no doubt recognize an uncanny similarity between the plot of *Soylent Green* and that of "A Madman's Diary," the famous work of social critique by Lu Xun, widely recognized as the father of modern Chinese literature. At the center of this 1918 short story is a man reputed to have been afflicted with a dreadful disease. Formally of a small, far-flung village, he has since recovered and now resides elsewhere, waiting to fill an official post. Aside from unsubstantiated hearsay, the only clues we have about the precise nature of the man's disease are contained in a prodigious diary he left behind. Full of incoherent ramblings, the diary appears to suggest that he suffered from a form of persecution complex, as he believed he belonged to a community of anthropophagites that saw him as next in line to be devoured.

He at first tries to pass the notion off as paranoia. So what if the neighbor's dog leered at him and the village children ogled him with iron-gray faces? But when his suspicion persists, he, like Detective Thorn, embarks on a dangerous, unauthorized investigation, carefully scrutinizing the words and actions of his fellow villagers and delving into the history, mythology, and science of cannibalism. The conclusion he reaches drives him to apparent madness. Not only is he convinced every village member, including his own family, is a cannibal, he is certain cannibalism is a four-thousand-year-old village tradition. Worse yet, he himself, in all likelihood, ate several pieces of his own sister's flesh served surreptitiously with rice—fed to him by his own brother, no less! Thus the Mad Diarist confronts his moral doom. He wonders how he can ever again "look real human beings in the eye" and whether "there are some children around who still haven't eaten human flesh." "Save the children," he begs.[8]

Whatever the method of butchering, stewing, or plating, cannibalism is not for the faint of heart. Humans have shunned the eating of human flesh to a degree matched only by the prohibition against incest. These two absolute taboos delineate the moral boundaries of what are arguably the two most potent human appetites, namely for food and for sex. As artistic works that caution against the utter corruptibility of man and society, *Soylent Green* and "A Madman's Diary" take us to the edge of the culinary abyss, a place cinematically visited by Peter Greenaway's *The Cook, the Thief, His Wife, and Her Lover* (1989), in which the titular Wife compels her husband (the Thief) to eat the body of her Lover (murdered by her husband) that the Cook (her friend) had roasted at the Wife's urging.

This is a place also visited by one of literary modernism's most important touchstones, Joseph Conrad's *Heart of Darkness*. In this 1902 novella, Marlow steams along the artery of the Congo teeming with savage and grotesque cannibals. He is in search of Kurtz, the supreme literary example of just how low a so-called civilized human can fall if given the right—or perhaps the wrong—conditions. Reputedly, Kurtz was once an eloquent and noble European who had succumbed to the savage call of the African jungle "by the inconceivable ceremonies of some devilish initiation." To his old age, Marlow is haunted by the specter of Kurtz presiding at "certain midnight dances ending with unspeakable rites" in which some unspecified "vestiges" were offered to him.[9] Whether these vestiges included human flesh, Marlow does not say outright. But given the depth of savagery to which Kurtz is reported to have descended, it appears more than likely it did. (Yes, "The horror! The horror!" indeed.)

Recall that the dread of anthropophagy is what finally drives Kurtz's literary progenitor, the title character of Daniel Defoe's *Robinson Crusoe* (1719), to the cusp of his own madness. After some twenty-four years of undeterred steadfastness in establishing a private fiefdom on a remote, godforsaken island, Crusoe's dreams are suddenly invaded by "eleven Savages coming to Land," bringing with them another savage "who they were going to kill, in Order to eat him."[10] To his great misfortune, the cannibals are not merely figments of nightmares but actual living souls who occasionally visit the island to engage in cannibalistic feasts. Given no choice, Crusoe is forced to slay a number of them while rescuing a special savage he famously names Friday in honor of the day of his deliverance.

In recent years the more notable examples of the deranged cannibal have been the make-believe Hannibal Lecter, who is perhaps best remembered for enjoying a census taker's liver with some fava beans and a nice Chianti, and the true-to-life Jeffrey Dahmer, who reportedly had a dietary predilection for young black and Asian men whom he first prepped by torturing, raping, and dismembering. But no discussion of psychotic cannibalism is complete without a mention of Armin Meiwes, a German citizen who, over the Internet in 2001, solicited a willing volunteer to be cannibalized. In one of his e-mail advertisements he wrote in rudimentary English, "I search for a boy, if i can real kill him and butchering him. I am a cannibal, a real cannibal." Answering his call—and on Valentine's Day, no less—was Bernd Jürgen Brandes. They flirted over e-mail at first: "What will you do with my brain?" queried Brandes. "I'll leave it, I don't want to split your scull," replied Meiwes. They met soon after and had sex. Then, reportedly at Brandes' request, Meiwes cut off the other's penis, which they fried and ate together, resulting in perhaps the only case of simultaneous anthropophagy and autophagy ever recorded in human history. Meiwes then slit Brandes' throat, again at the latter's request, and, as promised in the e-mail, butchered the body before freezing it. By the time he was finally arrested, Meiwes had consumed more than forty pounds of Brandes' flesh. Eventually Meiwes was sentenced to fifteen years in prison, where, the story goes, he converted to vegetarianism.[11]

Soylent Green and "A Madman's Diary" pose an unsavory question: is there anything more horrific than finding out after the fact that you unknowingly ingested—and possibly enjoyed—the meat of *Homo sapiens*? Judging by the magnitude of the shock, outrage, and, most of all, disgust generated internationally by a trivial yet well-publicized aspect of Asian gastronomy, it might be fair to say that the dread of unwittingly ingesting the meat of *Canis familiaris*, aka the domestic dog, comes pretty darned close.

Korea is a case in point. The fear of mistakenly consuming dogmeat while traveling in South Korea is so commonplace that the *Lonely Planet* travel guidebook devotes a special section to it. "Korea is famous—or perhaps infamous—for the tradition of eating dogmeat," the guide explains under the heading "Rough." "If the thought of it makes you squeamish, it's a sensitive topic for many Koreans too." The guide then lets us in on a pair of secrets: "first, the dogs used are a special breed, meaning you needn't worry about your pets. Second, dogmeat is only served in specialty restaurants, so it won't find its way onto your table unless you really want it there." Elsewhere, under the heading "We Dare You," dogmeat soup, along with silkworm larvae, fried grasshoppers, and live baby octopus, is suggested for the "more adventurous" tourist.[12]

Before achieving literary fame with his well-woven yarn about the origins of *The Oxford English Dictionary* and the eruption of an Indonesian volcano, Simon Winchester, the author of *The Professor and the Madman* and *Krakatoa,* fretted over the perils of dogmeat while trekking the entire length of South Korea, from the southernmost Jeju Island to the North Korean border, mostly on foot. In *Korea: A Walk through the Land of Miracles,* a travelogue published to coincide with the 1988 Seoul Olympics Games, Winchester describes a curious scene at a village market where a large dog, "just sold for some unspecified and unimaginable end use," was shoved into a plastic bag "for the journey back home to its fate." He immediately assumes the poor mutt is destined for someone's soup pot, or, more specifically, to be rendered into the famous Korean dogmeat soup *bosintang.* Overcome with disgust, he dashes away from the scene "without turning, until the shrieking of the terrified animal faded away." He is none too relieved nor convinced when told later by a "specialist on canine cuisine" that it was unlikely that this dog would end up as soup, given that "only medium-sized yellow dogs" are eaten. Later, the British writer frets over whether a hamburger he ate at a spa resort, "bearing in mind the Korean fondness for munching their way through roast dogs and dog soups," might in fact "have been fashioned from somebody's long-dead Rover." And during a stopover in Jindo, an island famous for a distinctive breed of dog named for it, he wonders whether the government's prohibition against removing the dogs from the island has less to do with maintaining a strict control over the dog's pedigree and more with protecting the nationally treasured breed from its own citizens, "who, as like it as not, would boil the dog up in a stew and serve it with onions and garlic."[13]

A common feature of these and other Korea-focused travel books is an expressed desire to educate the world about the uniqueness of Korea, the lesser-known and largely misunderstood neighbor of China and Japan. In doing so, the authors invariably allude to a timeless, more "authentic" Korea that has not yet succumbed entirely to modernization, urbanization, and globalization. Chief among their tasks is the search for and mapping of the "yet-to-be-domesticated" elements of Korean society, to turn back the clock, if you will, to a time before the Olympics, the Internet, blepharoplasty (cosmetic eyelid surgery), and hallyu (the Korean Wave) ruined it all. As such, these books commodify what Marc Manganaro, in his introduction to *Modernist Anthropology: From Fieldwork to Text*, calls "mythic consciousness," the notion that certain cultural productions have "access to a mythic condition that represents a return to a more vital, primal, and elemental human state."[14] This is a literary trope shared by canonical works that overlap both modernist anthropology, such as the ethnographic monographs of Bronislaw Malinowski, Franz Boas, and Ruth Benedict, and modernist literature, represented by luminaries such as Joseph Conrad, D. H. Lawrence, and T. S. Eliot.

These travel books also exhibit what Joannes Fabian, in *Time and the Other: How Anthropology Makes Its Object*, calls "denial of coevalness," a "persistent and systematic tendency to place the referent(s) of anthropology in a Time other than the present of the producer of the anthropological discourse."[15] The result is a temporal paradox, as the anthropologists interpret in the visage of the Other an earlier evolutionary version of themselves, even as the two parties stand face to face with one another at a given moment. When Margaret Mead, for example, observed and wrote about the sexual lives of Samoan adolescents in *Coming of Age in Samoa* (1928), she did so under the assumption that Samoa represented not only a simpler but also an earlier, less modern version of her own society. Samoan youths, therefore, amounted to less complicated analogs of American teenagers. And just as mythic consciousness is characteristic of both modernist anthropology and literature, so too is denial of coevalness. And nowhere is the literary example better illustrated than in *Heart of Darkness*, in which they—the black Africans—are described as lacking any "clear idea of time," of "still belonging to the beginning of time." As Marlow "penetrated deeper and deeper into the heart of darkness," Conrad writes, he could not help but intuit that he was a wanderer on "prehistoric earth," that he traveled in the "night of first ages, of those ages that are gone, leaving hardly a sign—and no memories."[16]

But in order for Mead to have observed the intimate goings-on of Samoans and for Marlow to have dodged the poison-tipped spears of devilish savages, they both first had to travel *to* them; that is to say, they boarded a vehicle that transported them from here to there—or, as Fabian puts it, from somewhere in the West to somewhere "Rest." In both modernist anthropology and literature, then, physical travel is often synonymous with temporal travel, and time is kept in accordance with the "Western clock," whose machinations are modeled after those of a time machine.[17] Not coincidentally, this is the same clock that contemporary tourists consult in their travels to faraway destinations advertised as historic, exotic, primitive, or primeval. In their quest to experience the "authenticity" of native life, tourists follow the ways of modernist anthropology and literature. In other words, they too deny the coevalness—or disregard the contemporaneousness—of the Native Other.

Seen through these theoretical lenses, the refusal of contemporary South Koreans to give up dogmeat is a cultural enigma, an atavistic behavior that requires anthropological rumination—or at least a close literary reading. Dogmeat is a reminder of globalization's limits: it is one thing for taco trucks in American urban centers to offer kimchi tacos; it is something altogether different for the tacos to contain dogmeat. If you find typical Korean fare, like *bibimbap* or sundubu jjigae, too tame for your taste, the travel literature suggests you leave the benign path of the tourist and venture into perilous eateries that specialize not merely in authentic cuisine but in hyper-authentic cuisine, which, in Korea, includes insects, live animals, and someone's loving pet. With our help, they tell us, it is possible to glimpse Korea's darker origins, its rapidly receding antediluvian ways of life. But only if you have the stomach for it. Time travel, like dog eating, like man eating, is not for the squeamish.

Culinary Myths and Racial Epithets

Some thirty years ago the anthropologist W. Arens created a row when he argued that often-repeated accounts of tribal cannibalism in faraway, so-called primitive places were not only greatly exaggerated but quite possibly entirely fabricated—or just short of it. In *The Man-Eating Myth: Anthropology and Anthropophagy,* first published in 1979, Arens contends that apart from periodic cases of survival cannibalism, he had been "unable to uncover adequate documentation of cannibalism as a custom in any form for any society." To the ire of many in his profession, he suggested that for both the general public and professional anthropologists alike "the idea of cannibalism exists prior to and thus independent of the evidence." Despite rumors, apprehensions, and accusations that abound, "no satisfactory first-hand accounts" of tribal or ritual cannibalism in fact existed.[18] Instead, what he found were, at best, accounts derived from preexisting accounts, which in many cases sprung from yet even earlier accounts. At worst he discovered hearsay, fantasy, and at times outright hoaxes. In effect, stories of cannibalism were nests of *matryoshka* dolls that progressively unpacked only to culminate as tiny, empty shells of the initial bloated versions. Cannibalism was, so to speak, the anthropological version of the alligator in the sewer, an urban legend of the discipline.

There is, furthermore, a double standard, Arens argued. While accounts of cannibalism taking place in Africa, Polynesia, and autochthonous America are "assumed to be in the realm of demonstrated fact," reports of early Christians, Jews, or any other European representatives resorting to this practice "are dismissed out of hand as prejudice and racism." There was an undeniable racial dimension to tales of anthropophagy in the annals of anthropology, Arens asserted. Ritual man eating was defined as a "tabooed practice" that the darker, savage races engaged in exclusively, and as nonexistent within the civilized, white, Judeo-Christian societies.[19]

Many—both in and beyond the discipline—took exception to Arens' thesis. Critics accused him of being in denial, of ignobly misreading or simply ignoring the empirical evidence before him. He was dismissed as someone more invested in absolving non-Europeans of the utterly vile offense of cannibalism than in staying true to his scientific principles. He, in other words, allowed political correctness to impair his scholarly judgment. One distinguished anthropologist, Marshall Sahlins, even went as far as to compare Arens to a Holocaust denier, as did the French historian Frank Lestringant, who railed against scholars falling into the trap of "spreading the denial of the cannibal through five continents."[20]

One notable anthropologist who chose not to criticize Arens was Gananath Obeyesekere. He refrained from doing so despite his belief that various forms of ritual anthropophagy in fact existed in several societies throughout history, "for the most part as a kind of sacrament associated with human sacrifice."[21] Obeyesekere, however, did concur with Arens on

An engraving depicting cannibalism among Tupinamba Indians of Brazil. From Theodor de Bry, *America* (Frankfurt, 1590).

a vital point. In *Cannibal Talk: The Man-Eating Myth and Human Sacrifice in the South Seas,* published in 2005, he characterizes the idea of cannibalism as a "colonial projection," similar in some respects to Edward Said's notion of Orientalism; both are "discourses on the Other."[22]

Like Arens, Obeyeskere contended that attributing cannibalism to non-Western peoples was a "Western obsession," and anthropological accounts of cannibalism served as justification for European colonial practices, which included not only conquest and proselytism, but at times the extermination of entire native societies. As such, Obeyesekere compared tribal cannibalism to sorcery and witchcraft. While many unfortunate souls throughout history have been accused of necromancy, the actual practice of it has been quite rare. "Witchcraft is entirely based on accusations and on peoples' belief in its reality," he notes.[23] Like witchcraft, the idea of cannibalism is first and foremost a projection, a chimera. People believe cannibalism is real because so-called civilized people (aka whites) have always accused so-called savage people (aka nonwhites) of practicing it. "This attitude toward native peoples has had a long run in Western thought particularly after the opening up of the New World," Obeyesekere adds.[24]

In fact, it was Christopher Columbus who initially confused the word Cariba—the root of Caribbean and the native name for the island on which he disembarked—with *cani-ba*, "or the 'canine' great Khan of Cathay, China, whose name in turn was confused with the Latin *canis* or dog."[25] (To his death, Columbus believed he had discovered an ocean passage to Cathay.) During and beyond the sixteenth century, *The Oxford English Dictionary* tells us, the word "Carib" was "often used with the connotation of *cannibal*." The dictionary's earliest cited example is 1555, when Richard Eden wrote of "The wylde and myscheuous people called *Canibales* or *Caribes*, whiche were accustomed to eate mannes flesche." We are told that etymologically, the letters l, n, and r "interchange dialectally in American languages" to produce Caniba, Caribe, and Calibi. And in 1610 William Shakespeare might very well have coined another variant of the word in bestowing the name Caliban upon a character in *The Tempest*.

It comes as no surprise that the specter of bloodthirsty headhunters and tattooed man-eaters run amok in the jungles of far-off parts of Africa, Asia, and Oceania proved shocking to Western bourgeois sensibilities. The fact that lurid tales of primitive cannibals not only shocked but also entertained the public did not escape shrewd, profit minded impresarios such as P. T. Barnum. From 1871 to 1873, in his tireless pursuit of newer and more exotic ways to titillate his customers, Barnum put on display at his American Museum and Traveling Show four living humans whom he advertised as "Fiji cannibals." These were not the first cannibals Barnum had ever showcased, however. Some thirty years earlier, in 1841, he had exhibited "Vendovi, a cannibal chief" at his American Museum. But Barnum conveniently omitted this fact in his publicity of the Fiji cannibals, whom he wanted to present to the public as the great, culminating find of his illustrious career. To that end, he even commissioned W. C. Crum to pen *The History of P. T. Barnum's Cannibals*, a book-length—and no doubt entirely fictional—exploit of how Barnum came to procure the ferocious Fiji man-eaters.[26]

In fact, the more lurid and fantastical the savage cannibal tales, the more lucrative it was for the purveyors and enjoyable for the buyers. Significantly, the purveyors included not only nineteenth-century showmen like Barnum, but also the authoritative pages of twenty-first-century *National Geographic* magazine. In March 2003, under the tantalizing headline "Cannibal Utensils, Fiji Islands, 1917," the magazine published a photograph of what appears to be some sort of wooden trident. Referring to the rolling-pin–sized scepter as a "cannibal fork, or *iculanibokola*," the caption in part reads, "For centuries in the Fiji Islands, tribal officials would bring out their best utensils for special people, not to serve them, but to eat them. The tribal officials were cannibals, and the special people were the meal." The caption also notes that while this grisly dietary practice ended by the end of the nineteenth century (due to "influence of Christianity"), the "Western fascination" for cannibalism had not. As a result, a brisk trade in counterfeit *iculanibokola,* which began in 1880, continues to this day. Although the magazine presents the cultural practice of cannibalism as a matter of apparent fact, the caption ends with a disclaimer that renders the truth of the matter somewhat less than definitive: "Our records don't say if this photograph, acquired by the Society in 1917, is of the real thing or not. It has never been before published in the *Geographic.*"[27] Thus it hardly matters that many—if not most—known reports and records of tribal cannibalism are second hand, third hand, or completely fabricated accounts. In the world of the ethnographic sideshow, whether under big circus tents or in the hallowed display rooms of museums, the thinness of the line between fact and fiction is matched only by the tenuous border that separates science from entertainment.

While the accused party in the widespread rumors of "man-eats-man" is the so-called savage (prompting Obeyesekere to devote a chapter of *Cannibal Talk* to "savagism"), the group in the crosshairs in the rampant tales of "man-eats-dog" is the so-called Oriental. Asians, particularly Southeast and East Asians (with the notable exception of the Japanese), are held under a dark cloud of culinary suspicion. This genie is loose as well, and there is no putting it back in the bottle again. Asians are dogeaters, we are told, so beware your pets.

The urban folklorist Jan Harold Brunvand contends that rumors of unsuspecting diners served dogmeat in Chinese restaurants are among the most recurrent food-based legends in the United States and Europe.[28] As an example, he relates an actual news story that Reuters circulated in 1971 and subsequently published in newspapers around the United States, including the front page of the *San Francisco Chronicle*. The story concerned a Swiss couple and their pet poodle named Rosa. While traveling as tourists in Hong Kong, the couple stopped at a restaurant, ordered their meal, and asked the waiter to bring something for Rosie as well. Due to the language barrier, the couple communicated using makeshift sign language, which consisted of alternately pointing to the menu, their mouths, and Rosa. When the waiter took Rosie away, the couple thought nothing of it, assuming the dog would be fed in the kitchen. A short while later, the waiter returned with their order covered by a large silver dome. Under the dome, bathed in chile sauce and cooked with bamboo shoots, was Rosa.[29]

Among those who immediately suspected this widely propagated story was a hoax was the US representative for the Hong Kong Tourist Association. "First of all, that alleged Swiss couple couldn't have been tourists because pets are quarantined for six months before they're allowed into Hong Kong," he explained. "And in the second place, pets are forbidden in Hong Kong restaurants, just as they are here [in the United States]."[30] Calling it an "outrageously silly urban legend," Brunvand asserts that the idea behind this utterly fictitious story—published in some newspapers under the headline "Roast Rosa"—is that "Orientals in general, and Chinese in particular, relish dogs as food." Brunvand draws a direct link between stories such as this and canards about Asian immigrants in the United States snaring and eating their neighbors' pets.[31]

Corresponding with the rise of Asian immigration following the 1965 Immigration Act, various local police officers, health officials, and journalists have investigated numerous reports of such stories, only to inevitably conclude that they are almost always entirely fabricated.[32] Susan McHugh, author of *Dogs*, sees this sort of "nativist backlash" as a "prominent vehicle for anti-immigrant and especially anti-Asian sentiments in the US."[33] In fact, in one of the extremely rare cases that resulted in a legal trial over dog eating, the defendant happened not to be even Asian. In 1992 an unrepentant California man received a three-year sentence for reportedly barbecuing the ribs of a neighbor's dog.[34]

To many East and Southeast Asians in the United States, no single food provokes emotional agony quite like dogmeat. Dog eating is such a vexatious subject that merely raising the issue is enough to elicit the ire of many Asian Americans. The author Jessica Hagedorn discovered this with the publication of her novel *Dogeaters* in 1990, when the otherwise critically acclaimed work was condemned by a small but vocal minority within the Filipino American community who took the Philippines-born writer to task for using such a derogatory term to refer to her Filipino characters. The filmmaker Michael Cho, meanwhile, had to take on a number of hostile Asian American audience members during college screenings of his 1991 documentary *Animal Appetites*, which examined the legal, racial, and moral issues that stemmed from an actual case of two Cambodian immigrants charged with slaughtering and eating a dog in Long Beach, California.

Of course, "dog-eater" is not the only food-related insult hurled at Asians over the course of their history in the United States. They have also been subjected to terms like chop suey, fortune cookie, mice-eater, chopstick, chow mein, chow, almond eye, rice belly, rice man, curry, curry breath, curry head, coconut, rotten coconut, banana, and Twinkie. But most of these are now either obsolete and quaint (like chop suey and fortune cookie) or relatively innocuous (like almond eye or banana), at least when compared to the acridity of dog-eater. Even mice-eater, no doubt as scurrilous an accusation as any, lacks the sting of dog-eater, since few really believe Asians eat micemeat.

Many, however, are convinced that Asians in fact commonly feast on dogmeat. This was made evident during the 2002 Winter Olympic Games when Jay Leno, host of NBC's *The Tonight Show*, was compelled to issue an apology to outraged Korean Americans. In one of his monologues, Leno joked that a South Korean short-track skater, Kim Dong-sung, upset at being disqualified in a race against the American Apolo Ohno, went home, kicked his dog, then ate it. Four years before, the comedian Joan Rivers had to apologize to Filipino Americans after signing off for a commercial break during the 1998 Emmy Awards—she was the emcee—with the following quip: "We're going to commercial break, so if you have time to feed your dog, or wash your dog or, if you're a Filipino, you can eat your dog!"[35] And as if to drive home the point that dog eating is a culturally dubious practice, the *New York Times* in 2009 reported that the Filipino boxer Manny Pacquiao left home at fourteen when his father, out of desperation and hunger, ate the family dog.[36]

Of course, Asians are not the only ethnic, racial, or religious group to have had food-based insults directed at them. The history of intercultural conflict in the United States is rife with taunts, digs, put-downs, and other forms of verbal abuse that in one way or another zero in on foodways strongly associated with another faction. Gastronomical pejoratives specific to African Americans, for example, have been numerous over the years: chocolate, chocolate drop, hot chocolate, licorice, skillet, stove lid, saucer lip, buckwheat, cantaloupe, conch, peanut, alligator bait, Oreo, banana, brown sugar, dark meat, and pork chop, among others. Mexicans, meanwhile, have been called taco, taco-eater, taco head, taco-bender, beaner, bean-eater, tamale, hot tamale, tio taco, coconut, chile-picker, enchilada-eater, frijole-guzzler, frito, Mexican dish, pepper, and pepper belly. In addition, food-related epithets for Italians, Catholics, Germans, Appalachians, French-Canadians, and countless other American groups have also been abundant.[37]

Genealogy of Dogmeat

As evidenced by the twentieth-century rise of the fast-food industry, and the McDonald's franchise in particular, there is no denying the hegemony of the hamburger, which has transformed the pitiable cow—*Bos taurus*—into the most used and abused animal in human history. What began as the quintessential symbol of American gastronomy is now global, as the supersized value meal, composed of a beef burger, French fries, and cola, threatens world domination. When it comes to meat, and the flesh of mammals in particular, the choice has narrowed. Current trends indicate that any meat source not deemed traditionally agrarian or pastoral is subject to an ever-increasing level of suspicion and proscription. In fact, to the US Department of Agriculture, the term "meat" refers only to the "muscle of cattle, pigs, sheep, and goats."[38] Conspicuously missing from this list is the dog, the first animal ever to be domesticated by humans.

The dog is the foremost example of a domestic animal, which Juliet Clutton-Brock, the eminent scholar of animal domesticity, defines as "one that has been bred in captivity for purposes of economic profit to a human community that maintains complete mastery over its breeding, organization of territory, and food supply."[39] As such, the dog is entirely a human invention. In this, dogs are not unlike all other domestic species, which include sheep, goats, cattle, pigs, horses, asses, mules, and hinnies. That is to say, these are all "man-made animals," which comprise "mammals that have been moulded by man for his personal satisfaction and gain." Moreover, domestic animals are defined as "*populations* that through direct selection by man have certain inherent morphological, physiological, or behavioural characteristics by which they differ from their ancestral stocks."[40]

By this definition, then, camels and llamas, for example, are not domestic but *domesticated* animals, which are "*individuals* that have been made more tractable or tame but whose breeding does not involve intentional selection." Other domesticated animals, which Clutton-Brock also calls "exploited captives," include elephants, reindeer, rabbits, ferrets, and many Asiatic cattle (excluding the zebu). The list also includes a number of rodents (such as guinea pigs, house mice, hamsters, and chinchillas) and carnivores (such as foxes and minks) that have been exploited by man for food and fur. The household cat, meanwhile, is a mammal that is neither completely domestic nor domesticated, but one that falls somewhere between the two categories. Clutton-Brock suggests calling the *Felis catus* "an exploiting captive" given that the cat is a "solitary carnivore that enjoys the company of man but is just as happy to return to Kipling's 'wet wild woods waving his wild tail and walking by his wild lone.'"[41]

Based on archaeological evidence, the dog, whose principle ancestor is the wolf, or *Canis lupus,* is believed to have been the first animal to be cultivated by humans some twelve thousand to fourteen thousand years ago.[42] It is generally assumed that nomadic hunters and gatherers, realizing that they and the wolf competed for the same prey, in a sense forced an alliance between the two species through the process of domestication. In doing so, humans appropriated the wolf's superb hunting ability, which they admired and envied. An alternate theory, however, flips this story on its head and asserts that the canine purposely gave up its wild ways in order to take advantage of human patronage. Accustomed to human hunters and scavenging after their remains, the dog, in the words of Frederick Simoons, was "a *volunteer* responsible for its own domestication."[43]

The most current research tends toward a third hypothesis: Ice Age humans domesticated the wolf to have a supply of fresh meat readily available. (This hypothesis is not new, however. Clutton-Brock noted in 1995 that prehistoric human hunters, in addition to killing wolves for skins, "would carry around a live pup that would often be eaten.")[44] For obvious reasons, this theory does not sit well with many in pet-owning societies, such as the United States, where dogs are often regarded as legitimate members of the family.

On September 7, 2009, the *New York Times* reported on a study conducted by a team of geneticists at the Royal Institute of Technology that appeared to locate southern China as the site of a single domestication event that gave rise to the dog. By sampling the mitochondrial DNA of dogs around the world, the research team concluded that every dog in the world is traceable to a single lineage, which indicates a single domestication event. Given the long history of dog-eating practices in southern China, along with archaeological remains that indicate cut marks on dog bones, the team proposed that the wolves of that region were initially domesticated for their meat. The spread of dogs to other parts of the world, however, indicates that the role dogs played in human communities rapidly diversified. Dogs were soon prized not only for their meat—in fact, in many places people abandoned dog eating altogether—but also for their capacity to work, be it guarding, shepherding, or pulling sleds.[45]

Classic sources reveal that ancient Carthaginians enjoyed dogmeat, and Hippocrates wrote of ancient Greeks regularly dining on it.[46] And according to Peter Lund Simmonds, author of *The Curiosities of Food or the Dainties and Delicacies of Different Nations Obtained from the Animal Kingdom,* first published in 1859, the meat of the canine was enjoyed by the "common people of Rome," as well as Turks, many South Sea Islanders, the Zanzibari, Australians, and, most notably, the Celestials of Canton, where "the hind quarters of dogs" could be seen "hanging up in the most prominent parts of the shops exposed for sale" and "consumed by both rich and poor."[47] Some of the most intriguing incidences of dog eating involve the Native Hawaiians. James King, who sailed with Captain James Cook on an expedition to Hawai'i, wrote in 1779 of the natives' fondness for dogmeat while at the same time treating the animal as a loving pet. He observed that the women even nursed the pups at their own breasts before slaughtering them, as the Hawaiians believed the practice produced the tastiest meat.[48]

Many are surprised to discover that contemporary Europeans, such as Belgians and people of various Alpine nations, are known to favor dogmeat. The Swiss, for example, dry the meat in varying temperatures for several months to prepare a dish called Gedörrtes Hunderfleisch. "In fact," Calvin Schawbe tells us, "the only two cases of human trichinosis diagnosed in Switzerland in recent years resulted from the patients eating their dogmeat too rarely cooked!" "It has been a traditional European belief," he reveals in *Unmentionable Cuisine,* "that dogmeat is a preventive of tuberculosis."[49] And less than a century ago widespread dog eating was reported in the German cities of Cassel and Chemnitz, as well as in the streets of Paris. Also, the existence of legislation ensuring safe dog slaughtering and marketing practices in several European countries is a strong indication that dog eating is not simply an exotic facet of Oriental gastronomy but possibly a quotidian Occidental tradition as well.[50]

Unlike man eating, then, dog eating is by no means entirely fictitious or completely a product of anthropological or urban mythology. (Frank Wu calls it "an international urban legend with some truth to the tale.")[51] There is no shortage of irrefutable evidence of dog eating as an immemorial human custom. Not only do humans eat dogs in many parts of the world today, but we have done so since the dawn of the human-dog relationship. That dogs have played a number of different functions in human societies since ancient times is common universal knowledge. In fact, their myriad roles—including as scavengers, hunters, guards, livestock herders, sled pullers, rescuers, soldiers, companion animals—are often celebrated.[52] That they have also functioned as food, on the other hand, is a reality that not only infuriates dog lovers everywhere, but also unnerves a legion of hungry tourists in search of a meal while visiting a locale reputed to include dogmeat as part of its local cuisine. Hong Kong, Taipei, Manila, and Seoul are cities that lead this list.

The preponderance of the evidence indicates that culinary use of dogmeat is more historically sweeping and globally widespread than most, especially those in the United States and Europe, would like to believe. Humans have eaten and continue to eat the meat of canines for a wide array of reasons, including religious, ceremonial, medicinal, survival, and, not least, culinary purposes. (The North American Oglala Sioux, for instance, still consume it during religious rituals.)[53] For all intents and purposes, dog eating is now narrowly classified as an Asian tradition above all else. Filipinos, Cambodians, and Vietnamese have all recently been targeted for ridicule and condemnation. As a result, in the Philippines today, one of the few legal ways left to enjoy dogmeat is ritual eating among tribal communities, such as the Igorots, Ilocanos, Pampangueños, and Pangasinenses. Although the archipelago's first animal welfare act curbing dog eating outside religious or tribal purposes was passed in 1998, the practice is still so widespread, especially among groups of imbibing men, that the ban is virtually impossible to enforce.[54]

Due to the global media spotlight on the 1988 Seoul Olympic Games and 2002 FIFA World Cup in South Korea, the image of the Korean dogeater has become preeminent. Commenting on the Western media's "occasional diatribe on the 'barbaric' practice of eating dog meat in Korea," Michael Pettid wonders why there is no discussion on why some Koreans enjoy the meat. "When the non-Korean is properly indoctrinated into the nuances and varieties of food in Korea," he asserts, "we rarely hear such generalizations or criticisms." For Pettid, the foreign obsession over dogmeat in the Korean diet is no more an accurate measure of the nation's multifarious gastronomy than is singling out the hot dog as the exemplar of American food or chop suey as that of Chinese food.[55]

And when the screen-goddess-turned-animal-rights-activist Brigitte Bardot infuriated an entire nation by calling South Koreans "barbaric" for their dogmeat proclivity, she did so not because she imagined it, but because, to put it frankly, many Koreans actually do relish dogs. Reportedly, the South Korean dogmeat industry encompasses around six thousand restaurants, 10 percent of the population, and one million dogs, the latter of which produce some nine thousand tons of meat a year.[56] (The 2001 South Korean film *Address Unknown*, directed by Kim Ki-duk, focuses on characters who, out of economic desperation and moral depravation, slaughter and butcher dogs and sell the meat to local restaurants.) During the run up to the 2002 FIFA World Cup, Bardot told a Korean radio interviewer that dogs were "not animals" but "friends," and added, "Cows are grown to be eaten, dogs are not. I accept that many people eat beef, but a cultured country does not allow its people to eat dogs."[57] A number of restaurants in South Korea responded to Bardot's criticism by giving bosintang, the most common type of dogmeat soup, a new name—Bardot soup.[58]

A dogmeat dish served at a restaurant in Seoul, South Korea. Photo by the author.

As for the peculiarity of a figure such as Bardot leading an international campaign against Korean dog eating, Frank Wu accuses the star of such classic films as Louis Malle's *Vie Privée* (1960) and Jean-Luc Godard's *Le Mépris* (1963) of connecting "mistreatment of animals with an influx of non-Western peoples [to France]." He argues that her calling Koreans barbaric is actually a cover for "her involvement with French right-wing groups that aim to curtail immigration for racial reasons."[59]

If true, then an identical political impulse was behind a more recent France-related incident involving another meat source that many in the world consider taboo. In 2006 soup kitchens associated with extreme right-wing groups served "pig soup"—aka "Identity Soup," after the Identity Bloc, a far-right nationalist movement—to Paris' downtrodden. Critics charged that the hearty soup, made of bacon and pigs' ears, feet, and tails, discriminated against observant Jews and Muslims, for whom consumption of pork is religiously proscribed. In defending the soup, a leader of the movement proclaimed, "Our freedom in France is being threatened. If we prefer European civilization and Christian culture, that's our choice." Groups in other French cities—Strasbourg and Nice, for example—soon followed Paris' example, as did those in neighboring Belgium—in Brussels, Antwerp, and Charleroi. A year later a Parisian administrative court rejected complaints filed by city authorities that attempted to close down the soup kitchens. The court ruled that while the distribution was "clearly discriminatory," it could not be blocked since the soup was offered to anyone, Christian, Jew, or Muslim, who asked for it.[60]

In her article "Dogs, Whales and Kangaroos: Transnational Activism and Food Taboos," Marianne Lien characterizes the structure of the international campaigns against South Korean dog eating as a rebuke by the "civilized world" on a "barbarian culture" that "may be read (and are read) as attacks on Korean national culture." She identifies the Korean response to these attacks as having three noticeable expressions. The first is the rise of home-grown animal rights activism in Korea, exemplified by groups such as the Korean Animal Protection Society that seek to pressure lawmakers into protecting pet animals from ending up in the nation's food supply. The second is a movement to define dog eating as a "unique culinary custom" that is an indelible part of Korean history, akin to eating kimchi or bulgogi. Fueling this effort is the growing indignation among those who see any foreign criticism as "an insult to all Koreans." The third response is "an interesting middle ground which tries to uphold

South Korea's honor as a modern nation by establishing a distinction between the shameful practices of the past, and a globalized modern South Korea."[61]

Dog eating, in other words, is perceived as an aged symptom of a bygone Korea that must vanish in order for the new Korea to rightfully share the stage—or the dinner table, rather—with other modern nations of the world. Perhaps John Feffer put it best when he identified the "greatest enemy" of bosintang to be not Brigitte Bardot but Colonel Sanders. After all, the practice of dog eating has always been and still is, at best, an intermittent aspect of Korean gastronomy. (As Pettid recounts, dogmeat is a prominent summer dish in Korea, as the spicy soup version of it "is believed to provide strength to the body to combat the hot and humid summer months.")[62] In a nation where the younger generation now comes of age with Dunkin' Donuts, Pizza Hut, and McDonald's as much as kimchi, the future of bosintang is, on the one hand, undeniably dim.[63] On the other hand, as South Korea propels itself along the information superhighway to the postindustrial future, dogmeat's destiny may not be so grim. The threat of prohibition has generated a redoubled effort by those who cherish the food to preserve and protect its legal welfare. It has also sparked a grassroots movement to keep dogmeat culturally relevant and an essential part of twenty-first-century Korean identity.

The Uses of Disgust

Question: how do you know if a Korean burglarized your home? Answer: someone finished your child's homework, cleaned your house, and ate your dog. The gist of this widely circulated joke—the third part of the punch line, at least—surfaced in HBO's *Curb Your Enthusiasm* starring Larry David, who is perhaps best known as the creator of the long-running NBC comedy *Seinfeld*. In a 2006 episode titled "The Korean Bookie," the mystery of a missing pet converges with a suspicious dietary predilection of a Korean American to refashion an urban legend into a contemporary television "gag" (pun intended).

Oscar, a genial German shepherd owned by Larry's manager, Jeff, mysteriously vanishes not long after Song, Larry's Korean bookie, meets the dog for the first time. During the meeting, a transfixed Song fawns excessively over the animal, describing it as "gorgeous," "beautiful," and "just

144   *Chapter 4*

right" before asking where the dog lives. When he first learns of Oscar's disappearance, Larry immediately suspects Song, played by the Korean American comedian Bobby Lee using a heavily accented English, as having had a hand, if not all of his teeth, in the crime. Larry's suspicion soon leads to a conversation with Jeff about rumors of a bizarre Korean food habit. Larry tells him that Song "drooled" over Oscar when he first saw the animal. When Jeff appears bemused, failing to connect the dots, Larry lets him in on a dirty little secret: "Well, you know what's not a myth. They do eat dogs. Yeah, some Koreans eat dogs." Jeff is utterly distraught. The implication is too grisly to bear, especially about a loving pet, which he considers a member of his family. In an attempt to assuage Jeff's anguish, Larry hastily apologizes and dismisses the idea.

Later, at a beachside wedding, the two men and dozens of other guests are seen enjoying a catered meal. In particular, everyone raves about an unfamiliar yet delicious meat dish. Larry calls it "fantastic" and "unbelievable." Jeff adds that he has "never tasted anything like it." Curious to know what the dish is, Larry asks the caterer, who replies that it is bulgogi, provided by the Korean florist, who just happens to be Larry's bookie, Song. With his mouth full of half-masticated food and his face contorted in disgust, Larry screams in horror: "Oscar! Bulgogi is Oscar! You're eating a dog!" He immediately spits and retches, which proves contagious. Each

Larry David in the "Korean Bookie" episode of *Curb Your Enthusiasm* (2005). Larry, wearing the hat, inquires about a mysterious meat dish. Publicity still from HBO.com.

and every guest, one by one at first, then en masse, expectorates, gags, and throws up. No one escapes the emetic tidal wave.

The field of behavioral psychology acknowledges disgust as one of six basic human emotions, along with anger, fear, sadness, happiness, and surprise. Of these, only disgust is directly tied to food and gustation. In fact, the word is derived from the sixteenth-century Italian *disgusto* (also French *desgoust*), which literally means aversion or negation (*dis-*) of taste (*gusto*) for food; it is synonymous with food-based nausea and loathing. In his study "Good Taste and Bad Taste: Preferences and Aversions as Biological Principles," Wulf Schiefenhövel contends that the physiological mechanism of the disgust response is part of a "complex cybernetical system" that regulates nausea and vomiting. Common stimuli that trigger the disgust response include "rotten substances with a putrid smell, body wastes, especially faeces, and slimy fluids."[64] Further, according to a team of researchers headed by Paul Rozin in an article titled "Disgust: Preadaptation and the Cultural Evolution of a Food-Based Emotion," with the exception of cow's milk and chicken's egg, virtually "all food-related disgust elicitors for Americans are animals or animal products," which includes rotten meat, insects, reptiles, rodents, simians, cats, and dogs.[65]

On a purely physical level, the disgust mechanism protects the body from harm by flagging toxic substances that might be ingested. Bitterness is thought to be "the prototype for eliciting this distaste response" and springs from "the gape response," characterized by the lowering of the sides of the mouth (to form an inverted U) and dropping of the lower jaw, often accompanied by jutting out of the tongue. In essence, the gape response is a ritualized vomit gesture; it is not limited to human adults but is also seen in newborns and even some animals. The disgust mechanism is often contagious, typically seen among groups of children when one child's theatrical outburst of disgust over a food item—which commonly manifests as the "eww" cry—triggers a domino effect. Somewhere along the evolutionary highway, however, the "neurobiology of the disgust-emotion shifted to become a purely social signal" in humans and thus extends "to a wide range of other socio-cultural markers, particularly ones which are subject to moral evaluation." In other words, although disgust was once strictly a matter of physiology and bodily instinct, it has, over time, evolved into a matter for the mind, soul, and spirit.[66]

Researchers have identified "three kinds of motive leading to rejection of potential foods by humans" vis-à-vis the disgust response. The first is "distaste," or "undesirable sensory properties," which includes foods that displease the nose, tongue, and eyes. This means, for example, avoiding the tropical fruit durian for its fetid smell; spitting out an astringent persimmon after a painful, "furry" bite; or returning a bloody, undercooked steak to the restaurant kitchen. The second is "anticipated consequences," or a fear of repeating a mistake. This means not going anywhere near a durian again, declining a second bite of the cottony persimmon, or ordering your steak well done the next time. The third motive for rejecting food is "conceptual," or knowledge "about the nature or origin of substances,"[67] which means converting to vegetarianism after witnessing first hand the industrial slaughter of farm animals, quitting fast food after reading Eric Schlosser's *Fast Food Nation*, not ordering anything meat-like at a Korean restaurant, or refusing to take another bite of Soylent Green after discovering its source. In this regard, Robert Thorn's "Soylent Green is people," the Mad Diarist's "Save the children," Kurtz's "The horror! The horror!" the *Lonely Planet*'s "Rough," Simon Winchester's pity for the large dog, and Larry David's "Bulgogi is Oscar" are not only expressions of dread, but the sounding of an alarm. Each expresses an anxiety about personal harm and, more importantly, warns others of danger—not necessarily physical danger, but moral.

Disgust is simultaneously "the strongest form of food rejection" and "a powerful principle leading to cultural diversity."[68] And, as strongly indicated by the existence of untold numbers of food-based ethnic insults and epithets, the food habits of others are often crudely mocked as disgusting. As Rozin et al. note, "Members of one ethnic group will often react with a disgust face and ritualized vomiting movements when speaking about other ethnic groups."[69] In other words, the foods—and the people who eat them—we mutually find disgusting can be the source of a social bond that distinguishes the in-group (or *our* group) from the out-group (or *their* group), a marker for not only preserving ethnic, racial, and class boundaries, but also creating new ones. If kosher and halal diets are indicative of ancient boundaries that circumscribed an in-group from an out-group, then elective vegetarianism and veganism, as well as raw food and no-gluten diets, are just few of the new borderlines that separate contemporary identities vis-à-vis the foods we choose either to eat or avoid.

The belief that Asians regularly consume disgusting foods, including outlandish animal flesh, abounds in the Western imagination and dates back to the start of the East-West encounter. Writing about his travels to

China between 1275 and 1292, Marco Polo expressed revulsion at the Chinese habit of consuming "brute beasts and animals of every kind which Christians would not touch for anything in the world," including dogs, snakes, and possibly crocodiles. Most shocking, however, was what he witnessed in Fuzhou. "The natives," he remarked, "even relish human flesh."[70] In his 1859 *Curiosities of Food*, Peter Lund Simmonds describes monkeys consumed by Malaysians, camels by Tartars, hyenas by Arabs, dogs by Turks, and rats by Chinese not only in China but also in San Francisco.[71] More recently, Jerry Hopkins, in his 2004 book *Extreme Cuisine: The Weird and Wonderful Foods That People Eat*, regales his readers with madcap stories of gecko-eating Thais, crocodile-munching Singaporeans, tarantula-chomping Cambodians, termite-devouring Japanese, and elephant-scoffing Indians.[72] In popular films such as Steven Spielberg's *Indiana Jones and the Temple of Doom*, obese Indians gorge themselves on live snakes, monkey brains, and giant beetles as a blond American woman looks on with aversion, while in the reality TV programs *Survivor* and *Fear Factor*, contestants battle their own gag reflexes by consuming as many balut—fertilized duck's egg with a developed zygote described as a Filipino aphrodisiac—as fast as they can or risk elimination.

The eccentricity of the Asian palate is such a cliché that even Chinese America's most respected writer famously flaunted it. In her 1975 book *The Woman Warrior: Memoirs of a Childhood among Ghosts*, Maxine Hong Kingston writes of her mother cooking "raccoons, skunks, hawks, city pigeons, wild ducks, wild geese, black-skinned bantams, snakes, garden snails, turtles that crawled about the pantry floor and sometimes escaped under refrigerator or stove, catfish that swam in the bathtub." She recalls hiding under her bed to avoid the horrors of her family kitchen, even holding candy over her nose to mask the smell of dismembered skunk on her mother's cutting board.[73] Not to be outdone, Frank Chin, Kingston's longtime literary nemesis, has boasted that a real badass Chinaman eats "toejam, bugs, leaves, seeds, birds, bird nests, treebark, trunks, fungus, rot, roots, and smut."[74]

The disgust some experience at the idea of dogmeat—or any other Asian food deemed disgusting by non-Asians—has little to do with food. Rather, it concerns an individual's sense of self within an imagined community against a perceived alien threat. It is less an expression of gustatory distaste than a signal to those in your in-group against external dangers. Specifically, the expression of disgust over the idea of dogmeat warns against the corrupting power of the primitive Orient, just as the horror over the idea of cannibalism warned the West against the corrosive possibility of the dark savage. And it matters not whether the Oriental resides there (in Asia) or here (in America). What matters is that we keep our loving pets from their perverse clutches, just as Crusoe protected his man Friday from the soup pot of the tattooed cannibals. By all means, however, we must avoid the fate of Larry David, who apparently failed to rescue Oscar from the ravenous clutches of the pidgin-speaking Korean florist. As we have seen, the consequences of his failure were horrific, as everyone in his group unwittingly ingested a member of Jeff's family, then vomited it out when told of the source. (In actuality, Larry David was wrong; bulgogi was not Oscar after all. The dog, alive and intact, makes a surprise appearance in the final scene of the episode.)

Domestic Animals in the Era of Postdomesticity

The defining feature of the human-animal relationship is overwhelmingly one of violence, suffering, and, above all else, death. The current of cruelty, misery, and slaughter flows in only one direction, however. In all but rare instances, it is man who delivereth death and the animal who receives. In all likelihood, the first meaningful gesture made toward an animal by a human at the dawn of our species' origin was to kill it. Juliet Clutton-Brock reminds us in *Domesticated Animals from Early Times* that "unlike remaining primates, man evolved as a carnivorous predator dependent on his mental and physical prowess to kill other animals for food."[75]

It is considered an anthropological truism that many human traits we take for granted today were a direct consequence of our evolutionary ancestors having added animal flesh to their diets. The ability to travel long distances, increased body size, heightened intelligence, and high-level intraspecies cooperation are just a few of the characteristics that marked the evolution of the genus *Homo* from its immediate predecessor, a bipedal primate known by the genus *Australopithecus*. Richard Wrangham, author of *Catching Fire: How Cooking Made Us Human*, believes this "meat-eating hypothesis" does not tell the entire story, however. Also known as the "Man-the-Hunter" theory, the hypothesis does not provide a full picture of human evolution unless the role of fire, and specifically the act of cooking, is taken into account.[76] If Wrangham is correct, what separates humans from other forms of life on earth is not necessarily a matter of language, as some linguists might insist, or cognition, as some psychologists might assert, but our species' unique ability to barbecue a hunk of animal flesh over an open fire.

To this day, humans continue to kill animals for a plethora of reasons, including subsistence (e.g., food, clothing, cosmetics), leisure (fishing, hunting), accident (deer on the highway, a titmouse crashed into a kitchen window), wagering (dog fights, cock fights), pity (a racehorse with a broken leg, a terminally sick pet), precautionary (pests, diseased livestock), and so forth. Whether regarded as pelts, pests, pets, or prizes, the vast majority of animals that cross paths with humans are fated for a painful demise. In the words of the Animal Studies Group, a consortium of British academics with backgrounds in different humanities disciplines and author of *Killing Animals*, "The killing of animals is a structural feature of all human-animal relations."[77]

To cite examples from a single human activity of animal farming, recently in the United Kingdom some 10 million animals were destroyed over concerns of bovine spongiform encephalopathy (aka mad-cow disease) and foot-and-mouth disease. In Hong Kong some 1.4 million fowls were dispatched during a single month to prevent the spread of the bird flu. In Australia the termination quota for kangaroos was 5.5 million. Here in the United States, some 45 million turkeys are killed each year for Thanksgiving, and workers in a hog factory can cut as many as a thousand porcine throats per hour.[78] And each year, a single Cargill Meat Solutions plant in Kansas reportedly slaughters about 1.5 million cattle.[79] It is estimated that, all told, nearly 10 billion domestic animals (mammals and fowls) are raised and killed each year in the United States for purposes of food production.[80] Carol J. Adams calculates that, on average, a nonvegetarian consumes "984 chickens, 37 turkeys, 29 pigs, 12 cattle, two lambs, one calf, and more than 1,000 fish" in a lifetime.[81] That death is the eventual outcome for any beast exposed to the machinations of humanity is a reality difficult for humans to refute and impossible for animals to escape. Piteously, this is true whether the beast is domestic, domesticated, wild, tamed, or feral.

For the most part humans, especially those of us who reside in industrial and postindustrial societies, do not care to dwell too deeply on what many animal rights activists see as nothing short of a holocaust. Given the choice, we would rather not know or be reminded where meats and other animal treats come from. If knowledge is power in human-human relationships, then ignorance (on the part of the human) is truly bliss in the human-animal interface.

In 2008, under threat of violence, both the San Francisco Art Institute and the Glasgow International Festival closed down an exhibit by the French-Algerian artist Adel Abdessemed that included a short video of livestock being slaughtered on a Mexican farm. In a multimedia installation titled "Don't Trust Me," a sheep, ox, pig, horse, deer, and goat are bludgeoned to death with a sledgehammer to the head. Abdessemed neither commissioned nor committed the acts himself; he was merely the documenter. Nevertheless, the video was considered too incendiary, and it was feared such graphic scenes of human-on-animal violence would unnecessarily provoke audiences on both sides of the Atlantic.[82] The fact that these types of violent acts take place daily in abattoirs across the developed world was irrelevant. So too was the reality that all of us, including those who profess disgust over these images, either tacitly empower or overtly condone the mass killing of animals for the sake of our collective need, pleasure, and whim.

Animals are known to kill in return, of course. They have done so since the beginning of human time and continue to do so today. In the waters off Hawai'i and Australia, sharks attack swimmers and surfers; in zoos and circuses around the world, elephants mow down their keepers and tigers savage their handlers;[83] on the hills of Southern California's San Fernando Valley, cougars pounce on hikers, joggers, and bikers; and in homes across the United States, seemingly gentle and loving pit bulls suddenly turn on their owners and maul little children. The psychic anxiety stemming from actual cases of animal attack serves as opportune fodder for wondrous stories in the human world. To the delight of packed theater audiences, films such as *The Birds* (1963), *Jaws* (1975), *Orca* (1977), *Cujo* (1983), *Jurassic Park* (1990), *Congo* (1995), *Snakes on a Plane* (2006), *Piranha* (2010, a remake of a 1978 film), and *The Grey* (2012) depict humans ruthlessly stalked and killed, in turn, by flocks of vicious birds, a colossal great white shark, a wayward killer whale, a rabid St. Bernard, a team of wily velociraptors, a pack of homicidal gorillas, a crateful of venomous snakes, a school of prehistoric man-eating fish, and a murderous pack of wolves. Graphic images of animals on the attack also abound on the small screen, in "reality" TV programs and pseudo-documentaries such as *The World's Most Dangerous Animals* (first aired in 1996), *When Animals At-*

tack (1996), and *When Good Pets Go Bad* (1998).[84] This trend endures: in 2009 Animal Planet premiered *I'm Alive*, which, according to the description on the network website, "features the death-defying and moving stories of people who—regardless of the obstacles or consequences—were determined to survive an animal attack."[85]

Despite their sensationalism, however, actual instances of animal-on-human violence occur so rarely that their ecological impact is all but meaningless. Moreover, they represent the most atypical of possible outcomes that stem from the human-animal relationship. Unquestionably, the most typical outcome is death and despair for animals at the hands of humans. In all but the rarest of instances, the ceaseless human endeavor for complete dominion over the natural world eventually brings devastation to every creature, great or small, beast or fowl or fish. If there are doubts, just ask the thylacine (extinct since the 1930s), the quagga (extinct since 1883), and, of course, the hapless dodo (extinct since the end of the seventeenth century).

Then again, it may be that these extinct species are the lucky ones; at least they have been put out of their misery, once and for all. The same cannot be said of animals whose very essence has been manipulated by human hands over the millennia to meet a single purpose—to serve humans. Perhaps the most wretched of all are the domestic and domesticated animals whose past, present, and future are permanently intertwined with the fate of humans who rely on them not only for food, clothing, and labor, but increasingly—especially in postindustrial societies—for companionship, if not love itself.

And, no doubt to Brigitte Bardot's relief, it appears many twenty-first-century South Koreans have come to realize the wide-ranging personal benefits in regarding dogs not merely as salubrious food, but also as mollycoddled pets. As *Korea Times* columnist John Huer puts it, "There's a wild race in Korea to see who can treat dogs best." Pet stores specializing in high-priced breeds have proliferated. Fashionable young women parade around town carrying trophy dogs in designer purses and coat pockets. Among the breeds most coveted by the trendy elite and often treated as if they were human babies are the smallest varieties, such as Chihuahuas, Shih Tzus, Yorkshire terriers, Maltese terriers, toy poodles, and dachshunds. These animals exist on the polar opposite end of the privilege barometer from those destined for the human food chain, either in restaurants through special channels or at private dog-eating parties in the countryside.[86]

But there is a third class of dogs caught between those pampered and those consumed in South Korea. These are the miserable mutts, mixed breeds, and mongrels of ignoble pedigree that are constantly leashed and given a mere square foot or two to roam for the better part of their inconsequential lives. Although technically pets, no one plays with these dogs or takes them for walks. They brave the cold of winter and heat of summer unsheltered as perpetually tethered creatures and subsist on the least desirable human refuse only.[87] What this relatively recent diversification of dog usage in South Korea signals is the rapid change undergone by the nation since the poverty-stricken days of the postwar era. Miraculously, South Korea now ranks as one of the most technologically and financially advanced societies on earth. Thus it was perhaps inevitable that even here some dogs are treated as honorary humans since South Korea, too, has transitioned into what could be called a postdomestic society.

Late- and postindustrial societies represent a new chapter in the long-running saga of human interaction with animals, an era that Richard Bulliet, in *Hunters, Herders, and Hamburgers: The Past and Future of Human-Animal Relationships,* calls postdomestic. During the prior "domestic" era, direct human contact with livestock—domestic animals—was commonplace. It was not that long ago, for example, that most Americans lived on or near farms, just as most of the developing world does today, and witnessed first hand the chain of events that rendered an animal into meat, hide, fiber, and other products. Today, while consuming these products in even greater abundance, the vast majority of Americans are shielded from the "births, sexual congress, and slaughter of these animals." The factory farms and industrial abattoirs where these processes take place are far removed both physically and psychologically. Yet these same people insist on the right to form intimate relationships with dogs and cats—pets or companion animals—and often relate to them "as if they were human." Consequently, postdomestic societies, which include large segments of the United States, Great Britain, Australia, and to a lesser degree, Europe, "are fully immersed in the emotional contradiction inherent in postdomesticity," argues Bulliet.[88]

The message that we might extrapolate by juxtaposing the concept of postdomesticity with the practice of dog eating has far-reaching consequences for both the dog lover and dogmeat lover alike: although we loathe being reminded of it, we know of the violence, suffering, and death that accompany a mouthful of hamburger and a closet full of leather jackets. Overwhelmed with guilt, shame, and, most of all, disgust over the inhumane treatment of animals we deem "livestock," we indulge, spoil, and pamper animals we deem "pet" and admonish whomever refuses to share our ritual of categorical purity, such as those who treat dogs as if they were livestock by eating them. Let us, therefore, compensate for the brutal treatment of the cow by turning the dog into an honorary human and equate dog eating with the most savage, prehistoric human behavior imaginable.

So what do we talk about when we talk about eating dog? Why, cannibalism, of course. Thus compared to the miserable cow, the dog appears to be the luckiest animal in the world in the postdomestic era. Scratch the surface, however, and you see an equally sad story. For every dog lovingly cared for by a human, many more face a miserable life and a silent death. For each diamond-studded collar that graces the neck of a cherished poodle there are many more choke collars that bite the skin of troublesome mutts. For every beloved pooch that sleeps on a human bed there are untold numbers put to sleep during the dark of night. And, as Susan McHugh and others have revealed, in the United States the remains of millions of euthanized dogs were once legally recycled into commercial dog food under benign euphemisms such as "meat meal" and "meat and bone meal" on package labels.[89] So it turns out Charlton Heston was wrong and Larry

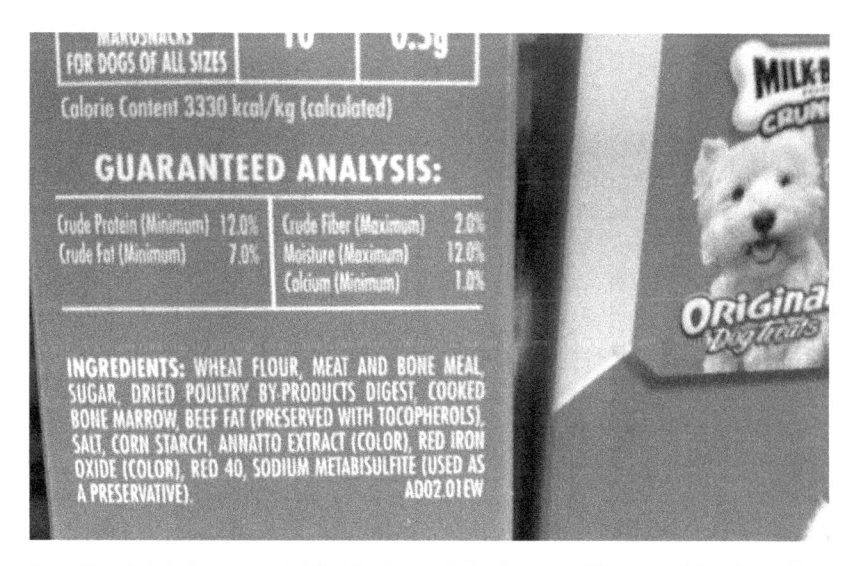

Ingredient label of commercial dog food containing "meat and bone meal," an ingredient that reportedly once consisted of euthanized dog remains.

David was right: Soylent Green isn't people after all. It is, rather, dog. Let's save the children.

Coda

I finally tried it on a rainy afternoon in Seoul as my two-week travel through South Korea with my wife and her parents drew to a close. The build up to it was excruciating. To our surprise, we were told repeatedly by casual acquaintances, including the hotel concierge, that there were no more of "those" places left in Seoul, that we had to travel outside the city, to small towns near the mountains, if we really wanted to find one. It was getting to be a bigger undertaking than we had anticipated. Just mentioning dogmeat to Seoulites invited suspicious, chastising looks. In general, there appeared to be great reluctance on the part of those we asked merely to acknowledge the existence of dogmeat, let alone engage in a discussion about which method of preparation might be best or which establishments were the locals' favorites. The matter was dropped or evaded as soon as it was raised, even by blue-collar types like cabdrivers, whom I assumed would be eager to boast about their enjoyment of it.

We had all but surrendered the idea, as the thought of making a special trip outside Seoul at this late stage in our travels just so that I could taste dogmeat for the first time seemed too bothersome, if not a bit creepy. (My father-in-law had eaten it on several occasions during earlier visits to Korea, usually after a round of golf with a group of men, and expressed a keen interest in doing so again when I first raised my desire to taste it.) Besides, it was not that big of a deal if I abandoned the idea altogether, or so I tried to inwardly rationalize. One did not necessarily have to eat dogmeat in order to write about it, did he?

Of course, from the get-go my wife and mother-in-law never entertained even the remotest possibility of trying it; they simply wanted to be good sports about it and humor the guys who clearly had something to prove. To be honest, the decision to give up on the search came to me entirely as a relief, as the theory of eating dogmeat was far more compelling than the potential practice of it. But just when I thought I was safely out of the woods, there it was, clearly visible through the rain-beaded cab window, right in the heart of Seoul, along a major boulevard, only a couple of blocks from the Ritz Carlton, no less—a bosintang restaurant, its signs prominently placed

Dogmeat restaurant in Seoul, South Korea. The word "bosintang," the most popular dogmeat dish in Korea, appears in large print. Photo by the author.

above and alongside the large wooden entrance for all the world to see. As the cab drove past, we quickly made note of its location and resolved to return for lunch the following day. There were only a couple days left before we returned to the United States, and we were feeling doubly lucky: first, I would finally be able to taste dogmeat for the first time, and second, we would be leaving Korea at the onset of the oppressive monsoon season, at the beginning of the dog days—pardon the pun—of summer.

A week or two later, back home in Binghamton, I confessed to one of my older Korean male colleagues my failure to enjoy dogmeat, of having nearly vomited the few bites I took, when the opportunity finally arrived. He shook his head and got me where it hurt the most when he teased: "That means you're not a true Korean man." That stung. That is to say, *not* being called a dogeater felt like a slur, and it bruised my ego. Outwardly, mostly out of deference and good humor, I agreed with him: "I guess you're right; maybe growing up in America diminished my Korean masculinity." Inwardly, I knew he was wrong. But at that moment, when it mattered most, I could not for the life of me come up with a reason why.

Part III
ARTIFICIAL GASTRONOMY

5 | Monosodium Glutamate

Since the late 1960s (April 4, 1968, to be exact) untold numbers of Americans have loudly and incessantly caviled about bodily discomforts stemming from Chinese food assumed to be juiced with perhaps the most dubious chemical food additive ever discovered—monosodium glutamate, aka MSG. Almost universally, they have taken their anger out on Chinese restaurants. One Chinese American, whose parents operated several restaurants in New York City in the 1970s, called it a nightmarish time. "Not because we used that much MSG—although of course we used some," she said, "but because it meant that Americans came into the restaurant with these suspicious, hostile feelings."[1]

It was during this time that Jonathan Blazon's family opened a Chinese restaurant in the small town of Hooksett, New Hampshire. Within a few years the restaurant was forced to stop adding MSG to its food in order to appease customers who groused about its ill effects. As the only nonwhites in town, Blazon's Chinese American family was used to being treated with some level of disrespect on a regular basis, but "nowhere was this racism more explicit and more vicious than when it was directed at [his family] by white customers in the restaurant," Blazon recalls. Many of Blazon's aunts and uncles "even wondered aloud whether the psychological and emotional damage that they all suffered might not have been so great and so permanent had the family merely lived among whites and had not chosen to serve food to them."[2]

Given that the popularity of Chinese food did not wane during this period—rather, it skyrocketed—these angry and impolite diners evidently complained with just one side of their mouths, as the other side was busy chewing the very food they claimed to revile. Consequently, the "No MSG"

NEW GARDEN

Szechuan • Hunan • Cantonese Cuisine

GETTYSBURG MARKETPLACE
20-44 NATURAL SPRINGS ROAD
GETTYSBURG, PENNSYLVANIA 17325

TEL: (717) 337-9995

OPEN HOURS
Mon. - Sun.: 10:30 am to 10:30 pm

Free Delivery

"No MSG" disclaimer on a take-out menu from a Chinese restaurant in Gettysburg, Pennsylvania.

disavowal, even by establishments that never used MSG to begin with, is now as much a universal feature of Chinese restaurant menus as is General Tso's chicken, pork fried rice, moo goo gai pan, and the cautionary red chile next to dishes deemed too spicy for the average American tongue.

"No MSG"

The rap against MSG is so scathing and universal that it is not unusual for eateries one might not ever think to associate with MSG, such as pizza parlors and sandwich shops, to display the "No MSG" sign. Moreover, the

MSG disclaimer is no longer limited to restaurants, but is also a common feature of grocery store items. This is not only the case with so-called Asian food products, such as chocolate-like blocks of instant Japanese curry roux, but with run-of-the-mill American staples such as canned soups.

In 2008 the two giants of US canned soups, Campbell's and Progresso, engaged in a smash-mouth ad war accusing each other of selling MSG-laden products while disclaiming the same practice. Campbell's fired the opening salvo in September 2008 via a full-color ad in the *New York Times*. The ad featured a picture of a Progresso soup can next to a Campbell's one. The caption "Made with MSG" was blazoned above the Progresso product while the words "Made with TLC" hovered over Campbell's. It did not take long for General Mills, the parent company of Progresso, to fire back with its own ad in the *Times*: "Campbell's has 95 soups made with MSG," it declared, and featured a group photo of each and every dubious Campbell's soup in question. Campbell's quickly responded with an ad that read, "Campbell's proudly offers 124 with *No MSG*." General Mills then released a bold announcement—Progresso will remove MSG from all eighty of its soups. The company challenged Campbell's to do the same. Campbell's replied by reminding the world that it already "proudly offers 124 soups with NO MSG."³

The ad war between Campbell's and Progresso did not go unnoticed by the mainstream media. ABC's *Good Morning America,* Fox News, and many other news outlets, both national and local, covered the dispute. The coverage often involved interviews with so-called MSG experts such as dieticians, physicians, or scientists, who expounded on either the alleged benefits or perils of MSG. So much media attention was given to the debate that Stephen Colbert of Comedy Central's *The Colbert Report* could not resist poking fun at it. In the November 17, 2008, episode, while referring to Progresso's ad that claimed ninety-five different Campbell soups contained MSG, Colbert remarked: "At first, I thought this was a pro-Campbell's ad." Then, referring to Campbell's ad that claimed its soups were made with TLC, he quipped, "They're introducing some kind of tasty new chemical; I'm hoping TLC stands for tetrodotoxin lithium chloride."

As the two companies went back and forth like this with additional ads, the industrial manufacturers of MSG did not see the humor and could not remain on the sidelines as the reputation of its prized product took a savage beating. The Glutamate Association, which, according to its

Stephen Colbert lampooning the ad war between Campbell's and Progresso. Frame enlargement from *The Colbert Report* (2008).

website, "is an association of manufacturers, national marketers, and processed food users of glutamic acid and its salts, principally the flavor enhancer, monosodium glutamate (MSG),"[4] weighed in with a public statement by its president: "It is a disservice to consumers to imply that the inclusion of MSG in canned soup is a detriment, when in fact, the use of MSG in canned soups has long been recognized as a safe, effective way to provide consumers with exactly what they want—a soup that tastes good."[5]

Despite this claim, and no doubt to the Glutamate Association president's great chagrin, MSG had been the bane of serious foodies and a source of headache—literally—for health enthusiasts for quite some time. More significantly, nearly half a century before the soup war, MSG began to become a source of unrelenting bellyaches—not necessarily in the sense of stomach pains (many complain of this too), but of noisy and persistent complaints. Among the thousands of chemical additives currently deployed by the US industrial food complex, MSG is routinely singled out as the embodiment of all that is wrong with the current state of human gastronomy. In effect, the dreaded white crystals have become, at best, a sign of culinary laziness, an ignominious shortcut taken by terrible cooks who generate nothing but cheap, lousy food. At worst, MSG is the epitome of culinary artificiality, of spurious gustation that is no longer limited to "bad" Chinese food and fifty-cent packs of instant ramen.

The makers of Campbell's and Progresso soups, in their attempts to gain a larger market share, resorted to battling each other over their competitor's use of MSG because both companies were fully aware of MSG's dubious reputation as an artificial food additive. To contemporary diners in the United States and increasingly beyond it, MSG is an apocryphal flavoring agent and the antithesis of culinary authenticity at a time when the seemingly unstoppable forces of technology and globalization appear to threaten both the sanctity of indigenous foodways and the integrity of the human food supply. But is it, really? What of the Glutamate Association's assurance that MSG not only makes canned soup taste good but is safe? That said, how are Campbell's and Progresso able to get away with talking, as it were, out of both sides of their mouths? How do they have the temerity to lambaste their main competitor for using MSG when the majority of their own products are awash with the substance? For that matter, what is MSG, anyhow? Whence did it arise and whence did it take on the stigma of dubiousness? Finally, what has Chinese food in the United States got to do with it?

The Birth of MSG

The story of MSG has at least two origins, each replete with its own cast of characters, discrete settings, and surprising turn of events. The protagonist of the first story is the legendary Japanese chemist Kikunae Ikeda. He was a scion of the Satsuma clan, which played a consequential role in introducing Western learning to Japan during the Meiji Restoration.[6] The clan not only promoted the study of science but also of Western culture by forming, for instance, the island nation's first brass band in 1869.[7] Born in Kyoto in 1864, Ikeda is universally recognized as the inventor of MSG and the discoverer of umami, the much-ballyhooed fifth basic taste. Despite its belatedness, and although first met with skepticism by the scientific community, especially in the West, umami now legitimately sits alongside the long-established foursome of sweet, salty, sour, and bitter.

In 1909, based on his investigation conducted a year earlier, Ikeda reported the successful isolation of metallic salts of glutamic acid from a type of kelp the Japanese call *konbu*.[8] The kelp is a class of brown seaweeds, usually in the genus *Laminaria*, of which there are numerous varieties. Common to the reef coasts of Hokkaido and northern Honshu, the highest quality konbu is said to come from the subarctic waters of Rebun Island in Hokkaido, and connoisseurs tend to covet "thick, wide leaves, a dark amber color in the dried product, and a whitish powder encrusting the surface."[9] Shizuo Tsuji, the author of *Japanese Cooking: A Simple Art* and founder of the Tsuji Culinary Institute in Osaka, sees magic in the white powder and warns against washing it away prior to cooking. He notes that the powder, which is essentially glutamate molecules that naturally crystallize during the drying process of konbu, "holds much of the flavor of this seaweed."[10] Harold McGee, meanwhile, simply calls the powder MSG.[11]

While the use of konbu in Japanese cuisine is manifold, its role in the preparation of *dashi*, Japan's indispensable soup stock and seasoning, ranks as the most essential. According to Tsuji, who counted M. F. K. Fisher among his numerous American devotees, dashi "stands figuratively if not literally at the right hand of every Japanese chef." More than any other ingredient, dashi "provides Japanese cuisine with its characteristic flavor, and it can be said without exaggeration that the success or failure (or mediocrity) of a dish is ultimately determined by the flavor and quality of the *dashi* that seasons it." "Making good *dashi*," Tsuji reveals, "is the first secret of the simple art of Japanese cooking."[12]

As with most culinary products, opinions vary as to what constitutes a proper dashi. While recipes and techniques are wide ranging, at its most fundamental dashi is composed of three ingredients: water, konbu, and *katsuobushi*, which is steam-processed bonito (a member of the mackerel family) fillets that have been dried, fermented, and aged to resemble a hard and heavy piece of "driftwood" or, as Naomichi Ishige describes it, "mahogany, so solid that it does not break even if struck with a hammer."[13] The ligneous fillet is shaved with a specially designed plane to form tissue-thin flakes and curls that, as Michael Ashkenazi and Jeanne Jacob put it, "look as if you had been playing rather extensively with a pencil sharpener."[14] The plane, called *katsuobushi kezuriki*, is a wooden rectangular box the size of a tissue box, with a built-in drawer to catch the shavings.

If dashi in fact is the essence of Japanese taste, what Ikeda essentially accomplished in his laboratory was to extract an essence (MSG) out of an essence (dashi). As Bernd Lindemann, Yoko Ogiwara, and Yuzo Ninomiya describe it in "The Discovery of Umami," an article published in 2002 in the journal *Chemical Senses,* Ikeda achieved this through the procedures of aqueous extraction; removal of contaminants such as mannitol, sodium chloride, and potassium chloride; lead precipitation; and numerous other steps of classic preparative chemistry. The final step of low-pressure evaporation culminated in the crystallization of a discrete substance, an amino acid known as glutamic acid, which has the mass formula $C_5H_9NO_4$.[15]

A German chemist, Karl Heinrich Leopold Ritthausen, while studying wheat proteins, first isolated glutamic acid (*Glutaminsäure*) as a pure substance in 1866, but he did not think to link it to a distinct taste. Although not directly analogous, he named glutamic acid after gluten, a major protein found in wheat. Essentially, MSG is the crystalline sodium salt of glutamic acid—hence the "monosodium" prefix. (Glutamic acid is one of twenty or so amino acids that are part of human nutrition; amino acids occur naturally in plants and animal tissues and are together known as the "building block of proteins.") Upon isolating the substance, Ikeda noted that the taste of this double essence was qualitatively different from the established sweet-salty-sour-bitter tetrad and was noticeable not only in the taste of dashi but in meats and cheeses as well.[16]

In one respect, MSG is to the umami taste what granulated sugar is to the sweet taste and table salt to the salty taste. All three are now industrially processed crystalline products that are the embodiments—rather than equivalents—of their respective tastes. Also, all three in their most commonly consumed forms are crystalline white, the color most often assigned to purity. (MSG was not always white, however. It was initially slightly off-white, which its first commercial manufacturer found ways to remedy when consumers appeared put off by the product's brown-gray hue.) But MSG differs from its counterparts in one crucial way: unlike sugar or salt, MSG on its own is considered devoid of taste. If anything, it imparts a slightly bitter taste if applied unadorned to the tongue. This is due to the fact that MSG is not a flavoring agent but a flavor enhancer. Specifically, it enhances and intensifies the taste of umami—but not any of the other four tastes—that is already present in food. But as Ruth Winter, author of *A Consumer's Dictionary of Food Additives,* warns, MSG is not a panacea; it cannot improve the taste of bad food. It does, however, make savory food more savory and meaty foods meatier, provided that it is applied in prudent amounts.[17]

Needing a word to describe the taste enhanced by MSG, Ikeda chose "umami," a term derived from the "colloquial masculine" word in Japanese meaning "tasty," and a term that was already in use during the premodern Edo period, or Tokugawa shogunate, which ran from 1603 to 1868.[18] In fact, umami—a word formed by the combination of the Japanese *umai*, meaning delicious, and *mi*, a suffix that forms abstract nouns from adjectives, akin to the English "-ness"—is a generic term used even by contemporary Japanese to refer to a wide range of foods, regardless of glutamic acid content, considered to have a balanced and appetizing taste. Umami also connotes a taste that is hidden, ineffable, or abstruse, a state of deliciousness that, while undeniably present, evades precise pinpointing. This is particularly true of foods that either have dashi as a foundation, like soups and sauces, or those that are simultaneously meaty and juicy, like a succulent steak. Foods that fall conspicuously outside umami's purview are confections, such as cakes, chocolate, or other dessert-like items. Not all sweet-tasting foods, however, are precluded—a savory dish with a sweet note, say, a fruit-based sauce or glaze, can and often does qualify. Curiously, among beverages, sake wears the description better than beer. A refreshing swig of beer, while appropriately deemed *umai* (tasty), would not fit the expression *umami ga aru* (there exists umami).[19]

Umami appears to have no exact non-Japanese language equivalent; the closest related English terms are "savory" (specifically the contradistinction to sweet), "meaty," and "broth-like." *The Oxford English Dictionary* cites 1971 as the earliest instance of the word's publication in English and defines it as a "category of taste corresponding to the 'savoury' flavor of free glutamates in various foods," a definition that is, at best, only a fraction complete, as numerous other substances beside glutamic acid trigger and enable the umami taste. (More on these other substances shortly.) That said, in 1825 Jean Anthelme Brillat-Savarin employed the term "osmazome" to describe what might have been a closely related precursor to the umami concept. Specifically, the French gastronome described the "sapid"—in contrast to the "extractive"—part of meat that is soluble in cold water. "It is osmazome which gives all their value to good soups," he wrote in *The Physiology of Taste*. It is "osmazome which, as it browns, makes the savory reddish tinge in sauces and the crisp coating on roasted meat." Moreover, it is the "infallible goodness of osmazome" that has led many employers to dismiss cooks who, ignorant of it, were prone to ruin a basic soup stock. He then reminded his readers of the maxim: "that in order to make a good bouillon the pot must only *smile* with heat."[20]

For all intents and purposes, despite its inclusion in both the OED and eighth edition of the *Dictionary of the French Academy,* the word osmazome is all but obsolete today. It appears only on rare occasions when someone notes its appearance in Brillat-Savarin's *Physiology* or (even rarer) in Alexandre Dumas' 1854 novel *Ingénue,* in which a character, during a lavish meal, quotes directly from Brillat-Savarin (without attributing him) when asked about the word's definition. Although the precise origin of osmozome is elusive (the word's source is Greek, formed by combining *osmo-,* meaning odor or scent, with *zomo,* meaning soup, typically made of meat), the earliest published use appears to be 1806 in French and 1814 in English. In both instances, it is terminology from nineteenth-century chemistry, which Brillat-Savarin appropriated essentially to mean superior stock made from animal flesh of a particular sort, "mainly in mature animals with red flesh, blackish flesh, or whatever is meant by well-hung meat, the kind that is never or almost never found in lambs, suckling pigs, pullets, or even in the white meat of the largest fowls"[21] In short, just as Ikeda detected umami in broth made from konbu and katsuobushi, Brillat-Savarin detected an analogous, if not directly related, essence that he called osmozome in broth made from meat—that is to say, in bouillon.[22]

Not so coincidentally, in due course, as the world's foods increasingly began to submit to industrialized processing in and beyond the twentieth century, bouillon and MSG would go on to form an inextricable partnership.

The Umami Taste

From 1899 to 1901 Ikeda studied at Leipzig University in the laboratory of the legendary German chemist Wilhelm Ostwald, who was awarded a Nobel Prize in 1909 in chemistry for his work on "catalysis, chemical equilibria and reaction velocities."[23] According to Jordan Sand, author of "A Short History of MSG: Good Science, Bad Science, and Taste Cultures," Ikeda "shared with his German colleagues a desire to develop a cheap and mass-manufactured source of nutrition."[24] Later in life Ikeda credited an article authored by a Japanese physician named Miyake Hide that linked flavorful foods to healthy digestion as having inspired his desire to remedy the regrettably poor diet of his nation. Only after reading Hide's article did it occur to him that "manufacturing a good, inexpensive seasoning to make bland, nutritious food tasty" might be a way to accomplish this objective.[25]

Of great influence on the work of Ikeda and his German colleagues at Leipzig was Justus von Liebig, generally considered one of the founders of the field of organic chemistry. In 1865, together with the German engineer George Giebert, Liebig founded a company that, at its Uruguayan factory, manufactured the commercial product Liebig's Extract of Meat, which he had invented five years earlier. Advertised as a nutritious supplement for those who could not afford the real thing, the extract—brown and syrupy with a potent beef aroma—was first sold through a physician's prescription. When the medical establishment was slow to vouch for the product's health benefits, Liebig set his sights on Europe's and the United States' domestic market, and women—that is, the home cook—in particular. This proved a financial boon. For those of us today who believe a decent broth is possible without devoting hours over a stockpot or that a respectable soup begins with the opening of a can or unwrapping of a bouillon cube, we have Liebig to thank. In fact, today's bouillon cube—which takes full advantage of MSG's flavoring magic—is a direct descendant of Liebig's extract, as Liebig's company was the originator of one of the earliest commercial bouillon products ever marketed, the OXO brand.[26]

Aside from the meat extract, Liebig's greatest contribution to modern gastronomy is perhaps in the area of culinary lore. Ranking up there with the myths that Catherine de' Medici revolutionized French cooking, that Marco Polo brought back pasta from China, and that medieval Europe used spices to render spoiled meat palatable (all three have been proven untrue) is Liebig's idea that searing meat with high heat "seals in" the juices. (Anyone who has watched a television cooking show has most likely heard this uttered by one cooking instructor or another.) It does not—at least according to science. Rather, it does the opposite, as the crust that forms on the surface of the seared meat is not waterproof, and high heat accelerates the rate of evaporation. Since he first proposed the notion in the 1850s, Liebig's theory has gained popularity among professional chefs and cookbook authors, and no less than the great Auguste Escoffier, considered by many to be the father of modern French cooking, promulgated the idea. Despite being scientifically disproved as early as the 1930s, Liebig's searing myth, in Harold McGee's words, "refuses to die."[27]

On the topic of culinary lore: while he is universally credited as such, to say that Ikeda "discovered" the umami taste is akin to saying that Isaac Newton discovered gravity or Christopher Columbus discovered America. Apples fell from trees long before Newton first become cognizant of the earth's gravitational principles, and millions upon millions inhabited the Americas before Columbus and his crew set sail on the Niña, Pinta, and Santa María. And for millennia prior to Ikeda's isolation of MSG, umami-rich, glutamate-laden foods and ingredients were fundamental to countless cuisines the world over.

A prime example is *garum,* a condiment made of fermented fish, which was foundational to the early Mediterranean diets of the Phoenicians and

Advertisement for Liebig Extract of Meat depicting a housewife using the product in her kitchen (ca. 1890).

Carthaginians as far back as the twelfth century BC. Commonly made of both the flesh and innards of fish mixed with aromatic herbs[28] and left to ferment in brine for months at a time, garum was an industrial operation that centered on Cádiz along the Punic coast. The ancient Greeks also consumed garum, as indicated by Hippocrates' *Diet,* which notes its production in Corinth and Delos prior to its appearance in Carthage and Rome. Archaeological evidence along the coasts of Iberia, Gaul, and Italy, as well as the northern shores of the Black Sea, strongly suggests that garum factories were a conspicuous presence in the Roman Empire.[29] For those interested in re-creating ancient Roman dishes today, Alan Davidson's *The Oxford Companion to Food* suggests substituting garum with fish sauces of Southeast Asia, such as the Vietnamese nuoc mam. Although separated by great geographic and cultural distances, the close culinary approximation of the two products was noted as early as 1822 by the German gastronome and author Karl Rumohr.[30]

Nuoc mam is just one of many fermented fish products ubiquitous to the assorted and wide-ranging cuisines of Southeast Asia. While its origin in the region is debated, its centrality to the region's diets is incontrovertible. Indonesians call fish sauce kecap ikan, the Thais call it nampla, and Filipinos know it as *patis*. And there appears to be an even greater variety of local names for fish paste, including bagoong (Philippines), *belachan* (Malaysia), kapi (Thailand), *ngapi* (Burma), padec (Laos), *prahoc* (Kampuchea), and *trassi* (Indonesia).[31] No matter the name, what these fermented fish products—which could very well include *shottsuru* (Japanese fish sauce), shiokara (Japanese fish paste) and *jeotgal* (Korean fish paste)—provide is a savory-salty taste, functioning essentially as a more complex-tasting, and umami-rich, salt substitute. They are, in this regard, closely related to another salt substitute that is rich in glutamates, namely soy sauce, which was established as a staple of East Asian and Southeast Asian cookery long before Ikeda's lifetime.[32]

In 1913, shortly after Ikeda's breakthrough isolation of glutamic acid in konbu, his disciple Shintaro Kodama identified the nucleotide inosine monophosphate (IMP) in the other dashi ingredient, katsuobushi, as a separate umami source. Since then additional umami triggers and umami synergizers have been discovered, including the nucleotides guanosine monophosphate (GMP) and adenosine monophosphate (AMP), as well as dozens of other substances.[33] Some speculate that the age-old practice of combining foods to make soups, stocks, and sauces might have achieved the desirable amalgam of glutamate and nucleotides, which greatly enhanced the umami taste. Among the more notable examples of this are the French use of meat (or fish) with mirepoix (aromatic vegetables such as onions, carrots, and celery), the Italian combination of tomatoes with cheese (especially Parmesan) or tomatoes with seafood, and the Japanese reliance on konbu and katsuobushi to make dashi.[34]

Like his mentor Leibig, Ikeda's talent as a chemist was equal only to his instincts as an entrepreneur. Immediately following his discovery of MSG, he acquired a patent for it and approached the newly established Suzuki Company, an iodine manufacturer based in Tokyo, to discuss a possible commercial venture.[35] Suzuki did not hesitate. It obtained a joint share of the patent and registered a trademark for the first brand-name MSG: Ajinomoto, a vernacular Japanese phrase meaning the "origin" or "foundation" (*moto*) of "taste" (*aji*). Only a year or so after its discovery, MSG was officially a commercial product with the launch of Ajinomoto on May 20, 1909.[36]

"Ajinomoto" was not the first name considered for the product, however. Suzuki first called it Misei, which proved unsuccessful.[37] Although rooted in the same Chinese characters, the two names had entirely different connotations. Whereas "Misei," due to its amorphous meaning, sounded ungainly to the Japanese ear, "Ajinomoto" suggested exactly what

An early Ajinomoto bottle (ca. 1909).

Ikeda and Suzuki wanted to convey—science, modernity, purity, and, most of all, deliciousness.[38]

The Chemical Miracle

The prevailing conventional wisdom of contemporary food discourse is that the food of today is a mere shadow of what it once was. Nostalgia is the sentiment of the moment, as one food writer after another laments the sorry state of our industrial and postindustrial gastronomy. Not only is the food most of us consume on a daily basis potentially toxic and pathogenic, but it also lacks depth of flavor and vitality of taste—or so we are told. As chronicled in *Food, Inc.*, Robert Kenner's 2008 documentary film, the pristine countenance of the grocery-store tomato—uniformly red, available year round, and still attached to the vine—belies the fact that it is typically grown in another country, harvested while green, ripened with ethylene gas, and merely approximates the taste of a proper tomato.[39] Hit the rewind button on a shrink-wrapped lump of bone- and sinew-less rib eye and it is not Old MacDonald's farm where we end up, but an assembly line of blood, death, and sharpened steel in factories run by giant, multinational corporations. For the sake of maximum profit, these modern meat factories substitute the natural grass diet of cattle with grain feeds, which, while cheaper to administer, not only render the ruminants' multicompartmental stomachs irrelevant and create an optimal breeding ground for harmful bacteria like *E. coli* O157:H7, but also result in bland-tasting cuts of meat. Diners who desire the full flavor of yesteryear must therefore turn to the farmer's market for organic heirloom tomatoes and boutique ranches for grass-fed beef—if you have the wherewithal to do so, that is. Despite Alice Waters' contention that the higher cost of organic produce and meats is justified because she feels she is "making a donation"[40] to small-scale farms and ranches, to most consumers who do not have the luxury of living within the loamy environment of Berkeley, or walking distance of the San Luis Obispo farmer's market, or even driving distance of a Whole Foods Market, these counter-mainstream foodstuffs are neither affordable nor sustainable, neither procurable nor desirable.

Large-scale factory farming of plants and animals is only one of several features that define the industrial and postindustrial foodscape typified by much of the United States, the United Kingdom, Australia, and, to a lesser degree, many European and Asian countries. Another important feature is the tireless pursuit of convenience in the form of ready-made foods. Often canned, frozen, highly processed, and chock full of chemical additives, these foods are designed first and foremost for profit and a long shelf life but peddled to the public as healthy and tasty. For the most part consumers do not care to dwell too deeply on this subject. Given the choice, we would rather not know or be reminded where our meals really come from. What we desire instead is what *Food, Inc.* calls the "spinning of the pastoral fantasy": although the foods we consume are increasingly a product of industrial factories, we pretend that our meals are still a product of Arcadia, of idyllic agrarianism, of small family farms that little children see pictures of in their cardboard books. The food industry deliberately drops a veil between us and the truth of where our meals come from, argues the film, because if we knew the truth, we might be too disgusted to eat their products.[41]

But even among those of us who believe ourselves to be enlightened, most would rather—to borrow a term from the Czech novelist Milan Kundera—willfully forget. "The will to forget is very different from a simple temptation to deceive," writes Kundera in *The Art of the Novel*, and adds that forgetting is "absolute injustice and absolute solace at the same time."[42] In other words, gastronomically speaking, it is far better to be in denial, to willingly acquiesce to false consciousness, than to have our appetites ruined. Recall that in the 1999 film *The Matrix*, when given the choice between staying loyal to his flesh-and-blood human comrades or dining on a big, fat, computer-simulated steak, Cypher, played by Joe Pantoliano, chooses the umami-rich steak.

While much has changed since the early days of our hunter-gatherer primogenitors, one thing has not: our food is composed of organic matter that is biologically volatile and unstable. Inherent enzymes that might benefit us by ripening fruit such as peaches or avocados after picking can also be detrimental by bringing about spoilage and rancidity. Yeasts and molds, useful in production of breads, beer, cheese, and tempeh, if left unchecked, release enzymes that render food toxic to humans. Bacteria can also act as either friend or foe, depending on whether we recruit microorganisms such as *Lactobacillus* to aid in the production of yogurt, butter, sauerkraut, olives, salami, and kimchi, or allow harmful varieties like

Salmonella to prevail.⁴³ But food spoilage need not necessarily involve microbes; mere contact with the air we breathe is enough to deteriorate our viands via chemical and biochemical reactions of oxidation.⁴⁴

Thus the history of food preparation is inseparable from the history of food preservation. Along with harnessing the power of fire, which not only makes food more palatable but provisionally safe by denaturing enzymes, humans have, over the millennia, devised myriad preservation methods through an endless cycle of trial and error. Primitive methods in northern climates, where winters equated to scarcity of food, included the slaughtering of livestock, game, or fish prior to the onset of winter and preserving the meat and organs by drying, salting, smoking, and fermenting. The lean months of winter were also offset by fruits and vegetables preserved via pickling and sugaring. Methods in the tropics, meanwhile, employed similar preservation strategies to deal not with the cold of winter but the excess of year-round heat. To these sure-fire, time-tested preservation methods, recent history has added canning, refrigeration, freezing, and irradiation.⁴⁵

Modern convenience, however, comes at a higher cost than what shows up on the grocery bill. Today, industrial food manufacturers have at their disposal an estimated three thousand additives they can add to their products in order to slow down the inevitable.⁴⁶ Like it or not, given the current state of food production, these additives are indispensable—not because they add nutritional value to foods (they do not), but because, as Ruth Winter puts it, "they feed our illusions." In effect, these chemicals make our industrial and postindustrial lifestyles possible by placing at our easy disposal foods that are cheap, convenient, visually pleasant, tasty, and resistant to early decay. The food industry thus fulfills our desire by, for example, dyeing the skin of oranges to make it more orange, feeding poultry a chemical to make the meat seem less pallid, and applying a slew of antispoilants such as fungicides, pesticides, and herbicides to fruit and vegetables to square them with our mental image of what unblemished produce ought to look like.⁴⁷

All told, the chemicals added to our foods are used as anticaking and free-flowing agents, antimicrobial agents or preservatives, antioxidants, coloring agents, curing and pickling agents, dough strengtheners, drying agents, emulsifiers, enzymes, firming agents, flavor enhancers, flavoring agents and adjuvants, flour-treating agents, formulation aids, humectants, leavening agents, lubricants and release agents, nonnutritive sweeteners, nutrient supplements, nutritive sweeteners, oxidizing and reducing agents, pH control agents, processing aids, propellants and aerating agents, solvents and vehicles, stabilizers and thickeners, surface-active agents, surface-finishing agents, synergists, texturizers, and yeast foods.[48] Ironically, the price of food skyrockets when no additives are added. The cost of unbleached flour is quadruple that of bleached, untreated tomatoes quintuple of canned, and unsulfured raisins six times more than treated ones. A typical loaf of supermarket bread contains up to sixteen "embalming agents" to keep it not only seemingly "fresh,"[49] but implausibly cheap. The iconic Wonder Classic White Bread, for example, lists the following ingredients that help to keep the product "fresh" and "soft" over an extended shelf life: calcium sulphate, vinegar, monoglyceride, dough conditioners (which include sodium stearoyl lactylate and calcium dioxide), diammonium phosphate, dicalcium phosphate, monocalcium phosphate, ammonium sulfate, and calcium propionate.[50]

Among the innumerable types of food additives that exist, the industry pays the greatest heed to flavoring agents and flavor enhancers. This is because an inevitable outcome of modern industrial food processing—that is, freezing, canning, pasteurizing—is destruction of flavor. (It is worth noting that the venerable preservation methods of yore, such as salting, sugaring, drying, smoking, and fermenting, intensified and in many instances improved flavors.) When it comes right down to it, given the choice, most people would rather spend their hard-earned money on foods that are tasty and cheap over those deemed healthy or beneficial to the environment. Although this may appear to be a false choice to a professional chef or serious home cook, in the world of industrial food production, matters of profit, health, and ecology are mutually exclusive.

Of the three thousand industrial food additives mentioned earlier, two thousand are flavoring agents, which is a rapidly growing market that approached $1.5 billion in 2006.[51] While some of these flavorings are considered "natural," such as fruit extracts, most—like anisyl phenylacetate (honey flavor), ethyl methylphenylglycidate (apple flavor), vanillin (vanilla flavor), and countless others—are synthetic products cooked up by enterprising chemists, geneticists, and other scientists. Eric Schlosser, of *Fast Food Nation* fame, reveals that the flavor manufacturing industry is "highly secretive" and will not "divulge precise formulas of flavor compounds or the identities of clients." What we do know is that each year in the United States some ten thousand new processed food products enter the market, and nearly all of them contain flavor additives. The cost of these additives is surprisingly low, often less than a product's packaging. A typical soft drink, for instance, contains a much higher percentage of flavor additives than most other products, but the cost of these additives amount to about half a cent in a twelve-ounce can of Coke.[52]

What might be an unlikely contributing factor to the escalation of flavor additives in the US food supply is the particular nature of immigration since 1965, which has diversified the American palate. This is not to imply, however, that the American foodscape prior to this time was in any way homogenous, monotonous, or insipid. The different regions of the country, due to a combination of wide environmental variations, settlement patterns of differing groups, and particular combinations of culinary fusion, gave rise to multifarious diets. Consider, for instance, as Sidney Mintz reminds us in *Tasting Food, Tasting Freedom: Excursions into Eating, Power, and the Past*, the broad culinary eclecticism of "the Southwest versus the Gulf Coast versus New England versus the Northwest Pacific."[53] Consider also the remarkable diversity of Louisiana Creole, Pennsylvania Dutch, and Tex-Mex, to merely scratch the surface. However, due to the rapid escalation of immigrants arriving from all over the world after 1965, and from Asia, Latin America, and the Caribbean in particular, the range of foods and flavor profiles Americans have access to today and can arguably call their own is dizzyingly heterogeneous.

Mintz observes that most middle-class Americans with some college education and familiarity with travel and eating out are generally open to new culinary experiences.[54] This is increasingly true even for those who do not fit Mintz's bourgeois demographic. In recent years consumers of all socioeconomic profiles, particularly those in urban areas, have learned about a United Nations of food (even if their knowledge is limited to one or two representational items per cuisine), including Japanese (sushi, tempura), Thai (pad Thai), Spanish (paella), Korean (*galbi*, kimchi), Lebanese (hummus, tabbouleh), Indian (curry, tandoori chicken), Vietnamese (*phở*), Cuban (Cuban sandwich), Ethiopian (injera, *doro wat*), Persian (*shireen polow, chelow kabab*), Moroccan (couscous, *tagine*), Greek (*tzatziki*, moussaka), and Turkish (*döner, dolma*). And it is no longer sufficient for mainstream supermarkets to carry a scant selection of goods. For instance, in the fresh produce section, more and more consumers expect to find a medley of leafy vegetables—not just iceberg, romaine, and spinach, but also chicory, radicchio, butterhead, escarole, watercress, and sorrel. They anticipate finding not just plain white cabbage and broccoli, but bok choy, kohlrabi, kale, and green cauliflower, among other brassicas. The same is true for mushrooms (not just button but shiitake, chanterelle, oyster, porcini, and morel), tropical fruits (not just bananas but prickly pears, mangos, kiwis, papayas, lychees, carambolas, and quinces), and herbs (not just curly parsley, rosemary, and thyme, but flat-leaf parsley, chervil, tarragon, cilantro, and culantro). Furthermore, Americans demand a wider array of spices to titillate their tongues. The diversification of American gastronomy requires the salt and pepper shaker atop the dinner table to make room for spices and spice mixtures once deemed foreign, if deemed at all: fenugreek, saffron, star anise, cardamom, Chinese five-spice, *garam masala,* and an astonishing variety of dried and powdered chiles from around the world.

What we have witnessed over the past fifty years, in other words, is the collision of the world's people and their varied diets with the inevitable industrial-level mass-production of these peoples' representational foods and flavors. Thus as "the popularity of ethnic-type foods continues to grow and diversify," posits Winter, "so do the new flavorings added to foods."[55] Today it is the chemist, more so than the spice merchant, farmer, or rancher, who is charged with injecting flavor into our foods, whether they be the "authentic" flavors of Mexico, Italy, Thailand, Lebanon, Spain, India, or, such is the case here, China. Viewed through this unsparing lens, MSG is but a drop in an ocean of chemicals, which leads to this question: why all the fuss over MSG? And, more significantly, why the all fuss over MSG in Chinese food?

The Myth of the Chinese Restaurant Syndrome

If the Japanese scientist Kikunae Ikeda, our intrepid discoverer of MSG, is the protagonist of the first story of MSG's origins, then Robert Ho Man Kwok, a Chinese American physician, certainly qualifies as the central character of the second story. It was he who wrote the letter that launched a thousand theories, conjectures, and complaints about the ill effects of MSG on the human body, mind, and soul. In a letter published in the April 4, 1968, issue of the *New England Journal of Medicine,* Kwok described "a strange syndrome" that usually began fifteen to twenty minutes after eating the first dish at a "Northern" Chinese restaurant and lasting for about two hours. (Reputedly, Kwok was a southern Chinese.)[56] Although the syndrome had no "hangover effect," the symptoms consisted of "numbness at the back of the neck, gradually radiating to both arms and the back, general weakness, and palpitation." When he heard similar complaints from his Chinese friends (all "well educated," he noted), they convened and narrowed the possible causes down to a few ingredients: soy sauce, cooking wine, MSG, and salt. Without offering a conclusive answer of his own, Kwok ended the letter by calling for the medical community to seek "more information about this rather peculiar syndrome."[57]

Thus was birthed the "Chinese restaurant syndrome," not because Kwok strung those three words together himself (he did not), but because the journal editors gave his letter that title. What followed in the journal's May 16 issue was a slew of responses by readers who recounted their own experiences with the syndrome. While some merely echoed Kwok's list of symptoms, many others added to what was quickly becoming an impossibly diverse inventory of ailments described in varying degrees of medical argot: a tightening of "masseter and temporalis muscles, lacrimation, periorbital fasciculation, numbness of the neck and hands, palpitation and syncope"; "severe aching in the muscles down both sides of the back of the neck and spread into the shoulders, shoulder blades and upper spine"; "profuse, cold sweat about the face and under the armpits"; "pounding, throbbing sensation in the head, vice-like in quality, but without real pain"; "palpitations and numbness above the diaphragm," and so forth. Among the letters was a particularly punctilious, if not pleonastic, enumeration by a Yale University gastroenterologist: "tightening of the face"; "unilateral numbness, usually intensified near the zygoma"; "weakness of the mouth" (but chewing unimpaired); a "sensation of dizziness"; "flushing and sweating"; "bandlike headache with orbital pain"; "facial anesthesia that often crossed the dermatome midline pattern"; "sinus tachycardia to a rate of 100"; "mild facial and cervical flushing"; "intense, heavy aching" in "biceps and triceps"; "extreme fatigue" in "the shoulder girdle"; "weakness of the muscles of mastication"; and "paresthesia and weakness in the upper extremities intense enough to suggest paralysis." Another letter simply called the ailment "our Chinese headache" that the writer eventually learned to accept as a customary "side dish" of a Chinese meal.[58]

Kwok's responders also speculated as to the precise component of the Chinese meal responsible for the syndrome. Along with the items previously suspected by Kwok, the growing list now included duck sauce, Chinese tea, imported mushrooms, frozen Chinese vegetables, and other potential "vasoconstrictor" substances. Curiously, what was conspicuously absent from the readers' list was MSG, which is mentioned just once in a single letter but is immediately ruled out as the cause since the writer used it (and soy sauce) at home with no ill effect. Meanwhile, an Atlanta doctor speculated that Kwok might have unwittingly ingested a potentially fatal Japanese delicacy, the puffer fish, which contains a potent neurotoxin that produces symptoms identical to those described by Kwok. (How Kwok might have accidentally eaten this in a Chinese restaurant the Atlanta doctor does not say.) Claiming that Captain James Cook unwittingly consumed the fish, to his great discomfort, during a 1774 voyage to New Caledonia, the letter writer urged Kwok to determine "the source of fish products in exotic foods." The writer also suggested, quite earnestly, that the Chinese restaurant syndrome be renamed either the "Japanese restaurant syndrome" or "Cook's syndrome."[59]

It was evident, even to the editors of the *New England Journal of Medicine,* that any uneasy feeling, both real and imagined, after a Chinese meal was being submitted as evidence of the Chinese restaurant syndrome and that there was something distinctly irrational, if not absurd, about the frenzied reaction to Kwok's letter. In jest, the journal offered an alternate name for the syndrome, one with an exaggeratedly specialized tone: "Post-Sino-Cibal Syndrome," or "sin-cib-syn" for short. "The threat of sin-cib-syn," quipped the editors, "according to the annals of anecdotal epidemiology, extends from California to New Hampshire; Hawaii and London as yet are not uninvolved." They noted that all the races—"Jew, Indian, WASP, no less than full Chinese"—appeared to be at risk and described the victims as at long last relieved at the public airing of the issue, as "their cries now reach co-tinglers' ears, and rehabilitated they stand, free of the charge of 'crock.' "[60]

Despite the teasing, the afflicted remained undeterred, and the letters kept pouring in. Less than two months later, in the July 11 issue, noting that Kwok's letter "has uncovered a legion of hitherto silent sufferers," the journal published three additional responses, along with an encapsulating summary of untold numbers of others that suggested as the causal agent everything from mustard, bean sprouts, and "Tit Goon Yum" (a type of tea) to muscarine (a poisonous compound found in some fungi), potassium depletion, and "myopathy of the facial and neck muscles induced when Westerners try to eat with chopsticks."[61] In keeping with the lighthearted tone taken by the editors, one of the three published letters professed incredulity at the whole affair and accused the journal of inventing Dr. Ho Man Kwok, noting the name's similarity to "Dr. Human Crock," and denounced the syndrome as "totally illusionary and nonexistent, except in the minds of readers who replied."[62]

For most of those who wrote in, however, the perils of Chinese food were no laughing matter. Indubitably, this was the moment when the unmitigated coupling of MSG to the Chinese restaurant syndrome was forevermore established. The two remaining letters in the July 11 issue were from separate teams of researchers, one from Albert Einstein College of Medicine and the other from New York University of Medicine, each claiming to have conducted carefully crafted experiments that strongly, if not conclusively, implicated MSG. The Einstein College team, headed by Herbert Schaumburg, asserted that "the dagger of suspicion" pointed at MSG and that further experiments confirmed this. (Ironically, it was Schaumburg who had previously ruled out MSG and soy sauce as the cause of the syndrome in his May 16 letter to the journal.) The team, however, cautioned that theirs was not the last word and that further experiments were currently in progress. The NYU team, meanwhile, did not prevaricate, announcing that Kwok's symptoms were "definitely" the result of MSG in Chinese food. They noted that Chinese cooks varied considerably in how liberally they used the chemical seasoning and referred to one family that had, though trial and error, "composed a list of 'safe' Chinese restaurants in town and a list of those that must be avoided." The team also vowed to conduct follow-up studies and bemoaned the absence of the matter in medical literature to date.[63]

This absence would be remedied on February 21, 1969—the moment the Chinese restaurant syndrome at last gained legitimacy as a documented medical condition, which would result in MSG becoming among the most scientifically scrutinized food additives ever invented. On this date the journal *Science* published the findings of a double-blind experiment conducted by a team of researchers headed by Herbert Schaumburg—the same Schaumburg whose letters had been twice published by the *New England Journal of Medicine* the previous year. The team's study presented two conclusions, one explicit and the other implicit. The explicit conclusion was that MSG was not "a wholly innocuous substance" and that "the Chinese restaurant syndrome was caused by MSG." The team reported that wonton soup that contained MSG repeatedly induced "burning, facial pressure, and chest pains" in human subjects while the soup prepared without MSG did not provoke an attack.[64]

The other, implicit conclusion, however, was not only more consequential, but altogether unforeseen despite being, if only in retrospect, glaringly self-evident. Given that the substance in question was MSG and not Chinese food per se (recall that the participants of Schaumburg's experiment were given wonton soup either with or without MSG and not, say, Campbell's chicken noodle soup), should it have mattered whether the mode of delivery was wonton soup or any other item on a Chinese restaurant menu? If there was indeed demonstrable proof linking MSG to determinable bodily discomforts, theoretically any food laced with MSG, regardless of its ethnic affiliation, should bring on symptoms of the Chinese restaurant syndrome, should it not? In fact, Schaumburg's team began their article by characterizing MSG as a food additive widely produced and consumed in the United States. Presumably, Chinese restaurants were not the only ones using the substance at that time. As such, the study failed to answer, let alone pose, a crucial question. In the words of Ian Mosby, "if a food product already in common use could quite easily trigger such a recognizable physiological reaction, why had the syndrome not been identified earlier?"[65] That is to say, why the deafening silence from the legions of sufferers prior to the publication of Kwok's letter?

This question is consequential and far reaching because of a simple fact: by the late 1960s the American food supply was already awash with the flavor-enhancing magic of MSG. In fact, from the mid-1930s until the Japanese attack on Pearl Harbor, the United States was the third largest purchaser of Ajinomoto in the world after Japan and Taiwan.[66] During much of the first half of the twentieth century the Ajinomoto brand dominated the MSG markets of Japan's East Asian colonies, including Taiwan, China, Korea, and Manchuria in a phenomenon that Keun-Sik Jung, author of "Colonial Modernity and the Social History of Chemical Seasoning in Korea," labels an "empire of taste." "The modernization of market under Japanese colonization," he writes, "comprises problems such as devices to generate new desires, experience of materialistic culture inherent in people, or the progression of unrealized desires." In terms of culinary culture, this meant not only the revamping of nutrition and table manners but the modernization of taste. Jung argues that the taste of modernity, reified as the Ajinomoto brand, was propelled across multiple national boundaries by the Japanese, who brought a commodified version of umami along on their empire-building missions across East Asia.[67]

In the colony of Taiwan, with its accompanying connotations of modernity and the "rhetoric of hygiene and efficiency," Ajinomoto was so firmly embraced by people of all classes that today the country leads the world in per capita consumption of MSG.[68] In South Korea, although the Ajinomoto monopoly vacated its markets after the country's liberation, the memory of and desire for MSG remained in the people's subconscious. When MSG was suddenly unavailable after nearly a half-century's presence on the peninsula, the Korean taste receptors collectively experienced withdrawal symptoms. The addictive power of MSG, introduced by Japanese colonialism, could not be actualized until it reemerged in the 1960s and 1970s with the establishment of domestic manufacturers, namely the Miwon and Mipung brands, both of which emulated and rehashed the advertising strategies pioneered by Ajinomoto during the colonial period.[69]

It was during this prewar period that the United States started down the road to its own MSG addiction. According to Jordan Sand there were two chief sources for the American demand of MSG in the 1930s: the first was the US military-industrial complex, which, taking its cue from the gustatory lesson observed by the Japanese military, acted on the understanding that "flavorless rations can undermine morale as quickly as any other single factor in military life." The second was American canned food companies, Campbell's Soup in particular, that "recognized the capacity of MSG to make bland, inexpensive foods flavorful."[70] Thus by the late 1960s US production of MSG was already in full swing as domestic manufacturers produced some sixty tons of it each year. Also by then, Ac'cent, the foremost American brand, had been in business for more than twenty years.[71]

In his discussion of the state of US gastronomy in the decades immediately following the end of World War II, Harvey Levenstein, author of *Paradox of Plenty: A Social History of Eating in Modern America,* places "the relentless pursuit of convenience" at the forefront. The nation's economic boom during this time paved the way for the unprecedented rise of the middle class. This, however, did not translate into the liberation of American women from their prescribed roles as stewards of family food preparation. Indeed, they were fettered more tightly than ever to the kitchen, a prevailing condition that was promoted and celebrated by magazines such as *Good Housekeeping, McCall's, Better Home and Gardens,* and *House Beautiful,* as well as TV shows like *Father Knows Best, Ozzie and Harriet,* and *The Honeymooners.*[72] Not surprisingly, the nation's major food and appliance manufacturers were quick to capitalize on what Betty Freidan would later label "The Feminine Mystique," the myth that postwar, middle-class American women's happiness was to be found not in professional fulfillment but in housework.[73]

During this period the rapidly expanding convenient-food sector directed its advertising apparatus squarely at the new American housewife, tempting her with a message that she found irresistible and the industry found profitable: why labor in the kitchen alone when America's food companies were there to lend a helping hand—or to use a more apt metaphor, meet her half way—in the form of ready-to-serve canned and frozen foods that the entire family could delight in? Thus was ushered in the "Golden Age for American food chemistry," a period that Levenstein finds synonymous with the "Golden Era of Food Processing." Fully aware that the consequences of mass production of food included not only compromised texture and appearance, but also the loss of flavor, the food industry turned to chemists and their twentieth-century powers of alchemy. The chemists would not disappoint, as they delivered exactly what everyone—maker, seller, and buyer—hankered for in food: enduring shelf life, unblemished visual appeal, affordability, and the reclamation of robust flavors associated with a fleeting past.[74]

The Stigma of MSG and the Triumph of Umami

Perhaps it was mere happenstance that the period in which MSG spread like wildfire across the processed food industry dovetailed with the proliferation of Chinese restaurants in the United States. Regardless, both managed to administer large doses of Ikeda's invention into the foods of all Americans, regardless of race, gender, class, or dietary fastidiousness. So the question remains: why was it that, for so long, only Chinese restaurants were blamed for the supposedly toxic repercussions of MSG?

In addressing this question, Ian Mosby, whose 2009 *Social History of Medicine* article, "'That Won-Ton Soup Headache': The Chinese Restaurant Syndrome, MSG and the Making of American Food, 1968–1980," is the best critical treatment of the subject to date, offers an explanation that is singularly persuasive. "Many of the basic assumptions about the Chinese restaurant syndrome," he argues, "were, at core, the product of a racialized discourse that framed much of the scientific, medical and popular discussions surrounding the condition." He buoys his argument with the works of scholars such as Nyan Shah and Susan Craddock, whose studies show how turn-of-the-twentieth-century San Francisco's Chinatown, identified as the source of disease and moral turpitude, was the target of "overtly racist laws and restrictions" that unabashedly exempted residents of white neighborhoods.[75]

From the late 1960s until well into the 1990s the majority of medical professionals and scientists, while making an awful din over MSG-laden Chinese fare, rarely uttered a peep about "American foods" that also contained MSG, such as cans of Campbell's soup that no doubt sat demurely in the pantries of their very homes. It is telling that over the same period of time that the *New England Journal of Medicine* published Kwok's and his responders' letters, the Campbell's Soup Company purchased a number of full-page color ads in the same journal touting the health benefits of its product. Placed amid ads for Keflin (sodium cephalothin), Surfak (dioctyl calcium sulfosuccinate), Ritalin (methylphenidate), and other pharmaceuticals, the Campbell's ads directly exhorted physicians, the journal's primary audience, to recommend Campbell's soup to their patients—"there's a soup for almost every patient and diet," boasted the copy—as well as to enjoy it themselves. Curiously, there were no letters of protest about the dangers of "Campbell's soup syndrome" published in the journal.

The sudden, unforeseen appearance of Kwok's letter and subsequent ballyhoo that followed "brought to the surface and, in a way, granted a renewed medical legitimacy to a number of long-held assumptions about the strangely 'exotic', 'bizarre' and 'excessive' practices associated with Chinese culture," posits Mosby.[76] The Chinese restaurant syndrome was, from the beginning, a creation of the medical profession, and the fact that its merits were first debated in the *New England Journal of Medicine,* the most prestigious of its kind in America, gave the syndrome automatic legitimacy, which the popular media wasted little time promulgating far and wide. On May 19, 1968, just three days after the publication of the first set of responses to Kwok's letter, the *New York Times* ran the first journalistic account of the Chinese restaurant syndrome. This would be followed over the next several years by dozens of others that in one way or another referenced the syndrome as a legitimate medical condition. The fact that no

Let's be specific about Campbell's Soups... and *prenatal diets*

CAMPBELL'S SOUPS IN PRENATAL DIETS*				
Soup	Calories	Protein gm.	Vit. A I.U.	Iron mg.
Beef	87	8.0	1067	0.9
Chicken Gumbo	49	2.2	179	0.6
Chicken with Rice	43	2.8	—	0.3
Consommé	28	4.7	—	0.7
Tomato	89	1.4	946	0.9
Vegetable Beef	91	6.0	2236	0.9
Vegetable	62	2.8	1945	0.9

*Average 7 oz. serving prepared with water according to label direction.
Nutritive analyses of all our soups are available for your convenience in planning diets. For your copy, write to Campbell Soup Company, Dept. 223, Camden, N.J. 08101.

Almost every one of the 4 million American women who will become pregnant this year could benefit from a physician's advice to include soup in their dietary regimens.

Soups are nourishing; they provide a wide variety of essential nutrients; and, above all, they are tasty and quickly prepared. But, even more importantly, soups can help provide additional nourishment without adding too many calories to the diet.

More than 20 of Campbell's Soups contain less than 75 calories in an average 7 oz. serving; nine contain over 3 gm. of protein; and 8 provide over 2,000 I.U. of vitamin A.

Recommend Campbell's Soups to your patients...and, of course, enjoy them yourself. Remember, there's a soup for almost every patient and diet...for every meal.

Advertisement for Campbell's soups that appeared in the April 25, 1968, edition of the *New England Journal of Medicine*. The ad boasted the soups' health benefits and urged physicians to recommend them to their patients.

one—not the journalists nor medical and science professionals—thought to scrutinize the supposed "Chineseness" of Chinese restaurant syndrome made it virtually certain that the general public did not as well. For Mosby, therefore, "the persisting strength of the association between Chinese cuisine and adverse reactions to the common additive MSG provides a lens into the ways in which, despite these larger changes in the American society, certain fears of a Chinese-American 'other' remained part of the popular imagination."[77]

Jeffrey Steingarten once famously asked, "Why Doesn't Everybody in China Have a Headache?" If MSG-laden Chinese food is the enormous bane of American diners as the mountain of anecdotal accounts makes it out to be, why was there no one in, say, Shanghai, "the largest Chinese settlement in the world," with a headache, despite the abundance of MSG on "practically every street corner"? He answered his own question by calling the complainers "psychologically troubled," "hypochondriacs," "crybabies," and sufferers of "phony food allergies and intolerances." To this he even included the "hapless 1 percent" who had been shown to legitimately develop symptoms "after consuming an oral dose of at least *three grams in the absence of food.*"[78] In other words, MSG-induced syndromes, including the Chinese restaurant variety, are not merely greatly exaggerated but are entirely fabricated.

To the dismay and disbelief of the unswayed multitude, Steingarten's proposition appears to be the current scientific consensus. Among those aboard Steingarten's bandwagon is Matthew Freeman, who, after reviewing forty years' worth of clinical trials beginning with the very first by Schaumburg's team, determined that there was no consistent link between "the assumption of MSG and the constellation of symptoms that comprise the syndrome." As a certified nurse practitioner writing for the *Journal of the American Academy of Nurse Practitioners,* Freeman thus advises his colleagues not to automatically assume MSG is the culprit when patients come to them complaining of symptoms such as headaches, migraines, and asthma after a Chinese meal. Noting that "MSG is not likely to be the cause of these symptoms," Freeman urges his fellow nurse practitioners to instead "concentrate their efforts on advising patients on the nutritional pitfalls"—such as high fat and sodium content—"of some Chinese restaurant meals and to seek more consistently documented etiologies for symptoms such as headache, xerostomia, or flushing."[79]

There are some who even suggest that the syndrome might have been a "hoax" from the very start. Given the fact that 43 percent of Americans regularly suffer some sort of bodily discomfort after a meal, MSG loaded or otherwise, one could reasonably conclude that Steingarten's harsh assessment is perhaps not harsh enough.[80] Marion Nestle, a leading voice in the growing demand for accountability of the government and the food industry in ensuring a safe food supply, believes there is "simply no clinical evidence" for the ill effects of MSG. In her voluminous *What to Eat,* a book in which she takes readers on a guided tour through every aisle of the supermarket, Nestle does not mention MSG once while devoting page upon page to the potential perils of everything from meat, margarine, and milk to myriad food additives. "I thought the issue was settled," she says, "though I know a lot of people will never believe that."[81] And add Julia Moskin of the *New York Times* to the growing number of those who now consider MSG a syndrome-benign substance. "Even now, after Chinese restaurant syndrome has been thoroughly debunked," she writes, "the ingredient has a stigma that will not go away."[82]

Then again, neither has MSG gone away. The reputation of MSG, due in large part to its positive association with the umami taste that Kikunae Ikeda discovered more than a century ago, is currently in the midst of a remarkable comeback. Not surprisingly, the MSG industry, and the Ajinomoto Group in particular, has been the most enthusiastic global promoter of the MSG-umami consanguinity. Surpassing even the glory of its East Asian colonial heyday, MSG is now all the rage the world over, from Asia to Latin America and from the United States to Europe. To the shock of many foodies, David Chang, the celebrated chef and proprietor of the Momofuku restaurants in New York City, revealed that he doused his restaurant's lobster roll in Kewpie mayonnaise, which, in his opinion, is the best tasting in the world due to the Japanese brand's MSG content. Meanwhile, other high-end chefs who might be less forgiving of MSG have no qualms about spotlighting umami on their menu. Jean-Georges Vongerichten offers what he calls "umami bombs" to his customers, while Rick Bayless, Daniel Boulud, Nobu Matsuhisa, Mary Sue Milliken and Susan Feniger, Ming Tsai, Norman Van Aken, and Alan Wong have all contributed recipes to a cookbook featuring umami-rich dishes.[83]

The United Kingdom's marmite, Thailand's Golden Mountain sauce, the Caribbean's Goya Sazon, Costa Rica's Salsa Lizano, America's spicy

Ajinomoto for Portuguese consumers. The label indicates that the product is the "essence of umami" and "enhances the flavor without salt."

tuna rolls, Thai noodles, Puerto Rican roast pork, and the Maggi products sold throughout the world are just the tip of the MSG-umami iceberg, with nary a murmur or complaint to show for it. But because there are legions still weary of it in the United States, the MSG industry has found a way to circumvent the policing gaze of the scrupulous label reader. Since the 1970s US food companies have legally cloaked MSG in myriad aliases, including but not limited to hydrolyzed protein, modified enzymes, yeast extracts, autolyzed yeast, soy concentrates, soy isolates, soy proteins, protein isolates, protein concentrates, natural flavors, natural flavorings, vegetable broth, and chicken broth.

This cloaking of MSG in different nomenclatural garbs took on an almost comic—if not Orwellian—feel during the ad war between Campbell's and Progresso soups discussed at the beginning of this chapter. In what can only be described as an inordinately cynical move on the parts of both parties, an asterisk accompanies every printed claim of non-MSG use in either company's products (e.g., the claim that Campbell's offers 124 soups without MSG and that Progresso will cease using MSG in all of their soups.) Follow the asterisk down to the bottom of the page and a disclaimer of the following sort appears in tiny print: "except that which occurs naturally in yeast extract and vegetable protein." It is perhaps worth repeating here Kundera's notion of willful forgetting, that the "will to forget is very different from a simple temptation to deceive," and that it is "absolute injustice and absolute solace at the same time." The soup companies' disavowal of MSG while cloaking the use of it in government-approved aliases is the ultimate apotheosis of Kundera's notion of willful forgetting served up in a bowl of soup. Yes, twenty-first-century gastronomy is not merely deceptive, but also unjust. It is, however, a solace.

In other words, in the postindustrial age that defines the United States today, the richest source of MSG, and the umami flavor, is no longer the Chinese restaurant—if it ever was to begin with—but your friendly neighborhood supermarket and fast-food outlet. These are foods that most Americans—and others in an increasingly postindustrial world—can no longer live without. Look for it in canned soups, low-fat yogurts and ice cream, McDonald's Sausage McGriddle, cold cuts, Goldfish crackers, onion soup mix, and "virtually everything ranch-flavored or cheese-flavored"—but designated as something other than MSG, of course.[84] But whatever you do, do not look for it for in a Chinese restaurant. The last place you will find MSG today is in a bowl of good, old-fashioned Chinese American wonton soup.

6 | SPAM

I love SPAM. No, not unwanted commercial e-mails but the canned meat product marketed by the Hormel Foods Corporation. Kimchi fried rice, kimchi *jjigae, budae jjigae,* musubi, *gimbap,* instant ramen—versions of these and other dishes laden with SPAM have been a regular part of my diet since childhood. Luckily, anyone curious enough to sample these sorts of dishes without actually having to travel to Hawai'i, where I grew up, can consult Ann Kondo Corum's *Hawaii's SPAM Cookbook.* Published in 1987, the book contains nearly fifty such SPAM-centered recipes. For good measure, Corum, who calls SPAM "Hawaii's soul food" and "king of the canned meats in Hawaii," includes more than forty additional recipes that take culinary advantage of three of the Islands' other favorite canned proteins—corned beef, sardines, and Vienna sausage. Together with SPAM, these potted goods are "a continuing part of local food culture," asserts Corum, and "very much a part of local residents' lives."[1]

In 2002 Corum published a sequel, *Hawaii's 2nd SPAM Cookbook,* which contains more than a hundred new recipes, including those from locally held SPAM cooking contests such as the SPAMARAMA in Honolulu and SPAM cook-offs in Maui.[2] More recently, in 2008, Muriel Miura, author of multiple cookbooks of local Hawai'i food and host of a pair of 1970s television cooking shows, published *Hawai'i Cooks with SPAM,* featuring recipes of more than 130 nouvelle-inspired, beautifully plated and photographed dishes organized along national lines—Chinese, Japanese, Filipino, French, Korean, Portuguese, Italian, Mexican, and so forth. Miura dedicates the book to "all who enjoy SPAM," and especially to her grandchildren, "who enjoy having regular servings of SPAM."[3]

Rachel Laudan, author of *The Food of Paradise: Exploring Hawaii's Culinary Heritage,* believes that to take on SPAM as a matter of discussion "is to pick at the ethnic seams of Hawaii." The culinary use of SPAM is universal to all groups while simultaneously unique to each. Laudan observes that locals of all backgrounds and persuasions "understandably regard SPAM as thrifty and tasty, a food of childhood, a food of family meals and picnics at the beach, a food of convenience." SPAM is the "motherhood-and-apple-pie of Hawaii, not specific to any ethnic group," she writes.[4]

SPAM I Am

Looking back, I cannot recall a time when there were no cans of SPAM in my mother's pantry, and there is rarely a time now when there is not one in my pantry. This is despite the fact that it has been nearly three decades—and some five thousand miles—since I last lived on the Islands. One of my favorite meals to this day is scrambled eggs and SPAM alongside a bowl of steaming rice. This was the default breakfast my perpetually overburdened mother turned to whenever she needed to rush her children out the door to school. (Her children preferred it to cold cereal and milk any day.) And I can think of no better lunch than the Zip Pac from Zippy's, a casual restaurant chain in Hawai'i that is probably more familiar to and beloved by locals than any other eating establishment in the state.[5] The Zip Pac is a supersized bento consisting of a piece of fried chicken (thigh meat), a breaded and fried mahi-mahi fillet, a palm-sized portion of beef teriyaki, and a slice of fried SPAM, all neatly nestled atop a bed of shredded cabbage. The assembly is served alongside a mound of white rice sprinkled with *furikake* and a slice of yellow takuan. Eating it, I usually saved the SPAM until the end, to make it my final, salty bite.

In a June 3, 2011, blog entry titled "The End of Spam Shame" that appeared on the website of *Hyphen,* an Asian American magazine, Sylvie Kim recalls that her childhood was "chock-full of nitrates, sodium, and an amalgam of four-legged animals chopped and cured into uniform cuts of salty goodness that was inexpensive, easy to heat, and lasted for damn near forever—key to a family of five with immigrant parents who were struggling financially."[6] By "salty goodness" she means hot dogs, Vienna sausages, and, above of all, SPAM. Kim writes that her "yen" for the canned meat was "inherited" from her mother, who grew up in impoverished postwar South Korea. Kim, on the other hand, grew up in the American Midwest, "where Asian faces weren't in abundance" and where she experienced a keen sense of shame over her family's reliance on a food product that was "synonymous with poverty or 'trashiness' in American pop culture." It was not until she moved to the San Francisco area, where SPAM musubi was shamelessly devoured by the large concentration of Asian and Pacific Islander Americans that resided there, that Kim was able to once and for all "cast off the onerous chains of Spam shame."[7] Some fifteen years earlier, another Korean American had written a confessional paean of sorts to SPAM. "In the popular imagination, this neatly tinned pink gelatinous substance straddles a gamut of associations from trashiness to status to kitsch," observes Sunyoung Lee in a 1997 essay titled "Spam I Am." But for "someone who, like me, grew up eating the stuff," she adds, "there's a personal consideration as well: Spam tastes good."[8]

I agree with and relate to both Kim and Lee completely. I also grew up with the stuff, and, despite the contradictory array of reputations that precedes it, I also find it delicious. Thus I too am SPAM—and in more ways than one. I trace my roots to Korea, where I was born, and Hawai'i, where I spent my formative years. Not so coincidentally, these two places occupy top spots on the list of the world's largest consumers of SPAM. According to one estimate, while Guam, at more than twelve pounds a year per person, leads in terms of per capita, South Korea is the largest bulk consumer (beyond the United States), accounting for more than ten million pounds and nearly $140 million in sales a year. That Hawai'i ranks first among US states is undisputed and well chronicled. By one count, nearly seven million cans are purchased on the Islands annually, which translates to about six cans—or four and a half pounds—a year for every man, woman, and child. This accounts for roughly 8 percent of all US domestic sales by a population that represents less than .44 percent of the total US population (based on 2010 US Census Bureau figures). Hawai'i residents on average consume several times more than Alaskans, who rank second as the biggest American consumer.[9]

No matter how you slice it, that's a whole lot of . . . what, exactly? SPAM is one of America's great dubious foods, one that epitomizes lamentable dining at a time when gastronomic authenticity is feared to be in decline due to relentless industrialization and globalization of the world's foodways. But while SPAM is widely regarded as vulgar, tacky, and farcical, a sizeable minority knowingly winks at its kitschy spectacle. And while SPAM to some is an affront to the very idea of real or whole food, others believe it to embody discrete indigenous cuisines or, alternatively, a luxury commodity—or simultaneously both. To its detractors, SPAM is less a comestible than a series of bothersome questions: what is it? Is it edible? Is it a joke? To devotees, it is simply delicious.

SPAM is the quintessential "mystery meat," not found at your local butchers but in the netherworld of the industrial food complex. While the hot dog, perhaps the prototypical mystery meat, has successfully shed that appellation to now stand alongside the hamburger as established exemplars of American gastronomy, SPAM has yet to enjoy the same fortune. In fact, it is a safe bet it never will. Long before G-M-Os menaced the American foodscape, S-P-A-M raised the eyebrows of many diners leery of the "Frankenfood" hermetically sealed inside the rectangular blue and yellow can with its distinctive rounded edges.[10]

Many of my friends, colleagues, and casual acquaintances find SPAM laughable. To be more precise, most of my non-Korean, non-Filipino, and those-not-from-Hawai'i peers find it laughable. At best they see SPAM as

A can of SPAM. Hormel first launched the product in 1937.

silly, like Cool Whip or Chicken McNuggets, and at worst as disgusting and otherworldly, like offal or dogmeat. Everyone knows of SPAM, but who has actually tasted it? Who admits to liking it? More important, what does it mean to consider SPAM an inalienable part of one's sense of self? While it exists mainly as an object of snooty condescension and a symbol of culinary unsophistication in most parts of the United States, the product is held in much higher regard elsewhere in the world.

As Ty Matejowsky, author of "SPAM and Fast-food 'Glocalization' in the Philippines," points out, consumers in such disparate settings as Guam, South Korea, the Philippines, and Japan treasure SPAM so much that "Western criticisms of the product are rendered all but irrelevant."[11] In the Philippines SPAM is considered an expensive delicacy, out of reach for most low-income families, but highly desired. Thus most Filipinos receive SPAM as *pasalubong* (homecoming gift) from friends, relatives, and other *balikbayans* (oversea Filipinos) returning home from other countries, where Filipinos by the millions live and work. The popularity of SPAM is so widespread throughout the archipelago that it is enjoyed even in Mindanao, which is predominantly Muslim, although there, diners opt for Turkey SPAM over the traditional pork version. "SPAM's appeal transcends social class so that wealthy, middle-class and working-class Filipinos all regularly consume it," writes Matejowsky, and adds, "That SPAM is viewed more as a dietary staple of the affluent and moderately affluent than that of the poor says a lot about its negotiated meaning outside the West."[12]

In South Korea, SPAM is among the more coveted American food products, equal in popularity to other iconic brands such as Coca-Cola and Kentucky Fried Chicken, but substantially outranking most in terms of status. In upscale department stores sleekly packaged SPAM regularly appears alongside fancy imported liquor and chocolates.[13] But this does not mean the product is beyond the reach of average consumers. Reportedly, SPAM represents over 50 percent of South Korea's entire canned food market, and the gifting of SPAM has become a megatrend during Chuseok, a three-day holiday held each year around the autumn equinox to celebrate the harvest.[14] As George H. Lewis notes in "From Minnesota Fat to Seoul Food: Spam in America and the Pacific Rim," SPAM for Koreans is a gift that reflects not only status but respect—"a far cry, indeed, from how it is viewed in America, its country of origin."[15]

The image of SPAM as an upscale, urbane product is evident in a pair of recent South Korean television commercials. In the first, the popular

SPAM has become a popular gift during the Korean holiday Chuseok.

leading actor Rae Won Kim, fresh off his role as a professional chef in the television drama *Shikgaek* (Gourmet), is in a gleaming new kitchen flamboyantly preparing elaborate dishes such as SPAM salad, SPAM sushi roll, and SPAM quiche. Although these are all delicious, says Kim, nothing tops the simplicity of fried SPAM with fresh, steaming rice. In the second commercial, a stylish young couple returns from a date. The young man tries to convince the woman to come up to his apartment with the lure of coffee or udon noodles. When she refuses, he has a sudden inspiration and asks whether she would like to come up for some SPAM with fresh, steaming rice. She immediately agrees.[16]

But how did it get this way? How is it that SPAM, a punch line to a joke in much of the continental United States, is a beloved comfort food in Hawai'i and a status symbol in the Philippines and South Korea? Moreover, to many Pacific Island cultures, such as those on the Gilbert Islands, Marshall Islands, and Tahiti, SPAM is said to function as a nonperishable form of meat currency "that could be stocked as wealth like money in the bank, saved up, or purchased and given as gifts."[17] For answers, we must reflect on the fact that, at its core, SPAM is a preserved food. Specifically, we must consider the role of food preservation—particularly the method of canning food—in the history of seafaring and the modern military, as well as situate the product within a rapidly globalizing industrial foodscape that began in earnest during the first half of the twentieth century.

Mystery Meat or Miracle Meat?

So what exactly is SPAM? Many have wondered this ever since Jay Hormel, whose father George founded the Hormel Company in 1891, first launched the product in 1937. If it was quarried from pigs, from what sinister limbs and innards is it made? The hoof, the ear, the snout, the skin, the gut? Perhaps it is something out of Upton Sinclair's muckraking literary abattoir—namely, remolded porcine floor scrap. If so, what manner of industrial alchemy aided its monstrous birth? What secretive polysyllabic additives give the pink blob its form, color, flavor, and texture? To many, SPAM is the epitome of horror in a can, a filthy amalgam of discarded orts of industrial animal slaughter and sinister chemical additives that require a doctorate in chemistry—or necromancy—to decipher. Based on its reputation in the United States, you might say SPAM is *The Jungle* meets *Frankenstein,* a grotesque concoction that resulted from the culinary collaboration of Jurgis Rudkus, the Lithuanian immigrant at the center of Upton Sinclair's naturalist masterpiece, and Victor Frankenstein, the creator of the unspeakable monstrosity that rampaged through the pages of Mary Shelley's gothic classic. SPAM is both unholy and unhealthy, a noxious culinary miscreant that is not only unnatural, but also unrepentant.

Or so many believe. This, I feel, is misguided. For me, SPAM is not so much a mystery meat as it is a "miracle meat." In fact, the latter was how the earliest print advertisements dubbed the product when it first entered the marketplace amid the Great Depression. The ads highlighted SPAM's miraculous capacity to not require "pampering in the refrigerator" as well as to make "any occasion more festive" and to save "kitchen work for the thousands."[18] Some seven decades later, I consider SPAM a miracle for a different set of reasons. First and foremost, SPAM is delicious—salty, sweet, and unmistakably porky. Second, SPAM is remarkably versatile, comfortably lending itself to any meal of the day (breakfast, lunch, or dinner) or cuisine (American, Korean, Japanese, Filipino, or even French).

And third, contrary to its ill repute, SPAM is surprisingly wholesome—as wholesome as any luncheon meat or sausage you might find in a deli counter, if not more so.

But how do we determine whether a food—and a canned product, no less—is in fact wholesome? One possible measure is provided in Michael Pollan's *In Defense of Food: An Eater's Manifesto,* which offers the pithy dictum, "Eat food. Not too much. Mostly plants." (This was in answer to the question of "what we humans should eat in order to be maximally healthy.") Pollan clarifies his dictum with a set of food rules geared to bring common sense—and pleasure—back to eating at a time when American consumers are bombarded by food industry propaganda designed not merely to confuse but blatantly mislead. The rule that arguably demonstrates SPAM's relative wholesomeness is the first under the chapter titled "Eat Food: Food Defined": "AVOID FOOD PRODUCTS CONTAINING INGREDIENTS THAT ARE A) UNFAMILIAR, B) UNPRONOUNCEABLE, C) MORE THAN FIVE IN NUMBER, OR THAT INCLUDE D) HIGH-FRUCTOSE CORN SYRUP."[19] By these criteria, SPAM scores a rather impressive three out of four. The only condition it fails to meet, I would argue, is the number of ingredients, and it misses this by a margin of only one.

In fact, SPAM's list of ingredients is testament to a minimalist vision that is antithetical to mass-produced foods engineered not only for a product's maximum shelf life, but also for a company's maximum profit. In total, SPAM contains a mere six ingredients: pork (mostly shoulder meat augmented by ham), salt, water, modified potato starch, sugar, and sodium nitrite. Originally there were only five ingredients, however. In 2001, to the delight of its more squeamish consumers, potato starch was added in an effort to minimize the thick layer of gelatin—or aspic—that completely coated every block of SPAM.[20]

Among the six ingredients that currently make up SPAM, only one can be considered a questionable additive—sodium nitrite, a "color fixative" commonly used in a wide array of cured meats, including bacon, hot dog, deviled ham, and bologna, as well as in smoke-cured fish such as tuna, shad, and salmon. According to Ruth Winter's *A Consumer's Dictionary of Food Additives,* sodium nitrite has a "particular ability to react chemically with the myoglobin molecule and impart red-bloodedness to processed meats, to convey tanginess to the palate, and to resist the growth of *Clostridium botulinum* spores."[21] In other words, the additive is ideally suited for preserved meats such as SPAM, whose pink hue would instead be a dull brown—something akin to the color of chopped chicken liver salad—without it. And of course, the ability of sodium nitrite to act as a preventive against botulism is an added bonus.

In comparison, consider a Hostess Twinkie. The list of ingredients for this popular spongy confection—an estimated half a billion sold each year—is so lengthy and perplexing that an entire book was devoted to deciphering them. In his prodigiously titled *Twinkie, Deconstructed: My Journey to Discover How the Ingredients Found in Processed Foods are Grown, Mined (Yes, Mined), and Manipulated into What America Eats*, Steve Ettlinger assigns a chapter to each of the two dozen or more ingredients in a Twinkie.[22] Most of these fall under the slippery category of "food additives" and include such mystifying—that is to say, "unfamiliar" and "unpronounceable" in Pollan's parlance—items as cellulose gum, sodium acid pyrophosphate, polysorbate 60, and calcium caseinate. Or, to compare a product ontologically closer to SPAM, there are no less than thirteen ingredients in Oscar Meyer Wieners, including sodium lactate, dextrose, sodium diacetate, and sodium nitrite. I say "no less than" thirteen because one of the ingredients is "flavor," an ambiguous if not completely meaningless and nonsensical term that could signify any number of things, from a single additive (e.g., monosodium glutamate) to a flavor cocktail consisting of untold numbers of chemical flavoring agents and flavor enhancers.

The most telling evidence of SPAM's relative wholesomeness, however, is a comparison with a disturbingly more mysterious meat product like the many "potted meats" that are typically placed next to SPAM on the supermarket shelf. The Armour Potted Meat Product, for example, deemed "America's Favorite" right on the label, contains the following ingredients:

> Mechanically Separated Chicken, Beef Tripe, Partially Defatted Cooked Beef Fatty Tissue, Beef Hearts, Water, Partially Defatted Cooked Pork Fatty Tissue, Salt. Less than 2 percent: Mustard, Natural Flavorings, Dried Garlic, Dextrose, Sodium Erythorbate, Sodium Nitrite.

It is thus easy to conclude that in comparison, SPAM is the apotheosis of wholesomeness.

Of course, technically speaking, SPAM, too, is a potted meat, if the term is broadly defined as any meat product preserved in a sealed "pot" such as a can or jar. Apparently, the food industry applies the term more narrowly and thus SPAM is precluded. What appears to define industrial potted meat is the truly frightening-sounding ingredient "mechanically separated chicken," among other residuum of industrial animal butchery, such as defatted fatty tissues and random organs of chickens, pigs, and cows. Mechanically separated chicken is a type of mechanically recovered meat (MRM) comprising remnants left on the animal carcass after the prime cuts have been removed. A high-powered machine pressure blasts the fleshy residue off of bones to produce a bubblegum-pink slurry, which is used by food companies to bulk up their meat products. In the case of commercial potted meats, MRM *is* the bulk of the product. And there is little doubt why MRM exists: it is incredibly cheap, a fraction of the price of other cuts.[23]

The intense scrutiny of and widespread misinformation about SPAM's actual ingredients are rivaled only by the public's niggling questions over its peculiar name. Even a monumental achievement that is Alan Davidson's *The Oxford Companion to Food* is confused about SPAM's composition, as it wrongly notes the inclusion of "other flavourings" in addition to salt and sugar.[24] This confusion is not surprising, as the two concerns—nature of substance and its name—are, in effect, different sides of the same slice. They both signify consumer anxiety about the precise makeup of a meat product that detours through an industrial factory rather than landing on your dinner table directly from a family farm or a neighborhood butcher.

According to one theory, SPAM is a shortened form of "Shoulder of Pork and Ham." This, however, is evidentially untrue; no authoritative document or account substantiates this. Another, more widely accepted notion claims that SPAM is a portmanteau of "Spiced" and "Ham"—this, too, is untrue. Hormel did in fact market a similar product under the name Spiced Ham prior to launching SPAM, but the two were distinct products. The former's main ingredient was "chopped ham," not pork shoulders, and included black pepper, fully justifying the "Spiced Ham" moniker. (In fact, in the 1937 design of the inaugural label, the descriptor "A New Hormel Meat" was placed below the word SPAM.) It turns out Spiced Ham is just one of many backronyms of SPAM—that is to say, a convenient expansion of the word after the fact. (Other, more tongue-in-cheek backronyms include "Something Posing as Meat" and "Specially Processed Artificial Meat.") More than a convenient expansion, the name is a fanciful one, given that there is no ingredient that might reasonably be classified as a spice in SPAM—that is, unless you consider salt or sugar a spice.

The most probable origin of the name SPAM is traced to Kenneth Daigneau, an actor who starred on Broadway and radio dramas during the 1930s. He was also a brother of the Hormel Company's vice president at the time. Having finally formulated a workable formula for the product after a long struggle of trial and error, Jay Hormel held a naming contest, offering a hundred dollar cash prize to the winner. Hundreds of entries poured in, including the early favorites Brunch, Baby Grand, and, despite already being a derogatory ethnic term at the time, Spic, but Hormel was dissatisfied with all of them. Thus, during a New Year's Eve party he offered a drink to any guest who took a stab at a name. A tipsy Daigneau blurted out "spam," which was crowned the winner. He was awarded the cash prize, and the name was officially trademarked a few months later, on May 11, 1937.[25]

Yet despite what I argue is its relative wholesomeness, SPAM is commonly derided as low-rent, "white trash," or simply ludicrous. "SPAM holds a paradoxical position in the United States," observes Matejowsky: on the one hand, the product is "associated with a lack of cultural sophistication and refinement due to its mass appeal and affordability." On the other, it is "celebrated as a definitive piece of Americana that resonates with society's populist inclinations."[26] To Lewis the pink block of pork is alternatively "good to think" and "bad to think," in the Lévi-Straussian sense, depending on the person slicing it. To some SPAM represents "thrift, native patriotism, and other conservative small town American values"—in other words, good to think. To others it has "the image of an artificially created product" and, unlike hamburgers or hot dogs, is not symbolic of "real animal meat." Thus SPAM is not only bad to think, argues Lewis, but "ridiculous to think" as well.[27]

During the economic crisis of 2008, while many US companies faced profit losses and downsized their workforce, it was reported that the Hormel Food Corporation increased SPAM production in order to meet a sudden rise in demand. Apparently many impecunious Americans were turning to SPAM as a cost-cutting substitute for "real" meat, which was rising in cost. The fact that SPAM made its debut during the Great Depression did not escape Andrew Martin of the *New York Times*, who referred to the product as "the emblematic hard-time food in the American pantry." He observed that Americans have historically turned to SPAM in times of war and economic downturn "as a way to save money while still putting something that resembles meat on the table."[28]

Question: if people turn to SPAM in times of hardship, what are they turning away from? What are they turning to and at what cost? As a meat product, SPAM is a contradiction: it is simultaneously the thing itself (meat) and a forgery of the thing (meat). It is at once something real and something simulated. And because the product straddles absolute categories, it confuses and therefore frightens. Of course, it also amuses.

SPAM is confusing, frightening, and amusing in all sorts of ways. For one, it is not entirely clear whether the pink block of meat is raw, cooked, or something in between. Of course, in reality, it is fully cooked. During its processing, raw pork is ground up and mixed with other ingredients. The slurry is poured into twelve-ounce cans, which are first sealed and then cooked. As such, to open up a can and fry a slice of SPAM is to double cook it. Be that as it may, there are those who believe the product's pink color uncannily resembles the skin tone of melanin-challenged humans. To eat it straight from the can without cooking it (again) therefore borders on the repulsive, something akin perhaps to cannibalism. The only way to ensure the meat no longer appears so human is to cook it. The *Honolulu Advertiser* once declared that to eat SPAM "raw" is not only "gross" but "socially unacceptable." To eat it uncooked was to violate the "Number 1 rule about Spam in Hawaii."[29]

Wonderful SPAM, Spam, Spa'am

As a common butt of jokes, insults, and parodies, SPAM has few food rivals. (Coincidentally, in butchery parlance, pork butt is the upper part of the pig's shoulder, which is the primary cut used in SPAM.) I know of no other food lampooned by both Monty Python and Weird Al Yankovic. In a classic 1970 Monty Python restaurant sketch, when asked about the bill of fare by a patron, a waitress gives an interminable list of SPAM-filled items: "well, there's egg and bacon; egg sausage and bacon; egg and spam; egg, bacon and spam; egg, bacon, sausage and spam; spam, bacon, sausage and spam," and so forth, ending with "or lobster thermidor aux crevettes with a mornay sauce served in a provençale manner with shallots and aubergines garnished with truffle pâté, brandy and a fried egg on top and spam." Nearby, a table of Vikings in horned helmets heartily sings, "spam,

spam, spam, spam, spam, lovely spam, wonderful spam." In the 1975 film *Monty Python and the Holy Grail,* the Knights of the Round Table dance to a song that includes the line, "we eat ham and jam and spam a lot." The film, and this line in particular, would later inspire the 2005 Broadway musical *Monty Python's Spamalot,* which would garner fourteen Tony Award nominations, winning three, including one for Best Musical.

In 1989 Yankovic released a parody of the alternative rock band R.E.M.'s "Stand." Yankovic's spoof, called "Spam," included lyrics that repeatedly called attention to the product's mystery-meat status: "wonder what's inside it now," "think about the stuff its made from," "think about the way it's processed, wonder if it's some kind of meat," and so forth. Apparently Yankovic, who first tasted fame in 1976 as a high-school student when one of his songs was aired on the Dr. Demento radio show, had a fondness for food-related song parodies. In 1995 he released a food-themed CD compilation under the title *The Food Album.* Included in the collection was "Spam" and several other spoofs of chart-topping hits, including "Fat" (a parody of Michael Jackson's "Bad"), "Lasagna" (Ritchie Valens' "La Bamba"), "I Love Rocky Road" (Joan Jett's "I Love Rock 'N Roll), "Eat It" (Michael Jackson's "Beat It"), "My Bologna" (The Knack's "My Sharona"), and "Rye or the Kaiser" (Survivor's "Eye of the Tiger").

SPAM's place in popular culture extends beyond Monty Python and Weird Al, of course. In the 1980s late-night television talk-show host David Letterman suggested "SPAM-on-rope" for people who might get hungry in the shower. In 1997 the ska punk band Save Ferris (the band's name alludes to John Hughes' 1986 film *Ferris Bueller's Day Off*) released a song called "Spam," which alleged the "pink" and "oval" "meat by-product" was "made in Chernobyl" and was eaten by a family that was too poor to "have the finer things in life to eat."

And in 1998 John Nagamichi Cho published *SPAM-ku: Tranquil Reflections on Luncheon Loaf,* a collection of haiku inspired by SPAM. Culled from a website started by Cho that contains nearly twenty thousand poems submitted by the public, the book contains such gems as

> Silken pig tofu,
> The color of spanked buttocks
> Blushing at my knife.

and

> Waxed my car with SPAM.
> The finish gleams, water beads,
> Hungry dogs chase it.[30]

Poems deemed too crass to be eligible for the book—Hormel had the right to preview the contents—but archived in the website include these two authored by Cho himself:

> SPAM as a sex toy:
> Soft, safe, self-lubricated.
> Afterwards: warm lunch.

and

> SPAM: Shit Pork All Mashed.
> Is there anything more gross?
> Vienna Sausage.[31]

Today the word spam (lowercase letters) is most strongly associated with unsolicited commercial missives that are the bane of e-mail inboxes everywhere. The *Oxford English Dictionary*—as do most Internet folklorists—conjectures that the etymology of e-mail spam is the aforementioned restaurant sketch of Monty Python, "set in a café where Spam was served as the main ingredient of every dish, and featuring a nonsense song whose lyrics consist chiefly of the word 'Spam' repeated many times over, at times interrupting or drowning out other conversation." The *OED*, however, also hints at another etymological possibility—a 1994 *Time* magazine article that implied that to "Spam the Net" is "a colorful bit of Internet jargon meant to evoke the effect of dropping a can of Spam into a fan and filling the surrounding space with meat."

Hormel Foods, all the while, did not see the humor in the name of its most important product transmogrifying into what was essentially a newly emerged cyber epithet. (Although Hormel sells about sixteen hundred different products, SPAM has long been the company's best selling and most profitable.) By the late 1990s the public and legislative outcry against e-mail spamming had reached a fever pitch. When a self-proclaimed "spammer" held a press conference—theatrically surrounded by cans of SPAM—to declare his constitutional right as an American to spam as much as he pleased, Hormel, which holds the trademark for

SPAM, sent him a cease-and-desist letter.³² The spam activist refused, arguing, "It's far too late to change the vocabulary of 25 million Internet users."³³ Hormel soon realized that it was far better to join rather than fight the juggernaut that was the Internet. In 1998 it launched the official SPAM website under a domain name, www.spam.com, acquired several years earlier.

But the company's magnanimity toward the e-mail use of the term was never absolute. In 2007 Hormel took a software company to court, charging that an anti-spam software product called Spam Arrest infringed on its trademark. Spam Arrest countered that the limited e-mail use of the word "spam" "will not detract from the fame associated with Hormel's meat products trademark." The court ruled in favor of Spam Arrest, opening the door for other anti-spam software companies to use the word in their product names.³⁴ Not willing to completely give up on the matter, Hormel declares on the SPAM website that the company does not object to the use of the "slang term" to describe unsolicited commercial e-mail, although it objects to the trademark use of the term. Moreover, the notice enjoins the public to use all lowercase letters when referring to e-mail spam "to distinguish it from our trademark SPAM, which should be used with all uppercase letters."³⁵

The company's ardent protectiveness toward the word "SPAM" was demonstrated even prior to the e-mail controversy against a more formidable foe. In 1996 Walt Disney Pictures, together with Jim Henson Productions, released *Muppet Treasure Island,* which featured a character named Spa'am. In a trademark infringement lawsuit filed in a federal court, Hormel Foods charged that the character, whose name was pronounced the same as their product, "was a noxious-appearing wild boar" intentionally portrayed as "evil in porcine form." In the film Spa'am is a savage priest in a tribe of wild boars that worship Miss Piggy, whom they call Queen Boom Sha-Ka-La-Ka-La.

The lawsuit also sought to stop Disney's plans to promote the character in McDonald's Happy Meals and Cheerios cereal boxes. Hormel's motivation to protect its brand was foreseeable, even if only in retrospect. In addition to the large revenue generated by the canned product itself, the company makes a tidy sum selling literally hundreds of kitschy merchandise—such as T-shirts, pajamas, cycling jerseys, ties, costumes, hats, golf balls, water bottles, piggy banks, stuffed pigs, baby bibs, mugs, fly swatters, Christmas tree ornaments, flip-flops, spoon lures, and watches—that feature the blue and yellow SPAM logo.

In response to the lawsuit, a Jim Henson spokesperson advised Hormel not to be so uptight, saying, "We are sorry that Hormel apparently does not share the Muppet sense of humor."[36] The court once again ruled against Hormel. It denied the company's request for a permanent injunction on federal trademark infringement, thereby balancing "Hormel's trademark rights in SPAM with Henson's desire to parody Hormel's product."[37] David Letterman joked about the lawsuit: "I'm thinking to myself, really, is there going to be much confusion between a puppet and a meat product? For one thing, the puppet automatically has a higher nutritional value."[38]

An Army Marches on Preserved Food

One way to understand SPAM's noteworthy place in today's culinary cultures of the Pacific, Pacific Rim, and among many Asians and Pacific Islanders in the United States is to travel two centuries back in time. The age of industrialization and dramatic rise of Europe's population during and after the eighteenth century coincided with improved food preservation methods of various sorts, from drying and smoking fish to pickling fruits and vegetables to canning meats. Stuart Thorne posits that 1860 was a "turning point" in the history of food preservation in the West. Prior to that, preserved foods were for the most part luxury items, expensive, and, because they were primarily produced in urban areas, out of reach of the rural poor. The establishment of new mass-production techniques after 1860 rapidly reduced the cost of preserved foods. A crucial factor in making these foods affordable was Europeans' increased reliance on major food imports, especially from Australia and South America, where raw materials were cheap and plentiful.[39]

It was, however, the long and epic sea voyages that gave rise to Europe's age of discovery that provided the entrepreneurial incentive needed for radical methodological improvements in food preservation. Until the end of the eighteenth century there was no greater diet-related bane of seafarers' lives than scurvy, a disease brought about by a deficiency of vitamin C. Minor scorbutic symptoms included fatigue, nausea, painful joints, and an overall feeling of discomfort. Left untreated, sufferers developed swollen and bleeding gums, and flesh wounds would fester badly. Generally credited with discovering the cure was James Lind, a surgeon in the Royal Navy of the United Kingdom; he famously found the cure in citrus fruits rich in vitamin C. Remarkably, Lind made the discovery despite having no idea what vitamins were. In what Thorne considers possibly the earliest "published recipe for a new process of preserving food," Lind described in detail a method for concentrating citrus juice that would keep for long periods at sea. The Royal Navy eventually adopted Lind's prevention and cure for scurvy (published as *Treatise on the Scurvy* in 1752) and added citrus as a regular part of the naval diet.[40]

"Exploration was important to the prestige of the major European nations in the early nineteenth century and both governments and commercial sponsors of these expeditions were more ready to encourage improvements in naval diet than in the diet of the poor at home," notes Thorne. As early as the 1750s the Dutch navy subsisted on beef preserved in fat and stored in iron canisters. The Dutch also established a salmon canning industry using a similar method. The Royal Navy had by this time adopted another invention of James Lind, a "portable soup" made from the offal, shins, and hooves of cattle. Stored as a thick, glue-like cake prior to being dissolved with boiling water to make a foul broth, the soup was detested by most seamen but considered essential by the higher ups. By 1757 no Royal Navy ship set sail to foreign waters without Lind's invention included in its provisions. (The Royal Navy required fifty pounds of the preserved soup cake for every hundred men aboard its ships.) Captain James Cook thought very highly of the soup and took it along on all his voyages. He flogged the men who refused it.[41] Cook himself most likely did not have to eat the soup, however, as naval custom called for officers not only dining apart from regular crewmen, but also dining on higher quality food.

More so than any other European power, it was the French who revolutionized large-scale food preservation and, in particular, the practice of thermal sterilization, which involves heating food in sealed, airtight containers such as jars and cans. The individual credited for perfecting this technique is a French pastry chef named Nicolas Appert. According to Giorgio Pedrocco's "Food Industry and New Preservation Techniques," during a series of experiments conducted in the 1790s Appert developed a "method that anticipated Pasteur's ideas and techniques, based on sterilizing food in order to kill living microorganisms, *les ferments*, and their spores."[42] And just as Lind discovered the effect of citrus on scurvy despite having no idea about the existence of vitamins, Appert was completely in the dark about the existence of microorganisms and thus did not know why his method worked—but work it did.

In 1804, eager to profit financially from his revolutionary technique, Appert set up a factory that employed fifty workers. Industrial-scale canning of food had now officially begun. The method of canning meat that Appert put into practice at his factory in Massy, France, is essentially identical to that employed some two centuries later at the SPAM plant in Austin, Minnesota, aka "Spamtown," which churns out nearly 150,000 cans of SPAM during a single daytime shift. In both instances, chunks of meat are placed into hermetically sealed cans that are then heated. Appert's factory heated them in vats of boiling water; the SPAM plant bakes them in a dry oven for three hours.

While Appert was busy refining his preservation method and launching a commercial factory, the French government in the meantime had been seeking ways to improve the diet of its men in uniform. It did so with the understanding that, to quote the famous adage attributed to none other than Napoleon Bonaparte, "an army marches on its stomach." Specifically, Bonaparte's army sought food that was economical, transportable, tastier, and more nutritious than the dried, salted, and smoked products that it had hitherto relied on.[43] Canned food turned out to be the answer.

Upon hearing of Appert's achievement, the French government investigated his methods and, in 1810, awarded him twelve thousand francs on the condition that he make public the details of his preservation method. Appert agreed and published a book, *The Art of Preserving All Kinds of Animal and Vegetable Substances for Several Years*.[44] According to Thorne the monetary award Appert received was not a prize for winning a government-sponsored contest for an invention that would ease the challenge of feeding the military, as often repeated in food lore. Rather, the "*ex gratia* payment that Appert received in return for the publication of his methods was the common practice of the French Government at the time."[45] Be that as it may, Appert continued to refine his process and began supplying canned foods to the French army and navy. This form of provisions had several obvious strategic and tactical advantages. As Tom Standage puts it in *An Edible History of Humanity*, "It allowed large numbers of rations to be prepared and stockpiled in advance, stored for long periods, and transported to combatants without the risk of spoiling." Moreover, it curtailed the difficulty of seasonal variations, allowing for military campaigns to be waged even in winter.[46]

Of course, Bonaparte's army was neither the first nor the last to recognize that the fitness of a standing army depended on the quality of food available to the rank and file. Food's capacity as a weapon and strategic tool has been recognized since ancient—if not prehistoric—times. The food policies of Alexander III of Macedon (aka Alexander the Great), for instance, were as instrumental to his countless battlefield successes as any other single strategic factor. In the fourth century AD the Roman military scholar Vegetius wrote, "Starvation destroys an army more often than does battle, and hunger is more savage than the sword." And, on the authority of a medieval Chinese military handbook: "If you occupy your enemies' storehouses and granaries and seize his accumulated resources in order to provision your army continuously, you will be victorious."[47]

Uncle "SPAM" Goes to War

Over the course of its history, the US military has also been keenly aware of the importance of a sound food policy. During the American War of Independence (1775–1783) the American army drove live cattle and hogs to campsites in order to provide soldiers with fresh meat, an arduous practice that lasted until the Spanish-American War of 1898. This sort of reliance on fresh food had serious drawbacks, however. For every soldier killed in battle during the Spanish-American War, a reported fourteen died of an illness linked either to a lack or spoilage of food. This prompted the US armed forces to revise its food policies in 1901, and thus was established the different purpose-dependent categories of military ration, such as garrison, field, and emergency.[48] Subsequently, the garrison ration was assigned the letter A, the field ration B, and emergency rations C, D, and K.[49]

In 1935, perhaps in anticipation of US involvement in World War II, a government directive mobilized all branches of food science to improve the quality of the existing combat ration. Specifically, the directive sought to stimulate production of an emergency ration that "(a) would be usable under any climactic conditions, (b) would provide the highest possible caloric value in the smallest possible package . . . and (c) would possess such palatability as would warrant its continuous daily use."⁵⁰ With the American entry into the war following the Japanese attack on Pearl Harbor, the efficacy of the American military's scientifically formulated ration would be thoroughly tested. It would pass with flying colors.

During World War II both allies and enemies of the United States were awestruck by the quality, quantity, and variety of food the American GIs had at their disposal. The British soldiers, who took pride at "making do" with limited provisions during wars and other difficult times, saw the Americans as "overfed." So did the Germans. As Harvey Levenstein notes in *Paradox of Plenty: A Social History of Eating in Modern America*, never in the history of mankind had an army been as abundantly supplied with food as the American army. For example, in 1942 an average American civilian male consumed 125 pounds of meat. The average soldier, meanwhile, consumed 360 pounds.⁵¹

Military chow provided far more than the minimum calories and nutrients the soldiers required. Despite their incessant complaints about the terrible and repetitive taste, the GIs thrived on it. (The complaints, moreover, were often good-natured.) A large swath of the war recruits hailed from humble if not impoverished backgrounds and, like the US population at large during the Great Depression, was typically malnourished. For many soldiers, therefore, military food, while not Mom's cooking, was literally the best—at least from the standpoint of nutrition—that they ever had on a regular basis. For instance, it was not uncommon for men stationed at the US Air Force base at Randolph Field, Texas, to gain ten to twenty pounds each month.⁵²

Accompanied by mobile field kitchens, the GIs ate reasonably well even near the field of battle. Instructed to provide their comrades with at least one hot meal each day, army cooks baked fresh bread daily in portable ovens and served it with hot soup and meat-filled stew. Ice cream machines were standard issue—a godsend for those stationed in the sweltering South Pacific. And for those directly engaged in combat there were the emergency rations, the bulk of which would not have been possible had it not been for Appert's contribution to the Napoleonic Wars. Each element of the rations was in one way or another preserved, with canned meats and vegetables playing the dominant role. The regular Army C ration consisted of six cans, two for each meal, containing meat, vegetables, beans, stew, hash, biscuits, candies, and instant coffee. The K ration, aka "parachute ration," was an improved version of the C ration. Developed by the Subsistence Research

Laboratory of the Chicago Quartermaster Depot, the K ration was packed in three separate boxes, each a complete meal containing canned meats, coffee tablets, concentrated bouillon, powdered lemon juice, biscuits, a chocolate bar, and chewing gum.[53]

As part of the nation's austerity measures to mobilize resources for the war, the federal government established a strict rationing system among the civilian population, which at times prompted hoarding frenzies. A year after the attack on Pearl Harbor, it was not uncommon for entire sections of grocery store shelves to remain bare. Citizens on the home front could no longer indiscriminately consume such commonplace items as gasoline, coal, tires, sugar, coffee, canned foods, and medicine. For the most part Americans tolerated such inconveniences with stoic patriotism. What appeared to perturb people most, however, was the rationing of fresh meat. In various parts of the country the police were called to quell panicky mobs at butcher shops and other outlets where meat was sold.[54]

And just as Appert's personal canning factory contributed to France's nineteenth-century war efforts, so did American private companies play a part in the United States' during World War II. It was during this period that Hormel, and its signature product, SPAM, came to national prominence. Faced with a shortage of fresh meat, the civilian population turned in droves to canned meats. This turned out be a boon for Hormel, as SPAM became America's substitute meat of choice. Sales of the product doubled between 1939 and 1942.[55]

SPAM also found international fame during this period. It began when Uncle Sam decided to include the canned product as part of the military's C ration. Soldiers consumed so much of it that they in short order began bellyaching about the drudgery of SPAM. Nevertheless, according to Ty Matejowsky, SPAM has remained a part of the military's ration in "every major US combat operation since World War II."[56] In a letter he wrote to Hormel in 1966, Dwight D. Eisenhower reflected that he, "along with millions of other soldiers," polished off his share of SPAM. He then confessed to making "a few unkind remarks about it—uttered during the strain of battle." But as a former commander in chief, "I believe I can still forgive you your only sin: sending us so much of it," he quipped.[57]

In addition to feeding US troops, SPAM also fed America's World War II Allies. In excess of fifty thousand tons were sent to both the Pacific and European theaters. One of the unique advantages of SPAM was its rectangular shape, which made it more easily stackable and thus more space sav-

Nikita Khrushchev on the cover of *Time* (November 30, 1953). In his memoir, the Soviet premier wrote about his troops subsisting on SPAM.

ing than cylindrical cans, and made the large-scale storage and transport of the product more efficient. Nikita Khrushchev, Soviet premier from 1958 to 1964, wrote in his memoir, "Without SPAM, we wouldn't have been able to feed our army." He also wrote that despite the many off-color jokes the soldiers made about the American product, "it tasted good."[58]

By 1944 Hormel exported some 90 percent of all its products overseas, including to Britain, where "SPAM became the biggest hit," according to Matthew Fort's *Guardian* article, "Play It Again, Spam." Faced with austerity measures that were far more severe than those faced by the Americans, the British fervently took to SPAM. It was included in sandwiches, fritters, and rarebits and was baked clove studded and glazed with brown sugar, mustard, and vinegar. Considered a luxury, SPAM was highly coveted during and for many years after the war. In fact, it was initially regarded as a quality product, especially when compared to most domestic sausages, whose ingredients were arguably more dubious, if not mysterious. This, however, did not stop SPAM from eventually ending up, as Fort puts it, "irredeemably low-rent, best fitted as bait for barbel and carp" for British satirists like Monty Python.[59]

As World War II drew to a close, SPAM found a home also in Asia and the Pacific, particularly in countries that played a major strategic role in US military endeavors during the twentieth century. Since 1898, when the United States first fought a significant battle in Asia against the Spanish navy in Manila Bay, the Asia-Pacific region has served as the backdrop for the majority of major US combat operations. Following on the heels of the Spanish-American War (1898) was the Philippine-American War (1899–1913), fought entirely on Philippines soil. The Boxer Rebellion (1900) took American soldiers to China, and they returned a number of times more over the next several decades to protect American citizens and interests during China's extended period of unrest. When the United States declared war against Japan during World War II (1941–1945), the entirety of Asia's Pacific Rim and almost every Pacific island turned into a single, enormous theater of war. During the Korean War (1950–1953) some thirty-seven thousand US soldiers died fighting on the Korean peninsula, and an additional fifty-eight thousand or so perished in the jungles of Vietnam, Cambodia, and Laos during the long duration of the Vietnam War (late 1950s to 1975).

In most cases the end of US combat operations did not mean the exit of US military personnel from the region. Rather, it often meant prolonged military occupation or even a permanent American presence with the establishment of bases, camps, stations, forts, and other military installations in such strategic locations as the Philippines, Okinawa, Japan, South Korea, Guam, and Hawai'i. The current culinary significance of SPAM to the cuisines of these places is thus directly linked to the history the US military in the twentieth century. What started out as emergency rations for American GIs during the war years eventually morphed into a symbol of American generosity and superiority for Asian and Pacific natives during the postwar years.

If a single dish were to be called upon to epitomize this, it has to be the Korean dish budae jjigae, a chile-based stew that includes various combinations of hot dogs, SPAM, canned Vienna sausage, canned baked beans, kimchi, ramen noodles, American cheese, bean curds, and whatever else is available. Literally translated as "army base stew," the dish reputedly originated during the Korean War in the impoverished neighborhoods of South Korea, where myriad US military installations were being established. Hungry natives would rummage through the garbage bins of army bases or rely on the handouts of soldiers to concoct the dish. John Feffer notes that because the war "destroyed crops and the Korean capacity for self-sufficiency, many citizens came to depend on what U.S. soldiers left behind." Thus Feffer finds it ironic that the name of the dish "suggests nourishment of warriors" and not what it really was in the beginning—the food of "scavengers." He observes that the new generation of South Koreans senses no "contradictory feelings" about the true origin of budae jjigae, which is now "a popular dish enjoyed by couples and groups at middle-class restaurants."[60]

George Lewis posits that the "successes of the Allied military effort in the Pacific theater during World War II gave an intense and up-close introduction to many Pacific cultures of things American." This includes such items as beer, chocolate, chewing gum, and military rations like SPAM, which "became valuable artifacts of the most recent occupying culture, and prized as such by the locals."[61] And despite any feelings of ambivalence or lingering resentment the natives might have toward the US military, SPAM remains a local favorite to this day.[62] Unlike in Britain, where the product fell out of favor among the people within a generation or two after its introduction, SPAM has not lost any of its luster for many people of Asia and the Pacific. Nor is that luster lost for many in the United States, as evidenced by the popularity of SPAM among many in the Asian and Pacific Islander American communities.

Japanese Americans are one such community; their affection for SPAM began during what was surely the most troubling and painful period in Japanese American history—their internment in concentration camps during World War II.[63] As featured in "Weenie Royale: Food and the Japanese Internment," a story produced by National Public Radio's *Morning Edition*, many of the dishes today's Japanese Americans consider comfort food originated in the camps. Akemi Tamaribuchi, a third-generation Japanese American interviewed in the program, is positive that the first time her family ate Weenie Royale, her favorite dish, was at Tule Lake Internment Camp. To this day the dish, made of "sliced hot dogs mixed with eggs with soy sauce and a little oyster sauce, stir-fried in with some onions over rice," is a regular Sunday morning family meal.

Jimi Yamaichi, who spent three years at Tule Lake, recalls that "carloads of hot dogs" would be brought to camp and they would "eat hot dogs for days." Frank Kukuchi, who was interned in Manzanar, recounts that although no one ever starved, the food was dreary and boring, especially for a meat-loving young man like himself. "Meat was a precious item,"

Kukuchi recalls. "No one ever got meat." Instead of steaks, the government brought in weenies (hot dogs) and bologna.

The government also brought in SPAM. Howard Ikemoto, who remembers the difficulty of having to subsist on a heavy dose of potatoes in camp (and it was especially difficult for his parents, who "ate rice every day of their life"), recalls what happened after the war when "a lot of the Japanese came back to places like Sacramento":

> They had no jobs, and a lot of them got pickup trucks and became gardeners. When I was twelve year old, I would go every Saturday to work with my father. Every lunch, all the Japanese gardeners would meet in front of people that they were mowing lawns for. We used to eat rice with one plum in the middle. And then we have a slice of SPAM, corned beef hash out of a can. That was part of our main diet in camp. And while they were having their lunch, they will talk about the camps, which was the prime of their life.

Jackie Yamashita, a secretary at the Watsonville Buddhist Temple in California, believes "SPAM became very popular during the war because it was a canned meat." She describes how the current generation of young Japanese Americans devours "SPAM sushi" during lunchtime. "There's gotta be Shoyu Weenies! There's gotta be SPAM sushi! It's just tradition," she proclaims.[64] "The temple serves SPAM sushi in a couple of ways—either makizushi style, rolled as a filling, or nigirizushi style, as a topping. Some of the kids, meanwhile, just wrap it [in nori] and eat it like a burrito."[65]

Culinary Hawai'i: Global, Local, Personal

There is one SPAM dish in particular from my Hawai'i childhood that stands out from the rest, one I personally concocted when I was a teenager and often shared with my younger brother when the two of us were left home alone to our own devices. Although I did not have a name for the dish then, if pressed I would today call it "Chili, SPAM, and Egg Rice Bowl." The recipe (for two) goes something like this: in a small saucepan, heat a fifteen-ounce can of chili with beans (preferably the Hormel brand). Meanwhile, brown to a dark crisp four slices of SPAM (each about a quarter-inch thick) in a nonstick pan with a tiny bit of vegetable oil. Remove SPAM from the pan and fry two eggs over easy. Mound the desired amount of steaming, freshly cooked white rice in two large bowls and place two SPAM slices over each. Divide the chili over the SPAM, then top with a fried egg. Sprinkle with chopped raw onions and several dashes of Tabasco. Serve with kimchi on the side.

No doubt this is a recipe that Sam Choy, the jovial Hawai'i restaurateur who often features SPAM on his menus, would greatly appreciate. A 2004 recipient of the James Beard Foundation Award, Choy is one of the twelve celebrated "founders" of Hawaiian Regional Cuisine. Begun in 1991, this was a culinary movement, so to speak, that attempted to ennoble the humble, quotidian food of Hawai'i and transform it into a high-end commodity, to place it on a more upscale track that might cater better to local gastronomes and affluent tourists who flock to Hawai'i by the thousands each day. The Hawai'i Visitors and Convention Bureau website describes Hawaiian Regional Cuisine as an inventive blend of "Hawaii's diverse, ethnic flavors with the cuisines of the world." It utilizes "the freshest island ingredients: cattle raised on the islands' upland pastures, fruits and vegetables grown from rich, volcanic soil, and fish from one of the best managed fisheries around." The website, featuring eye-catching photos of beautiful food and a video profile of another Hawaiian Regional Cuisine founder, Alan Wong, encourages potential tourists and convention attendees to "Start making your reservations."[66]

Along with Choy and Wong, the latter of whom defines Hawaiian Regional Cuisine as a "contemporary style of cooking in Hawai'i today that borrows from all the ethnic influences you find in Hawai'i,"[67] the ten other pioneers constitute a Who's Who of local culinary lore: Roger Dikon, Amy Ferguson-Ota, Mark Ellman, Beverly Gannon, Jean Marie Josselin, George Mavrothalassitis, Peter Merriman, Philippe Padovani, Gary Strehl, and Roy Yamaguchi. Rachel Laudan notes, however, that the movement "was created by forces quite different from those that drive Local Food"—that is, from the everyday food of the Islands' long-time residents.[68]

In other words, Hawaiian Regional Cuisine was not meant for the likes of me, a local boy who had come to Hawai'i not as a tourist or for business but as an immigrant with his working-class family. And neither was it meant for the majority of my childhood friends, who, unlike me, were mostly Hawai'i-born descendants of plantation workers who had arrived a century ago from such diverse places as Japan, Okinawa, China, the Philippines, Korea, Portugal, and Puerto Rico. My friends were also Pacific

Islanders—Hawaiians, Tongans, Samoans, Fijians, Chamorros. Still others were haoles. More often than not, my peers were a motley mixture of any of the above, say, half Japanese, a quarter Puerto Rican, an eighth Native Hawaiian, and an eight Scottish—which happens to be the ancestral combination boasted by my closest high school friend.

The food we grew up on was not the likes of "Day Boat Catch Bourride 'Moderne'" ("medallion poached in bourride, leek and onion étuvée, aïoli sabayon, sea asparagus tempura") or "Big Island Goat Cheese Bavaroise" ("crusted with marcona almonds, toasted pain d'épice, house sour cherries, braised celery and tarragon, cherry glaze"), served at George Mavrothalassitis' Honolulu restaurant. Rather, we thrived on simple, unpretentious fare typified by anything that could easily accommodate SPAM as a component, such as musubi (the SPAM version is popular enough in Hawai'i for 7-Eleven stores to sell it) or saimin (commonly served with a slice of SPAM floating atop the steaming bowl of broth and noodles).

Above all, we came of age on the plate lunch, perhaps the most emblematic framework for a local restaurant meal there is. The archetypal plate lunch consists of two "scoops" (literally from an ice scream scooper) of white rice, a scoop of mayonnaise-doused macaroni salad, and usually an entrée of an Asian-style meat—Japanese *katsu,* Filipino adobo, Korean galbi, and the like. The entrée is not always Asian inflected, however. American-style beef stew or chili with a frankfurter (hot dog sans bun) is hugely popular, as are Native Hawaiian dishes like *laulau* and *kalua* pig. And as Alan Wong is fond of repeating, "Hawaii is probably the only place in the world where you can get spaghetti and meat sauce, garlic bread, two scoops of rice and a macaroni salad all on one plate."[69]

The origin of the plate lunch is in Hawai'i's pineapple and sugar plantations, many of which were established in the nineteenth century by the haole descendants of American missionaries. These plantations flourished after Hawai'i, then a sovereign kingdom, signed the Reciprocity Treaty with the United States in 1875. The treaty allowed Hawai'i to export sugar and other goods to the United States duty free in return for tariff-free importation of American products such as cotton, lumber, salt, meat, and books. (In an 1887 addendum to the treaty, the United States also acquired the land that later became Pearl Harbor.) Not satisfied with Native Hawaiian workers (the indigenous population was at a precipitous decline, and those enlisted to work were tagged as ill disciplined), the sugar and pineapple industries looked to China, Japan, Korea, the Philippines, and beyond for labor pools willing to endure the backbreaking work the plantations required. For those toiling under the harsh conditions of the tropics, hearty food was a must, and over time the representative foods of the various ethnic groups began to merge onto a single plate. The centerpiece was the pairing of starchy rice (*Oryza sativa* var. *japonica*) that the Japanese and Koreans favored with a variety of meat-based dishes affiliated with different culinary traditions.

The plate lunch "evolved from a cross of the lunch wagon and the bento, the traditional Japanese packed lunch that the plantation workers took out into the field," speculates Laudan.[70] If so, the lunch wagons eventually gave way to food stalls and the *okazuya,* Japanese American delicatessens in which diners point and pick from premade foods on display. While the term is Japanese (*okazu* refers to food served with rice and *ya* means store), okazuya is uniquely of Hawai'i. It began before World War II, offering foods that ran the gamut of the Islands' wide-ranging multiethnic populations.[71] In "Shifting Plates: Okazuya in Hawai'i," Christine Yano describes okazuya as "an expression of local Japanese American identity in Hawai'i," one that, "like many other social institutions and cultural practices introduced in Hawai'i by Native Hawaiians and plantation period immigrants," has become "local (a panethnic identity expressive of an appreciation of the cultures, people and land of Hawai'i) in their clientele, workers, owners, and in the mixture of food offered."[72] Eventually the plate lunch became the principal merchandise of stand-alone restaurants, followed by chains such as the L&L Drive-Inn franchise, with dozens of locations throughout Hawai'i, and, since 1999, increasingly elsewhere, including in California, Nevada, Oregon, New York, Texas, Alaska, New Zealand, American Samoa, and Japan.[73]

The restaurants my friends and I grew up with were not Roy Yamaguchi's in Hawai'i Kai or Beverly Gannon's Hali'imaile General Store on Maui, but establishments that served humble, no-frills, affordable local fare. This included places like the aforementioned Zippy's and, my personal favorite, Grace's Inn on Kapiolani Boulevard in Honolulu, where I could completely satiate my youthful, bottomless appetite on the cheap. We also frequented national food chains, or fast-food establishments—we were typical Americans, after all. We were no strangers to Pizza Hut (especially the all-you-can-eat lunch buffet), Taco Bell, and, of course, McDonald's, where I usually paired an order of Big Mac, fries, and a Coke with saimin.

L&L Hawaiian Barbecue Restaurant's promotional poster featuring SPAM musubi. From L&L Hawaiian Barbecue Facebook page.

Served in a foam cup (à la Cup O' Noodles, the Nissin-brand instant ramen invented by Momofuku Ando in 1971),[74] McDonald's saimin comes garnished with reconstituted *kamaboko,* nori, char siu, and *tamago.* In 1976 saimin became the first region-specific menu item ever to be offered in any of McDonald's franchises. Poland's McKielbasa, India's McAloo Tiki Burger, France's Croque McDo, South Korea's Bulgogi Burger, the Philippine's McSpaghetti, and Canada's McLobster all represent McDonald's corporate strategy, first introduced in Hawai'i, of expanding its standardized menu at a given location with locally identified foods. Not surprisingly, another menu item unique to McDonald's in Hawai'i is SPAM, served as the meat alternative to Portuguese sausage (another offering unique to the Islands) in a breakfast order with rice and eggs. McDonald's introduced SPAM to its Hawai'i menu in 2002. Not to be outdone, Burger King followed suit in 2007.[75]

On special family occasions, my parents took their children out to what were basically cloth-napkin versions of Zippy's that served slightly upscale types of plate lunch, like, say, one of the Flamingo restaurants, where I worked as a bus boy, dishwasher, and janitor during college summer breaks. (The restaurant owners were the grandparents of a high school friend, meaning I had a summer job whenever I needed it.) More typically, however, my parents opted for something much closer to their roots: my father invariably insisted on Korean restaurants for *naengmyeon*, while my mother preferred Korean-style Chinese places for jjajangmyeon, *jjamppong*, and *tangsuyuk*. Their divergent preferences were neither arbitrary nor matters of idiosyncratic taste; rather, they were nostalgic. My father is originally from what is now North Korea, where naengmyeon originated, and my mother hails from Incheon, the South Korean port city where Korean Chinese cuisine was born.

In a 2008 article, "Carbo-Loading, Hawaiian Style," *New York Times* reporter Jennifer Steinhauer writes that a few months before he was elected president of the United States, Barack Obama proclaimed a longing for a plate lunch while vacationing in Hawai'i, his birthplace. Included in his "must-get-to list" that summer was Zippy's, where "he likes to indulge in the culinary treats of his youth," and Rainbow Drive-In, where for "less than $7 one can fill up on the teriyaki beef plate, which some like to top with chili, or the 'mix, all over,' which is a plate of teriyaki beef, breaded mahi-mahi and fried chicken, smothered in brown gravy 'all over.' "[76] That the Obamas take pleasure dining at some of the country's most high-end and highly priced restaurants—Spiaggia in Chicago, Blue Hill in New York City, and Equinox in Washington, D.C.—is a well-known fact. Curiously, Steinhauer makes no mention of any of the more swanky restaurants associated with Hawaiian Regional Cuisine as being a part of Obama's culinary destination. It is likely that candidate Obama evoked the plate lunch while vacationing on O'ahu for the same reason that he might have evoked a hot dog with "the works" while campaigning in Chicago:[77] to appeal to a working-class, locally identified, populist voting bloc. Even so, Laudan finds the current "cross fertilization" between the two types of eateries (local food and Hawaiian Regional Cuisine) "nothing but mutually beneficial, creating a firm regional base for the cuisine of the restaurants and increasing sophistication for the cuisine of the home and the street."[78]

Although I failed to realize it then, my childhood SPAM and chili recipe, while a poor facsimile of Hawaiian Regional Cuisine, is a reasonable permutation of the loco moco, the uniquely local Hawai'i dish traditionally composed of rice topped with a hamburger patty, fried egg, and gobs of brown gravy. As legend has it, the dish came into existence in 1949 on the Big Island and was the brainchild of Nancy and Richard Inouye, the proprietors of Hilo's Lincoln Grill. The dish was first created for a teenage boy who, on behalf of his hungry friends, requested something not so American as a sandwich but less fussy than something Asian—and also filling and cheap. The boy and his friends belonged to an informal organization called the Lincoln Wreckers Athletic Club and played in the local "barefoot" football league. They also hung out regularly at the Lincoln Grill. The Inouyes answered the teens' entreaty by improvising what became the loco moco. The dish was named for the nickname of the boy—known as Loco among his friends for his wild and reckless approach to football—who made the request. The word "loco," meaning "crazy," is from the Portuguese *louco* and is an established part of the Islands' vernacular. "Moco" was chosen randomly simply because it rhymed with loco, and the teens thought the two words sounded great together—far better than loco with soko, doko, or koko.[79]

An alternate but decidedly less-prescribed-to legend locates the origin of the dish, or at least the dish's name, to an eatery called Café 100 in Hilo, first opened in 1946 by Richard and Evelyn Miyashiro. The restaurant was named after the army unit in which Richard Miyashiro served during World War II. This unit, the 100th Infantry Battalion, an all–Asian American (mostly Japanese American) combat team, later merged with the 442nd Regimental Combat Team, composed also mostly of nisei. Having earned 18,143 individual decorations, including 47 Distinguished Service Crosses, 810 Bronze Stars, 350 Silver Stars, 1 Congressional Medal of Honor, and more than 3,600 Purple Stars while fighting in Europe, the 442nd is considered "the most decorated unit in United States military history."[80] Whether it was the Miyashiros or Inouyes who invented the dish and the name, with more than thirty different permutations of the loco moco on its menu, Café 100, in the words of one restaurant reviewer, "certainly provides the widest array of this local favorite to be found anywhere."[81]

Not surprisingly, the loco moco figures prominently on Sam Choy's menus. At his Breakfast, Lunch & Crab restaurant in Honolulu, diners can choose from a number of variations, including "Da Hilo Original" (with grilled onions) and a "Vegetarian Moco" (made with tofu, spinach, and mushrooms). Customers can also request substitutions, such as a slice of

Screenshot of the loco moco page of Café 100's website. Featuring more than thirty varieties, including a SPAM version, the restaurant sells about nine thousand bowls of loco moco each month.

SPAM for the hamburger patty, which makes the dish resemble my SPAM and chili concoction even more. At his signature restaurant on King Street, Alan Wong features a decidedly more refined version, sans SPAM—a "Mini Loco Moco" starter of mocha-crusted *unagi* meat loaf, sunny-side quail egg, and wasabi *kabayaki*. And for those who wish to prepare a no-frills version at home, "Sam Choy's SPAM Loco Moco" recipe, made with SPAM, chopped onions, packaged brown gravy mix, rice, and eggs, appears in *The SPAM Cookbook* by Linda Eggers, who dedicates the book "to those who eat SPAM Luncheon Meat simply because it tastes good."[82] This would certainly include me and virtually everyone else whose gastronomic identity came of age in Hawai'i.

Coda

As a Korean immigrant who grew up in Hawai'i, I find SPAM to be much more than just a preposterous luncheon meat or a punch line to a joke. (Of course, it is also those things, in spades). It is as apt a gastronomic symbol as any of what I am as a transnational, diasporic product, simultaneously situated within a nation-state (namely, the United States) while straddling the conceptual borders of multiple cultural identities, an amalgam of Korean, Hawai'i local, and Asian American. I am, in other words, not unlike SPAM, a hybrid, a muddler of categories. Thus to point out that I am neither authentically Korean nor Hawaiian, neither authentically Asian nor American, matters very little, if at all. So what, I say—just as I say "so what" to those who insist SPAM is not real food, that it is a dubious meat wannabe.

What James Watson, editor of *Golden Arches East: McDonald's in East Asia,* said about the proliferation of McDonald's restaurants in East Asia easily applies to SPAM: "the Golden Arches have always represented something other than food."[83] To some the Big Mac is the epitome of cultural imperialism, the embodiment of vulgar Americanism, the defiler of fragile indigenous foodways. To others it is a soft alloy, malleable enough to take exacting shapes desired even by the most persnickety of localities. To those who distrust the power of corporate machinations, McDonald's is the apotheosis of dubious food in an age of globalization, capitalist repetition, and industrial standardization. And to those bewitched by the siren of modernity, there is nothing tastier than a Big Mac, fries, and Coke. Moreover, McDonald's "symbolizes different things to different people at different times in their lives," argues Watson, including, "predictability, safety, convenience, fun, familiarity, sanctuary, modernity, culinary tourism, and 'connectedness' to the world beyond." And he adds, "Few commodities can match this list of often contradictory attributes."[84]

I believe SPAM is one of the few global commodities that can. SPAM, which Matejowsky calls "one of the most successful foods of modern times,"[85] is much more than a mere comestible to the devoted legions of South Koreans, Filipinos, Pacific Islanders, and Asian Americans, especially those of Korean, Filipino, or Japanese ancestry. It is no less integral to their identity than, say, Jamón serrano is to some Spaniards, prosciutto di Parma is to Italians, haggis is to Scots, or their respective features of the hot dog is to New Yorkers and Chicagoans. Thus, given that Asian Americans do not necessarily "eat racially," meaning a cuisine that might be called "Asian American," is it possible to elevate SPAM (alongside rice, of course) as a rare example of a food that unites Asian America? After all, Asian Americans who grew up with the stuff do not consider SPAM a dubious food. So might we consider SPAM a food that has "crossed over" to become an "authentic" Asian American one?[86]

Perhaps, perhaps not—I cannot say. Then again, does it even matter? What I do know is that with every bite of SPAM I consume layers of overlapping histories, zigzagging and crisscrossing migrations, and elaborate cultural transformations. With it are consumed calamitous political turmoil, military conflicts, and other global upheavals that shaped much of the twentieth century. Those of us who love SPAM do so not despite but precisely because of what it is. That is to say, SPAM is not a substitute for something else shamefully consumed during moments of desperation, but the real thing consumed in order to experience moments of gustatory pleasure. As Joyce Carol Oates once said about the bloody sport of pugilism, "boxing really isn't a metaphor, it is the thing in itself." [87] Likewise, SPAM is not a metaphor—for, say, real meat, real pork, or real food. Rather, it is what it is. Ridiculous as it may sound, SPAM and I go together like Thanksgiving and pumpkin pie or pastrami with mustard on rye. And in this, I am not alone. Vast swaths of the Pacific, Pacific Rim, and Asian America sit alongside me at the table.

Conclusion

Appearing a few years ago on the dinner menu of Blue Ginger, celebrity chef Ming Tsai's "Asian fusion" restaurant in Wellesley, Massachusetts, was an entrée item that baffled the mind as much as it promised to titillate the tongue: "Grilled Harissa Glazed New Zealand Lamb Rack with Coconut Raita," accompanied by "Summer Vegetable Couscous Salad and Thai Basil-Mint Puree." At first glance, this dish appears to epitomize Tsai's culinary philosophy of "East Meets West." His first television show, which aired on the Food Network in 1998, was called *East Meets West with Ming Tsai,* and his first cookbook, published in 1999, made direct references to both his restaurant and TV show via the title *Blue Ginger: East Meets West Cooking with Ming Tsai.* He has starred in additional TV shows since (*Ming's Quest* and *Simply Ming*) and authored a handful of other cookbooks (*Simply Ming, Ming's Master Recipes,* and *Simply Ming One-Pot Meals*). And there is much more to Tsai's achievements: included among his many claims to fame, culinary or otherwise, are making *People Magazine*'s "Most Beautiful People" list in 2000 and a victory over Bobby Flay in a duck challenge during a 2005 episode of *Iron Chef America.*

As a once-upon-a-time Ph.D. student in English, I cannot help but be reminded of a certain canonical British writer when I ruminate on the first titles of Tsai's book and TV show. I am referring, of course, to perhaps the most imperial of Britain's imperial writers, Rudyard Kipling, who once wrote, "Oh, East is East and West is West, and never the twain shall meet." Would Tsai's harissa-lamb offering be a dish that once and for all debunks Kipling's famous—or, depending on your point of view, notorious—poetic sentiment? Or will it reaffirm the imperialistic ballast of the verse? In the introduction to his first cookbook, Tsai tells the reader what he professionally "strives" for: "Successful East-West cooking... just the right, harmonious way to combine culinary approaches."[1] Is this lamb dish the apotheosis of such a laudable if not noble culinary endeavor? Had Kipling lived long enough to partake of the dish, would he have felt compelled to retract or rewrite that bit of poetry?

Before we even begin to ponder these questions, perhaps it will be helpful to determine what exactly goes into the making of the dish. Harissa, according to Alan Davidson's *The Oxford Companion to Food*, could mean one of at least three things: a fiery red paste, common to kitchens throughout North Africa, made of chiles, garlic, coriander, caraway, salt, and olive oil; a Tunisian dish made of pounded green bell peppers, tomatoes, onions, garlic, coriander, and caraway; or a thick porridge of wheat and lamb, also called *haleem*, found in many Arab countries, including Syria, Lebanon, and Iraq.[2] Given that harissa is used as a meat glaze in Tsai's dish, it is reasonable to assume that the first meaning applies here. While New Zealand is a major exporter of lamb, the country is not known for *raita*, a heat-soothing relish of yogurt mixed with any number of vegetables (such as cucumber) and herbs (such as fresh mint or cilantro), and common accompaniment to pungent Indian fare. In point of fact, the word "yogurt" is rooted in Turkish for a fermented milk product whose origins are believed to be multiple sites but centers on and near Central or West Asia.[3]

The origin of the coconut remains a hotly debated topic. While most botanists cite the East Indies and Melanesia, a vociferous minority argues for the American tropics, the west coast of the Isthmus of Panama in particular.[4] Among the most utilitarian fruits in the world, the coconut in any number of forms—dried, juiced, grated, oiled, as a syrup, etc.—appears in equatorial cuisines that circumnavigate the globe. The grain product couscous is a dietary staple of the Amazigh people (Berbers), whose habitation of North Africa adjacent to the Mediterranean predates the current predominantly Arab population. Soon after it was invented, sometime during the Middle Ages, couscous was taken to the Middle East and Europe by Arabs. The product is now ubiquitous not only in North Africa and the Middle East, but also in nearby African nations from Chad to Senegal. It is also common in Europe—for example, in France and Italy—as well as Brazil.[5]

According to Ben-Erik van Wyk's encyclopedic *Food Plants of the World*, Thai basil is a variety of basil characterized by purplish bracts beneath the flowers. Numerous types of basil are found throughout

Africa, the Middle East, and South Asia. The herb was first used in food preparation in India before it spread to the Mediterranean diets of the Near East, Africa, and southern Europe.[6] Mint, meanwhile, is an herb that might have originated in Europe or Asia, depending on the variety, and frequently appears in recipes of Thai, Vietnamese, Malaysian, and Indian dishes,[7] not to mention in toothpastes, mouthwashes, and chewing gums. In England, mint as a sauce or jelly often accompanies lamb dishes, which explains the seventeenth-century English herbalist John Gerard's contention that "the smell of mint does stir up the minde and the taste to a greedy desire of meat."[8]

There are, of course, many other ingredients enlisted in the construction of Tsai's lamb dish that are not directly referenced in the dish's name. For example, there is no mention of which specific summer vegetables are included, but one could imagine a medley of zucchini, sweet corn, tomato, and red bell pepper—all New World plant foods unknown outside the Americas prior to 1492, when Columbus became flummoxed upon the ocean blue. Add to this an assortment of miscellaneous ingredients ubiquitous among most professional kitchens—oils, salts, black pepper, sugar, stocks and reductions, flat-leaf parsley and other herbs, vinegars, lemon juice, wine, a variety of alliums (e.g., garlic, onions, leeks, chives, shallots), etc.—and the resulting dish, exquisitely plated and garnished, is quite literally the world upon a plate. That is, for a modest thirty-five dollars and a week-long wait for a table.

As this brief inventory of a single menu item and its global origins indicates, what Ming Tsai markets as a culinary expression of "East Meets West"—or "Asia Meets Europe," "Orient Meets Occident," or what have you—may in fact ignore a large chunk of the globe, along with two equally important compass points. This dish, as with most items on Blue Ginger's menu, is perhaps better served by the description "East Meets West Meets North Meets South" or "Asia Meets Europe Meets Africa Meets the Americas Meet Australasia." Although he fails to acknowledge it, deeply invested as he is with his culinary philosophy, the East-West binary vanishes into the proverbial thin air of modernity—or was it postmodernity?—when closely interrogated. In this regard, and although he may reject the idea outright as preposterous, Tsai's edible creations are discursively if not spiritually linked to the culinary subjects of this book—namely, California roll, Chinese take-out, kimchi, dogmeat, MSG, and SPAM.

Whatever Tsai's food is, it will not be considered traditionally or authentically Asian in the eyes of culinary purists. (Of course, this is the whole point of Tsai's cooking.) Legions may laud, admire, and gush over it, given Tsai's considerable culinary pedigree and skills, but even his most loyal devotees will be hard pressed to call it "authentic." Tsai's creations are dubious, albeit in an upscale, gentrified way. But, as I have tried to demonstrate in this book, dubiousness is not necessarily a bad thing. It can be, as the Queen of Dubious Foods, Rachel Ray, might say, "yummo!" and "very delish!" But there is another, equally important motive for this book: to show that even the most ostensibly authentic foods—such as sushi, kimchi, and dogmeat—are and have always been products of fusion, adaptation, experimentation, and globalization.

What is now considered authentic was once upon a time apocryphal; what is now considered traditional was once considered fusion; and what is now considered legitimate was once considered dubious. To take this further, what is now decried as apocryphal, fusion, or dubious very well might in the future be defended, celebrated, and mandated as authentic, traditional, or legitimate. In other words, authenticity has always been and continues to be the analog of the apocryphal. To return to the cultural linguistic analogy I evoked in the introduction, what is now considered pidgin or creole might be considered standard or proper in the future; in fact, this might well describe most, if not all, so-called standard languages that exist today.

An example of this process currently playing itself out is Hawaiian Creole English, aka "pidgin English." (Although technically a creole, the locals mistakenly, albeit affectionately, refer to the island vernacular as pidgin).[9] Only a generation or so ago pidgin English was labeled "broken English" by both nonusers and users alike; it symbolized a lack of education, laziness, delinquency, and most other traits that supposedly kept the majority of locals from achieving social mobility.[10] Today, pidgin has become a source of local pride. The written form is the foundation of a veritable literary tradition, as an ever-increasing number of local writers—Darrell H. Y. Lum, Lois-Ann Yamanaka, R. Zamora Linmark, Gary Pak, and Lee A. Tonouchi are just a few notable examples—use it as an essential component of their works of fiction or poetry.[11] As such, Hawaiian Creole English—the syntax, morphology, and orthography—has become increasingly codified and, dare I say, standardized.

Here I am reminded of Eric Hobsbawm's idea that traditions "which appear or claim to be old are often quite recent in origin and sometimes invented."[12] Every tradition has a beginning, a moment when it emerged from nothingness or a dubious combination of disparateness. If you are not convinced, look no further than the traditional Caesar salad, which came into existence out of desperation and depleted provisions. According to culinary lore, the romaine-anchovy-Parmesan-crouton concoction was invented by an Italian American named Caesar Cardini in Tijuana in 1924. He chanced upon the combination when some hungry friends dropped by his restaurant late one evening—over the Fourth of July weekend—and he was forced to scramble to find something decent to feed them. By 1948 the salad had become such a sensation that Cardini took out a patent on the dressing.[13] Julia Child added considerable mythological heft to the story when she wrote in her cookbook *From Julia Child's Kitchen,* published in 1975, "One of my early remembrances of restaurant life was going to Tijuana in 1925 or 1926 with my parents, who were wildly excited that they should finally lunch at Caesar's Restaurant." Child also stoked the fires of debate when she insisted that Cardini never used a particular ingredient strongly associated with the salad: "No! No anchovies!"[14] Today the Caesar salad is perhaps the most popular salad in America—it certainly ranks above the Waldorf, Niçoise, Cobb or any other salad named after a reputed origin or originator. (Legend has it that it ranks first as the most commonly ordered item in American sit-down restaurants.) This naturally leads to considerable discussion of and dispute over what constitutes an authentic version. Must it be prepared tableside in a wooden bowl rubbed with raw garlic? Is the dressing made with raw or coddled eggs? Is it just the yolk or the entire egg? Are anchovies really necessary? Is it sacrilegious to top it with grilled chicken?

For Hobsbawm, the notion of invented tradition represents "a set of practices, normally governed by overtly or tacitly accepted rules and of a ritual or symbolic nature, which seek to inculcate certain values and norms of behaviour by repetition, which automatically implies continuity with the past."[15] Those who seek authentic Asian cuisine yearn for a connection with a useable past, even if—or particularly if—the past is someone else's. The industrialized world's cherishing of the ritual of mourning the passing of traditional, indigenous, or native cultures, for example, is inculcated through the language shared by the discourse of taste and commodity fetishism. Nostalgia for the endangered or extinct past is expressed through conservation and cultivation of taste—the taste of personal style, spirituality, environmentalism, travel, tourism, and gastronomy, which is the sort of bourgeois New Age alchemy that leads to the creation of works such as Elizabeth Gilbert's much praised and equally panned *Eat, Pray, Love: One Woman's Search for Everything across Italy, India and Indonesia*. Eating foods advertised as authentic offers pleasures and thrills similar to those of commercialized safaris in present-day Kenya, where "wild" lions and giraffes conveniently pose for your digital cameras, and San Diego's Sea World, where Shamu the Killer Whale leaps into the air to the delight of audiences aged three to ninety-three.

Ming Tsai, however, thrills his audiences using a strategy that is diametrically opposed to that of safari tourism and Sea World. As a leading culinary innovator of "Asian fusion cuisine," he relies on imagination and improvisation instead of rhetorical acuity of authenticity to wow the crowd. No, Blue Ginger's menu items are not paragons of "just right," "harmonious," or "successful East-West cooking" that Tsai strives for. To call it those things would be to sell his culinary talents short. Rather, Tsai's dubious but delectable creations epitomize successful global gastronomic amalgamation.

But I do not mean to uncritically celebrate the phenomenon of culinary Asian fusion. There is a crucial, if not fundamental, difference between the dubiousness of the sort of food identified with Tsai (as well as with Masaharu Morimoto, Jean-Georges Vongerichten, Wolfgang Puck, and countless other Asian fusion practitioners) and the foods that I have highlighted in this book. Simply put, the difference between, say, Tsai's harissa-lamb dish on the one hand and SPAM musubi on the other is a matter of cultural status and economic class.

In "Model Minorities Can Cook: Fusion Cuisine in Asian America," Anita Mannur observes that Asian fusion cuisine is "heralded as the democratic melding of cuisines ... a type of culinary multiculturalism that seems to challenge the rigidity of national boundaries and fixity." It is also "seen as the apparent tribute to successful multiculturalism in the United States," she asserts, "and it is often described as a fusion of different national styles." That may all be well and good, but Mannur cautions against digesting uncritically "the myth that fusion culinary discourse can be separated from the political terrain on which consumers of cuisine are located." In the case of Ming Tsai, this would be to imagine him as the "future of America—a figure who takes the 'best' of the east and incorporates it into his Western culinary offerings." Mannur argues that "Ming Tsai emerges as the model minority chef who inhabits a newer stereotype—that of the hyperassimilated, attractive, and yuppified Asian American who seamlessly integrates into American cultural life."[16]

In other words, Tsai is regarded as the opposite of the unassimilable Chinese immigrant alien who toils in the kitchens and behind the counters of the tens of thousands of Chinese take-outs scattered throughout the United States. Of course, this latter image—which was the earlier Chinese American male stereotype of pidgin English, buck teeth, and goofy laugh—was one that Martin Yan performed brilliantly to his great profit. ("If Yan can cook, so can you!" he promised.) Authenticity might be big bucks, but so are racial stereotypes. Often the two are one and the same. The costumes and accents might differ, as do the ingredients, recipes, and menus, but both performances rely on the same illusion of an authentic Asia, a fixed and stable notion of Asia that is dangled before the eyes of hungry diners longing for the true taste of the Orient. Thus the choice of Asian tradition or Asian fusion joins the ranks of other choices dogging the modern consumer: "Coke or Pepsi?" "Big Mac or Whopper?" "Soup or salad?"

Notes

Introduction

1. I use the terms "Orient" and "Oriental" ironically and as anachronisms. By Orient I evoke a Eurocentric, colonialist view of Asia. By Oriental I mean an antiquated if not offensive descriptor of Asians akin to the use of "negro" to refer to African Americans.

2. For an in-depth discussion of the Standard English debate, see James Milroy, "The Consequences of Standardization in Descriptive Linguistics," Peter Trudgill, "Standard English: What It Isn't," and several other chapters in *Standard English: The Widening Debate,* edited by Tony Bex and Richard J. Watts (London: Routledge, 1999).

3. Trudgill, "Standard English," 124.

4. Arjun Appadurai, "On Culinary Authenticity," letter, *Anthropology Today* 2, no. 4 (August 1986): 25.

5. I borrow the pluralized form of English from Tom McArthur's *The English Languages* (Cambridge: Cambridge University Press, 1998). Given the immense diversity and pluralism of English globally, McArthur asks whether it may be linguistically prudent to consider English as a family of languages in its own right.

6. David Crystal, *English as a Global Language* (Cambridge: Cambridge University Press, 1997), 61.

7. Bharati Mukherjee, *Jasmine* (New York: Grove, 1989), 101.

8. David Henry Hwang, *M. Butterfly* (New York: Plume, 1989), 94–95.

9. Ibid.

10. Ibid., 98.

11. Edward Said, *Orientalism* (New York: Vintage, 1979), 2.

12. Ibid.; emphasis added.

13. Lisa Lowe, *Immigrant Acts: On Asian American Cultural Politics* (Durham, N.C.: Duke University Press, 1996).

14. Matthew Frye Jacobson, *Barbarian Virtues: The United States Encounters Foreign Peoples at Home and Abroad, 1876–1917* (New York: Hill and Wang, 2001), 62.

Chapter 1: California Roll

1. Quoted in Theodore C. Bestor, "How Sushi Went Global," in *The Cultural Politics of Food and Eating,* ed. James L. Watson and Melissa L. Caldwell (Malden, Mass.: Blackwell, 2005), 14.

2. Jay McInerney, "Raw," *New York Times*, August 10, 2007, accessed October 14, 2011, http://www.nytimes.com/2007/06/10/books/review/McInerney-t.html.

3. Indeed, the number of type of sushi rolls in America is limited only by the imagination of the sushi chef and the diners willing to try a new combination. On the website of the Rock and Roll Sushi Restaurant in Dallas, for example, the house special signature sushi rolls include the following innovative if not whimsical concoctions: Volcano Roll (creamy baked scallops over California roll), Cajun Roll (crawfish tail, cucumber, spicy sauce), Spicy Rock n' Roll (spicy tuna, shrimp tempura, cucumber, potato wrapped in soybean sheet), Triple Roll (fried calamari, crabmeat, smelt egg, potato, cucumber), Dallas Stars Roll (fried calamari, eel, dried vegetable flakes), Mavericks Roll (spicy tuna, avocado, spicy mayonnaise, chile sauce), Longhorn Roll (shrimp tempura, avocado, tuna, spicy mayonnaise, chile sauce), and Fried Jalapeño Roll (panko-battered, deep-fried roll with fried calamari, jalapeño, cream cheese, sweet and spicy sauce).

4. Rumi Sakamoto and Matthew Allen, "There's Something Fishy about That Sushi: How Japan Interprets the Global Sushi Boom," *Japan Forum* 23, no. 1 (2011): 114.

5. David Kamp, *The United States of Arugula: How We Became a Gourmet Nation* (New York: Broadway, 2006), 316.

6. In a July 15, 2007, *New York Times* article, Stephen A. Shaw writes that although American obstetricians routinely advise pregnant women to avoid raw fish (along with alcohol and unpasteurized cheeses), his "friends in Japan laugh at the notion of avoiding sushi when they're expecting." (And French women commonly drink wine and eat unpasteurized cheese during pregnancy.) In fact, "in Japan, eating raw fish is considered part of good neonatal nutrition," writes Shaw. "The Japanese government is fanatical about public health, and Japanese medical scientists are among the best in the world. You can be sure that, were there documented complications resulting from pregnant women eating sushi in Japan, there would be swift government intervention. Yet, in the United States, it is taboo for a pregnant woman to eat raw fish." Shaw contends the US medical establishment's fear over sushi's potential harm to unborn children (due to "speculative risk of food-borne illness, especially parasites") is scientifically unfounded.

7. Julia Moskin, "Game Food that Intercepts Nachos," *New York Times*, February 1, 2006, accessed November 10, 2011, http://www.nytimes.com/2006/02/01/dining/01supe.html.

8. Kamp, *United States of Arugula*, 316.

9. Harold McGee, *On Food and Cooking: The Science and Lore of the Kitchen* (New York: Scribner, 2004), 218.

10. Kim Severson, "Global Food Fight? Why, Soytainly!" *San Francisco Chronicle*, August 25, 2002, accessed January 15, 2006, http://www.sfgate.com/cgi-bin/article.cgi?f=/c/a/2002/08/25/MN70302.DTL.

11. Ibid.

12. Alan Davidson, *The Oxford Companion to Food* (Oxford: Oxford University Press, 1999), 740.

13. W. Mark Fruin, *Kikkoman: Company, Clan, and Community* (Cambridge, Mass.: Harvard University Press, 1983), 262–263.

14. Chris Hawley, "Chinese Chili Pepper Invasion Making Some Mexicans Hot," *USA Today*, November 22, 2005, accessed January 15, 2006, http://www.usatoday.com/news/world/2005-11-21-pepper-war_x.htm.

15. Sophie D. Coe, *America's First Cuisines* (Austin: University of Texas Press, 1994), 61.

16. Dave DeWitt, *The Chile Pepper Encyclopedia* (New York: William Morrow, 1999), 184.

17. Houyuan Lu et al., "Culinary Archaeology: Millet Noodles in Late Neolithic China," *Nature* 437 (October 13, 2005): 967–968.

18. Steve Conner, "Chinese Take Away the Credit for Inventing Noodles," *Independent*, October 13, 2005, accessed October 15, 2005, http://www.independent.co.uk/news/science/chinese-take-away-the-credit-for-inventing-noodles-510722.html; and Lachlan Cartwright, "4000-Year-Old Noodles," *Sun*, October 13, 2005, accessed October 15, 2005, http://www.thesun.co.uk/sol/homepage/news/112432/4000-year-old-noodles.html.

19. Thomas H. Maugh II and Karen Kaplan, "Neolithic Chinese Used Their Noodles," *Los Angeles Times*, October 13, 2005, accessed October 15, 2005, http://articles.latimes.com/2005/oct/13/science/sci-noodles13.

20. Davidson, *Oxford Companion to Food*, 413.

21. M. F. K. Fisher, introduction to *Japanese Cooking: A Simple Art*, by Shizuo Tsuji (Tokyo: Kodansha International, 1980), 8–9.

22. Michael Ashkenazi and Jeanne Jacob, *The Essence of Japanese Cuisine: An Essay on Food and Culture* (Philadelphia: University of Pennsylvania Press, 2000), 160.

23. Ibid., 202.

24. Ibid., 205.

25. Theodore C. Bestor, *Tsukiji: The Fish Market at the Center of the World* (Berkeley: University of California Press, 2004), 238.

26. Ashkenazi and Jacob, *Japanese Cuisine*, 205–206.

27. Kinjiro Omae and Yuzuru Tachibana, *The Book of Sushi* (Tokyo: Kodansha, 1981), 122–123.

28. Sasha Issenberg, *The Sushi Economy: Globalization and the Making of a Modern Delicacy* (New York: Gotham, 2007), 111.

29. Linda Nochlin, "Why Have There Been No Great Women Artists?" *Art News* 69, no. 9 (January 1971): 22–39.

30. Bestor, *Tsukiji*, 126.

31. Ashkenazi and Jacob, *Japanese Cuisine*, 211.

32. Trevor Corson, *The Zen of Fish: The Story of Sushi, from Samurai to Supermarket* (New York: HarperCollins, 2007), 53.

33. Naomichi Ishige, *The History and Culture of Japanese Food* (London: Kegan Paul, 2001), 228.

34. Corson, *Zen of Fish*, 53.

35. Ashkenazi and Jacob, *Japanese Cuisine*, 211.

36. Ishige, *History and Culture of Japanese Food*, 206–207.

37. Ashkenazi and Jacob, *Japanese Cuisine*, 211.

38. Ishige, *History and Culture of Japanese Food*, 228.

39. Corson, *Zen of Fish*, 54.

40. Eric Asimov, "Quiet, Please: Sushi Being Served," restaurant review of Sushi Yasuda, *New York Times*, November 15, 2011, accessed November 15, 2011, http://www.nytimes.com/2011/11/16/dining/reviews/sushi-yasuda-nyc-restaurant-review.html?ref=dining.

41. Ibid.

42. Katy McLaughlin, "Sushi Bullies," *Wall Street Journal,* October 24, 2008, accessed January 4, 2012, http://sec.online.wsj.com/article/SB122480233710964683.html.

43. Ashkenazi and Jacob, *Japanese Cuisine,* 202 (italics in the original).

44. Coe, *America's First Cuisines,* 28. A diverting side note: the word "avocado" is derived from the word *ahuacatl,* which in Nahuatl (the Aztec language) means testicle, in reference to the fruit's shape, which was thought to resemble that part of the male anatomy. Coe notes that the *Oxford English Dictionary's* claim that the word comes from the Spanish for "advocate" is most certainly fallacious (28).

45. Ligaya Mishan, "If Fish Liked Nightclubs," restaurant review of Catch, *New York Times,* June 5, 2012, accessed June 5, 2012, http://www.nytimes.com/2012/06/06/dining/reviews/restaurant-review-catch-in-meatpacking-district.html?ref=dining.

46. John F. Mariani, *The Dictionary of American Food and Drink* (New York: Hearst, 1994), 52.

47. Raymond Sokolov, *Why We Eat What We Eat: How Columbus Changed the Way the World Eats* (New York: Summit, 1991), 238; Katarzyna J. Cwiertka, *Modern Japanese Cuisine: Food, Power and National Identity* (London: Reaktion, 2006), 196.

48. Quoted in Sakamoto and Allen, "There's Something Fishy," 115.

49. Cwiertka compares the American California roll to the asparagus *nigiri* and kamikaze roll that are common in Britain, not so much to portray these as symbols of culinary debasement but to point out the consequence of sushi's globalization, in which the notion of authenticity often seems to be the last thing that matters.

50. James L. Watson, ed., *Golden Arches East: McDonald's in East Asia* (Stanford, Calif.: Stanford University Press, 1997), 4–5.

51. Youchi Shimemura, "Globalization vs. Americanization: Is the World Being Americanized by the Dominance of American Culture?" *Comparative Civilizations Review* 47 (Fall 2002): 81.

52. Donald E. Pease, "New Perspectives on U.S. Culture and Imperialism," in *Cultures of United States Imperialism,* ed. Amy Kaplan and Donald E. Pease (Durham, N.C.: Duke University Press, 1994), 26.

53. Davidson, *Oxford Companion to Food,* 771.

54. Sonoko Kondo, *The Poetical Pursuit of Food: Japanese Recipes for American Cooks* (New York: Clarkson Potter, 1986), 147. Also, according to Roberta Strippoli, a scholar of premodern Japanese literature, California roll was ubiquitous in Japan when she first visited there in the late 1980s. She had previously lived in Rome and was unaware of California roll's backstory. Only when she moved to the United States a few years later did she realize that California roll was regarded by "serious" American sushi aficionados as thoroughly "American" and thus not fit for consumption.

55. Injoo Chun, Jaewoon Lee, and Youngran Baek, *Authentic Recipes from Korea* (Singapore: Periplus, 2004), 78; and "Korean Barbecued Flank Steak on Hot and Sour Slaw Salad," Food Network, accessed June 13, 2007, http://www.foodnetwork.com/food/recipes/recipe/0,1977,FOOD_9936_30793,00.html.

56. Ernest Hemingway, *The Sun Also Rises* (New York: Scribner, 1926), 251.

57. Michael Pollan, *The Ominvore's Dilemma: A Natural History of Four Meals* (New York: Penguin, 2006), 3.

58. Hemingway, *Sun Also Rises,* 136–137.

59. Henri Kamer, "De l'authenticité des sculptures africaines," *Arts d'Afrique Noire* 12 (1974): 38, quoted in Sally Price, *Primitive Art in Civilized Places* (Chicago: Chicago University Press, 1989), 13.

60. Milan Kundera, *The Unbearable Lightness of Being* (New York: Harper and Row, 1984), 32–35.

61. Appadurai, "On Culinary Authenticity," 24–25.

62. John Berger, *Ways of Seeing* (London: Penguin, 1972), 7–34.

63. Appadurai, "On Culinary Authenticity," 24–25.

64. Edward Said, *Beginnings: Intention and Method* (New York: Columbia University Press, 1985), 6, 142, 316, 357, 372–373.

65. Sylvia Lovegren, *Fashionable Food: Seven Decades of Food Fads* (Chicago: Chicago University Press, 2005), 286, 288, 292.

66. Bestor, *Tsukiji*, 141.

67. Ishige, *History and Culture of Japanese Food*, 42.

68. Omae and Tachibana, *Book of Sushi*, 151.

69. Bestor, *Tsukiji*, 141.

70. For an example of a type of sushi that belies the popular idea that sushi by its nature is bite-sized and consists of raw fish and rice (à la nigirizushi or makizushi), consider *chirashizushi* ("scattered sushi"), which is essentially a bowl of rice. A common presentation consists of a bowlful of seasoned rice artistically topped with an assortment of sashimi and a variety of garnishes, both cooked and raw.

71. Corson, *Zen of Fish*, 27.

72. Bestor, *Tsukiji*, 141.

73. Omae and Tachibana, *Book of Sushi*, 152.

74. Bestor, *Tsukiji*, 141.

75. Omae and Tachibana, *Book of Sushi*, 153–154.

76. Ishige, *History and Culture of Japanese Food*, 42.

77. Richard Hosking, *A Dictionary of Japanese Food: Ingredients and Culture* (Tokyo: Tuttle, 1995), 138.

78. Corson, *Zen of Fish*, 27–29.

79. Issenberg, *Sushi Economy*, 89.

80. Molly O'Neill, "The Chop Suey Syndrome: Americanizing the Exotic," *New York Times*, July 26, 1989, accessed January 12, 2012, http://www.nytimes.com/1989/07/26/garden/the-chop-suey-syndrome-americanizing-the-exotic.html?scp=20&sq=%22california+roll%22&st=nyt.

81. For a comprehensive genealogy of chop suey, see Andrew Coe, *Chop Suey: A Cultural History of Chinese Food in the United States* (New York: Oxford University Press, 2009).

82. Iris-Aya Laemmerhirt, "Imagining the Taste. Transnational Food Exchanges between Japan and the United States," *The Japanese Journal of American Studies* 21 (2010): 233.

83. Kamp, *United States of Arugula*, 314.

84. Corson, *Zen of Fish*, 82.

85. Issenberg, *Sushi Economy*, 88–90.

86. Ibid., 90–91.

87. Ibid., 91.

88. Kamp, *United States of Arugula*, 315; italics added.

89. Ibid., 315–316.

90. Florence Fabricant, "Dining Out: Japanese Food with Inventiveness," *New York Times*, March 7, 1982, accessed January 10, 2012, http://www.nytimes.com/1982/03/07/nyregion/dining-out-japanese-food-with-inventiveness.html?scp=1&sq=%22california+roll%22&st=nyt.

91. Corson, *Zen of Fish*, 82.

Chapter 2: Chinese Take-Out

1. Lukas I. Alpert, "Georgia Woman Calls 911 to Report Delivery of a Wrong Order from Chinese Food Restaurant," *New York Daily News*, June 15, 2011, accessed June 27, 2011, http://articles.nydailynews.com/2011-06-15/news/29681628_1_georgia-woman-wrong-order-wrong-food.

2. Indigo Som, "Chinese Restaurant Drive-Thru," in *Alien Encounters: Popular Culture in Asian America*, ed. Mimi Thi Nguyen and Thuy Linh Nguyen Tu (Durham, N.C.: Duke University Press, 2007), 150.

3. Kara Kelly Hallmar, *Encyclopedia of Asian American Artists* (Westport, Conn.: Greenwood, 2007), 202.

4. Davidson, *Oxford Companion to Food*, 316–317; Joel Denker, *The World on a Plate: A Tour through a History of America's Ethnic Cuisine* (Boulder, Colo.: Westview Press, 2003), 75–76.

5. Judy Yung, Gordon H. Chang, and Him Mark Lai, eds., *Chinese American Voices: From the Gold Rush to the Present* (Berkeley: University of California Press, 2006), 9; and Samantha Barbas, "'I'll take Chop Suey': Restaurants as Agents of Culinary and Cultural Exchange," *Journal of Popular Culture* 36, no. 4 (2003): 671.

6. Daniel Ostrow, David Ostrow, and Mary Sham, *Manhattan's Chinatown* (Charleston, S.C.: Arcadia, 2008), 43, 59–61; and Harley Spiller, "Chow Fun City: Three Centuries of Chinese Cuisine in New York City," in *Gastropolis: Food and New York City*, ed. Annie Hauck-Lawson and Jonathan Deutsch (New York: Columbia University Press, 2009), 135.

7. Robert G. Lee, *Orientals: Asian Americans in Popular Culture* (Philadelphia: Temple University Press, 1999), 3.

8. Barbas, "'I'll take Chop Suey,'" 684.

9. Frank Wu, *Yellow: Race in America beyond Black and White* (New York: Basic, 2002), 223.

10. Margot Adler, "Chinese Restaurant Workers in U.S. Face Hurdles," *NPR*, May 8, 2007, accessed March 15, 2009, http://www.npr.org/templates/story/story.php?storyId=10069448.

11. Jan Harold Brunvand, *The Choking Doberman and Other "New" Urban Legends* (New York: Norton, 1984), 121–122; Brunvand, *The Mexican Pet: More "New" Urban Legends and Some Old Favorites* (New York: Norton, 1986), 103; Brunvand, *The Vanishing Hitchhiker: American Urban Legends and Their Meanings* (New York: Norton, 1981), 83; and Brunvand, *Encyclopedia of Urban Legends* (New York: Norton, 2002), 70–71.

12. Several Internet sources mistakenly attribute "Cats in the Kettle" to a more renowned song parodist, Weird Al Yankovic.

13. Jeffrey Steingarten, *It Must've Been Something I Ate* (New York: Vintage, 2002), 97–98.

14. Manny Fernandez, "When Pennies Fail to Pay the Bill, A Bronx Man Pushes for Change," *New York Times*, May 4, 2007, accessed June 12, 2007, http://select.nytimes.com/search/restricted/article?res=F70A10FD3A5A0C778CDDAC0894DF404482.

15. Toni Morrison, *Playing in the Dark: Whiteness and the Literary Imagination* (Cambridge, Mass.: Harvard University Press, 1992), xxi.

16. Ibid., 46–47.

17. Quoted in ibid., 72.

18. Morrison, *Playing in the Dark*, 72–73.

19. For a detailed account of the Vincent Chin case and its aftermath, including the formation of a nationwide Asian American protest movement as a response to the case, see Helen Zia, *Asian American Dreams: The Emergence of an American People* (New York: Farrar, Staus and Giroux, 2001), 55–81.

20. Michael Moore, "The Man Who Killed Vincent Chin," *Detroit Free Press*, August 30, 1987, posted on Michael Moore (blog), accessed June 24, 2012, http://www.michaelmoore.com/words/must-read/man-who-killed-vincent-chin-michael-moore#.

21. "CME Beginnings (From Tender Plant to Sturdy Tree)," Christian Methodist Episcopal Church, accessed June 8, 2012, http://www.c-m-e.org/core/roots.htm.

22. For a detailed account and analysis of the discord between African American customers and Korean merchants in New York City during the 1980s and 1990s, see Claire Jean Kim, *Bitter Fruit: The Politics of Black-Korean Conflict in New York City* (New Haven, Conn.: Yale University Press, 2003). For an analysis of the Los Angeles riots of 1992, see Nancy Abelmann and John Lie, *Blue Dreams: Korean Americans and the Los Angeles Riots* (Cambridge, Mass.: Harvard University Press, 1997). For a fictional account of the Black-Korean discord centered on a Korean small business in Queens, New York, see Leonard Chang's novel, *The Fruit 'N Food* (Seattle: Black Heron, 1996).

23. This is dramatically illustrated in the 2004 film *Take Out*, directed by Sean Baker and Shih-Ching Tsou, which captures a day in the life of an illegal Chinese immigrant working as a deliveryman for a New York City Chinese take-out restaurant.

24. I thank Jennifer Ann Ho for reminding me of this important culinary relationship.

25. Dareh Gregorian, "Panel Woks Away: Drops Menu-Bias Rap," *New York Post*, May 1, 2007, accessed June 12, 2007, http://www.nypost.com/seven/05012007/news/regionalnews/panel_woks_away_regionalnews_dareh_gregorian.htm; Michael Saul, "Restaurant Serves Deal in Price Clash," *New York Daily News*, May 1, 2007, accessed June 12, 2007, http://www.nydailynews.com/news/restaurant-serves-deal-price-clash-article-1.253169.

26. For a glimpse into the extent of how Chinese food has become global, see Sidney Cheung and David Y. H. Yu, eds., *Globalization of Chinese Food* (London: Routledge, 2004).

27. For a fascinating discussion of the origins of General Tso chicken and whether or not an "authentic" version even exists, see Fuchsia Dunlop, "Strange Tale of General Tso," in *Authenticity in the Kitchen: Proceedings of the Oxford Symposium on Food and Cookery 2005*, ed. Richard Hosking (Blackawton, UK: Prospect Books, 2006), 165–177.

28. For a discussion of authenticity and tourism, see Dean MacCannell, *The Tourist: A New Theory of the Leisure Class* (Berkeley: University of California Press, 1999);

and John Urry, *The Tourist Gaze: Leisure and Travel in Contemporary Societies* (London: Sage Publications, 1990). For a discussion of authenticity and tourism within the context of food, see Jennie Germann Molz, "Tasting an Imagined Thailand: Authenticity and Culinary Tourism in Thai Restaurants," in *Culinary Tourism: Eating and Otherness*, ed. Lucy Long (Lexington: University of Kentucky Press, 2004), 53–75.

29. E. N. Anderson, *Food of China* (New Haven, Conn.: Yale University Press, 1988), 173.

30. In the Binghamton area of New York, where I currently live and work, there are no less than thirty Chinese restaurants within a ten-mile radius of my home. The majority of them are take-outs, meaning restaurants that do not provide table service. There are also several enormous buffet-type restaurants, which appears to be the direction Chinese food as a business is trending nationwide. Then there are two or three places considered authentic enough for "foodies" to brag about to visitors to the area. While each of these places fills a different consumerist niche, none serves the type of food Anderson describes. In his defense, perhaps the quality of Chinese food in the United States has changed for the better since Anderson published his book in 1988. However, my personal recollection of having regularly eaten Chinese food since the 1970s is that Chinese food in this country, like any other type of food, varies widely enough in type and quality as to not warrant the wholesale dismissal of Chinese food in America.

31. "The Legacy," Trader Vics, accessed June 11, 2007, http://www.tradervics.com.

32. Anderson, *Food of China*, 170–172.

33. Ibid., 173–174; emphasis added.

34. Nina Zagat and Tim Zagat, "Eating beyond Sichuan," *New York Times*, June 15, 2007, accessed June 22, 2011, http://www.nytimes.com/2007/06/15/opinion/15zagat.html.

35. Jennifer 8. Lee, *The Fortune Cookie Chronicles: Adventures in the World of Chinese Food* (New York: Twelve, 2008), 49.

36. Coe, *Chop Suey*, 176–177.

37. David M. Lubin, *Titanic* (London: British Film Institute, 1999), 8.

38. Kenneth Turan, "You Try to Stop It," *Los Angeles Times*, March 21, 1998, accessed January 18, 2010, http://articles.latimes.com/1998/mar/21/entertainment/ca-31050.

Chapter 3: Disreputable Gastronomy

1. Martin F. Manalansan IV, "The Empire of Food: Place, Memory, and Asian 'Ethnic Cuisines,'" in *Gastropolis: Food and New York City*, ed. Annie-Hauck-Lawson and Jonathan Deutsch (New York: Columbia University Press, 2009), 93.

2. Edwin G. Burrows and Mike Wallace, *Gotham: A History of New York City to 1898* (New York: Oxford University Press, 1999), 5.

3. Kenneth T. Jackson, ed., *The Encyclopedia of New York City* (New Haven, Conn.: Yale University Press, 1995), 966.

4. Sarah Kershaw, "Protector of the Long Departed; Historian Restores Early Burial Plots in Queens," *New York Times*, December 29, 2000, accessed June 9, 2011, http://www.nytimes.com/2000/12/29/nyregion/protector-of-the-long-departed-historian-restores-early-burial-plots-in-queens.html.

5. Jeff Berglund, *Cannibal Fictions: American Explorations of Colonialism, Race, Gender, and Sexuality* (Madison: University of Wisconsin Press, 2006), 3.

6. W. Arens, *The Man-Eating Myth: Anthropology and Anthropophagy* (Oxford: Oxford University Press, 1979), 44.

7. Jean Andrews, *Peppers: The Domesticated Capsicums* (Austin: University of Texas Press, 1995), 4.

8. Jack Turner, *Spice: The History of a Temptation* (New York: Knopf, 2005), 11.

9. Andrews, *Peppers*, 4.

10. Also called "nightshades" (from the Latin *Solanum*), the most significant Old World food that belongs to this family of flowering plants is the eggplant.

11. Coe, *America's First Cuisines*, 60.

12. Andrews, *Peppers*, 5.

13. Mark Miller, *The Great Chile Book* (Berkeley, Calif.: Ten Speed, 1991), 6.

14. Andrews, *Peppers*, 11.

15. Dave DeWitt and Paul W. Bosland, *Peppers of the World: An Identification Guide* (Berkeley, Calif.: Ten Speed, 1996).

16. Alfred W. Crosby Jr., *The Columbian Exchange: Biological and Cultural Consequences of 1492* (Westport, Conn.: Praeger, 2003), 31.

17. Jean Andrews, "The Peripatetic Chili Pepper: Diffusion of the Domesticated Capsicums since Columbus," in *Chilies to Chocolate: Food the Americas Gave the World*, ed. Nelson Foster and Linda S. Cordell (Tucson: University of Arizona Press, 1992), 82.

18. Ben-Erik van Wyk, *Food Plants of the World* (Portland, Ore.: Timber, 2005), 116; and DeWitt, *Chile Pepper Encyclopedia*, 239.

19. Andrews, "Peripatetic Chili Pepper," 82–83.

20. Amal Naj, *Peppers: A Story of Hot Pursuits* (New York: Random House, 1992), 3.

21. On June 25, 2009, BBC News reported that India's defense scientists were working on a "chilli grenade" containing Bhut Jolokia, the hottest variety on record. The device "will be used to control rioters and in counterinsurgency operations" as well as "spread on the fences around army barracks in the hopes the strong smell will keep out animals." http://news.bbc.co.uk/2/hi/south_asia/8119591.stm.

22. DeWitt, *Chile Pepper Encyclopedia*, 176.

23. Mi-ok Kim, "Yeongyang Chili Pepper Market," *Koreana* 14, no. 3 (Autumn 2000): 64. There are ten botanically cataloged hybrids in Korea, all resembling the North American cayenne chile and introduced to South Korea between 1979 and 1985. Prior to the mid-1970s, only open-pollinated land varieties existed in Korea.

24. DeWitt, *Chile Pepper Encyclopedia*, 176.

25. Michael J. Pettid, *Korean Cuisine: An Illustrated History* (London: Reaktion, 2008), 48.

26. Manjo Kim, "A Korean Original: Kimchi," *Koreana* 11, no. 3 (Autumn 1997): 64; and Kim, "The Origins and History of Kimchi," in *Kimchi, Thousand Years*, vol. 1, ed. Man-Jo Kim, Kyou-Tae Lee, and O-Young Lee (Seoul: Design House, 1997), 120.

27. Pettid, *Korean Cuisine*, 45.

28. Man-jo Kim, "Origins and History of Kimchi," 121.

29. Lizzie Collingham, *Curry: A Tale of Cooks and Conquerors* (New York: Oxford University Press, 2006), 50–54.

30. Andrews, "Peripatetic Chili Pepper," 86–90.

31. Dave DeWitt and Nancy Gerlach, *The Whole Chile Pepper Book* (Boston: Little, Brown, 1990), 277. The popular jalapeño, in comparison, registers between 2,500 to 15,000 SHUs, while the habañero and Scotch bonnet range between 100,000 and 500,000 SHUs. The Santaka, a cayenne-type that the Japanese began cultivating soon after the chile was introduced to the islands, ranges between 50,000 and 100,000 SHUs.

32. Martin Robinson, Andrew Bender, and Rob Whyte, *Lonely Planet: Korea* (Victoria, Aus.: Lonely Planet, 2004), 50.

33. Mi-ok Kim, "Yeongyang Chili Pepper," 62, 64.

34. Chun Ja Lee, Hye Won Park, and Kwi Young Kim, *The Book of Kimchi* (Seoul: Korean Information Service, 1998), 18–19.

35. Kyung-Koo Han, "Some Foods Are Good to Think: Kimchi and the Epitomization of National Character," *Korean Social Science Journal* 27, no. 1 (2000): 223.

36. Pettid, *Korean Cuisine*, 45–46.

37. Cherl-Ho Lee, *Fermentation Technology in Korea* (Seoul: Korea University Press, 2001), 92; and The Korea Food Research Institute, accessed June 2, 2007, http://kimchi.kfri.re.kr/html.

38. Manjo Kim, "Kimchi: The Secret Korean Flavor of the Centuries," *Korean and Korean American Studies Bulletin* 6, no. 1 (Spring 1995): 26.

39. Lee, Park, and Kim, *Book of Kimchi*, 17.

40. The Korea Food Research Institute, http://kimchi.kfri.re.kr/html.

41. Man-jo Kim, "Origins and History of Kimchi."

42. Manjo Kim, "Secret Korean Flavor of the Centuries," 29.

43. Lee, Park, and Kim, *Book of Kimchi*, 43–48.

44. Ibid., 49–52.

45. Ibid., 27. The importance of seafood is most evident in the fact that kimchi can also be prepared with squid, cutlass fish, flounder, crab, or some other sea creature as the central ingredient. Given kimchi's incredible diversity, it is perhaps not surprising to learn that even meat-based kimchi, most notably made of pheasant, was not uncommon during the early Joseon period.

46. Young C. Lee, "Kimchi: The Famous Fermented Vegetable Product in Korea," *Food Reviews International* 7, no. 4 (1991): 400.

47. Man-jo Kim, "Origins and History of Kimchi," 112–113.

48. Ibid., 132; Kun-Young Park and Cheigh Hong-Sik, "Kimchi," in *Handbook of Food and Beverage Fermentation Technology*, ed. Y. H. Hui et al. (New York: Marcel Dekker, 2004), 621; Lee, Park, and Kim, *Book of Kimchi*, 32.

49. Man-jo Kim, "Origins and History of Kimchi," 132.

50. McGee, *On Food and Cooking*, 291–292.

51. Man-jo Kim, "Origins and History of Kimchi," 136.

52. In this, kimchi is semi-analogous to "Hawai'i," a term that can denote either one specific island (the Big Island) or all the islands that make up the Hawaiian archipelago, including the seven inhabited islands and hundreds of uninhabited islets and atolls.

53. Frank J. Prial, "Wine Talk," *New York Times*, December 25, 1991, accessed June 9, 2011, http://www.nytimes.com/1991/12/25/garden/wine-talk-425591.html.

54. Since the airing of the *60 Minutes* feature, the *New York Times*, for example, has published an abundance of articles stating, implying, or debating the associa-

tion between a modest intake of red wine with a whole host of healthy outcomes, including lowering cholesterol (August 14, 1991), improving the heart (February 17, 1993), reducing the risk of prostate cancer (September 28, 2004), increased endurance (November 17, 2006), extending the human life span (June 4, 2008), cutting the risk of fatty liver disease (June 10, 2008), curbing fat cells (June 17, 2008), reducing inflammation (November 9, 2009), slowing and reversing aging (November 27, 2008), and speeding up metabolism and reducing weight gain in women (March 8, 2010).

55. Prial, "Wine Talk," December 25, 1991.

56. Frank J. Prial, "Wine Talk," *New York Times*, October 20, 1993, accessed June 9, 2011, http://www.nytimes.com/1993/10/20/garden/wine-talk-735893.html.

57. Marian Burros, "Eating Well," *New York Times*, March 4, 1992, accessed June 9, 2011, http://www.nytimes.com/1992/03/04/garden/eating-well.html.

58. Frank J. Prial, "Wine Talk," *New York Times*, May 15, 1996, accessed June 10, 2011, http://www.nytimes.com/1996/05/15/garden/wine-talk-frank-j-prial.html.

59. Ibid.

60. Burros, "Eating Well."

61. Georgia Dullea, "No Two Kimchis Taste Alike," *New York Times*, July 29, 1987, accessed June 10, 2011, http://www.nytimes.com/1987/07/29/garden/no-two-kimchis-taste-alike.html.

62. Nick B. Williams Jr., "Potent Side Dish Kimchi: The Spice of Life to Koreans," *Los Angeles Times*, November 10, 1987, accessed June 10, 2011, http://articles.latimes.com/1987-11-10/news/mn-19948_1_side-dish.

63. Joan Raymond, "The World's 5 Healthiest Foods," *Health*, March 2006, 171.

64. Mei Chin, "The Art of Kimchi," *Saveur*, November 2009, 76.

65. Mary Katherine Schmidl and Theodore Peter Labuza, *Essentials of Functional Foods* (Gaithersburg, Md.: Aspen, 2000), 381.

66. R. Chadwick et al., *Functional Foods* (Berlin, Ger.: Springer, 2004), 32.

67. Glenn R. Gibson and Christine M. Williams, *Functional Foods: Concept to Product* (Boca Raton, Fla.: CRC, 2000), 1.

68. Clare M. Hasler, *Regulation of Functional Foods and Nutraceuticals: A Global Perspective* (Ames, Iowa: Blackwell, 2005), 169.

69. Kun-Young Park and Sook-Hee Rhee, "Functional Foods from Fermented Vegetable Products: Kimchi (Korean Fermented Vegetables) and Functionality," in *Asian Functional Foods*, ed. John Shi, Chi-Tang Ho, and Fereidoon Shahidi (Boca Raton, Fla.: CRC, 2005), 346, 349.

70. The "Patent IH-22 Lactic Acid Bacteria" proclamation appears not only on the kimchi jar, but is evident throughout Kum Gang San Restaurant—on menus, posters, and placements.

71. Raymond, "World's 5 Healthiest Foods," 171.

72. Stuart Thorne, *The History of Food Preservation* (Totowa, N.J.: Barnes and Noble, 1986), 15

73. Davidson, *Oxford Companion to Food*, 296.

74. Ibid., 296.

75. Patricia Rain, "Vanilla: Nectar of the Gods," in *Chiles to Chocolate: Food the Americas Gave the World*, ed. Nelson Foster and Linda S. Cordell (Tucson: University of Arizona Press, 1992), 36–37.

76. Coe, *America's First Cuisines*, 53.

77. Norimitsu Onishi, "From Dung to Coffee Brew with No Aftertaste," *New York Times*, April 17, 2010, accessed June 10, 2011, http://www.nytimes.com/2010/04/18/world/asia/18civetcoffee.html.

78. Barbara Demick, "Koreans' Kimchi Adulation, with a Side of Skepticism," *Los Angeles Times*, May 21, 2006, accessed June 10, 2011, http://articles.latimes.com/2006/may/21/world/fg-kimchi21.

79. "Korean Scientists Say Kimchi Can Prevent Food Poisoning," *Chosun Ilbo*, October 31, 2004, accessed January 12, 2007, http://english.chosun.com/w21data/html/news/200408/200408310015.html.

80. "S Korea's LG Sells Kimchi Air Conditioner Which Kills Bird Flu Virus," *Forbes*, February 14, 2006, accessed October 12, 2007, http://www.forbes.com/business/feeds/afx/2006/02/14/afx2523633.html.

81. Demick, "Koreans' Kimchi Adulation."

82. Curiously, the bottle makes no mention of "Dok-do" in the Korean portion of the text, either when mentioning Dr. Kang or when stating that the contents are more nutritious when aged longer.

83. Although there is no exact English equivalent, *han* might best be defined as a state of sadness, melancholy, and resentment that is specific to the Korean experience, akin to how the "blues" might sum up the often doleful struggle of the African American experience.

84. Charles Scanlon, "S Korean Fury over Island Dispute," *BBC News*, March 14, 2005, accessed January 20, 2007, http://news.bbc.co.uk/2/hi/asia-pacific/4347851.stm; and Norimitsu Onishi, "Dispute Over Islets Frays Ties between Tokyo and Seoul," *New York Times*, March 22, 2005, accessed June 10, 2010, http://www.nytimes.com/2005/03/22/international/asia/22korea.html.

85. Sean Fern, "Tokdo or Takeshima? The International Law of Territorial Acquisition in the Japan-Korea Island Dispute," *Stanford Journal of East Asian Affairs* 5, no. 1 (Winter 2005): 78.

86. Ibid., 85.

87. Sung-jae Choi, "The Politics of the Dokdo Issue," *Journal of East Asian Studies* 5 (2005): 468.

88. Rather confusingly, back then Japan referred to Takeshima as Matsushima, while another nearby island, South Korea's Ulleungdo, was called Takeshima.

89. Jon M. Van Dyke, "Legal Issues Related to Sovereignty over Dokdo and Its Maritime Boundary," *Ocean Development & International Law* 38 (2007): 167–168.

90. Ibid., 180.

91. In addition to Takeshima, Japan is currently mired in another territorial dispute over a different group of islands, this time in the East China Sea, which it claims to have taken possession of as *terra nullius* in 1895. These islands, too, have at least three names: Senkaku in Japanese, Diaoyu in Chinese, and Pinnacle Islands in English. The sovereignty of these tiny islands, situated between Okinawa and Taiwan, has been bitterly contested since the early 1970s, when the presence of hydrocarbon deposits on the islands' seabed was predicted. Battling Japan for ownership—at times in harmony and at other times in discordance—is both the People's Republic of China and the Republic of China. See Steven Wei Su, "The Territorial Dispute over the Tiaoyu/Senkaku Islands: An Update," *Ocean Development & International Law* 36 (2005): 47.

92. Van Dyke, "Legal Issues," 165–167.

93. Fern, "Tokdo or Takeshima?" 85.

94. Ibid., 86–87.

95. Collectively fanning the fire of South Korea's "Dokdo movement," these include the National Headquarters of Defending Dokdo, the Korea Dokdo Research and Preservation Association, the Council of Dokdo Residents, and the Headquarters for Making Dokdo an Inhabited Island, among countless others. And in August 2000 the establishment of the Dokdo Love Society by twenty-nine lawmakers became a clear signal that Dokdo was no longer just a populist crusade, but also a vital domestic political issue. See Choi, "Politics of the Dokdo Issue," 469–470.

96. Fern, "Tokdo or Takeshima?" 79; Choi, "Politics of the Dokdo Issue," 475.

97. "LP-X Dokdo (Landing Platform Experimental) Amphibious Ship," Global Security, accessed November 1, 2007, http://www.globalsecurity.org/military/world/rok/lp-x.htm.

98. "Seoul Regrets Japan's Protest over Ship's Name," *Yonhap News Agency*, July 13, 2005, accessed November 1, 2007, http://www.accessmylibrary.com/coms2/summary_0286-9439250_ITM.

99. Seung-woo Kang, "Unified Team at Crossroads," *Korea Times*, October 31, 2007, accessed November 1, 2007, http://www.koreatimes.co.kr/www/news/include/print.asp?newsIdx=12849.

100. North Korea chose not to qualify for the games and ignored FIFA's request to host tournament matches. See Jeré Longman, "North Korea Trying for Unexpected in World Cup Again," *New York Times*, June 1, 2010, accessed June 2, 2011, http://www.nytimes.com/2010/06/02/sports/soccer/02korea.html.

101. Julia Moskin, "Culinary Diplomacy with a Side of Kimchi," *New York Times*, September 23, 2009, accessed September 24, 2009, http://query.nytimes.com/gst/fullpage.html?res=9C0CE0D8103FF930A1575AC0A96F9C8B63.

102. William Franklin Sands, *Undiplomatic Memories* (New York: McGraw-Hill, 1930), quoted in Martin Uden, *Times Past in Korea: An Illustrated Collection of Encounters, Events, Customs and Daily Life Recorded by Foreign Visitors* (London: Korea Library, 2003), 21.

103. Homer Hulbert, *The Passing of Korea* (New York: Doubleday, Page, 1906), 17.

104. H. B. Drake, *Korea of the Japanese* (London: Bodley Head, 1930), quoted in Uden, *Times Past in Korea*, 69.

105. Goldie Baron Schwarz, "Unpretty Pickle," *New York Times Magazine*, November 26, 1950, SM11.

106. Cornelius Osgood, *The Koreans and Their Culture* (New York: Ronald, 1951), 83.

107. Simon Winchester, *Korea: A Walk through the Land of Miracles* (New York: Harper Perennial, 2005), 59, 192–193.

108. Han, "Some Foods Are Good to Think," 225.

109. Ibid.

110. "Korea-Japan Battle Sprouts over Cabbage Patch," *The Korea Society Quarterly* (Spring 2000): 35; "Korea Challenged in Global Kimchi Market," *Korea Times*, October 26, 2003, accessed June 6, 2003, http://times.hankooki.com/lpage/biz/200310/kt2003102619194811860.htm.

111. John Feffer, "Food Fight," *Gastronomica* 1, no. 3 (Summer 2001), 3–4; Richard Lloyd Parry, "Kimchi War Erupts as Korea Rises Up against Old Enemy Japan,"

Independent–London, October 9, 2000, accessed November 1, 2007, http://findarticles.com/p/articles/mi_qn4158/is_20001009/ai_n14350525; "Korea-Japan Battle," 35; and Song Jung A, "Hot Rivals," *Far Eastern Economic Review* 163, no. 21 (May 25, 2000): 83.

112. Headquartered in Rome, the commission has "Contact Point" offices in each of its 183 member countries, including in not-so-surprising places such as the United States, France, Italy, and Japan, and in less-than-expected places like Kiribati, Seychelles, Dominica, and North Korea. According to the commission's website, the main purposes of the program are "protecting health of the consumers and ensuring fair trade practices in the food trade, and promoting coordination of all food standards work undertaken by international governmental and non-governmental organizations." http://www.codexalimentarius.net/web/index_en.jsp.

113. Feffer, "Food Fight," 3.

114. "Current Official Standards," Codex Alimentarius, accessed June 2, 2010, http://www.codexalimentarius.net/web/standard_list.do?lang=en. Standards have been established for foods such as olive oil (adopted in 1981), canned pineapple (1981), quick-frozen finfish (1981), honey (1981), canned chestnuts (1985), food-grade salt (1985), mango chutney (1987), whole and decorticated pearl millet grains (1989), soy protein products (1989), formula foods for use in weight-control diets (1991), shark fins (1993), litchi (1995), bananas (1997), cheeses in brine (1999), asparagus (2001), bottled/packaged drinking waters (2001), fermented milks (2003), instant noodles (2006), fat spreads and blended spreads (2007), and live and raw bivalve mollusks (2008).

115. "Korean *Kimchi* Beats Out Its Japanese Rival," *The Korea Society Quarterly* (Fall 2000): 41; and Ting-I Tsai, "Korea Swallows Its Pride in Chinese Kimchi War," *Asia Times Online,* November 22, 2005, accessed November 1, 2007, http://www.atimes.com/atimes/China_Business/GK22Cb05.html; Korea Food Research Institute.

116. "Codex Standard for Kimchi" (CODEX STAN 223-2001), Codex Alimentarius, accessed June 3, 2010, http://www.codexalimentarius.net/web/standard_list.do?lang=en.

117. Shizuo Tsuji, *Japanese Cooking: A Simple Art* (Tokyo: Kodansha International, 2006), 315.

118. Ishige, *History and Culture of Japanese Food,* 253.

119. Ibid., 255. I know the truth of this from personal experience. Growing up in Hawai'i, I have eaten quite a bit of onigiri—called *musubi* in Hawai'i—with an umeboshi nucleus. My mouth waters even as I write this sentence.

120. Tsuji, *Japanese Cooking,* 321.

121. Calvin Sims, "Cabbage Is Cabbage? Not to Kimchi Lovers; Koreans Take Issue with a Rendition of Their National Dish Made in Japan," *New York Times,* February 5, 2000, accessed June 10, 2011, http://www.nytimes.com/2000/02/05/business/cabbage-cabbage-not-kimchi-lovers-koreans-take-issue-with-rendition-their.html.

122. Ashkenazi and Jacob, *Essence of Japanese Cuisine,* 45.

123. Collingham, *Curry,* 252–253.

124. "Korea Challenged in Global Kimchi Market."

125. Ibid.

126. Don Lee, "Trade Spat Ferments over Spicy Cabbage," *Los Angeles Times,* November 24, 2005, accessed June 10, 2011, http://articles.latimes.com/2005/nov/24/business/fi-kimchi24; and "The Kimchi Wars," *The Economist,* November 19, 2005, 44.

127. Alina Tugend, "If Only the Flier in Front of You Were a Fan of Miss Manners," *New York Times*, August 2, 2005, accessed June 10, 2011, http://www.nytimes.com/2005/08/02/business/02etiquette.html?n=Top%2FNews%2FBusiness%2FSmall%20Business%2FBusiness%20Travel.

128. D. J. Waldie, "Taken for a Ride," *Los Angeles Times*, May 18, 2008, accessed June 10, 2011, http://articles.latimes.com/2008/may/18/opinion/op-waldie18.

129. Karen Crouse, "A Culture Clash for South Korean Players on the L.P.G.A. Tour," *New York Times*, November 2, 2008, accessed June 10, 2011, http://www.nytimes.com/2008/11/02/sports/golf/02lpga.html.

130. Moskin, "Culinary Diplomacy."

131. Ju-min Park, "South Korean Creates Kimchi That Won't Smell," *Los Angeles Times*, July 23, 2009, accessed June 10, 2011, http://articles.latimes.com/2009/jul/23/world/fg-korea-kimchi23.

132. That year, the United States agreed to finance the supply of C rations specially tailored for the forty-seven thousand South Korean combat troops fighting alongside American troops in South Vietnam. The $7.1 million commitment, lasting from December 1967 through June 1968, was an effort to improve the morale of the Korean troops, who had complained that the American meals they received thrice daily were too greasy to endure. They also groused incessantly about the absence of kimchi, the culinary equivalent of oxygen for Koreans stranded abroad. The newly constituted C rations included kimchi formulated and canned by the Korean Foods Company, based in Seoul, which would become the first to mass produce kimchi. See "Koreans to Send Troops a Delicacy," *Sunday Special to the New York Times*, November 19, 1967, 3.

133. Park, "South Korean Creates Kimchi That Won't Smell."

134. Sang-Hun Choe, "Star Ship Kimchi: A Bold Taste Goes Where It Has Never Gone Before," *New York Times*, February 24, 2008, accessed June 10, 2011, http://www.nytimes.com/2008/02/24/world/asia/24kimchi.html.

135. Quoted in Barbara Kirshenblatt-Gimblett, *Destination Culture: Tourism, Museums, and Heritage* (Berkeley: University of California Press, 1998), 30.

Chapter 4: Dogmeat

1. Even Drellich, "Assembly Meeting Ends with Police," *Pipe Dream*, April 28, 2009, accessed July 12, 2010, http://ww.bupipedream.com/Prints/11606.

2. Psyche A. Williams-Forson, *Building Houses out of Chicken Legs: Black Women, Food, and Power* (Chapel Hill: University of North Carolina Press, 2006), 2, 5.

3. Wu, *Yellow*, 225–227.

4. Frederick Simoons, *Eat Not This Flesh: Food Avoidances from Prehistory to the Present* (Madison: University of Wisconsin Press, 1994), 252.

5. James Serpell, "From Paragon to Pariah: Some Reflections on Human Attitudes to Dogs," in *The Domestic Dog: Its Evolution, Behaviour and Interactions with People*, ed. James Serpell (Cambridge: Cambridge University Press, 1995), 254.

6. Nick Fiddes, *Meat: A Natural Symbol* (London: Routledge, 1991), 133.

7. Lynette A. Hart, "Dogs as Human Companions: A Review of the Relationship," in Serpell, *The Domestic Dog*, 161–178.

8. Lu Xun, "Diary of a Madman," *Diary of a Madman and Other Stories* (Honolulu: University of Hawai'i Press, 1990).
9. Joseph Conrad, *Heart of Darkness* [1902] (Mineola, N.Y.: Dover, 1990), 45.
10. Daniel Defoe, *Robinson Crusoe* [1719] (New York: Modern Library, 2001), 183.
11. Roger Davis, "*You* Are What You Eat: Cannibalism, Autophagy and the Case of Armin Meiwes," in *Territories of Evil*, ed. Nancy Billias (Amsterdam: Rodopi, 2008), 151–152; and Mark Morton, "Joie de Mort," *Gastronomica* 9, no. 1 (Winter 2009): 11.
12. *Lonely Planet: Korea*, 6th ed. (Victoria, Aus.: Lonely Planet, 2004), 51, 53.
13. Winchester, *Korea*, 69, 84–85, 224.
14. Marc Manganaro, "Textual Play, Power, and Cultural Critique: An Orientation to Modernist Anthropology," in *Modernist Anthropology: From Fieldwork to Text*, ed. Marc Manganaro (Princeton, N.J.: Princeton University Press, 1990), 12.
15. Johannes Fabian, *Time and the Other: How Anthropology Makes Its Object* (New York: Columbia University Press, 1983), 31.
16. Conrad, *Heart of Darkness*, 31–32, 44.
17. Fabian, *Time and the Other*, 1–35.
18. Arens, *Man-Eating Myth*, 19–22.
19. Ibid., 19–20.
20. Quoted in Gananath Obeyesekere, *Cannibal Talk: The Man-Eating Myths and Human Sacrifice in the South Seas* (Berkeley: University of California Press, 2005), 2.
21. To be fair, Arens had not entirely ruled out the possibility of cannibalism having existed, a fact that Obeyesekere acknowledges. Arens merely pointed out that its prevalence was vastly overstated and the anthropological evidence for it was woefully lacking.
22. Obeyesekere, *Cannibal Talk*, 1–2
23. Ibid., 15.
24. Ibid., 1–2.
25. Susan McHugh, *Dog* (London: Reaktion, 2004), 52.
26. Berglund, *Cannibal Fictions*, 29–76.
27. "Cannibal Utensil, Fiji Islands, 1917," from Flashback, March 2003, *National Geographic*, accessed April 4, 2009, http://photography.nationalgeographic.com/photography/enlarge/cannibal-utensil_pod_image.html.
28. Brunvand, *Choking Doberman*, 121.
29. Ibid., 95.
30. Jan Harold Brunvand, *Too Good to Be True: The Colossal Book of Urban Legends* (New York: Norton, 2001), 54.
31. Brunvand, *Choking Doberman*, 96.
32. Brunvand, *Encyclopedia of Urban Legends*, 129.
33. McHugh, *Dog*, 34.
34. Wu, *Yellow*, 219.
35. Quoted in Marcie Griffith, Jennifer Wolch, and Unna Lassiter, "Animal Practices and the Racialization of Filipinas in Los Angeles," *Society & Animals* 10, no. 3 (2002): 235–236.
36. Greg Bishop, "Out of Chance Meeting, a Formidable Pairing," *New York Times*, November 7, 2009, accessed November 8, 2009, http://www.nytimes.com/2009/11/08/sports/08pacquiao.html?scp=1&sq=manny%20pacquiao%20family%20dog&st=cse.

37. Irving Lewis Allen, *The Language of Ethnic Conflict: Social Organization and Lexical Culture* (New York: Columbia University Press, 1983); Philip Herbst, *Color of Words: An Encyclopaedic Dictionary of Ethnic Bias in the United States* (Yarmouth, Me.: Intercultural Press, 1997). Additional food-related epithets include the following for Italians (spaghetti, spaghetti-eater, spaghetti-bender, spag, spiggoty, garlic breath, macaroni, pizza man, banana-peddler, grape-stomper, lukschen, meatball, wino), Catholics (fish-eater, mackerel-snapper, guppy-gobbler), Jews (bagel, bagel-bender, herring-punisher, motza, motzer), Germans (sauerkraut, kraut, cabbagehead, sausage, hans-wurst, hop-head, metzel, pretzel, limburger), Appalachians (clay-eater, corn-cracker), French-Canadians (French fries, frog, Johnny cake, Johnny peasoup, Pepsi), Russians (cabbage-eater, candle-eater), Native Americans (apple, hooch, smoked ham), Irish (spud, whiskey mick, boiled dinner, potato-eater, potatohead), Dutch (buttermouth, cabbagehead, pickleherring), American Southerners (butternut, clay-eater, cracker, corn-cracker), Northerners (bean-eater, pumpkinhead), and whites in general (vanilla, white bread, cracker, soda cracker, white meat, marshmallow, milk, buttermilk-swallower, hay-eater, rosin-chewer, wheat folks). Other miscellaneous insults include pineapple (Pacific Islanders), goulash (Hungarians), mushroom-picker (Czechs), beef-eater (English), frog (French), herring-destroyer (Norwegians and Swedes), pork and beans (Portuguese), and spinach (Spaniards).

38. Irma Rombauer, Marion Rombauer Becker, and Ethan Becker, *Joy of Cooking* (New York: Scribner, 1997), 637.

39. Juliet Clutton-Brock, *Domesticated Animals from Early Times* (Austin: University of Texas Press, 1981), 21.

40. Ibid., 104; emphasis in the original.

41. Ibid., 104.

42. McHugh, *Dog*, 16.

43. Simoons, *Eat Not This Flesh*, 200; italics added.

44. Juliet Clutton-Brock, "Origins of the Dog: Domestication and Early History," in Serpell, *The Domestic Dog*, 8.

45. Nicholas Wade, "In Taming Dogs, Humans May Have Sought a Meal," *New York Times*, September 7, 2009, accessed September 10, 2009, http://www.nytimes.com/2009/09/08/science/08dogs.html?scp=1&sq=china%20dog%20domestication&st=cse.

46. Antonella Spanò Giammellaro, "The Phoenicians and the Carthaginians: The Early Mediterranean Diet," in *Food: A Culinary History from Antiquity to the Present*, ed. Jean-Louis Flandrin and Massimo Montanari (New York: Penguin Books, 2000), 61; and Marie-Claire Amouretti, "Urban and Rural Diets in Greece," in Flandrin and Montanari, *Food*, 82.

47. Peter Lund Simmonds, *The Curiosity of Food: Or the Dainties and Delicacies of Different Nations Obtained from the Animal Kingdom* (Berkeley, Calif.: Ten Speed, 2001), 55.

48. Marvin Harris, *The Sacred Cow and the Abominable Pig: Riddles of Food and Culture* (New York: Simon and Schuster, 1985), 183.

49. Calvin W. Schwabe, *Unmentionable Cuisine* (Charlottesville: University Press of Virginia, 1979), 168–175.

50. Simoons, *Eat Not This Flesh*, 240.

51. Wu, *Yellow*, 218.

52. Douglas Brewer, Terence Clark, and Adrian Phillips, *Dogs in Antiquity: Anubis to Cerberus, the Origin of the Domestic Dog* (Warminster, UK: Aris and Phillips, 2001), 1.
53. McHugh, *Dog,* 31.
54. Ibid., 32.
55. Pettid, *Korean Cuisine,* 9.
56. William Saletan, "Wok the Dog," *Slate,* January 16, 2002, accessed May 12, 2008, http://www.slate.com/id/2060840; and John Huer, "Dog's Life in Korea," *Korea Times,* March 27, 2009, accessed June 12, 2009, http://www.koreatimes.co.kr/www/news/opinon/2009/06/272_42111.html.
57. Saletan, "Wok the Dog."
58. Boudewijn Walraven, "Bardot Soup and Confucians' Meat," in *Asian Food: The Global and the Local,* ed. Katarzyna Cwiertka and Boudewijn Walraven (Honolulu: University of Hawai'i Press, 2001), 106.
59. Wu, *Yellow,* 226.
60. Craig S. Smith, "Poor and Muslim? Jewish? Soup Kitchen is Not for You," *New York Times,* February 28, 2006, accessed June 8, 2011, http://www.nytimes.com/2006/02/28/international/europe/28soup.html; "World Briefing: Pork Soup Handouts Not Racist, Court Says," *New York Times,* January 3, 2007, accessed June 8, 2011, http://query.nytimes.com/gst/fullpage.html?res=9405E3DA1730F930A35752C0A9619C8B63.
61. Marianne Elisabeth Lien, "Dogs, Whales and Kangaroos: Transnational Activism and Food Taboos," in *The Politics of Food,* ed. Marianne Elisabeth Lien and Briggitte Nerlich (Oxford: Berg, 2004), 183–184.
62. Pettid, *Korean Cuisine,* 62. Interestingly, the Chinese consume dogmeat during the winter months, believing that it warms the body. In both cases men are the primary consumers, as dogmeat is said benefit male "potency." That said, it is an open secret in Hong Kong and Taiwan that the euphemism "fragrant meat" stands for dogmeat.
63. John Feffer, "The Politics of Dog," *The American Prospect,* June 2, 2002, accessed June 2, 2011, http://prospect.org/cs/articles?article=the_politics_of_dog.
64. Wulf Schiefenhövel, "Good Taste and Bad Taste: Preferences and Aversions as Biological Principles," in *Food Preferences and Taste: Continuity and Change,* ed. Helen Macbeth (Providence, R.I.: Berghahn, 1997), 55–58.
65. Paul Rozin et al., "Disgust: Preadaptation and the Cultural Evolution of a Food-Based Emotion," in Macbeth, *Food Preferences and Taste,* 68.
66. Schiefenhövel, "Good Taste and Bad Taste," 56–62; Rozin et al. "Disgust," 62–66.
67. Rozin et al., "Disgust," 66–67.
68. Ibid., 67; Schiefenhövel, "Good Taste and Bad Taste," 55.
69. Rozin et al., "Disgust," 67.
70. Quoted in J. A. G. Roberts, *China to Chinatown: Chinese Food in the West* (London: Reaktion, 2002), 28–29.
71. Simmonds, *Curiosity of Food.*
72. Jerry Hopkins, *Extreme Cuisine: The Weird and Wonderful Foods That People Eat* (Hong Kong: Periplus, 2004).
73. Maxine Hong Kingston, *The Woman Warrior: Memoirs of a Childhood among Ghosts* [1975]. (New York: Vintage, 1989), 90–91.

74. Frank Chin, "Eat and Run Midnight People," *The Chinaman Frisco and R.R. Co.* (Minneapolis: Coffeehouse, 1988), 11.
75. Clutton-Brock, *Domesticated Animals*, 9.
76. Richard Wrangham, *Catching Fire: How Cooking Made Us Human* (New York: Basic, 2009), 1–14.
77. Animal Studies Group, *Killing Animals* (Urbana and Chicago: University of Illinois Press, 2006), 4.
78. Ibid., 1–2.
79. Betty Fussell, *Raising Steaks: The Life and Times of American Beef* (Orlando, Fla.: Harcourt, 2008), 212.
80. Erin E. Williams and Margo DeMello, *Why Animals Matter: The Case for Animal Protection* (Amherst, N.Y.: Prometheus, 2007), 73.
81. Carol J. Adams, "Eating Animals," in *Eating Culture*, ed. Ron Scapp and Brian Seitz (Albany: State University of New York Press, 1998), 63.
82. Elisabetta Povoledo, "Exhibition with Disturbing Videos of Animals Leads to Protests in Italy," *New York Times*, February 27, 2009, accessed June 9, 2011, http://www.nytimes.com/2009/02/28/arts/design/28anim.html; Ilana DeBare, "Art Institute Halts Exhibition Showing Killing of Animals," *San Francisco Chronicle*, March 30, 2008, accessed February 20, 2009, http://www.sfgate.com/cgibin/article.cgi?f=/c/a/2008/03/29/BAGNVSRME.DTL.
83. The issue of the fate of a circus elephant under the control of a brutal keeper is explored in the 2011 film *Water for Elephants*, directed by Francis Lawrence. Based on Sara Gruen's 2006 novel, the story touches on the human qualities of revenge and resentment as played out among humans and a domesticated animal within the institutional structure of a professional traveling circus.
84. Chris Wilbert, "What Is Doing the Killing? Animal Attacks, Man-Eaters, and Shifting Boundaries and Flows of Human-Animal Relations," in Animal Studies Group, *Killing Animals*, 39–42.
85. *I'm Alive*, Animal Planet, accessed January 8, 2011, http://animal.discovery.com/tv/im-alive/.
86. Huer, "Dog's Life in Korea."
87. Ibid.
88. Richard W. Bulliet, *Hunters, Herders, and Hamburgers: The Past and Future of Human-Animal Relationships* (New York: Columbia University Press, 2005), 3.
89. McHugh, *Dog*, 34.

Chapter 5: Monosodium Glutamate

1. Quoted in Julia Moskin, "Yes, MSG, the Secret behind the Savor," *New York Times*, March 5, 2008, accessed Feb, 16, 2010, http://abcnews.go.com/Health/Diet/wireStory?id=2968836.
2. Jonathan Blazon, e-mail correspondence, July 26, 2009.
3. Campbell's also aired television commercials to press the point of Progresso's MSG use. In one such commercial a woman is subjected to what is obviously a mock blindfold tasting of the two brands. A voice off camera asks her to describe the two soups. After tasting the Progresso, she answers with a knowing look, "MSG." After tasting the Campbell's, she answers, "Chicken, one-hundred percent natural." Then, after a brief pause, "the Peterson-Jacob's farm, I believe."

4. "About TGA," The Glutamate Association, accessed June 18, 2012, http://www.msgfacts.com/About_TGA.aspx.

5. Quoted in Rosie Mestel, "MSG and the Soup Wars," *Los Angeles Times*, November 3, 2008, accessed June 18, 2012, http://latimesblogs.latimes.com/booster_shots/2008/11/with-all-thats.html.

6. Masao Katayama, "Professor Kikunae Ikeda," *Bulletin of the Chemical Society of Japan* 1, no. 1 (1926): 1.

7. Mari Yoshihara, *Musicians from a Different Shore: Asian Americans in Classical Music* (Philadelphia: Temple University Press, 2007), 16.

8. Bruce Halpern, "What's in a Name? Are MSG and Umami the Same?" *Chemical Senses* 27 (2002): 845.

9. Tsuji, *Japanese Cooking*, 147.

10. Ibid.

11. McGee, *On Food and Cooking*, 342.

12. Tsuji, *Japanese Cooking*, 146.

13. Ishige, *History and Culture of Japanese Food*, 221.

14. Ashkenazi and Jacob, *Essence of Japanese Cuisine*, 71.

15. Bernd Lindemann, Yoko Ogiwara, and Yuzo Ninomiya, "The Discovery of Umami," *Chemical Senses* 27 (2002): 843.

16. David Kasabian and Anna Kasabian, *The Fifth Taste: Cooking with Umami* (New York: Universe, 2005), 14; and George K. York and Stephan H. O. Gruenwedel, "Food Additives in the Human Food Chain," in *Chemicals in the Human Food Chain*, ed. Carl K. Winter, James N. Seiber, and Carole F. Nuckton (New York: Van Nostrand Reinhold, 1990), 114. Amino acids are categorized as either essential or nonessential. Glutamic acid is a nonessential amino acid, meaning the human body can produce it on its own. In contrast, essential amino acids, which the body cannot produce, must be obtained through diet. Essential amino acids include histidine, isoleucine, leucine, lysine, methionine, phenylalanine, threonine, tryptophan, and valine. Nonessential amino acids include alanine, arginine, asparagine, aspartic acid, cysteine, glutamic acid, glutamine, glycine, proline, serine, and tyrosine.

17. Ruth Winter, *A Consumer's Dictionary of Food Additives* (New York: Three Rivers, 2004), 38; York and Gruenwedel, "Food Additives," 15.

18. Jordan Sand, "A Short History of MSG: Good Science, Bad Science, and Taste Cultures," *Gastronomica* 5, no. 4 (Fall 2005): 38.

19. I would like to thank Yuki Taguchi for her help in explicating the meaning of umami.

20. Jean Anthelme Brillat-Savarin, *The Physiology of Taste* [1825], trans. M. F. K. Fisher (New York: Counterpoint, 1949), 66–67; italics in original.

21. Ibid., 66.

22. I would like to thank Elisa Camiscioli for her help in explicating the meaning of osmozome.

23. Katayama, "Professor Kikunae Ikeda," 1; "Wilhelm Ostwald—Biography," Nobel Prize, accessed May 2, 2009, http://nobelprize.org/nobel_prizes/chemistry/laureates/1909/ostwald-bio.html.

24. Sand, "Short History of MSG," 38–39.

25. Quoted in Sand, "Short History of MSG," 38.

26. William H. Brock, *Justus von Liebig: The Chemical Gatekeeper* (Cambridge: Cambridge University Press, 1997); and Mark R. Finlay, "Quackery and Cookery: Justus von Liebig's Extract of Meat and the Theory of Nutrition in the Victorian Age," *Bulletin of the History of Medicine* 66, no. 3 (Fall 1992): 405.
27. McGee, *On Food and Cooking*, 161.
28. Modern science has shown that enzymes present in the digestive systems of fish allow for necessary fermentation.
29. Carl S. Pederson, *Microbiology of Food Fermentations* (Westport, Conn.: AVI, 1971), 242; Giammellaro, "The Phoenicians and the Carthaginians," 55, 61; and Amouretti, "Urban and Rural Diets in Greece," 82.
30. Davidson, *Oxford Companion to Food*, 332.
31. Ko Swan Djien, "Indigenous Fermented Foods," in *Fermented Foods*, ed. A. H. Rose, Economic Microbiology 7 (London: Academic Press, 1982), 22.
32. For an account of soy sauce's history and the economic significance of Kikkoman, the world's most profitable brand, see Fruin, *Kikkoman*.
33. Kasabian and Kasabian, *Fifth Taste*, 15–16.
34. Shizuko Yamaguchi and Kumiko Ninomiya, "The Use and Utility of Glutamates as Flavoring Agents in Food," *The Journal of Nutrition* 130, no. 4 (April 1, 2000): 922S.
35. Keun-Sik Jung, "Colonial Modernity and the Social History of Chemical Seasoning in Korea," *Korea Journal* 45, no. 2 (Summer 2005): 14.
36. "Ajinomoto Group History," Ajinomoto, accessed November 20, 2009, http://www.ajinomoto.com/about/history/index.html.
37. Jung, "Colonial Modernity," 14.
38. I would like to thank Rumiko Sode for explaining this distinction.
39. *Food, Inc.*, directed by Robert Kenner, Magnolia Pictures, 2008.
40. Quoted in Maureen Dowd, "The Aura of Arugulance," *New York Times*, April 18, 2009, accessed June 8, 2009, http://www.nytimes.com/2009/04/19/opinion/19dowd.html.
41. *Food, Inc.*
42. Milan Kundera, *The Art of the Novel* (New York: Harper and Row, 1988), 130.
43. Davidson, *Oxford Companion to Food*, 633.
44. Thorne, *History of Food Preservation*, 14.
45. Davidson, *Oxford Companion to Food*, 633–634; Thorne, *History of Food Preservation*, 13–16.
46. Winter, *Consumer's Dictionary of Food Additives*, 32.
47. Ibid., 2.
48. York and Gruenwedel, "Food Additives," 117–126.
49. Winter, *Consumer's Dictionary of Food Additives*, 32.
50. See Winter's *Consumer's Dictionary of Food Additives* for detailed definitions and industrial applications of these ingredients.
51. Ibid., 2, 38.
52. Eric Schlosser, *Fast Food Nation: The Dark Side of the All-American Meal* (New York: Perennial, 2002), 121–125.
53. Sidney Mintz, *Tasting Food, Tasting Freedom: Excursions into Eating, Power, and the Past* (Boston: Beacon, 1996), 109–111.
54. Ibid., 116.

55. Winter, *Consumer's Dictionary of Food Additives*, 38.

56. Ian Mosby, "'That Won-Ton Soup Headache': The Chinese Restaurant Syndrome, MSG and the Making of American Food, 1968–1980," *Social History of Medicine* 22, no. 1 (2009): 136.

57. Robert Ho Man Kwok, letter, "Chinese Restaurant Syndrome," *New England Journal of Medicine* 278, no. 14 (April 4, 1968): 796.

58. H. Schaumburg, Thomas J. McCaghren, Matthew Menken, William Migden, Elizabeth Kirk Rose, Jogeswar Rath, Elissa L. Beron, Stephen R. Kandall, Martin E. Gordon, Nicholas E. Davies, letters, "Correspondence: Chinese-Restaurant Syndrome," *New England Journal of Medicine* 278, no. 20 (May 16, 1968): 1122–1124.

59. Ibid.

60. Editorial, *New England Journal of Medicine* 278, no. 20 (May 16, 1968): 1122.

61. Editorial, *New England Journal of Medicine* 279, no. 2 (July 11, 1968): 106.

62. William C. Porter, letter, "Correspondence: Sin Cib-Syn: Accent on Glutamate," *New England Journal of Medicine* 279, no. 2 (July 11, 1968): 106.

63. Herbert H. Schaumburg, Robert Byck, Marjorie Ambos, Nancy R. Leavitt, Lynne Marorek, and Susan B. Wolschina, letters, "Correspondence: Sin Cib-Syn: Accent on Glutamate," *New England Journal of Medicine* 279, no. 2 (July 11 1968): 105.

64. Herbert H. Schaumburg et al., "Monosodium L-Glutamate: Its Pharmacology and Rule in the Chinese Restaurant Syndrome," *Science* 163, no. 3869 (February 21, 1969): 826–828.

65. Mosby, "That Won-Ton Soup Headache," 138.

66. Sand, "Short History of MSG," 43.

67. Jung, "Colonial Modernity," 11–12.

68. Sand, "Short History of MSG," 42.

69. Jung, "Colonial Modernity," 12.

70. Sand, "Short History of MSG," 43–44.

71. Mosby, "That Won-Ton Soup Headache," 139.

72. Harvey Levenstein, *Paradox of Plenty: A Social History of Eating in Modern America* (New York: Oxford University Press, 1993), 101–118.

73. Betty Friedan, *The Feminine Mystique* (New York: Dell, 1963).

74. Levenstein, *Paradox of Plenty*, 101–118.

75. Mosby, "That Won-Ton Soup Headache," 134–135.

76. Ibid., 134.

77. Ibid., 134–135.

78. Steingarten, *It Must've Been Something I Ate*, 97–98; italics in original.

79. Matthew Freeman, "Reconsidering the Effects of Monosodium Glutamate: A Literature Review," *Journal of the American Academy of Nurse Practitioners* 18 (2006): 482–485.

80. York and Gruenwedel, "Food Additives," 117.

81. Quoted in Moskin, "Yes, MSG."

82. Moskin, "Yes, MSG."

83. Katy McLaughlin, "A New Taste Sensation," *Wall Street Journal*, December 8, 2007, accessed March 2, 2009, http://online.wsj.com/article/SB119706514515417586.html; Sara Dickerman, "Could MSG Make a Comeback?" *Slate*, May 3, 2006, accessed March 2, 2009, http://www.slate.com/id/2140999/.

84. Moskin, "Yes, MSG"; McLaughlin, "New Taste Sensation"; Dickerman, "Could MSG Make a Comeback?"

Notes to Pages 190–200   253

Chapter 6: SPAM

1. Ann Kondo Corum, *Hawaii's SPAM Cookbook* (Honolulu: Bess Press, 1987), xv–xvii.

2. Ann Kondo Corum, *Hawaii's 2nd SPAM Cookbook* (Honolulu: Bess Press, 2001).

3. Muriel Miura, *Hawai'i Cooks With SPAM* (Honolulu: Mutual, 2008).

4. Rachel Laudan, *The Food of Paradise: Exploring Hawaii's Culinary Heritage* (Honolulu: University of Hawai'i Press, 1996), 66–69.

5. To thousands of Hawai'i expatriates living elsewhere, the mere mention of Zippy's evokes both fond memories and pangs of nostalgia.

6. Sylvie Kim, "The End of Spam Shame: On Class, Colonialism, and Canned Meat," *Hyphen* (blog), June 3, 2011, accessed June 20, 2011, http://www.hyphenmagazine.com/blog/archive/2011/06/end-spam-shame-class-colonialism-and-canned-meat.

7. Ibid.

8. Sunyoung Lee, "Spam I Am," *MUÆ* 2 (1997): 78.

9. Judith Rehak, "Spam! Spam! Spam! Lovely Spam! Wonderful Spam!" *International Herald Tribune,* March 9, 2002, accessed October 1, 2008, http://www.iht.com/articles/2002/03/09/mhorn_ed3_.php; Jane Han, "Koreans' Endless Love for Spam," *Korea Times,* December 6, 2007, accessed October 1, 2008, http://www.koreatimes.co.kr/www/news/biz/2007/12/123_15098.html; and "SPAM," Hormel Foods, accessed October 1, 2008, http://www.hormelfoods.com/brands/Spam.

10. Although the use of "Frankenfood" most often refers to genetically modified organisms (GMO) in the human food chain, the term can also be used more generally to mean any food that does not seem completely natural—i.e., a food that is synthetic or artificial, a product of a factory or laboratory.

11. Ty Matejowsky, "SPAM and Fast-food 'Glocalization' in the Philippines," *Food, Culture, Society* 10, no. 1 (2007): 28–30.

12. Ibid..

13. George H. Lewis, "From Minnesota Fat to Seoul Food: Spam in America and the Pacific Rim," *Journal of Popular Culture* 34, no. 2 (Fall 2000): 96.

14. Han, "Koreans' Endless Love for Spam."

15. Lewis, "From Minnesota Fat," 102.

16. I thank Joseph Jeon for alerting me to the second commercial.

17. Lewis, "From Minnesota Fat," 96.

18. Carolyn Wyman, *SPAM: A Biography* (New York: Harcourt Brace, 1999), 57.

19. Michael Pollan, *In Defense of Food: An Eater's Manifesto* (New York: Penguin, 2008), 1, 150.

20. Dan Armstrong and Dustin Black, *The Book of Spam* (New York: Atria, 2007), 26–28.

21. Winter, *Consumer's Dictionary of Food Additives,* 293–294.

22. Steve Ettlinger, *Twinkie, Deconstructed: My Journey to Discover How the Ingredients Found in Processed Foods are Grown, Mined (Yes, Mined), and Manipulated into What America Eats* (New York: Plume, 2008).

23. "What is Mechanically Recovered Meat?" *BBC News,* August 9, 2001, accessed January 17, 2010, http://news.bbc.co.uk/2/hi/health/1482140.stm.

24. Davidson, *Oxford Companion to Food,* 742.

25. Wyman, *SPAM,* 7–10; Armstrong and Black, *Book of Spam,* 63–65.

26. Matejowsky, "SPAM and Fast Food," 27.

27. Lewis, "From Minnesota Fat," 83.

28. Andrew Martin, "Spam Turns Serious and Hormel Turns Out More," *New York Times*, November 15, 2008, accessed June 21, 2011, http://www.nytimes.com/2008/11/15/business/15spam.html.

29. "Spam," in *Hawaii Newcomer's Guide 2007–08, Honolulu Advertiser*, accessed June 12, 2008, http://ssl.honoluluadvertiser.com/livinginparadise/2007/spam. The paper has now merged with *Honolulu Star-Bulletin* to form *Honolulu Star-Advertiser*.

30. John Nagamichi Cho, *SPAM-ku: Tranquil Reflections on Luncheon Loaf* (New York: HarperCollins, 1998), 57, 76.

31. John Nagamichi Cho, *SPAM Haiku* (online posting), accessed June 20, 2011, http://mit.edu/jync/www/spam/mine.html.

32. Amy Harmon, "The American Way of Spam," *New York Times*, May 7, 1998, accessed June 21, 2011, http://www.nytimes.com/1998/05/07/technology/the-american-way-of-spam.html.

33. Tom Zeller, "Ideas & Trends: Spamology," *New York Times*, June 1, 2003, accessed June 21, 2011, http://www.nytimes.com/2003/06/01/weekinreview/ideas-trends-spamology.html.

34. Steve Alexander, "Spam Lawsuit's Last Laugh Is at Hormel's Expense," *Minneapolis-St. Paul Star Tribune*, November 29, 2007, accessed June 21, 2011, http://www.startribune.com/business/11904166.html.

35. "About SPAM Brand," SPAM, accessed June 25, 2010, http://www.spam.com/about/internet.aspx.

36. James C. McKinley Jr., "Hormel Sues over a Boarish Film Muppet," *New York Times*, July 26, 1995, accessed June 21, 2011, http://www.nytimes.com/1995/07/26/nyregion/hormel-sues-over-a-boarish-film-muppet.html.

37. Pamela C. Chalk, "A Pig by Any Other Name Would Smell as Sweet," *Journal of Contemporary Legal Issues* (2001): 340.

38. James C. McKinley Jr., "Spa'am, a Boar (And a Boor) Riles Hormel," *New York Times*, July 30, 1995, accessed June 20, 2011, http://www.nytimes.com/1995/07/30/weekinreview/july-23-29-spa-am-a-boar-and-a-boor-riles-hormel.html.

39. Thorne, *History of Food Preservation*, 16–19.

40. Ibid., 19–20.

41. Ibid., 21.

42. Giorgio Pedrocco, "Food Industry and New Preservation Techniques," in Flandrin and Montanari, *Food: A Culinary History*, 486.

43. Tom Standage, *An Edible History of Humanity* (New York: Walker & Co., 2009), 159.

44. H. G. Muller, "Industrial Food Preservation in the Nineteenth and Twentieth Centuries," in *Waste Not, Want Not: Food Preservation from Early Times to the Present Day*, ed. C. Anne Wilson (Edinburgh: Edinburgh University Press, 1991), 123–125.

45. Thorne, *History of Food Preservation*, 31–33.

46. Standage, *Edible History*, 162.

47. Ibid., 145–148.

48. Alissa Hamilton, "World War II's Mobilization of the Science of Food Acceptability: How Ration Palatability Became a Military Research Priority," *Ecology of Food and Nutrition* 42 (2003): 327–328.

49. "12,000,000 Meals a Day," *Popular Mechanics*, February 1943, 85.
50. Hamilton, "World War II's Mobilization," 326.
51. Levenstein, *Paradox of Plenty*, 89.
52. Ibid., 90.
53. "12,000,000 Meals a Day," 85–86.
54. Levenstein, *Paradox of Plenty*, 80–83.
55. Matthew Fort, "Play It Again, Spam," *Guardian*, July 7, 2000, accessed February 10, 2008, http://www.guardian.co.uk/theguardian/2000/jul/07/features11.g2.
56. Matejowsky, "SPAM and Fast Food," 26.
57. Dirk Johnson, "A Feast from the Can: Honors for SPAM at 50," *New York Times*, July 5, 1987, accessed June 21, 2011, http://www.nytimes.com/1987/07/05/us/a-feast-from-the-can-honors-for-spam-at-50.html.
58. Fort, "Play It Again, Spam."
59. Ibid.
60. John Feffer, "Korean Food, Korean Identity: The Impact of Globalization on Korean Agriculture," Shorenstein APARC (2005): 40, accessed July 30, 2012, http://ksp.stanford.edu/publications/korean_food_korean_identity_the_impact_of_globalization_on_korean_agriculture/.
61. Lewis, "From Minnesota Fat," 93.
62. Matejowsky, "SPAM and Fast Food," 26.
63. For an extended discussion of the role food played in the lives of those interned, see Jane Dusselier, "Does Food Make Place? Food Protests in Japanese American Concentration Camps," *Food and Foodways* 10, no. 3 (2002): 137–165.
64. Shoyu Weenies are made of hot dogs cut into slices, fried with onions and soy sauce, and served atop rice. "Shoyu" is the Japanese term for soy sauce.
65. The Kitchen Sisters, "Weenie Royale: Food and the Japanese Internment," recording of program and archived interviews, NPR *Morning Edition*, December 20, 2007, accessed June 22, 2012, http://www.npr.org/templates/story/story.php?storyId=17335538.
66. "Hawaii Regional Cuisine," Hawaii Visitors and Convention Bureau, accessed February 2, 2010, http://www.gohawaii.com/about_hawaii/plan/things_to_do_in_hawaii/dining/founders_cuisine.
67. "Hawai'i Regional Cuisine with Chef Alan Wong," online video, Hawaii Visitors and Convention Bureau, accessed July 19, 2010, http://www.gohawaii.com/stories/stories.html?video=15.
68. Laudan, *Food of Paradise*, 8.
69. Marian Burros, "From Quail Egg to Fried Egg: Hawaii High and Low," *New York Times*, February 17, 1999, accessed June 21, 2011, http://www.nytimes.com/1999/02/17/dining/from-quail-egg-to-fried-egg-hawaii-high-and-low.html.
70. Laudan, *Food of Paradise*, 20.
71. Betty Shimabukuro, "Okazuya: 'Cause You Hungry, Yah?" *Honolulu Star-Bulletin*, May 24, 2000, accessed July 8, 2010, http://archives.starbulletin.com/2000/05/24/features/story1.html.
72. Christine Yano, "Shifting Plates: Okazuya in Hawai'i," *Amerasia Journal* 32, no. 2 (2006): 37–38.
73. "About L&L," L&L Hawaiian Barbecue, accessed July 8, 2010, http://hawaiianbarbecue.com/live/about-ll/.

74. Momofuku Ando also invented the first instant ramen in 1958. Born in Taiwan on March 5, 1910, Ando moved to Japan at the age of twenty-three and established the Nissin Food Company.

75. James Song, "Burger King Puts Spam on the Menu," *USA Today,* June 11, 2007, accessed July 20, 2010, http://www.usatoday.com/money/industries/food/2007-06-11-bk-spam_N.htm.

76. Jennifer Steinhauer, "Carbo-Loading, Hawaiian Style," *New York Times,* November 12, 2008, accessed June 21, 2011, http://www.nytimes.com/2008/11/12/dining/12plate.html?.

77. The classic Chicago-style hot dog consists of an all-beef hot dog topped with yellow mustard, neon-green pickle relish, dill pickle, chopped onions, tomato slices, and pickled sport peppers sprinkled with celery salt in a poppy seed bun.

78. Laudan, *Food of Paradise*, 7–8.

79. James L. Kelly, "Loco Moco: A Folk Dish in the Making," *The Taste of American Place: A Reader on Regional and Ethnic Foods,* ed. Barbara G. Shortridge and James R. Shortridge (Lanham, Md.: Rowman and Littlefield, 1998), 39–43; and Linda Stradley, "Hawaiian Loco Moco—Hawaii's Feel Good Food," *What's Cooking America* (online positing), assessed January 15, 2010, http://whatscookingamerica.net/History/LocoMocoHistory.htm.

80. Ronald Takaki, *Strangers from a Different Shore: A History of Asian Americans* (Boston: Little, Brown, 1989), 400–402.

81. Jonathan Botticelli, review of Café 100 Restaurant, Kulshan (online posting), October 16, 2006, accessed June 21, 2010, http://hawaii.kulshan.com/Hawaii/Hawaii%20County/The%20Big%20Island/Hilo/Restaurants/Cafe100.htm. On its website, Café 100 cites "either Lincoln Grill or May's Fountain, both long gone," as possible places of origin: "People then started to request Loco Moco at Café 100 and by 1949 it was on our menu. Café 100 does not claim to have invented Loco Moco, but we surely helped to popularize it." For Café 100's fuller exposition of the dish, see http://www.cafe100.com/the-loco-moco.html.

82. Linda Eggers, *The SPAM Cookbook: Recipes from Main Street* (Marietta, Ga.: Longstreet, 1998).

83. James L. Watson, "Introduction: Transnationalism, Localization, and Fast Food in East Asia," in Watson, *Golden Arches East*, 38.

84. Ibid.

85. Matejowsky, "SPAM and Fast Food," 24.

86. I thank Jennifer Ann Ho for pointing out this possibility.

87. Joyce Carol Oates, *On Boxing* (New York: HarperCollins, 2006), 102.

Conclusion

1. Ming Tsai and Arthur Boehm, introduction to *Blue Ginger: East Meets West Cooking with Ming Tsai* (New York: Clarkson Potter, 1999), np.

2. Davidson, *Oxford Encyclopedia of Food*, 371.

3. Ibid., 859.

4. Ibid., 199.

5. Ibid., 220.

6. van Wyk, *Food Plants of the World*, 265.

7. Ibid., 245.

8. Quoted in Davidson, *Oxford Encyclopedia of Food*, 508.

9. To understand the differences among pidgins, creoles, and standard languages, see Mark Sebba, *Contact Languages: Pidgins and Creoles* (New York: St. Martin's, 1997).

10. For a fuller exploration of the politics of pidgin in Hawai'i, see Rosina Lippi-Green, *English with an Accent: Language, Ideology, and Discrimination in the United States* (New York: Routledge, 1997), 41–52.

11. See Darrell H. Y. Lum, *Pass On, No Pass Back!* (Honolulu: Bamboo Ridge, 1990); Gary Pak, *The Watcher of Waipuna and Other Stories* (Honolulu: Bamboo Ridge, 1992); Lois-Ann Yamanaka, *Saturday Night at the Pahala Theatre* (Honolulu: Bamboo Ridge, 1993); R. Zamora Linmark, *Rolling the R's* (New York: Kaya Production, 1995); and Lee A. Tonouchi, *Da Word* (Honolulu: Bamboo Ridge, 2001).

12. Eric Hobsbawm, introduction to *The Invention of Tradition*, ed. Eric Hobsbawm (Cambridge: Cambridge University Press, 1983), 1.

13. Marc Lacey, "Wary Tourists Toss Aside a Chance to Taste History," *New York Times*, October 21, 2008, accessed January 5, 2012, http://www.nytimes.com/2008/10/22/world/americas/22tijuana.html?scp=1&sq=caesar%20salad%20tijuana%20cardini&st=cse; and Barbara Ann Kipfer, *The Culinarian: A Kitchen Desk Reference* (New York: Wiley), 79–80.

14. Julia Child, *From Julia Child's Kitchen* (New York: Knopf, 1975).

15. Hobsbawm, introduction to *Invention of Tradition*, 1.

16. Anita Mannur, "Model Minorities Can Cook: Fusion Cuisine in Asian America," in *East Main Street: Asian American Popular Culture,* ed. Shilpa Davé, LeiLani Nishime, and Tasha G. Oren (New York: New York University Press, 2005), 72–77. For a fuller treatment of the cultural politics of Asian fusion cuisine, see Mannur, *Culinary Fictions: Food in South Asian Diasporic Culture* (Philadelphia: Temple University Press, 2010), 186–216.

Glossary of Food Terms

(Primary national or regional affiliation in parentheses)

adobo—(Philippines) A dish of pork or chicken cooked in vinegar, often with soy sauce, garlic, peppercorns, and bay leaves. Considered the national dish of the Philippines.

aebleskiver—(Denmark) Golf-ball sized, spherical pancakes traditionally made of wheat flour, buttermilk, eggs, and sugar.

anago—(Japan) Saltwater eel, such as conger. Used in sushi, tempura, and other dishes.

asazuke—(Japan) A lightly or quickly pickled type of preserved vegetables. Categorized as a *tsukemono*.

baechu—(Korea) A variety of cabbage. Also known as Chinese cabbage or napa cabbage. The basis for the most common type of kimchi.

baek kimchi—(Korea) A type of kimchi made without red chiles. Literally "white kimchi."

bagoong—(Philippines) A paste made of fermented fish or shrimp.

balut—(Philippines) Fertilized or embryonated duck eggs. Usually consumed boiled.

bento—(Japan) A meal served in a compartmented box.

berbere—(Ethiopia/Eritrea) A mixture of ground spices such as chiles, ginger, coriander, nutmeg, and fenugreek.

Bhut Jolokia—(India) A type of chile from Assam, India. Considered among the hottest in the world.

bibim naengmyeon—(Korea) A dish of buckwheat-based noodles in a *gochujang* sauce. Served cold with a variety of garnishes, such as sliced meat, pears, and boiled egg.

bibimbap—(Korea) A dish of rice mixed with a medley of ingredients such as sliced beef, seasoned vegetables, and chile paste, topped with a fried egg.

bosintang—(Korea) A pungent soup made of dogmeat. Among the most common dogmeat dishes in Korea.

budae jjigae—(Korea) Literally "army-base stew." Originally made of surplus foods from US military instillations in South Korea. A chile-based stew that includes various combinations of hot dogs, SPAM, canned Vienna sausage, canned baked beans, kimchi, ramen noodles, American cheese, bean curds, and whatever else is available.

bulgogi—(Korea) Grilled meat, principally beef, that has been marinated.

California roll—(Japan/United States) A type of *makizushi* made of avocado, crabmeat, and cucumber. Also a type of *uramaki*.

ceviche—(Central and South America) A dish of raw seafood marinated in vinegar or citrus, olive oil, chiles, herbs, and other ingredients.

char siu—(China) Roasted meat, typically pork.

chelow kabab—(Iran) Skewered grilled meat served with saffron rice. Considered the national dish of Iran.

chile de árbol—(Mexico, Central America) A variety of chile commonly used in many Mexican dishes.

chirashizushi—(Japan) A type of sushi. Commonly served in a bowl consisting of seasoned rice topped with an assortment of sashimi and a variety of garnishes.

chop suey—(China/United States) A Chinese-style dish of various chopped ingredients such as meat, onions, bean sprouts, water chestnuts, and bamboo shoots.

chorizo—(Spain, Latin America) Chile-spiced sausages.

chotkal—(Korea) Seafood fermented in salt.

couscous—(North Africa) Granules of crushed and rolled whole grains such as semolina or durum wheat.

daikon—(Japan) A type of white radish.

danmuji—(Korea) A pickle made of radish. Called *takuan* in Japanese.

dashi—(Japan) Soup stock, traditionally made of *katsuobushi* and *konbu* heated in water. A fundamental element of traditional Japanese cuisine.

dolma—(Turkey/Greece/Middle East) Grape leaves or cabbage stuffed with a variety of ingredients such as rice, meat, vegetables, herbs, and spices.

doro wat—(Ethiopia and Eritrea) Chicken stew spiced with *berbere* and *niter kibbeh*. Also called *tsebhi*.

dosa—(India) Crepes made of fermented rice and lentils.

edomaezushi—(Japan) Another name for *nigirizushi*. Named for Edo, where it originated.

funazushi—(Japan) A type of *narezushi* made with a freshwater fish called *funa*, a type of carp. A regional sushi from Shiga prefecture.

furikake—(Japan) A garnish for rice. Often a mixture of nori, *katsuobushi*, sesame seeds, and salt.

galbi—(Korea) Grilled ribs, principally beef, that have been marinated.

garam masala—(India) A spice mixture. Typically made of ground cardamom, cloves, chiles, cinnamon, cumin, fennel, and other spices.

garum—(Ancient Greek and Rome) A sauce made of flesh and innards of fish fermented with aromatic herbs.

General Tso's chicken—(China/United States) A dish of deep-fried chicken pieces in a sweet and spicy sauce. Among the most popular Chinese take-out items in the United States.

gimbap—(Korea) Rice and other ingredients, such as seasoned vegetables, meat, and omelet, rolled in *gim*, or dried seaweed or laver in sheet form, called nori in Japanese. A type of *makizushi*.

goulash—(Hungary) A paprika-spiced stew of meat and vegetables.

harissa—(North Africa) A sauce or condiment typically made of chiles, garlic, oil, coriander, and other spices.

hummus—(Middle East) A spread of ground chickpeas, tahini, garlic, and lemon juice.

injera—(Ethiopia and Eritrea) Flatbread made of yeast-risen teff flour. Considered a national dish of Ethiopia and Eritrea.

jeotgal—(Korea) Seafood fermented in salt.

jjajangmyeon—(Korea) A dish of noodles topped with a sauce made of black soybean paste. The most popular Chinese-style dish in Korea.

jjamppong—(Korea) A dish of noodles in chile-based soup. Typically includes seafood. A popular Chinese-style dish in Korea.

kabayaki—(Japan) A sweet-tasting sauce made from soy sauce.

kalua pig—(Hawai'i) Pork, often an entire pig, roasted in an underground oven called *imu*.

kamaboko—(Japan) A type of *surimi*.

kanpachi—(Japan) A type of fish, usually amberjack or yellowtail.

kapi—(Thailand) A paste made of fermented fish.

karee pan—(Japan) Bread stuffed with curried filling.

karee raisu—(Japan) Rice topped with curry sauce.

karee udon—(Japan) Noodles topped with curry sauce.

kasuzuke—(Japan) Vegetables pickled in sake lees. Categorized as a *tsukemono*.

katsu—(Japan) A cutlet or flat croquette made of sliced meat that is breaded, typically in *panko,* and fried.

katsuobushi—(Japan) Dried bonito shavings.

kecap ikan—(Indonesia) A sauce made of fermented fish.

kimchi—(Korea) A variety of fermented vegetables. Considered the national dish of Korea.

kimuchi—(Japan) Kimchi in Japan. Often milder than the Korean counterpart.

kojizuke—(Japan) Vegetables pickled in rice mold. Categorized as a *tsukemono*.

konbu—(Japan) A type of brown seaweed. Principally used to make *dashi*.

kung pao—(China) A dish typically of chicken, vegetables, chiles, Sichuan peppercorns, and peanuts.

laulau—(Hawai'i) A dish of pork or other meats bundled in taro leaves with salted butterfish. Traditionally cooked in ti leaves in an underground oven called *imu*.

loco moco—(Hawai'i) A dish of rice topped with a hamburger patty, fried eggs, and brown gravy.

lutefisk—(Scandinavia) Dried whitefish, usually cod or ling, soaked in lye.

makizushi—(Japan) A type of sushi that is rolled into a cylinder and cut into bite-sized pieces. Made using a bamboo mat called *makisu*, except with *temakizushi,* which is hand rolled.

mirepoix—(France) A mixture of sautéed aromatic vegetables such as onions, celery, and carrots. A foundational element of various sauces and dishes.

miso—(Japan) A paste made of fermented soybean, barley, and rice malt.

misozuke—(Japan) Vegetables pickled in miso. Categorized as a *tsukemono*.

mole—(Mexican) A sauce of chiles, dried fruit, nuts, chocolate, and other ingredients. Widely varies from region to region.

moo goo gai pan—(China) A dish of chicken, mushrooms, and vegetables.

moussaka—(Eastern Mediterranean/Middle East) A dish typically of lamb, eggplant, tomatoes, and cheese.

musubi—(Japan) A type of *onigiri*.

naengmyeon—(Korean) Buckwheat-based noodles in a chilled broth. Served with a medley of garnishes, including sliced meat, pear, and boiled egg. Originated in northern Korea.

nampla—(Thailand) A sauce made of fermented fish.

narezushi—(Japan) Among the oldest types of sushi. Made of fish fermented in rice.

ngapi—(Burma) A paste made of fermented fish.

nigirizushi—(Japan) A type of sushi consisting of a small ball of rice typically topped with raw or cooked seafood. Also called *edomaezushi*.

nori—(Japan) Dried seaweed or laver, typically in sheet form and used in sushi preparation. Called *gim* in Korean.

nukazuke—(Japan) Vegetables pickled in rice bran. Categorized as a *tsukemono*.

nuoc mam—(Vietnam) A sauce made of fermented fish.

ojingeo bokkeum—(Korea) Stir-fried squid in a chile sauce.

onigiri—(Japan) Rice balls with various fillings such as *umeboshi*, bonito shavings, tuna mixed with mayonnaise, or other salty, sour, or savory ingredients.

otoro—(Japan) The fattiest portion of *toro*, the belly of the bluefin tuna. Among the most highly prized and priced cuts of fish used for sushi or sashimi.

pad Thai—(Thailand) A stir-fried noodle dish of eggs, meat, and a variety of condiments such as bean sprouts, peanuts, lime, and herbs. A popular street food and considered a national dish of Thailand.

padec—(Laos) A paste made of fermented fish.

paella—(Spain) A dish of rice cooked in a shallow pan with a variety of ingredients such as meat, seafood, sausage, snails, and vegetables.

patis—(Philippines) A sauce made of fermented fish.

phở—(Vietnam) A dish of rice noodles in a rich broth, typically beef, garnished with a variety of condiments such as bean sprouts, basil, mint, and lime.

poi—(Hawaiʻi) A paste made of pounded and fermented taro.

prahoc—(Cambodia) A paste made of fermented fish.

ramen—(Japan) A dish of wheat noodles in a hot broth garnished with a variety of ingredients.

roux—(France) A mixture of fat, such as butter, and flour cooked to a paste. A fundamental element of a variety of sauces and dishes.

saimin (Hawaiʻi) A dish of wheat noodles in a flavorful broth, similar to Japanese ramen. Garnishes typically include *kamaboko, char siu*, wontons, SPAM, egg, and green onions.

sake—(Japan) An alcoholic beverage made of fermented rice.

sashimi—(Japan) Fresh raw fish and other seafood sliced into bite-sized pieces. Typically garnished with a mound of white radish cut into long, thin strands.

seolleongtang—(Korea) A soup made of ox bones simmered for hours until the broth becomes milky white. Typically garnished at the table with salt, black pepper, and scallions.

shiokara—(Japan) A paste made of fermented fish.

shiozuke—(Japan) Vegetables pickled in salt. Categorized as a *tsukemono*.

shireen polow—(Iran) A festive rice dish made of saffron, orange peels, almonds, and pistachios.

shottsuru—(Japan) A sauce made of fermented fish.

shoyuzuke—(Japan) Vegetables pickled in soy sauce. Categorized as a *tsukemono*.

siu ngaap—(China) Roast duck.

soy sauce—(East and Southeast Asia) A sauce made of fermented soybeans.

stinky tofu—(China/Taiwan) Fermented bean curds with a strong odor.

sukiyaki—(Japan) A hotpot dish of thinly sliced beef and other ingredients cooked at the table.

sundubu jjigae—(Korea) A spicy stew of silken, custard-soft bean curds cooked with a variety of ingredients such as seafood, beef, pork, and vegetables.

surimi—(Japan) A fish product made from pollock and other fish that has been minced, cooked, formed into various shapes, and dyed. Often made to mimic the flavor, texture, and look of specific seafood such as crabmeat.

sushi—(Japan) A dish of seasoned rice paired with other ingredients, chiefly but not exclusively raw and cooked seafood. An umbrella term that includes *chirashizushi, makizushi, narezushi,* and *nigirizushi.*

suzuke—(Japan) Vegetables pickled in vinegar. Categorized as a *tsukemono*.

tabbouleh—(Middle East) A salad made of bulgur, chopped herbs, principally parsley and mint, and vegetables such as tomato and cucumber. Dressed with olive oil and lemon juice.

tagine—(Morocco/North Africa) Dishes named for the conical earthenware vessel in which they are cooked. Usually lamb or chicken with a variety of vegetables and spices.

takuan—(Japan) A pickle made from radish. Called *danmuji* in Korean.

tamago—(Japan) A type of sweet omelet often used in sushi.

tandoori—(India) Dishes named for the cylindrical clay oven called tandoor in which they are cooked. Principally meat and bread.

tangsuyuk—(Korea) Fried pork or beef with vegetables in a sweet and sour sauce. A popular Chinese-style dish in Korea.

tekkamaki—(Japan) A type of *makizushi* filled with raw tuna.

temakizushi—(Japan) A type of *makizushi* that is hand-rolled, often into a conical shape.

tempura—(Japan) Vegetable, fish, shrimp, and other seafood lightly battered and deep fried.

tom yum—(Thailand/Southeast Asia) A hot and sour soup often containing shrimp or prawn and flavored with lemon grass, chiles, lime, kaffir lime leaves, and various herbs.

tonkatsu—(Japan) A *katsu* made with pork.

toro—(Japan) The belly of the bluefin tuna. Commonly used for sushi or sashimi.

trassi—(Indonesia) A paste made of fermented fish.

tsukemono—(Japan) A general term for pickled foods. Includes *asazuke, kasuzuke, kojizuke, misozuke, nukazuke, shiozuke, shoyuzuke*, and *suzuke*.

tzatziki—(Greece/Turkey) Yogurt that is strained and flavored with a variety of ingredients such as garlic, cucumber, and herbs.

umeboshi—(Japan) A pickled apricot common in Japan called *ume*. Often called "pickled plum" in English. A type of *shiozuki*.

unagi—(Japan) Freshwater eel. Used in sushi, tempura, and other dishes.

uramaki—(Japan) An "inside-out" sushi roll such as California roll, in which the rice forms the outer layer and the filling is surrounded by nori inside. A type of *makizushi*.

vindaloo—(India) A highly spiced dish of meat, traditionally pork but also lamb or chicken, characterized by the sour taste of vinegar and heat of chiles and other spices. Originally of the Portuguese-influenced Goa region.

yuja—(Korea) A tart, grapefruit-like citrus. Called *yuzu* in Japanese.

yukgaejang—(Korea) A spicy soup made of shredded beef, chiles, scallions, and other vegetables.

Bibliography

Abelmann, Nancy, and John Lie. *Blue Dreams: Korean Americans and the Los Angeles Riots*. Cambridge, Mass.: Harvard University Press, 1997.
Adams, Carol J. "Eating Animals." In *Eating Culture*, ed. Ron Scapp and Brian Seitz, 60–75. Albany: State University of New York Press, 1998.
Alegre, Edilberto N. *Inumang Pinoy*. Manila: Anvil, 1992.
Alegre, Edilberto N, and Doreen G. Fernandez. *Kinilaw: A Philippine Cuisine of Freshness*. Manila: Bookmark, 1991.
Alejandro, Reynaldo. *The Philippine Cookbook*. New York: Perigree, 1982.
Allen, Irving Lewis. *The Language of Ethnic Conflict: Social Organization and Lexical Culture*. New York: Columbia University Press, 1983.
Amouretti, Marie-Claire. "Urban and Rural Diets in Greece." In *Food: A Culinary History from Antiquity to the Present*, ed. Jean-Louis Flandrin and Massimo Montanari, 79–89. New York: Penguin Books, 2000.
Anderson, E. N. *Food of China*. New Haven, Conn.: Yale University Press, 1988.
Andrews, Jean. *Peppers: The Domesticated Capsicums*. Austin: University of Texas Press, 1995.
———. "The Peripatetic Chili Pepper: Diffusion of the Domesticated Capsicums since Columbus." In *Chilies to Chocolate: Food the Americas Gave the World*, ed. Nelson Foster and Linda S. Cordell, 81–93. Tucson: University of Arizona Press, 1992.
Animal Studies Group. *Killing Animals*. Urbana and Chicago: University of Illinois Press, 2006.
Appadurai, Arjun. "How to Make a National Cuisine: Cookbooks in Contemporary India." *Comparative Studies in Society and History* 30, no. 1 (1988): 3–24.
———. Letter. "On Culinary Authenticity." *Anthropology Today* 2, no. 4 (1986): 24–25.
Arens, W. *The Man-Eating Myth: Anthropology and Anthropophagy*. Oxford: Oxford University Press, 1979.
Armstrong, Charles K. *The Koreas*. New York: Routledge, 2007.
Armstrong, Dan, and Dustin Black. *The Book of Spam*. New York: Atria, 2007.
Ashkenazi, Michael, and Jeanne Jacob. *The Essence of Japanese Cuisine. An Essay on Food and Culture*. Philadelphia: University of Pennsylvania Press, 2000.

Barbas, Samantha. "'I'll take Chop Suey': Restaurants as Agents of Culinary and Cultural Exchange." *Journal of Popular Culture* 36, no. 4 (2003): 669–686.
Berger, John. *Ways of Seeing.* London: Penguin, 1972.
Berglund, Jeff. *Cannibal Fictions: American Explorations of Colonialism, Race, Gender, and Sexuality.* Madison: University of Wisconsin Press, 2006.
Besa, Amy, and Romy Dorotan. *Memories of Philippine Kitchens: Stories and Recipes from Far and Near.* New York: Stewart, Tabori & Chang, 2006.
Bestor, Theodore C. "How Sushi Went Global." In *The Cultural Politics of Food and Eating: A Reader,* ed. James L. Watson and Melissa L. Caldwell, 13–20. Malden, Mass.: Blackwell, 2005.
———. *Tsukiji: The Fish Market at the Center of the World.* Berkeley: University of California Press, 2004.
Bex, Tony, and Richard J. Watts, eds. *Standard English: The Widening Debate.* London: Routledge, 1999.
Brewer, Douglas, Terence Clark, and Adrian Phillips. *Dogs in Antiquity: Anubis to Cerberus, the Origin of the Domestic Dog.* Warminster, UK: Aris and Phillips, 2001.
Brillat-Savarin, Jean Anthelme. *The Physiology of Taste* [1825]. Trans. M. F. K. Fisher. New York: Counterpoint, 1949.
Brock, William H. *Justus von Liebig: The Chemical Gatekeeper.* Cambridge: Cambridge University Press, 1997.
Brunvand, Jan Harold. *The Choking Doberman and Other "New" Urban Legends.* New York: Norton, 1984.
———. *Encyclopedia of Urban Legends.* New York: Norton, 2002.
———. *The Mexican Pet: More "New" Urban Legends and Some Old Favorites.* New York: Norton, 1986.
———. *Too Good to Be True: The Colossal Book of Urban Legends.* New York: Norton, 2001.
———. *The Vanishing Hitchhiker: American Urban Legends and Their Meanings.* New York: Norton, 1981.
Bulliet, Richard W. *Hunters, Herders, and Hamburgers: The Past and Future of Human-Animal Relationships.* New York: Columbia University Press, 2005.
Burrows, Edwin G., and Mike Wallace. *Gotham: A History of New York City to 1898.* New York: Oxford University Press, 1999.
Chadwick, R. et al. *Functional Foods.* Berlin, Ger.: Springer, 2004.
Chalk, Pamela C. "A Pig by Any Other Name Would Smell as Sweet." *Journal of Contemporary Legal Issues* 12 (2001): 340–344.
Chang, Leonard. *The Fruit 'N Food.* Seattle: Black Heron, 1996.
Cheung, Sidney, and David Y. H. Yu, eds. *Globalization of Chinese Food.* London: Routledge, 2004.
Child, Julia. *From Julia Child's Kitchen.* New York: Knopf, 1975.
Chin, Frank. *The Chinaman Frisco and R.R. Co.* Minneapolis: Coffeehouse, 1988.
Chin, Mei. "The Art of Kimchi." *Saveur,* November 2009, 74–83.
Cho, John Nagamichi. *SPAM-ku: Tranquil Reflections on Luncheon Loaf.* New York: HarperCollins, 1998.

Choi, Sung-jae. "The Politics of the Dokdo Issue." *Journal of East Asian Studies* 5 (2005): 465–494.
Chu, Young-ha. "Origins and Change in *Kimch'i* Culture. *Korea Journal* 35, no. 2 (1995): 18–33.
Chun, Injoo, Jaewoon Lee, and Youngran Baek. *Authentic Recipes from Korea*. Singapore: Periplus, 2004.
Clutton-Brock, Juliet. *Domesticated Animals from Early Times*. Austin: University of Texas Press, 1981.
Coe, Andrew. *Chop Suey: A Cultural History of Chinese Food in the United States*. New York: Oxford University Press, 2009.
Coe, Sophie D. *America's First Cuisines*. Austin: University of Texas Press, 1994.
Coleman, Craig S. *American Images of Korea*. Elizabeth, N.J.: Hollym, 1997.
Collingham, Lizzie. *Curry: A Tale of Cooks and Conquerors*. New York: Oxford University Press, 2006.
Collins, Kathleen. *Watching What We Eat: The Evolution of Television Cooking Shows*. New York: Continuum, 2009.
Conrad, Joseph. *Heart of Darkness* [1902]. Mineola, N.Y.: Dover, 1990.
Corson, Trevor. *The Zen of Fish: The Story of Sushi, from Samurai to Supermarket*. New York: HarperCollins, 2007.
Corum, Ann Kondo. *Hawaii's SPAM Cookbook*. Honolulu: Bess Press, 1987.
———. *Hawaii's 2nd SPAM Cookbook*. Honolulu: Bess Press, 2001.
Craddock, Susan. *City of Plagues: Disease, Poverty, and Deviance in San Francisco*. Minneapolis: University of Minnesota Press, 2004.
Crosby, Alfred W., Jr. *The Columbian Exchange: Biological and Cultural Consequences of 1492*. Westport, Conn.: Praeger, 2003.
Crystal, David. *English as a Global Language*. Cambridge: Cambridge University Press, 1997.
Cwiertka, Katarzyna J. *Modern Japanese Cuisine: Food, Power and National Identity*. London: Reaktion, 2006.
Cwiertka, Katarzyna, and Boudewijn Walraven, eds. *Asian Food: The Global and the Local*. Honolulu: University of Hawai'i Press, 2001.
Czarra, Fred. *Spices: A Global History*. London: Reaktion, 2009.
Davidson, Alan. *The Oxford Companion to Food*. Oxford: Oxford University Press, 1999.
Davis, Roger. "*You* Are What You Eat: Cannibalism, Autophagy and the Case of Armin Meiwes." In *Territories of Evil*, ed. Nancy Billias, 151–170. Amsterdam: Rodopi, 2008.
Defoe, Daniel. *Robinson Crusoe* [1719]. New York: Modern Library, 2001.
Den Hartog, Adel P. "Acceptance of Milk Products in Southeast Asia: The Case of Indonesia as a Traditional Non-Dairying Region." In *Asian Food: The Global and the Local*, ed. Katarzyna Cwiertka and Boudewijn Walraven, 34–45. Honolulu: University of Hawai'i Press, 2001.
Denker, Joel. *The World on a Plate: A Tour through a History of America's Ethnic Cuisine*. Boulder, Colo.: Westview Press, 2003.

DeWitt, Dave. *The Chile Pepper Encyclopedia*. New York: William Morrow, 1999.

DeWitt, Dave, and Paul W. Bosland. *Peppers of the World: An Identification Guide*. Berkeley, Calif.: Ten Speed, 1996.

DeWitt, Dave, and Nancy Gerlach. *The Whole Chile Pepper Book*. Boston: Little, Brown, 1990.

Djien Ko Swan. "Indigenous Fermented Foods." In *Fermented Foods*, ed. A. H. Rose, 15–38. Economic Microbiology 7. London: Academic Press, 1982.

Dunlop, Fuchsia. "Strange Tale of General Tso." In *Authenticity in the Kitchen: Proceedings of the Oxford Symposium on Food and Cookery, 2005*, ed. Richard Hosking, 165–177. Blackawton, UK: Prospect, 2006.

Dusselier, Jane. "Does Food Make Place? Food Protests in Japanese American Concentration Camps." *Food and Foodways* 10, no. 3 (2002): 137–165.

Eggers, Linda. *The SPAM Cookbook: Recipes from Main Street*. Marietta, Ga.: Longstreet, 1998.

Ettlinger Steve. *Twinkie, Deconstructed: My Journey to Discover How the Ingredients Found in Processed Foods are Grown, Mined (Yes, Mined), and Manipulated into What America Eats*. New York: Plume, 2008.

Fabian, Johannes. *Time and the Other: How Anthropology Makes Its Object*. New York: Columbia University Press, 1983.

Feffer, John. "Food Fight." *Gastronomica* 1, no. 3 (Summer 2001): 3–4.

Fern, Sean. "Tokdo or Takeshima? The International Law of Territorial Acquisition in the Japan-Korea Island Dispute." *Stanford Journal of East Asian Affairs* 5, no. 1 (Winter 2005): 78–89.

Fiddes, Nick. *Meat: A Natural Symbol*. London: Routledge, 1991.

Fine, Gary Alan. *Kitchens: The Culture of Restaurant Work*. Berkeley: University of California Press, 1996.

Finlay, Mark R. "Quackery and Cookery: Justus von Liebig's Extract of Meat and the Theory of Nutrition in the Victorian Age." *Bulletin of the History of Medicine* 66, no. 3 (Fall 1992): 404–418.

Fisher, M. F. K. Introduction. In Shizuo Tsuji, *Japanese Cooking: A Simple Art*, 11–21. Tokyo: Kodansha International, 1980.

Flandrin, Jean-Louis, and Massimo Montanari, eds. *Food: A Culinary History from Antiquity to the Present*. New York: Penguin, 2000.

Foster, Nelson, and Linda S. Cordell, eds. *Chiles to Chocolate: Food the Americas Gave the World*. Tucson: University of Arizona Press, 1992.

Freeman, Matthew. "Reconsidering the Effects of Monosodium Glutamate: A Literature Review." *Journal of the American Academy of Nurse Practitioners* 18 (2006): 482–486.

Friedan, Betty. *The Feminine Mystique*. New York: Dell, 1963.

Fruin, W. Mark. *Kikkoman: Company, Clan, and Community*. Cambridge, Mass.: Harvard University Press, 1983.

Fussell, Betty. *Raising Steaks: The Life and Times of American Beef*. Orlando, Fla.: Harcourt, 2008.

Giammellaro, Antonella Spanò. "The Phoenicians and the Carthaginians: The Early Mediterranean Diet. In *Food: A Culinary History from Antiquity to the Present*, ed.

Jean-Louis Flandrin and Massimo Montanari, 55–65. New York: Penguin Books, 2000.
Gibson, Glenn R., and Christine M. Williams. *Functional Foods: Concept to Product.* Boca Raton, Fla.: CRC, 2000.
Gilbert, Elizabeth. *Eat, Pray, Love: One Woman's Search for Everything across Italy, India and Indonesia.* New York: Penguin, 2007.
Grew, Raymond, ed. *Food in Global History.* Boulder, Colo.: Westview, 1999.
Griffith, Marcie, Jennifer Wolch, and Unna Lassiter. "Animal Practices and the Racialization of Filipinas in Los Angeles." *Society & Animals* 10, no. 3 (2002): 221–248.
Haber, Barbara. *From Hardtack to Home Fries: An Uncommon History of American Cooks and Meals.* New York: The Free Press, 2002.
Hahm, Hanhee. "Rice and Koreans: Three Identities and Meanings." *Korea Journal* 45, no. 2 (Summer 2005): 89–106.
Hallmar, Kara Kelly. *Encyclopedia of Asian American Artists.* Westport, Conn.: Greenwood, 2007.
Halpern, Bruce. "What's in a Name? Are MSG and Umami the Same?" *Chemical Senses* 27 (2002): 845–846.
Hamilton, Alissa. "World War II's Mobilization of the Science of Food Acceptability: How Ration Palatability Became a Military Research Priority." *Ecology of Food and Nutrition* 42 (2003): 325–356.
Hamilton, Angus. *Korea.* New York: Scribner's, 1904.
Han, Kyung-Koo. "Some Foods Are Good to Think: Kimchi and the Epitomization of National Character." *Korean Social Science Journal* 27, no. 1 (2000): 221–235.
Harris, Marvin. *The Sacred Cow and the Abominable Pig: Riddles of Food and Culture.* New York: Simon and Schuster, 1985.
Hart, Lynette A. "Dogs as Human Companions: A Review of the Relationship." In *The Domestic Dog: Its Evolution, Behaviour and Interactions with People,* ed. James Serpell, 161–178. Cambridge: Cambridge University Press, 1995.
Hasler, Clare M. *Regulation of Functional Foods and Nutraceuticals: A Global Perspective.* Ames, Iowa: Blackwell, 2005.
Hemingway, Ernest. *The Sun Also Rises.* New York: Scribner, 1926.
Herbst, Philip. *Color of Words: An Encyclopaedic Dictionary of Ethnic Bias in the United States.* Yarmouth, Me.: Intercultural, 1997.
Ho, Jennifer Ann. *Consumption and Identity in Asian American Coming-of-Age Novels.* New York: Routledge, 2005.
Hobsbawm, Eric, ed. *The Invention of Tradition.* Cambridge: Cambridge University Press, 1983.
Hopkins, Jerry. *Extreme Cuisine: The Weird and Wonderful Foods That People Eat.* Hong Kong: Periplus, 2004.
Hosking, Richard, ed. *Authenticity in the Kitchen: Proceedings of the Oxford Symposium on Food and Cookery 2005.* Blackawton, UK: Prospect, 2006.
———. *A Dictionary of Japanese Food: Ingredients and Culture.* Tokyo: Tuttle, 1995.
Hulbert, Homer. *The Passing of Korea.* New York: Doubleday, Page, 1906.
Hwang, David Henry. *M. Butterfly.* New York: Plume, 1989.

Ishige, Naomichi. *The History and Culture of Japanese Food.* London: Kegan Paul, 2001.

Issenberg, Sasha. *The Sushi Economy: Globalization and the Making of a Modern Delicacy.* New York: Gotham, 2007.

Jackson, Kenneth T., ed. *The Encyclopedia of New York City.* New Haven, Conn.: Yale University Press, 1995.

Jacobson, Matthew Frye. *Barbarian Virtues: The United States Encounters Foreign Peoples at Home and Abroad, 1876–1917.* New York: Hill and Wang, 2001.

Jung, Keun-Sik. "Colonial Modernity and the Social History of Chemical Seasoning in Korea." *Korea Journal* 45, no. 2 (Summer 2005): 9–36.

Kamp, David. *The United States of Arugula: How We Became a Gourmet Nation.* New York: Broadway, 2006.

Kaplan, Amy, and Donald E. Pease, eds. *Cultures of United States Imperialism.* Durham, N.C.: Duke University Press, 1994.

Kasabian, David, and Anna Kasabian. *The Fifth Taste: Cooking with Umami.* New York: Universe, 2005.

Katayama, Masao. "Professor Kikunae Ikeda." *Bulletin of the Chemical Society of Japan* 1, no. 1 (1926): 1–2.

Kelly, James L. "Loco Moco: A Folk Dish in the Making." In *The Taste of American Place: A Reader on Regional and Ethnic Foods,* ed. Barbara G. Shortridge and James R. Shortridge, 39–43. Lanham, Md.: Rowman and Littlefield, 1998.

Kim, Claire Jean. *Bitter Fruit: The Politics of Black-Korean Conflict in New York City.* New Haven, Conn.: Yale University Press, 2003.

Kim, Elaine. *Asian American Literature: An Introduction to the Writings and Their Social Context.* Philadelphia: Temple University Press, 1982.

Kim, Manjo. "Kimchi: The Secret Korean Flavor of the Centuries." *Korean and Korean American Studies Bulletin* 6, no. 1 (Spring 1995): 26–31.

———. "A Korean Original: Kimchi." *Koreana* 11, no. 3 (Autumn 1997): 62–67.

Kim, Man-Jo, Kyou-Tae Lee, and O-Young Lee, eds. *Kimchi, Thousand Years.* 2 vols. Seoul: Design House, 1997.

Kim, Mi-ok. "Yeongyang Chili Pepper Market." *Koreana* 14, no. 3 (Autumn 2000): 62–67.

Kingston, Maxine Hong. *The Woman Warrior: Memoirs of a Childhood among Ghosts* [1975]. New York: Vintage, 1989.

Kipfer, Barbara Ann. *The Culinarian: A Kitchen Desk Reference.* New York: Wiley, 2011.

Kirshenblatt-Gimblett, Barbara. *Destination Culture: Tourism, Museums, and Heritage.* Berkeley: University of California Press, 1998.

Kondo, Sonoko. *The Poetical Pursuit of Food: Japanese Recipes for American Cooks.* New York: Clarkson Potter, 1986.

Kundera, Milan. *The Art of the Novel.* New York: Harper and Row, 1988.

———. *The Unbearable Lightness of Being.* New York: Harper and Row, 1984.

Kwok, Robert Ho Man. Letter. "Chinese Restaurant Syndrome." *New England Journal of Medicine* 278, no. 14 (April 4, 1968): 796.

Laemmerhirt, Iris-Aya. "Imagining the Taste: Transnational Food Exchanges between Japan and the United States." *The Japanese Journal of American Studies* 21 (2010): 231–250.

Laudan, Rachel. *The Food of Paradise: Exploring Hawaii's Culinary Heritage.* Honolulu: University of Hawai'i Press, 1996.

Lee, Cherl-Ho. *Fermentation Technology in Korea.* Seoul: Korea University Press, 2001.

Lee, Chun Ja, Hye Won Park, and Kwi Young Kim. *The Book of Kimchi.* Seoul: Korean Information Service, 1998.

Lee, Jennifer 8. *The Fortune Cookie Chronicles: Adventures in the World of Chinese Food.* New York: Twelve, 2008.

Lee, Robert G. *Orientals: Asian Americans in Popular Culture.* Philadelphia: Temple University Press, 1999.

Lee, Sunyoung. "Spam I Am." *MUÆ* 2 (1997): 78–83.

Lee, Young C. "Kimchi: The Famous Fermented Vegetable Product in Korea." *Food Reviews International* 7, no. 4 (1991): 399–415.

Levenstein, Harvey. *Paradox of Plenty: A Social History of Eating in Modern America.* New York: Oxford University Press, 1993.

Lewis, George H. "From Minnesota Fat to Seoul Food: Spam in America and the Pacific Rim." *Journal of Popular Culture* 34, no. 2 (Fall 2000): 83–105.

Lien, Marianne Elisabeth. "Dogs, Whales and Kangaroos: Transnational Activism and Food Taboos." In *The Politics of Food,* ed. Marianne Elisabeth Lien and Briggitte Nerlich, 179–198. Oxford: Berg, 2004.

Lien, Marianne Elisabeth, and Briggitte Nerlich, eds. *The Politics of Food.* Oxford: Berg, 2004.

Lindemann, Bernd, Yoko Ogiwara, and Yuzo Ninomiya. "The Discovery of Umami." *Chemical Senses* 27 (2002): 843–844.

Linmark, R. Zamora. *Rolling the R's.* New York: Kaya Production, 1995.

Lippi-Green, Rosina. *English with an Accent: Language, Ideology, and Discrimination in the United States.* New York: Routledge, 1997.

Long, Lucy M., ed. *Culinary Tourism: Eating and Otherness.* Lexington: University of Kentucky Press, 2004.

Lovegren, Sylvia. *Fashionable Food: Seven Decades of Food Fads.* Chicago: Chicago University Press, 2005.

Lowe, Lisa. *Immigrant Acts: On Asian American Cultural Politics.* Durham, N.C.: Duke University Press, 1996.

Lu, Houyuan et al. "Culinary Archaeology: Millet Noodles in Late Neolithic China." *Nature* 437 (October 13, 2005): 967–968.

Lubin, David M. *Titanic.* London: British Film Institute, 1999.

Lum, Darrell H. Y. *Pass On, No Pass Back!* Honolulu: Bamboo Ridge, 1990.

MacCannell, Dean. *The Tourist: A New Theory of the Leisure Class.* Berkeley: University of California Press, 1999.

Manalansan, Martin F. IV. "The Empire of Food: Place, Memory, and Asian 'Ethnic Cuisines.'" In *Gastropolis: Food and New York City,* ed. Annie Hauck-Lawson and Jonathan Deutsch, 93–107. New York: Columbia University Press, 2009.

Manganaro, Marc, ed. *Modernist Anthropology: From Fieldwork to Text*. Princeton, N.J.: Princeton University Press, 1990.

———. "Textual Play, Power, and Cultural Critique: An Orientation to Modernist Anthropology." In *Modernist Anthropology: From Fieldwork to Text*, ed. Marc Manganaro, 3–49. Princeton, N.J.: Princeton University Press, 1990.

Mannur, Anita. *Culinary Fictions: Food in South Asian Diasporic Culture*. Philadelphia: Temple University Press, 2010.

———. "Model Minorities Can Cook." In *East Main Street: Asian American Popular Culture*, ed. Shilpa Davé, LeiLani Nishime, and Tasha G. Oren, 72–94. New York: New York University Press, 2005.

Mariani, John F. *The Dictionary of American Food and Drink*. New York: Hearst, 1994.

Matejowsky, Ty. "SPAM and Fast-food 'Glocalization' in the Philippines." *Food, Culture, Society* 10, no. 1 (2007): 24–41.

Mazumdar, Sucheta. "The Impact of New World Food Crop on the Diet and Economy of China and India, 1600–1900." In *Food in Global History*, ed. Raymond Grew, 58–78. Boulder, Colo.: Westview Press, 1999.

McArthur, Tom. *The English Languages*. Cambridge: Cambridge University Press, 1998.

McGee, Harold. *On Food and Cooking: The Science and Lore of the Kitchen*. New York: Scribner, 2004.

McHugh, Susan. *Dog*. London: Reaktion, 2004.

Miller, Mark. *The Great Chile Book*. Berkeley, Calif.: Ten Speed, 1991.

Mintz, Sidney. *Tasting Food, Tasting Freedom: Excursions into Eating, Power, and the Past*. Boston: Beacon, 1996.

Miura, Muriel. *Hawai'i Cooks With SPAM*. Honolulu: Mutual, 2008.

Molz, Jennie Germann. "Tasting an Imagined Thailand: Authenticity and Culinary Tourism in Thai Restaurants." In *Culinary Tourism: Eating and Otherness*, ed. Lucy Long, 53–75. Lexington: University of Kentucky Press, 2004.

Morrison, Toni. *Playing in the Dark: Whiteness and the Literary Imagination*. Cambridge, Mass.: Harvard University Press, 1992.

Morton, Mark. "Joie de Mort." *Gastronomica* 9, no. 1 (Winter 2009): 9–11.

Mosby, Ian. "'That Won-Ton Soup Headache': The Chinese Restaurant Syndrome, MSG and the Making of American Food, 1968–1980." *Social History of Medicine* 22, no. 1 (2009): 133–151.

Mukherjee, Bharati. *Jasmine*. New York: Grove, 1989.

Muller, H. G. "Industrial Food Preservation in the Nineteenth and Twentieth Centuries." In *Waste Not, Want Not: Food Preservation from Early Times to the Present Day*, ed. C. Anne Wilson, 104–133. Edinburgh: Edinburgh University Press, 1991.

Naj, Amal. *Peppers: A Story of Hot Pursuits*. New York: Random House, 1992.

Nestle, Marion. *Food Politics: How the Food Industry Influences Nutrition and Health*. Berkeley: University of California Press, 2002.

———. *What to Eat*. New York: North Point, 2006.

Nguyen, Mimi Thi, and Thuy Linh Nguyen Tu, eds. *Alien Encounters: Popular Culture in Asian America*. Durham, N.C.: Duke University Press, 2007.

Nochlin, Linda. "Why Have There Been No Great Women Artists?" *Art News* 69, no. 9 (January 1971): 22–39.

Oates, Joyce Carol. *On Boxing*. New York: HarperCollins, 2006.

Obeyesekere, Gananath. *Cannibal Talk: The Man-Eating Myths and Human Sacrifice in the South Seas*. Berkeley: University of California Press, 2005.

Ohnuki-Tierney, Emiko. "The Ambivalent Self of the Contemporary Japanese." *Cultural Anthropology* 5, no. 2 (May 1990): 197–216.

———. *Rice as Self: Japanese Identities through Time*. Princeton, N.J.: Princeton University Press, 1993.

Okihiro, Gary Y. *Margins and Mainstreams: Asians in American History and Culture*. Seattle: Washington University Press, 1994.

———. *Pineapple Culture: A History of the Tropical and Temperate Zones*. Berkeley: University of California Press, 2010.

Omae, Kinjiro, and Yuzuru Tachibana. *The Book of Sushi*. Tokyo: Kodansha, 1981.

Osgood, Cornelius. *The Koreans and Their Culture*. New York: Ronald, 1951.

Ostrow, Daniel, David Ostrow, and Mary Sham. *Manhattan's Chinatown*. Charleston, S.C.: Arcadia, 2008.

Pak, Gary. *The Watchers of Waipuna and Other Stories*. Honolulu: Bamboo Ridge, 1992.

Park, Kun-Young, and Hong-Sik Cheigh. "Kimchi." In *Handbook of Food and Beverage Fermentation Technology*, ed. Y. H. Hui et al., 714–754. New York: Marcel Dekker, 2004.

Park, Kun-Young, and Sook-Hee Rhee. "Functional Foods from Fermented Vegetable Products: Kimchi (Korean Fermented Vegetables) and Functionality." In *Asian Functional Foods*, ed. John Shi, Chi-Tang Ho, and Fereidoon Shahidi, 341–380. Boca Raton, Fla.: CRC, 2005.

Pease, Donald E. "New Perspectives on U.S. Culture and Imperialism." In *Cultures of United States Imperialism*, ed. Amy Kaplan and Donald E. Pease, 22–37. Durham, N.C.: Duke University Press, 1994.

Pederson, Carl S. *Microbiology of Food Fermentations*. Westport, Conn.: AVI, 1971.

Pedrocco, Giorgio. "Food Industry and New Preservation Techniques." In *Food: A Culinary History*, ed. Jean-Louis Flandrin and Massimo Montanari, 481–491. New York: Penguin, 2000.

Pettid, Michael J. *Korean Cuisine: An Illustrated History*. London: Reaktion, 2008.

Pollan, Michael. *In Defense of Food: An Eater's Manifesto*. New York: Penguin, 2008.

———. *Omnivore's Dilemma: A Natural History of Four Meals*. New York: Penguin, 2006.

Porter, William C. Letter. "Correspondence: Sin Cib-Syn: Accent on Glutamate." *New England Journal of Medicine* 279, no. 2 (July 11, 1968): 106.

Price, Sally. *Primitive Art in Civilized Places*. Chicago: Chicago University Press, 1989.

Rain, Patricia. "Vanilla: Nectar of the Gods." In *Chiles to Chocolate: Food the Americas Gave the World*, ed. Nelson Foster and Linda S. Cordell, 35–46. Tucson: University of Arizona Press, 1992.

Rath, Eric C., and Stephanie Assman, eds. *Japanese Foodways Past and Present*. Urbana: University of Illinois Press, 2010.
Ray, Krishendu. "Domesticating Cuisine: Food and Aesthetics on American Television." *Gastronomica* 7, no. 1 (Winter 2007): 50–63.
Roberts, J. A. G. *China to Chinatown: Chinese Food in the West*. London: Reaktion, 2002.
Robinson, Martin, Andrew Bender, and Rob Whyte. *Lonely Planet: Korea*. Victoria, Aus.: Lonely Planet, 2004.
Rombauer, Irma, Marion Rombauer Becker, and Ethan Becker. *Joy of Cooking*. New York: Scribner, 1997.
Rose, A. H., ed. *Fermented Foods*. London: Academic, 1982.
Rozin, Paul et al. "Disgust: Preadaptation and the Cultural Evolution of a Food-Based Emotion." In *Food Preferences and Taste: Continuity and Change*, ed. Helen Macbeth, 65–82. Providence, R.I.: Berghahn, 1997.
Said, Edward. *Beginnings: Intention and Method*. New York: Columbia University Press, 1985.
———. *Orientalism*. New York: Vintage, 1979.
Sakamoto, Rumi, and Matthew Allen. "There's Something Fishy about That Sushi: How Japan Interprets the Global Sushi Boom." *Japan Forum* 23, no. 1 (2011): 99–121.
Sand, Jordan. "A Short History of MSG: Good Science, Bad Science, and Taste Cultures." *Gastronomica* 5, no. 4 (Fall 2005): 38–49.
Scapp, Ron, and Brian Seitz, eds. *Eating Culture*. Albany: State University of New York Press, 1998.
Schaumburg, H., Thomas J. McCaghren, Matthew Menken, William Migden, Elizabeth Kirk Rose, Jogeswar Rath, Elissa L. Beron, Stephen R. Kandall, Martin E. Gordon, and Nicholas E. Davies. Letters. "Correspondence: Chinese-Restaurant Syndrome." *New England Journal of Medicine* 278, no. 20 (May, 16, 1968): 1122–1124.
Schaumburg, Herbert H., Robert Byck, Marjorie Ambos, Nancy R. Leavitt, Lynne Marorek, and Susan B. Wolschina. Letters. "Correspondence: Sin Cib-Syn: Accent on Glutamate," *New England Journal of Medicine* 279, no. 2 (July 11, 1968): 105.
Schaumburg, Herbert H. et al. "Monosodium L-Glutamate: Its Pharmacology and Rule in the Chinese Restaurant Syndrome." *Science* 163, no. 3869 (February 21, 1969): 826–828.
Schiefenhövel, Wulf. "Good Taste and Bad Taste: Preferences and Aversions as Biological Principles." In *Food Preferences and Taste: Continuity and Change*, ed. Helen Macbeth, 55–64. Providence, R.I.: Berghahn, 1997.
Schlosser, Eric. *Fast Food Nation: The Dark Side of the All-American Meal*. New York: Perennial, 2002.
Schmidl, Mary Katherine, and Theodore Peter Labuza. *Essentials of Functional Foods*. Gaithersburg, Md.: Aspen, 2000.
Schwabe, Calvin W. *Unmentionable Cuisine*. Charlottesville: University Press of Virginia, 1979.

Sebba, Mark. *Contact Languages: Pidgins and Creoles.* New York: St. Martin's, 1997.
Serpell, James, ed. *The Domestic Dog: Its Evolution, Behaviour and Interactions with People.* Cambridge: Cambridge University Press, 1995.
———. "From Paragon to Pariah: Some Reflections on Human Attitudes to Dogs." In *The Domestic Dog: Its Evolution, Behaviour and Interactions with People,* ed. James Serpell, 245–256. Cambridge: Cambridge University Press, 1995.
Shah, Nayan. *Contagious Divides: Epidemics and Race in San Francisco's Chinatown.* Berkeley: University of California Press, 2001.
Shi, John, Chi-Tang Ho, and Fereidoon Shahidi, eds. *Asian Functional Foods.* Boca Raton, Fla.: CRC, 2005.
Shibusawa, Naoko. *America's Geisha Ally: Reimagining the Japanese Enemy.* Cambridge, Mass.: Harvard University Press, 2006.
Shimemura, Youchi. "Globalization vs. Americanization: Is the World Being Americanized by the Dominance of American Culture?" *Comparative Civilizations Review* 47 (2002): 80–91.
Shiva, Vandana. *Stolen Harvest: The Hijacking of the Global Food Supply.* Cambridge, Mass.: South End Press, 2000.
Shortridge, Barbara G., and James R. Shortridge, eds. *The Taste of American Place: A Reader on Regional and Ethnic Foods.* Lanham, Md.: Rowman and Littlefield, 1998.
Simmonds, Peter Lund. *The Curiosity of Food: Or the Dainties and Delicacies of Different Nations Obtained from the Animal Kingdom.* Berkeley, Calif.: Ten Speed, 2001.
Simoons, Frederick. *Eat Not This Flesh: Food Avoidances from Prehistory to the Present.* Madison: University of Wisconsin Press, 1994.
Siskind, Janet. "The Invention of Thanksgiving: A Ritual of American Nationality." *Critique of Anthropology* 12, no. 2 (1992): 167–191.
Sokolov, Raymond. *Why We Eat What We Eat: How Columbus Changed the Way the World Eats.* New York: Summit, 1991.
Som, Indigo. "Chinese Restaurant Drive-Thru." In *Alien Encounters: Popular Culture in Asian America,* ed. Mimi Thi Nguyen and Thuy Linh Nguyen Tu, 150–160. Durham, N.C.: Duke University Press, 2007.
Spiller, Harley. "Chow Fun City: Three Centuries of Chinese Cuisine in New York City." In *Gastropolis: Food and New York City,* ed. Annie Hauck-Lawson and Jonathan Deutsch, 132–150. New York: Columbia University Press, 2009.
Standage, Tom. *An Edible History of Humanity.* New York: Walker & Co., 2009.
Steingarten, Jeffrey. *It Must've Been Something I Ate.* New York: Vintage, 2002.
Su, Steven Wei. "The Territorial Dispute over the Tiaoyu/Senkaku Islands: An Update." *Ocean Development & International Law* 36 (2005): 45–61.
Swislocki, Mark. *Culinary Nostalgia: Regional Food Culture and the Urban Experience in Shanghai.* Stanford, Calif.: Stanford University Press, 2009.
Takaki, Ronald. *Strangers from a Different Shore: A History of Asian Americans.* Boston: Little, Brown, 1989.
Thorne, Stuart. *The History of Food Preservation.* Totowa, N.J.: Barnes & Noble, 1986.
Tonouchi, Lee A. *Da Word.* Honolulu: Bamboo Ridge, 2001.

Trudgill, Peter. "Standard English: What It Isn't." In *Standard English: The Widening Debate,* ed. Tony Bex and Richard J. Watts, 117–128. London: Routledge, 1999.
Tsai, Ming, and Arthur Boehm. *Blue Ginger: East Meets West Cooking with Ming Tsai.* New York: Clarkson Potter, 1999.
Tsuji, Shizuo. *Japanese Cooking: A Simple Art.* Tokyo: Kodansha International, 2006.
Tuchman, Gaye, and Harry Gene Levine. "New York Jews and Chinese Food: The Social Construction of an Ethnic Pattern." *Journal of Contemporary Ethnography* 22, no. 3 (October 1993): 382–407.
Turner, Jack. *Spice: The History of a Temptation.* New York: Knopf, 2005.
Uden, Martin. *Times Past in Korea: An Illustrated Collection of Encounters, Events, Customs and Daily Life Recorded by Foreign Visitors.* London: Korea Library, 2003.
Urry, John. *The Tourist Gaze: Leisure and Travel in Contemporary Societies.* London: Sage Publications, 1990.
Van Dyke, Jon M. "Legal Issues Related to Sovereignty over Dokdo and Its Maritime Boundary." *Ocean Development & International Law* 38 (2007): 157–224.
van Wyk, Ben-Erik. *Food Plants of the World.* Portland, Ore.: Timber, 2005.
Wallace, David Foster. *Consider the Lobster and Other Essays.* New York: Back Bay, 2006.
Walraven, Boudewijn. "Bardot Soup and Confucians' Meat." In *Asian Food: The Global and the Local,* ed. Katarzyna Cwiertka and Boudewijn Walraven, 95–114. Honolulu: University of Hawai'i Press, 2001.
Watson, James L., ed. *Golden Arches East: McDonald's in East Asia.* Stanford, Calif.: Stanford University Press, 1997.
Wilbert, Chris. "What Is Doing the Killing? Animal Attacks, Man-Eaters, and Shifting Boundaries and Flows of Human-Animal Relations." In Animal Studies Group, *Killing Animals,* 30–49. Urbana and Chicago: University of Illinois Press, 2006.
Williams, Erin E., and Margo DeMello. *Why Animals Matter: The Case for Animal Protection.* Amherst, N.Y.: Prometheus, 2007.
Williams-Forson, Psyche A. *Building Houses out of Chicken Legs: Black Women, Food, and Power.* Chapel Hill: University of North Carolina Press, 2006.
Wilson, C. Anne, ed. *Waste Not, Want Not: Food Preservation from Early Times to the Present Day.* Edinburgh: Edinburgh University Press, 1991.
Winchester, Simon. *Korea: A Walk through the Land of Miracles.* New York: Harper Perennial, 2005.
Winter, Carl K., James N. Seiber, and Carole F. Nuckton, eds. *Chemicals in the Human Food Chain.* New York: Van Nostrand Reinhold, 1990.
Winter, Ruth. *A Consumer's Dictionary of Food Additives.* New York: Three Rivers, 2004.
Wrangham, Richard, *Catching Fire: How Cooking Made Us Human.* New York: Basic, 2009.
Wu, Frank. *Yellow: Race in America beyond Black and White.* New York: Basic, 2002.
Wyman, Carolyn. *SPAM: A Biography.* New York: Harcourt Brace, 1999.
Xu, Wenying. *Eating Identities: Reading Food in Asian American Literature.* Honolulu: University of Hawai'i Press, 2008.

Xun, Lu. "Diary of a Madman." In *Diary of a Madman and Other Stories*. Honolulu: University of Hawai'i Press, 1990.

Yamaguchi, Shizuko, and Kumiko Ninomiya. "The Use and Utility of Glutamates as Flavoring Agents in Food." *The Journal of Nutrition* 130, no. 4 (April 1, 2000): 922S-996S.

Yamanaka, Lois-Ann. *Saturday Night at the Pahala Theatre*. Honolulu: Bamboo Ridge, 1993.

Yano, Christine. "Shifting Plates: Okazuya in Hawai'i." *Amerasia Journal* 32, no. 2 (2006): 37-45.

Yoshihara, Mari. *Musicians from a Different Shore: Asian Americans in Classical Music*. Philadelphia: Temple University Press, 2007.

Yung, Judy, Gordon H. Chang, and Him Mark Lai, eds. *Chinese American Voices: From the Gold Rush to the Present*. Berkeley: University of California Press, 2006.

Zia, Helen. *Asian American Dreams: The Emergence of an American People*. New York: Farrar, Staus and Giroux, 2001.

Index

adobo, 216, 259
aesthetic taste, 23. *See also* taste
African Americans, 4, 58–59, 62–63, 121, 136
Ajinomoto, 171–172, 181–182, 187, 188
Albert Einstein College of Medicine, 180
Alexander the Great, 208
American food, 52; diversity of, 176–177; MSG in, 181–182, 184
Americanization: of equatorial cuisines, 33–34; of food, 4, 8, 23, 33–34, 69, 76; of Japanese food, 33; of Korean men, 124; and US hegemony, 34
American literature, 58–60
American studies, 10
anago, 259
Anderson, E. N., 68–71, 73
Ando, Momofuku, 218
animal farming, 149. *See also* factory farming
anthropophagy, 86, 126–127, 130–134. *See also* cannibalism
anti-Asian sentiments, 135
anti-Chinese sentiments, 57
anti-immigrant sentiments, 135
Appert, Nicolas, 206–207, 209
Armour Potted Meat Product, 198
asazuke, 112, 259, 265
Asian American activists, 60–61
Asian American audience, 135
Asian American community, 61, 213

Asian American groups, 61
Asian American magazine, 191
Asian Americans, 6, 8, 9, 61, 135; assimilability of, 13; and citizenship, 60, 62, 63; conflicts with African Americans, 63; insults against, 135–136; as perpetual foreigners, 61, 63; protests by, 61, 121; racial slurs about, 120–122; racist imageries of, 121; violence against, 61
Asian American scholars, 60–61
Asian American students, 120–121
Asian American studies, 10, 120
Asian communities, 5
Asian cuisines, 228
Asian cultures, 122
Asian diaspora, 4, 6
Asian foods, 4, 5–9, 11, 13, 71, 147, 161; globalization of, 3–4
Asian gastronomy, 5, 127
Asian identities, 5
Asian immigrants, 7, 52, 135
Asians, 8, 9, 10, 52, 63, 85, 134, 146; in American Midwest, 61, 192; and dog eating, 54, 121–122, 123, 134–136; racial slurs about, 120–122; stereotypes of, 11; in the United States, 60–61, 135
Asian studies, 10
Asian tradition, 140, 230
Asimov, Eric, 30
authenticity, 2–3, 5–6, 8–9, 35–39, 48, 227; analogy to language, 227–228; challenge

281

authenticity (cont.)
to, 4, 6; discursive strategy of, 35; and modernity, 36, 38; as narrative of origin, 39; of native life, 130; as prescribed order of things, 37
avocado, 32, 89, 173; in California roll, 19, 21, 23, 32, 33, 43–44, 45–48; in Japan, 6; in sushi rolls, 19, 21, 31

bagoong, 42, 170, 259
balut, 10, 147, 259
basil, 224, 225–226, 263
Bayless, Rick, 22, 187
bento, 112, 191, 217, 259
berbere, 90, 259, 260
Bhut Jolokia, 92, 259
bibim naengmyeon, 92, 259
bibimbap, 130, 260
Bigler, John, 52, 226
Binghamton, New York, 81, 84, 155
Binghamton University, 120–121
black pepper, 86–87, 91, 119, 199, 226
Bloomberg, Michael, 64
Blue Ginger restaurant, 26, 224, 226, 229
bok choy, 35, 177
Bonaparte, Napoleon, 207
borders: conceptual, 222; geographic, 1, 69, 74, 94
bosintang, 128, 141, 143, 154–155, 260
bouillon, 167, 168, 210
Bourdain, Anthony, 36
Boxer Rebellion, 212
Bradshaw, Terry, 17–18
Breakfast Club (Hughes), 17, 18
Brillat-Savarin, Anthelme, 1, 166, 167
Bronx, New York, 57, 62, 64, 67, 85
budae jjigae, 190, 212–213, 260
Buffalo wings, 25
bulgogi, 35, 142, 144–148, 218, 260
Burger King restaurants, 53, 218
Burma, 170, 260

cabbage, 177, 191, 260; *baechu* variety of, 95, 96–97, 259
Caesar salad, 228
California roll, 19, 48, 226; absence of raw fish, 22, 23; analogy to chop suey, 44, 45; appeal of, 21, 22; authenticity of, 8, 31, 34–35, 44–45, 48; avocado in, 32, 33; crabmeat in, 23; creation of, 43, 44–47; criticism of, 7, 22–23, 31, 32–35, 43; a dubious food, 6, 7, 11, 23, 48; a gateway dish to Japanese cuisine, 22; ingredients for, 21, 23, 35; popularity of, 7
Cambodia, 212
Cambodian cuisine, 42
Cambodians, 135, 140, 147
canned meat, 6, 190, 209–210, 214
cannibalism: and colonialism, 132; examples of, 127; fabrication of, 130–132; in film and literature, 124–127, 133–134; naming of, 132–133
Cantonese cuisine, 68–71
Cargill Meat Solutions, 149
ceviche, 22, 260
Chan, Michael Paul, 60
Chang, David, 187
char siu, 69, 218, 260, 263
chelow kabab, 176, 260
Chicago, 22, 50, 118, 210, 219
Chicagoans, 222
Child, Julia, 228
chile de árbol, 24–25, 26, 260. *See also* chile pepper
chile pepper, 24–25, 34, 35, 82; and Christopher Columbus, 86–87, 119; in cuisines of the world, 90; in early human diet, 25, 90–91; early trade of, 91; hotness scale, 91–92; Korean consumption of, 90–91, 92–93; naming of, 86–88, 119; origin of, 25, 89–90; varieties of, 25, 88
Chin, Vincent, 61
China, 6, 34; chile pepper exports from, 24; chile pepper production in, 90; consumption of dogmeat in, 138; food of, 68–69; kimchi exports from, 114; laborers from, 22, 215, 216; and MSG, 181, 186; origin of soy sauce in, 24; pickling in, 95; prehistoric noodles in, 25–26; restaurant chains in, 70; travel writings of, 146–147; US military in, 212
Chinatown: in Monterey Park, 74; in New York City, 52, 64–67, 74; in San Francisco, 74, 184

Chinese American community, 85
Chinese Americans, 50, 52, 57, 72, 73, 77; racism towards, 159; stereotypes of, 230; violence against, 61
Chinese culinary visa program, 72–73
Chinese food, 9, 140; Americanization of, 8, 68–69, 72, 76; authenticity of, 8, 66–67, 75, 76–77; and Chinese people, 52–53, 63, 72, 73, 77; commonness of, 50; criticism of, 68–69, 69–73, 75, 163; culture of complaint surrounding, 7, 49, 53, 55–56, 71, 76–77; in daily life, 53; as a dubious food, 6, 7, 73–75, 163; foreignness of, 50, 52, 56–57, 63; and MSG, 6, 7, 8, 55–56, 159 (*see also* Chinese restaurant syndrome; MSG); parodies of, 54; popularity of, 7, 49, 52, 159; portrayals in popular culture of, 53–55; and racial attitudes, 52, 56–57; urban legends of, 53–55, 134–135
Chinese literature, 125
Chinese restaurant: American character of, 50; cultural expectations of, 65–66; culture of complaint surrounding, 49, 53; early restaurants in the United States, 52; menus of, 55, 56, 64–66, 160; and MSG, 8, 159, 160, 177, 179, 189 (*see also* Chinese restaurant syndrome; MSG); number of, 53, 74; take-out restaurants (*see* Chinese take-out); ubiquity of, 49–50, 53, 67
Chinese Restaurant Project, 50–51
Chinese restaurant syndrome: causes of, 178–179, 180, 186–187; racialized discourse of, 184–186; studies of, 180–181, 186; symptoms of, 56, 177–178
Chinese take-out, 6, 8, 49, 55, 59, 60, 62, 63, 226, 230; and African American versus Chinese conflict, 57–58, 62–63, 67; and menu controversy, 64–65, 66–68
chirashizushi, 260, 264
chop suey, 43, 71, 72, 140, 260; analogy to California roll, 44, 45; foreignness of, 50; popularity of, 74; as racial slur, 136; urban legend about, 53–54
chorizo, 90, 101, 260
chotkal, 95, 260

chow mein, 50, 53, 54, 71, 136
Choy, Sam, 215, 220–221, 72
Chun King, 24
citizenship, 60, 62
Clavel, James, 20
Coca-Cola, 34, 194
coconut, 32, 136, 224, 225
Codex Alimentarius Commission, 24, 110–111
Codex Standards, 110, 111, 114
Columbian Exchange, 88–89
Columbus, Christopher, 169; and Asia, 133; and black pepper, 86–87, 119; and cannibals, 132; and chile pepper, 86–87, 88, 90; and Old and New World biological exchanges, 32, 88–89, 226
combat rations, 208–210
ConAgra Foods, 24
Coney Island, 50
Conrad, Joseph, 126, 129
cookbooks, 3, 13; of Hawaiian food, 190; of Korean food, 93; by Ming Tsai, 224, 225, 228; and MSG, 187; of SPAM, 190, 221
cooking shows, 3, 13, 168, 190
Cool Whip, 194
Corum, Ann Kondo, 190
couscous, 176, 224, 225, 260
Cruise, Tom, 29
cuisines, 30, 35, 37, 49, 176, 196; analogy to language, 4–6; authenticity of, 2–4; popular in America, 49; of the world, 2, 90, 109, 169, 215
culinary adaptation, 45. *See also* Americanization
culinary authenticity. *See* authenticity
culinary tradition, 9, 38, 112, 217. *See also* tradition
cultural citizenship, 1
cultural identities, 222
cultural imperialism, 10, 34, 222
cultural politics, 4
cultural power, 4, 38
cultural studies, 10
Curb Your Enthusiasm, 143–145

Daigneau, Kenneth, 200
daikon, 112, 260

danmuji, 112, 260, 264
dashi, 164–166, 170–171, 260, 262
delicatessens, 217
Detroit, 25, 61
diaspora, 4, 6
diasporic communities, 119
diasporic dynamic, 13
diasporic product, 221
diasporic taste, 77
disgust: over animal treatment, 150, 153; over Asian food, 7, 17, 144; over dog eating, 8, 124, 126, 128, 147; human emotion of, 145–146; and sense of self, 147–148
dogmeat, 194, 226, 227; and anti-Asian stereotypes, 135–136; consumption, 139–140; consumption in Korea, 124, 128, 130, 140–143, 154–155; disgust at, 124, 128, 147–148; as a dubious food, 6, 8, 11; joke in *Curb Your Enthusiasm*, 143–145; and Korean manhood, 124, 155; and postindustrial societies, 153–153; racial imageries of, 121; served in Chinese restaurants, 54, 134; taboos against, 123; trial over, 135
dogs: domestication of, 138–139; as pets, 123, 128, 135, 148, 151–152
Dok Island. *See* Dokdo Island
Dokdo Island, 105–108, 114
dolma, 176, 260
Doosan Corporation, 113
doro wat, 176, 260
dosa, 2, 101, 260
Do the Right Thing (Lee), 62
dubious Asian foods, 6–8, 10, 13, 192, 227; and Asian people, 9; chemicals, 159; gone mainstream, 19
Dutch navy, 206

East Asia. *See* China; Japan; Korea
East Asian food, 9–10, 170
East Asians, 134, 135, 170
East-West binary, 13
Ebens, Ronald, 61–62
Edo, 42. *See also* Tokyo
edomaezushi, 42, 261
eggrolls, 63, 73

EIWA Group, 44
English language, 4–5, 64, 67, 103, 227
epicurean, 2, 12, 22, 84
equatorial cuisine, 33–34, 225
Escoffier, Auguste, 168–169
ethnic affiliation, 5, 181
ethnic boundaries, 146
ethnic cuisines, 3
ethnic dishes, 43, 113
ethnic eateries, 53, 54
ethnic entrepreneurs, 3
ethnic foods, 7, 49, 177
ethnic groups, 9, 11, 136, 146, 191, 217
ethnic identity, 1
ethnic influences, 215
ethnic insults, 146
ethnicity, 68

factory farms, 149, 152, 172, 199
Falling Down (Schumacher), 59–60
fermentation, 41, 101–102, 111
fifth taste. *See umami*
Filipino American community, 135
Filipino Americans, 6, 136
Filipino cuisine, 42, 212
Filipinos, 22, 60; and dogmeat, 140; and SPAM, 194, 196, 222
Fisher, M. F. K., 26, 164
flavor enhancers, 174, 175–176, 198; in kimchi, 111. *See also* MSG
Flutie, Doug, 17–18
Food, Inc. (Kenner), 172, 173
food additives, 173, 174–176, 187, 196; in kimchi, 111; in SPAM, 197; used by US food industries, 162–163, 198. *See also* MSG
Food and Agriculture Organization of the United Nations (FAO), 110
food-based insults, 135–136, 146
food preservation, 96, 101, 174–175, 196, 205, 206, 207
food studies, 10
French cooking, 168–169
French diet, 98–99
French food, 30, 74, 98
French fries, 50, 137
French government, 98, 99, 207

funazushi, 40, 41, 261
functional food, 100
furikake, 191, 261
fusion cuisine, 2, 23, 176, 227; of Asian foods, 224, 229, 230

galbi, 176, 216, 261
garam masala, 177, 261
garum, 169–170, 261
General Tso's chicken, 55, 66, 73, 76, 77, 160, 261
Giebert, George, 168
gimbap, 112, 190, 261
globalization, 119; of Asian food, 3; and authenticity, 8, 129, 130, 227; of food, 38, 65; and industrialization, 192, 222; and technology, 163; and US imperialism, 34
Glutamate Association, 161–162, 163
goulash, 90, 261
Great Depression, 196, 200, 209
Guam, 6, 192, 194, 212
gustatory taste. *See* taste

hamburger: as American dishes, 50, 193; artificiality of, 200; and beef production, 137, 152; in Hawaiian dishes, 220, 221, 262
harissa, 2, 90, 224, 225, 229, 261
Hart-Celler Act. *See* Immigration Act of 1965
haute cuisine, 21
Hawai'i, 150; Barack Obama's visit to, 219; Chinese restaurant syndrome in, 179; dog eating in, 139; fast food chains in, 217–218; food in, 215–221; natives of 139, 216, 217; origins of plantation workers in, 215, 216–217; plantations in, 216–217; restaurants in, 215, 217, 219–221; SPAM consumption in, 6, 190–191, 192, 195, 201, 215, 216, 218, 221; US military in, 212
Hawaiian Regional Cuisine, 215–216, 219
Hawai'i Visitors and Convention Bureau, 215
Heart of Darkness (Conrad), 126, 129
Hemingway, Ernest, 11, 35, 58–59
Henson, Jim, 204, 205
Hide, Miyake, 168

honor, 28, 143
Hormel, George, 196
Hormel, Jay, 196, 200
Hormel Food Corporation, 190; merchandise of, 204; naming of SPAM, 200; production of SPAM, 200; product launch of SPAM, 196; versus Spam Arrest, 204; SPAM exports of, 211; SPAM trademark of, 203; versus Walt Disney Corporation, 204–205; and World War II, 210
Hostess Twinkie, 136, 198
hot dog, 50, 113, 140, 191, 193, 197, 200; in Hawai'i, 216, 219; and identity, 222; and Japanese internment, 213–214; in Korean dishes, 212
hummus, 176, 261
Hwang, David Henry, 11–12, 13

Ikeda, Kikunae, 163–164, 169, 170; identification of *umami*, 166, 167; isolation of glutamic acid, 164, 165, 170; and mass-manufactured seasoning, 167–168, 171–172
imagined community, 147
Imaizumi, Teruo, 44–47
immigrants, 2, 13, 43, 52, 85, 176
Immigration Act of 1965, 74, 135
Indian cuisine, 1
injera, 101, 176, 261
International Academic Conference of Food Science and Engineering, 96
International Hydrolyzed Protein Council, 24
Iron Chef, 3, 224
Italian cuisine, 49

James Beard Foundation, 215
Japan, 34, 77, 129, 163; chile pepper in, 91, 119; colonies of, 6, 181; curry consumption in, 113, 161; fish preservation in, 41; in global kimchi trade, 113; introduction of foods to, 40; introduction of sushi to, 42–43; kimchi consumption in, 117; kimchi makers of, 111; laborers from, 216, 217; and MSG, 6, 7, 163, 181; restaurant chains in, 70, 217; rice

Japan (cont.)
cultivation in, 41; soy sauce from, 26, 28; soy sauce lobby of, 24; SPAM consumption in, 194; sushi in, 22, 27; territorial claims of, 104–108, 113–114; US military in, 212; World Cup in, 108; in World War II, 105, 212

Japanese American community, 213

Japanese colonialism, 103, 105, 108, 114, 182, 187

Japanese cuisine, 1, 17, 22, 26, 30, 112, 164, 212; American discourse on, 26–27, 30–31

Japanese immigrants, 44; in Hawai'i, 215, 216; after interment, 214

Japanese internment, 213–214

Japanese kimchi. See *kimuchi*

Japanese restaurants: in Japan, 30; in the United States, 19, 20

Japan Pickle Producers Association, 113

jeotgal, 170, 261

jjajangmyeon, 112, 219, 261

jjamppong, 219, 261

kabayaki, 221, 261

kalua pig, 216, 261

kamaboko, 218, 261, 263

kanpachi, 30, 261

kapi, 42, 170, 261

kasuzuke, 112, 262, 265

katsu, 216, 262

katsuobushi, 164, 167, 170, 171, 260, 261, 262

kecap ikan, 42, 170, 262

Kentucky Fried Chicken, 194

Kewpie mayonnaise, 187

Khrushchev, Nikita, 211

Kikkoman, 24

Kim, Rae Won, 195

Kim, Sylvie, 191

kimchi: *baechu* variety of, 97, 101, 112, 118; *baek* variety of, 118, 259; cabbage in, 95, 96–97; characteristics of, 82; chile peppers in, 82, 90–91, 93; Chinese versus Korean trade in, 114; definition of, 96–97, 111; as a dubious food, 6, 8, 11; etymology of, 95–96; fermentation process for, 101; health value of, 99–101, 102; ingredients in, 82, 90, 94; international trade standards for, 110–111; Japanese versus Korean trade in, 110, 111, 113–114; made in Flushing (Queens), 81, 84, 86, 103, 118; as national dish of Korea, 6, 82; origin of, 95; refrigerator for, 116–117; smell of, 109–110, 115; taste of, 82; trade in, 110, 113–114; types of, 93–95

kimuchi, 110, 111–112, 113, 114, 117, 262

Kipling, Rudyard, 138, 224, 225

Kodama, Shintaro, 170

kojizuke, 112, 262, 265

konbu, 164, 167, 170, 171, 260, 262

Korea: chile pepper consumption, 90; chile pepper production in, 90; dogmeat consumption (*see* dogmeat); government of, 93, 99, 100, 108, 109, 111, 114, 117; under Japanese colonialism, 6, 103, 181, 182; kimchi producers from, 113, 114; laborers from, 22, 215, 216; pet dogs in, 151–152; regions of, 94, 95; SPAM consumption in, 6, 192, 194–195; territorial dispute with Japan, 103–108; US military in, 212

Korean community, 81, 119

Korean food, 6, 8, 71, 74, 117, 219; Americanization of, 92; and authenticity, 92, 130; chile pepper in, 90–91, 91–92; dogmeat in (*see* dogmeat); influence of US military on, 212–213; international trade standards for, 111; kimchi (*see* kimchi); and manhood, 125, 155; and MSG, 182; and pickling, 112; portrayed in US popular culture, 136, 140, 143–146, 148; research on, 93–94, 100; SPAM in, 6, 192, 194–195, 196; spiciness of, 91, 93, 109; and territorial dispute with Japan, 103, 108, 114; travel writings of, 109–110, 128–129

Korean Food Research Institute, 93, 94

Korean manhood, 124, 155

Koreans, 54; in American Midwest, 192; employment of Latinos, 118–119; in Hawai'i, 190, 192, 215, 216, 221, 222; honor of, 143; identity of, 119, 143; and

pet dogs, 151–152; portrayed in US popular culture, 59–60, 136, 140; in Queens, 84; in the United States, 118, 119
Korean restaurants, 81, 108, 118, 146
Korean War, 212–213, 215
kung pao, 1, 54, 69, 90, 262
Kwan, Michelle, 61
Kwok, Robert Ho Man, 177, 178, 179, 180, 181, 184

La Choy, 24
Ladies' Home Journal, 17
Lakshmi, Padma, 21
lamb, 35, 149, 167; in Ming Tsai's recipe, 224, 225, 226, 229, 262, 264, 265
Laudan, Rachel, 191, 215, 217, 219
laulau, 216, 262
Lee, Sunyoung, 192
Leipzig University, 167, 168
Letterman, David, 202, 205
Liebig, Justus von, 168
Lin, Jeremy, 61
Lind, James, 206, 207
linguistics, 4, 5, 227
Lipinski, Tara, 61
literary studies, 10
Little Tokyo, 44, 48
loco moco, 219–221, 262
Lu, Xun, 125
lutefisk, 115, 262
Lyte Funky Ones, 55

M. Butterfly (Hwang), 11–12
Madman's Diary (Lu), 125–126, 127
makizushi, 19, 45, 46, 47, 112, 214, 260, 261, 262, 264, 265
Manzanar Internment Camp, 213
Mashita, Ichiro, 44–47
Matrix (Wacowski Brothers), 173
Matsumoto, Yoshiichi, 41, 42
McDonaldization, 3
McDonald's restaurants, 22, 34, 53, 143, 217, 218, 222; burgers, 75; franchise, 137, 218
McInerney, Jay, 19
mechanically recovered meat, 199
Medici, Catherine de, 168

Mexican chile pepper, 24–25, 48
Mexican cuisine, 22
Mifune, Toshiro, 20
Ming, Yao, 61
mint, 224, 225, 226, 263, 264
mirepoix, 171, 262
Mishima, Yukio, 29
miso paste, 101, 112, 262; soup from, 31
misozuki, 112, 262, 265
Miura, Muriel, 190
model minority, 230
modernity, 1, 38, 113, 172, 181–182, 222, 226
mole, 24, 90, 262
Monosodium Glutamate. *See* MSG
Monty Python, 201–202, 203, 211
moo goo gai pan, 160, 262
Morimoto, Masaharu, 19, 229
Morrison, Toni, 58–59, 60
MSG: ad war over, 161, 163; in American food, 181, 184; chemistry of 165; and Chinese food, 159–160; and high-end chefs, 188; ill effects on humans, 177–181; manufacture of, 171–172; other names for, 188; reputation of, 163; and sense of taste (see *umami*); taste of, 165–166
multiculturalism, 34, 122, 229
Muppet Treasure Island, 204–205
musubi, 190, 192, 216, 218, 229, 262
mystery meat, 8, 54, 193, 196, 202

naengmyeon, 219, 262
nampla, 42, 170, 262
Napoleonic Wars, 209
narezushi, 40, 41, 42, 261, 262, 264
Nashville, Tennessee, 19
National Basketball Association, 61
national cuisines, 3
New England Journal of Medicine, 178, 179, 180, 184, 185
New York City: Chinese restaurants in, 57, 62, 72, 159; elected officials of, 57; food in, 5, 30, 66, 74, 77; Japanese restaurants in, 19, 30, 31; Korean restaurants in, 118; mayor of, 64; restaurants using MSG in, 187

New Yorkers, 55, 222
New York State, 81, 217
New York University of Medicine, 180
New York World's Fair, 85
ngapi, 170, 263
Nitz, Michael, 61
noodles, 48, 113, 188, 195, 212, 216; prehistoric samples of, 25–26
nostalgia, 2, 36, 39, 124, 172, 228
nukazuke, 112, 263, 265
nuoc mam, 42, 170, 263

Obama, Barack, 219
okazuya, 217
Okinawa, 215
Olympic Games, 61, 99, 128, 129, 136, 140
Orient, 1, 2, 3, 5, 12, 13, 35, 86, 148, 226; cuisines of, 1; flavors of, 1, 3, 148; taste of, 230
Oriental gastronomy, 139
Orientalism, 12–13, 132
Oriental people, 1, 7, 11, 121, 134, 135
Oscar Meyer Wieners, 198
osmazome, 166–167
Ostwald, Wilhelm, 167
otoro, 82, 263

Pacific Islander, 205, 212, 213
Pacquiao, Manny, 136
padec, 42, 170, 263
Park, Kun-Young, 100–101
patis, 170, 263
pepper. *See* black pepper; chile pepper
Philippine-American War, 212
Philippines, 106; coffee from, 102; dog eating in, 140; food from, 84; food in, 77, 218; labor from, 22, 215, 216; SPAM consumption in, 6, 194, 195; US military in, 212
pickling, 96, 112, 174, 205
pizza, 49, 50, 113, 118
Pizza Hut restaurants, 143, 217
plate lunch, 216–217, 219
poi, 101, 263
Pollan, Michael, 36, 197, 198
Polo, Marco, 147, 168
postmodernity, 1, 226

potted meat, 198–199
Pusan National University, 100–101

Queens, New York, 84–86; Flushing section of, 5, 74, 81; kimchi from, 81, 86, 97, 101, 103, 117, 118; Koreans in, 114, 117, 118

race, 179, 183; in American literature, 58; and multiculturalism, 34
racial anxieties, 52
racial boundaries, 146
racial discrimination, 62, 67
racial groups, 11, 136
racialized discourses, 184
racial slurs, 120
racial stereotypes, 230
racism, 131, 159
raita, 224, 225
ramen, 22, 163, 190, 212, 218, 260, 263
ready-made foods, 173
Reciprocity Treaty, 216
red wine, 97–99
regional cuisines, 3, 49
restaurant chains, 21, 191
rice cultivation, 41
Ritthausen, Karl Heinrich Leopold, 165
Rivers, Bob, 54
Rivers, Joan, 136
roux, 161, 263
Royal Navy (British), 206

Said, Edward, 12–13, 38–39, 132
saimin, 216, 217, 218, 263
sake, 26, 32, 166, 263
San Francisco, 25, 52, 74, 147, 184, 192
Schaumburg, Herbert, 180–181, 186
Scoville Heat Unit (SHU), 91–92, 93
seafood, 21, 22, 28, 31, 42, 95, 111, 112, 171
Seinfeld, 55
Sex in the City, 55
shiokara, 42, 170, 264
shiozuke, 112, 264
shireen polow, 176, 264
Shogun (Clavell), 20
shottsuru, 170, 264
shoyuzuke, 112, 264, 265
Simmonds, Peter Lund, 139, 147

sodium nitrate, 197–198
Som, Indigo, 49–51
Sopranos, 19
South Asia, 9, 10, 113, 226
Southeast Asia, 42, 91, 102; dogmeat consumption in, 6; fermented fish products in, 170
Southeast Asians, 134, 135
South Korea. *See* Korea
South Korean food. *See* Korean food
Soylent Green (Fleischer), 124–125, 126, 127, 146, 154
soy sauce: as cause of Chinese restaurant syndrome, 178, 179, 180; in Chinese food, 68; as curing agent, 94; fermentation of, 101, 102; international trade standard for, 23–24; from Japan, 26, 48; in Japanese internment food, 213; in kimchi, 94; MSG in, 170; for pickling, 112; with sushi, 31
SPAM: additive in, 197–198; and authenticity, 8, 192; cookbooks on, 190; cook-offs with, 190; as currency, 195; dishes based on, 190–191; exports of, 211; as gifts, 194; ingredients for, 197, 199; largest consumers of, 192; as luxury commodity, 193, 211; merchandise for, 204; name of, 199–200; parodies of, 201–202; product launch of, 196; reputation of, 192, 193–194, 196; sushi based on, 214; trademark for, 203–205; US consumption of, 7; wholesomeness of, 197, 198
spam (e-mail), 203–204
Spanish-American War, 208, 212
Steingarten, Jeffrey, 56, 186, 187
stinky tofu, 115, 264
sukiyaki, 40, 264
sundubu jjigae, 92, 130, 264
surimi, 23, 45, 261, 264
sushi: American discourse on, 27, 30–31; avocado in, 32–33; definition of, 41; etiquette of eating, 31–32; intimidation factor of, 32; origin of, 26, 40–43; popularity of, 18–19, 20; prestige of, 18–19; raw fish in, 17; reputation makeover of, 19–20; in US popular culture, 17–18, 19

sushi bars, 19
sushi chefs, 29, 32, 41; apprenticeship to become, 27–28; female, 28, 29–30; and manliness, 29; as sushi bullies, 31; in the United States, 30
sushi knife, 28–29
Sushi Nozawa restaurant, 31
sushi rice, 41, 42
sushi rolls, 21, 47, 195. *See also* California roll
suzuke, 112, 264
Suzuki Company, 171

tabbouleh, 176, 264
taboos, 123, 126, 131, 142
Taco Bell restaurants, 50, 217
tagine, 174, 264
Takeshima Island, 105–108, 114
takuan, 112, 191, 260, 264
tandoori, 176, 264
taste, 36–37, 65, 75–76, 228–229; and authenticity, 67, 77, 92; basic taste senses, 164–165; discourse of, 228; and military food, 209; and modernity, 181–182
tekkamaki, 19, 264
temakizushi, 47, 262, 264
tempura, 22, 40, 176, 216, 264, 265
Thai cuisine, 42
Titanic (Cameron), 75, 76
Tokyo, 5, 19, 30, 42, 44, 67, 171
Tokyo Kaikan restaurant, 44–45, 47
tom yum, 90, 265
tonkatsu, 113, 265
toro, 45, 47–48, 263, 265. *See also* tuna
Trader Vic's restaurant, 68, 69, 70
tradition, 24, 227–229. *See also* culinary tradition
transnational capital, 1
transnational labor, 1
Tsai, Ming, 26, 187, 224–225, 226–227, 229–230
tsukemono, 112, 259, 262, 263, 264, 265
Tule Lake Internment Camp, 213
tuna, 17, 21, 22, 45, 46, 47, 197. *See also toro*
turkey (animal), 89, 149, 194
Turks, 86, 139, 147
tzatziki, 176, 265

umami, 11; chemical components of, 170–171; discovery of, 163–164, 165; food rich in, 169–170; Japanese meaning of, 166; and MSG, 164, 165, 187–188, 189
umeboshi, 112, 263, 265
unagi, 221, 265
United Nations, 24, 110, 176
uramaki, 45, 47, 260, 265
US Department of Agriculture, 137
US military, 182, 208–210, 212–213, 220; all Asian American unit, 220

Vienna sausage, 190, 191, 203, 212, 260
Vietnamese cuisine, 42, 71, 226
Vietnamese people, 54, 140
Vietnam War, 212
vindaloo, 1, 35, 90, 265
Vongerichten, Jean-Georges, 115, 187, 229

Walt Disney Pictures, 34, 204
Waters, Alice, 172
Winchester, Simon, 109, 128, 146
Wong, Alan, 187, 215, 216, 221
working-class, 194, 215, 219
World Health Organization (WHO), 110
World War II, 212, 213; combat rations during, 208–210; and loco moco, 220; and SPAM, 210–211, 217

Yan, Martin, 26, 230
Yankovic, Weird Al, 201, 202
Yohei, Hanaya, 42
yuja, 94, 265

Zagat, Nina, 71–73
Zagat, Tim, 71–73
Zevon, Warren, 53, 70
Zip Pac, 191

About the Author

ROBERT JI-SONG KU is associate professor of Asian American Studies at Binghamton University of the State University of New York. He is co-editor of *Eating Asian America: A Food Studies Reader*. Born in Korea, he spent his childhood in Hawai'i.

Production Notes for Ku | *Dubious Gastronomy*

Jacket design by Julie Matsuo-Chun

Text design by University of Hawai'i Press production staff with display type in Bakersignet and text type in Minion

Composition by Westchester Publishing Services

Printing and binding by Sheridan Books, Inc.

Printed on 60 lb. House White, 444 pi.